Tomás Rivera
The Complete Works

Edited by
Julián Olivares

Arte Público Press
Houston, Texas
1992

Acknowledgements

This volume is made possible through a grant from the National Endowment for the Arts, a federal agency.

Arte Público Press
University of Houston
Houston, Texas 77204-2090

Cover Design and Photograph by Mark Piñón

Rivera, Tomás, 1935–1984
   [Works. 1991]
   Tomás Rivera: the complete works / Tomás Rivera: edited by Julián Olivares
      p.   cm.
   Includes bibliographical references.
   ISBN 1-55885-153-4
   I. Title.
PQ7079.2.R5 1991
863–dc20   91-12328
                                    CIP

The paper used in this publication meets the requirements of the American National Standard for Permanence of Paper for Printed Library Materials Z39.48-1984. ∞

En memoria de Tomás
y para nuestros hijos:
Javier, Iracema e Ileana.

—Concha Rivera

To my brother Ernest who was a searcher all his life.

—Julián Olivares

Contents

Tomás Rivera
The Complete Works

Introduction

🌿

> *It is impossible to imagine Chicano lit-*
> *erature without the migrant worker*
>
> —Tomás Rivera[1]

Tomás Rivera's ... *y no se lo tragó la tierra / ... And the Earth Did Not Part* (1971),[2] winner of the Quinto Sol Literary Prize in 1970, is a product of the Chicano social movement of the 1960's and a landmark in Chicano literary history. This novel gave considerable impetus to Chicano writers and brought wide recognition to the Hispanic creative presence of the United States. Taking place within the context of the experiences of the Chicano migrant farmworkers between 1945 and 1955, the novel's theme deals with a boy's quest of his identity. Functioning as the novel's central conscious—either as protagonist, narrator protagonist, narrator witness or as a character who overhears but does not narrate—, the boy recuperates his past, discovers his history and affirms his own singular being and his identity as a collective person. By discovering who he is, this adolescent becomes one with his people. Through his quest, he embodies and expresses the collective conscious and experiences of his society.[3]

Tomás Rivera was born to a family of migrant farmworkers in the south Texas town of Crystal City, on December 22, 1935. His mother, Josefa Hernández Gutiérrez, and her family immigrated to Texas in 1920.[4] Rivera's grandfather, Apolino Hernández, had been an officer in the Mexican army and a union organizer in the mines of northern Mexico. In order to avoid reprisals from political enemies, he fled to Dallas, then moved to Houston, and finally settled in Crystal City, where he bought a truck and became an agricultural crew leader. The winter garden areas provided work for only half the year, so the migrant labor experience became regularized, as he took the family to California or the midwestern states. Rivera's grandfather continued this type of work until his death. Rivera recalls that his grandfather "would become angered when he heard of people returning to 'nuestra tierra' ('our native land'). He would say 'Tu tierra es donde vives y donde trabajas' ('Your native land is where you live and where you work')" ("Immigrants," 6H).

Florencio Rivera Martínez, Rivera's father, was ten-years old when the Mexican Revolution of 1910 erupted. In order to avoid the turbulence of the Revolution, his family fled to northern Mexico from the central

Mexican state of Aguascalientes. At fifteen he went to Texas, where he worked on the railroads. For the next fifteen years, his occupations took him to California, the midwest and to west Texas, where he worked as a cowboy. Passing through Crystal City on his way to visit his family in Mexico, Florencio Rivera met and married Josefa Hernández, and took on the migrant labor life. Rivera recalls that his father "had tempered a philosophy of work: 'La mejor vida es la del que sabe trabajar' ('The best life is that of the person who likes to work')" ("Immigrants," 6H).

From his early years until 1954, Tomás Rivera traveled with his family, joining the migrant stream that left Crystal City around mid-April, searching for farmwork as far north as Michigan and Minnesota, and returning around the beginning of November. This nomadic life required that Rivera make up much school work upon his return to Crystal City, which became impossible when he began junior college in 1954. He could only then join his family during the summer months.[5] Years later, in much of his writings, and especially in his novel ... *y no se lo tragó la tierra*, he would document the experiences that he underwent and witnessed as a migrant worker.

The concern that Rivera felt for his people and their education motivated him to seek a career as a teacher. After receiving his B.S. in English Education in 1958 from Southwest Texas State University, he taught high school in San Antonio, Crystal City and League City, teaching English and Spanish. He returned to Southwest Texas State, where he received an M.Ed. in 1964, and continued his graduate studies at the University of Oklahoma, receiving his Ph.D. in Romance Literatures in 1969.

Rivera's ascent through the professorial ranks and into university administration was rapid. Beginning as an Associate Professor of Spanish at Sam Houston State University in 1969, he became a Professor of Spanish and Director of Foreign Languages at The University of Texas, San Antonio, in 1971. By 1976, Rivera had become Vice President for Administration, leaving this post in 1978 for The University of Texas, El Paso, where he assumed the position of Executive Vice President. One year later Rivera became Chancellor of the University of California, Riverside, a position he held for five years until his sudden death on May 16, 1984.

Rivera's concern for education, especially that of minorities, and his extensive administrative duties curtailed his creative efforts. After the publication of *Tierra*, he published but five short stories, two of which were episodes he omitted from the novel, a chap book containing thirteen poems, titled *Always and other poems*, and thirteen more poems, including his epic "The Searchers." It is believed that Rivera was working on a second novel, *La casa grande del pueblo* (*The People's Mansion*), when he suffered a fatal heart attack in Fontana, California.

This edition contains Tomás Rivera's entire literary production, including two short stories and five vignettes—excluded from *Tierra*—and twenty-six poems, which remained unpublished at the time of his death but which appeared posthumously.[6] In addition, the Appendix of this edition of the complete works contains two brief works not published until now, "La casa grande del pueblo"—which appears to have been the introduction to his projected second novel—and a literary cameo, "Era muy llorón." Also appearing here are Rivera's influential critical essays, including "Critical Approaches to Chicano Literature and its Dynamic Intimacy," previously unpublished.

... y no se lo tragó la tierra/ ... And the Earth Did Not Devour Him[7]

Tomás Rivera wrote three literary essays that have been instrumental in the ethical and esthetic appreciation of much of the Chicano literature of the 1970's. These are "Into the Labyrinth: The Chicano in Literature," "Chicano Literature: Fiesta of the Living," and "Recuerdo, descubrimiento y voluntad en el proceso imaginativo literario" ["Remembering, Discovery and Volition in the Literary Imaginative Process"].[8] They are especially relevant in the critical appreciation of Rivera's own literary production.

In "Into the Labyrinth: The Chicano in Literature," Rivera reminds us that the *search*—as noted above—is the essential characteristic of both labyrinth and life: "We need to make the analogy between the Greek myth of Daedalus and Minos, and our own lives ... the labyrinth ... is a man-made structure full of intricate passageways ... the important element here is that the labyrinth provided a setting for a search ... toward the exterior or the interior. In either case, the setting provided not only a setting for a search but also a setting for tension." Consequently, the labyrinth, "a man-made structure," and literature, man's artifice, share a preoccupation for the search:

> Literature provide[s] tension. Literature represents man's life; it also reflects his inner search and his outward search. It is, in a sense, an intricate maze to provide either exteriorization or internalization of the human involvement and evolvement [evolution] ... And the search can only exist if there is an impulse into the labyrinth of the human totality of conditions. Thus, the search and labyrinth complement each other to bring forth a vicarious sensibility to the perceiver.

For Rivera, the labyrinth is also the means by which one searches for one's *alter ego*, the *other*: "it is a vicarious notion of humanity, or man, to attempt to search for the other alter ego in order to better comprehend himself.... [T]he labyrinth ... is a mold wherein he can place his life. In essence, is it not life in search of form—a conquest, a labyrinth in which to reflect his human condition?" In the search for the form in which to mold the Chicano experience, the Chicano, newly arrived to this enterprise, invents his own labyrinth:

> This brings us to the Chicano who also wishes to create a labyrinth, who wishes to invent himself in the labyrinth ... where he can vicariously live his total human condition. However, since he has perceived continually the development of the North American and the Mexican literatures, literatures which have reached great heights of intricateness and sophistication for their counterparts, more stress is given to finding form or forms for expression. So we find Chicano literature and the Chicanos in fiction as simply life in search of form.

Rivera develops the concept of the *other* in "Chicano Literature: Fiesta of the Living." Here Rivera affirms, "for me the literary experience is one of total communion, an awesome awareness of the *other*, of one's potential self. I have come to recognize my *other* in Chicano literature." The search for the *other* represents "an exact, pure desire to transform what is isolated in the mind into an external form," so that the creative process is "A personal ritual, a constant means of establishing contact with humanity and with one's origins." The *other*, for Rivera, then, is the recognition of one's people, *la raza*, and its collective experience.

Implied in these discussions are the assertions of Rivera's third essay, "Remembering, Discovery and Volition in the Literary Imaginative Process." Through memory, the Chicano recuperates the past, discovers his history and affirms his own singular being and his identity as a collective person. With this cultural awareness, he applies his volition in the quest for intellectual and spiritual development. In the realm of creative expression, volition is indispensable for literary invention, crucial for the quest of a form in which to express one's being and identity. Critical awareness, then, of the concepts of the labyrinth, of the *other*, and of memory, discovery and volition are indispensable in the appreciation of Chicano literature, especially of Rivera's literary production.

... *y no se lo tragó la tierra* begins with a brief narrative, "El año perdido" ("The Lost Year"), in which we note the psychological drama of an alienated boy who struggles to recall the events of the preceding year, of which he has no memory: "Aquel año se le perdió" ["That year was lost to him"].[9] In the boy's confusion, we perceive a struggle whose ultimate resolution depends on his capacity to discover and give form to his past by means of words, but which dissipate at the point where the past begins to become clear: "A veces trataba de recordar y ya para cuando creía que se estaba aclarando un poco se le perdían las palabras" ["At times he tried to remember and, just about when he thought everything was clearing up some, he would be at a loss for words"]. This lack of self-expression has caused him to lose himself; he is unable, therefore, to recover his history and to encounter his being and identity. Nonetheless, his *other* calls him, urging the boy to search for him, to search for himself: "Siempre empezaba todo cuando oía que alguien le llamaba por su nombre pero cuando volteaba la cabeza a ver quién era el que le llamaba, daba una vuelta entera y así quedaba donde mismo . . . luego . . . Se dio cuenta de que él mismo se había llamado" ["It always began when he would hear someone calling him by his name but when he turned his head to see who was calling, he would make a complete turn, and there he would end up—in the same place . . . then . . . He realized that he had called himself"]. The *other* reveals himself in the perception, barely glimpsed by this protagonist, of the collective conscious of his people that he carries within his own as yet unconscious. In the boy's mind, the collective conscious and experience struggle for their recognition. This adolescent, who cannot escape from the whirlwind of his thoughts, now finds himself at the entrance to a labyrinth in search of his authentic history and being.

"El año perdido" is followed by twelve stories and thirteen vignettes[10] which portray the lives of migrant workers, each story representing a month of the child's lost year. It becomes clear as the work proceeds that these months and year are not fixed chronologically but are to be conceived symbolically by the reader. The temporal dimension of some of the episodes indicate a past more remote than one year; hence, the months and year are to be taken as stages of existence and, in some cases, as an individual's or even a group's entire past.[11]

It is clear that Rivera arranged the sequence of the stories in *Tierra*, so that the four stories following "El año perdido" would present the main themes, which would be explored and developed in the remaining stories.[12] Thus, the second story, "Los niños no se aguantaron" ("The Children Couldn't Wait"), through an omniscient narrator, immediately presents the principal subject of the migrant workers and the theme of social injustice; "El rezo" ("A Prayer"), the third story, offers a first-person monologue of a woman who prays for her son missing in action in the Korean war. Thus, "Los niños no se aguantaron" portrays the Chicano in the cropfield where the landowner kills a child, and "El rezo" is a story of the Chicano away from the fields but killed (as we learn in "El retrato" ["The Portrait"]) in North Korea. However, "El rezo" has the additional function of introducing the theme of religion, which will be developed in three central and consecutive stories, "La noche estaba plateada" ("A Silvery Night"), "...y no se lo tragó la tierra" ("...And the Earth Did Not Devour Him") and "Primera comunión" ("First Communion"). The fourth story, "Es que duele" ("It's That It Hurts"), portrays the Chicano in school and develops the theme of discrimination. The next story, "La mano en la bolsa" ("Hand in His Pocket") presents as the elements of oppression those Chicanos who prey upon their own people. Consequently, in *Tierra* there are two classes of obstacles that the child, and collectively the Chicano people, must overcome: the external and the internal. The former are the obstacles of racism, discrimination, injustice and exploitation; while the latter are religion, in the sense that religion can inculcate fatalism and resignation to a life of poverty, and consequently submission to the external elements of oppression;[13] and victimization at the hands of those members of one's own culture/ethnic group.[14]

The boy's encounter of his identity is the result of a dialectic of the personal and the collective, and depends on what José Saldívar calls a "dawning sense of solidarity with other members of [his] class and race."[15] The freedom from the oppressing symbols and ideologemes of his society's world order allows this adolescent to begin thinking for himself and to determine his own destiny. Nowhere is this liberation more manifested than in the stories, "La noche estaba plateada" and "...y no se lo tragó la tierra." In the former, the child summons the devil, but he does not come. The devil's failure to appear causes the child to postulate the possibility of the devil's non-existence. However, since in Christianity—and particularly in the Chicano's Catholic formation—good and evil coexist, the the devil's non-existence logically implies God's non-existence: "Pero si no hay diablo tampoco hay... No, más vale no decirlo" ["But if there's no devil neither is there... No, I better not say it"]. This story's thrust is not an atheistic denial of God, but to put the child on the road to self-determination. This development is advanced in the next story.

In the title story the boy's father has suffered a sunstroke from working in a hot and parched Texas cotton field. These same brutal working conditions had also debilitated his aunt and uncle, making them fall to tuberculosis. When the boy sees his mother lighting candles for the father and praying for him, rationalizing their existence by believing that the poor go to heaven, the child rails against this religious escapism:

—¿Qué se gana, mamá, con andar haciendo eso? ¿Apoco cree que le ayudó mucho a mi tío y a mi tía? ¿Por qué es que nosotros estamos aquí como enterrados en la tierra? O los microbios nos comen o el sol nos asolea.... Y todos los días trabaje y trabaje. ¿Para qué?... Tanto darle de comer a la tierra y al sol y luego, zas, un día cuando menos lo piensa cae asoleado. Y uno sin poder hacer nada. Y luego ellos rogándole a Dios...si Dios no se acuerda de uno...yo creo que ni hay... No, mejor no decirlo, a lo mejor empeora papá. (...) N'ombre, a Dios le importa poco de uno de los pobres (...) ¿Dígame usted por qué? ¿Por qué nosotros nomás enterrados en la tierra como animales sin ningunas esperanzas de nada?

["What's to be gained from doing all that, Mother? Don't tell me you think it helped my aunt and uncle any. How come we're like this, like we're buried alive? Either the germs eat us alive or the sun burns us up.... And every day we work and work. For what?... All the time feeding the earth and the sun, only to one day, just like that, get knocked down by the sun. And there you are, helpless. And them, begging for God's help...why, God doesn't care about us...I don't think there even is... No, better not say it, what if Dad gets worse. (...) God could care less about the poor. (...) Tell me, Mother, why? Why us, buried in the earth like animals with no hope for anything?"]

The next day the boy and his two younger brothers go to work the cotton fields. In the afternoon, in the sweltering heat, the sun drops his youngest brother. As he rushes home carrying his brother, "...empezó a echar maldiciones. Y no supo ni cuándo, pero lo que dijo lo había tenido ganas de decir desde hacía mucho tiempo. Maldijo a Dios" ["he started cursing. And without even realizing it, he said what he had been wanting to say for a long time. He cursed God"]. At this moment, with years of his people's religious indoctrination operating in his conscious, he believes that the earth will open up and devour him: "Al hacerlo sintió el miedo infundido por los años y por sus padres. Por un segundo vio que se abría la tierra para tragárselo" ["Upon doing this he felt that fear instilled in him by the years and by his parents. For a second he saw the earth opening up to devour him"]. But the earth does not part. Having cursed and defied God, and not having suffered any retribution, he feels the earth more solid than ever beneath his feet, and curses God again: "Luego se sintió andando por la tierra bien apretada, más apretada que nunca. Entonces le entró el coraje de nuevo y se desahogó maldiciendo a Dios" ["Then he felt his footsteps against the earth, compact, more solid than ever. Then his anger swelled up again, and he vented it by cursing God"]. The next day both his father and brother recover. God has not punished them either. This liberation from the restrictions of good and evil permits his realization of self-determination and his movement towards class solidarity. His self-analysis, as Ramón Saldívar notes, "is less a demand to abandon religion than a plea to give up a condition that requires illusions…. His iconoclastic act, cursing God, speaking the unspeakable, is motivated by a double urgency: to liquidate oppressive idols and to articulate the power of self-determination."[16] These two central stories, much more than an invective against religion,[17] "dramatize that the making of a working-class consciousness is at least in part a reaction to a pacifying combination of imaginary, psychological, religious, and economic formations working to protect the status quo" (R. Saldívar, 84–85). The child's iconoclastic act is a requisite for a people's liberation from those myths and attitudes that sustain social hegemony and make them the victims of an agribusiness that literally forces them to their knees.

The trajectory from the personal experiences and tragedies of the migrant workers to an awareness of class solidarity is noted in the penultimate story, "Cuando lleguemos" ("When We Arrive"). In the development of *Tierra*, Rivera had three stories in which the migrant theme was central. In the work's initial stage, Rivera had written the drafts of "Los niños no se aguantaron" and "…y no se lo tragó la tierra,"[18] with the latter combining the theme of the migrant worker experience with the religious theme. In the second stage, he added "Los quemaditos" ("The Little Burnt Victims"), which deals with the inadequate housing provided to the migrant workers; here a couple's shack catches fire while they are working in the field, and two of their three children perish. At the third stage, Rivera must have been aware that he needed not only a fourth story on the migrant theme, but also one that dealt with a collective experience and that gave emphasis to the migrant workers' nomadic existence. "Cuando lleguemos" was the last story that Rivera wrote for *Tierra*. At first he placed it as the sixth story, following "La primera comunión" and preceding "La mano en la bolsa." In the fourth and final stage, Rivera placed the story in the penultimate position, where it simultaneously represents an awareness of collective oppression and sums up the cycle of the migrant-worker experience.[19]

"Cuando lleguemos" deals with a number of Chicano families and individuals, around forty people, who are packed into a truck which takes them from Texas to the Minnesota beet and onion fields. After constant traveling without any stops, around 4:00 in the morning the truck breaks

down in Iowa. What the reader then hears is a chorus of interior monologues, as various individuals address their individual dilemmas, all connected by the refrain, "Cuando lleguemos." At first the refrain refers to
their arrival in Minnesota and what their plans are when they arrive, but
then it comes to signify that which is never reached, neither their dreams
nor the end of their journey: "Cuando lleguemos, cuando lleguemos, ya,
la mera verdad estoy cansado de llegar. Es la misma cosa llegar que partir porque apenas llegamos y... Mejor debería decir, cuando no lleguemos porque es la mera verdad. Nunca llegamos" ["When we arrive,
when we arrive, the real truth is that I'm tired of arriving. Arriving and
leaving, it's the same thing because we no sooner arrive and...I really
should say when we don't arrive because that's the real truth. We never
arrive"]. "Cuando lleguemos" thus represents an endless cycle of
exploitation and broken dreams, the awareness of which is expressed collectively through the ensemble of the interior monologues, and which is
manifested in the trajectory from first- and third-person narrations to a
first-person plural narrative. Yet the awareness of the workers' collective
exploitation and victimization is qualified by their silence. Each is only
speaking to him or herself. One of the functions of the novel, then, is to
raise class consciousness through writing, expressing the characters' individual and collective experience.

In the conclusion, Rivera sets forth the conditions necessary for the
demand for social and civil rights, and for group solidarity (unity). These
are allegorically represented in the child's discovery that his individual
identity is contingent on his social identity. He must first discover *what*
he is before he can affirm *who* he is. This is the revelation that he experiences in the novel's concluding story, "Debajo de la casa" ("Beneath the
House"). The boy is beneath the house: "De donde estaba nada más se
veía una línea blanca de luz todo alrededor" ["From where he was all he
could make out was a white strip of daylight...all around"]. This dark
place serves as a concrete projection of the character's psychological state.
It is within the dark solitude of his mind that the boy enters the labyrinth
of self-discovery: "Aquí no está mal. Me podría venir aquí todos los
días... Puedo pensar a gusto" ["It's not bad here. I could come here every
day... I can think in peace"]. It is in this concrete and psychological
space that the boy finds his way and recovers the fragments of the lost
year; and, upon discovering the links that unite him with his people, he
arrives at self-discovery.[20] And it is beneath the house that the reader
becomes aware that this space has been the temporal point from which the
previous stories have emanated. Here the events related in the previous
episodes pass through the boy's mind in a stream of conscious. It is in

this manner that the child who, as noted above, is not actually present or narrating in all of the novel's episodes, functions, affirms Ramón Saldívar, "as what Bakhtin has termed a chronotopic point—a figural intersection of time and space—around which the collective subjective experience of Rivera's Texas-Mexican farmworkers coalesce, forming a communal oral history" (75). The twelve episodes, along with the vignettes that echo the themes and actions of the episodes, constitute, then, the personal and collective past of a character who functions as a chronotope/central conscious of the work. His experience is not limited to what he has seen or personally experienced, but includes what he has heard from his father— who "le contaba cuentos" ["used to tell him stories"] from his mother, grandparents, relatives, from the troubadour Bartolo and all the workers on the roads and in the fields of the migratory life, each contributing from his/her own harvest of wisdom and experience to the child's maturation process and final epiphany. The collective conscious, the *other* at first scarcely perceived in the depths of the protagonist's being, at the conclusion comes to the surface of his conscious. The recapitulation of prior events—provoking the reader's own epiphany—reintegrates the work's apparent fragmentary structure, bestowing structural unity to the work and giving it a novelistic sense of completeness.

The boy crawls out from under the house, emerging from the darkness and the dark labyrinth of his mind. In an interior monologue he declares his wish to see united all those people that have passed through his mind and to be able to embrace them:

> Quisiera ver a toda esa gente junta. Y luego si tuviera unos brazos bien grandes los podría abrazar a todos. Quisiera poder platicar con todos otra vez, pero que todos estuvieran juntos. Pero eso apenas es un sueño. Aquí sí que está suave porque puedo pensar en lo que yo quiera. Apenas estando uno solo puede juntar a todos. Yo creo que es lo que necesitaba más que todo. Necesitaba esconderme para poder comprender muchas cosas. De aquí en adelante todo lo que tengo que hacer es venirme aquí, en lo oscuro, y pensar en ellos. Y tengo en tanto que pensar y me faltan tanto años. Yo creo que hoy quería recordar este año pasado. Y es nomás uno. Tendré que venir aquí para recordar los demás.

> [I would like to see all of the people together. And then, if I had great big arms, I could embrace them all. I wish I could talk to all of them again, but all of them together. But that, only in a dream. I like it right here because I can think about anything I please. Only by being alone can you bring everybody together. That's what I needed

to do, hide, so that I could come to understand a lot of things. From now on, all I have to do is to come here, in the dark, and think about them. And I have so much to think about and I'm missing so many years. I think today what I wanted to do was recall this past year. And that's just one year. I'll have to come here to recall all of the other years.]

This narrative and the book close with the voice of the omniscient narrator:

Había encontrado. Encontrar y reencontrar y juntar. Relacionar esto con esto, eso con aquello, todo con todo. Eso era. Eso era todo. Y le dio más gusto. Luego cuando llegó a la casa se fue al árbol que estaba en el solar. Se subió. En el horizonte encontró una palma y se imaginó que ahí estaba alguien trepado viéndolo a él. Y hasta levantó el brazo y lo movió para atrás y para adelante para que viera que él sabía que estaba allí.

[He had made a discovery. To discover and rediscover and piece things together. This to this, that to that, all with all. That was it. That was everything. He was thrilled. When he got home he went straight to the tree that was in the yard. He climbed it. He saw a palm tree on the horizon. He imagined someone perched on top, gazing across at him. He even raised one arm and waved it back and forth so that the other could see that he knew he was there.]

In the concluding story, through memory, the fragments of the lost year coalesce in the child's mind, and he comes to discover the *other*, that is, he discovers that humanity and collective conscious that he carried within himself, and that is symbolically represented in the form of another youngster whom he discovers looking at him from a palm tree. The protagonist arrives at the realization of his own being by virtue of the experiences that, little by little, but in the span of one day, he threads together. And with this thread, like that of Daedalus, he emerges from the labyrinth with his being and identity. He becomes one with his people.

For a greater appreciation of the formal and symbolic originality of . . . *y no se lo tragó la tierra*, we return to Rivera's essay, "Chicano Literature: Fiesta of the Living," where he says the writer has "a desire to transform what is isolated in the mind into an external form." The context is the following: "To perceive what people had done through this process and to come to realize that one's own family group or clan is not represented in literature is a serious and saddening realization." The Chicano working class experience remained isolated, retained in the collective conscious, preserved to be sure in its oral literature, yet it had not encountered its external form, a form forged in a written literature. Rivera in this work externalizes the images isolated in the mind—in his own as well as in the child's mind—and gives them coherence in the form of a young boy in search of his own being. We venture to add that this being is, in turn, the *other* that Rivera himself encounters; the boy is also the central conscious through which the author relives—and we arrive at—the Chicano experience. The youngster, on the narrative level, strings together the histories which make up a year of his life, but which, essentially, because of the *forms* preserved, are *all* his life and *all* the life of his people. Structurally, this gives unity to the stories, and the work is resolved thematically in the protagonist's epiphany when he discovers himself. On an allegorical level, the youngster symbolizes the struggles and efforts of the creative process, and the unity to which this process leads. Furthermore, in a parallel allegorical plane, the adolescent's awareness of self and society points to the formation of a political conscious, as J. Saldívar notes: "Class consciousness . . . in *Tierra* is utopian insofar as it expresses the unity of a collectivity; yet it must be stressed that this proposition is an allegorical one" (103). It, nevertheless, has political implications and underscores the call for Chicano unity in the social and political context when Rivera was writing *Tierra*.

With regard to the allegorical level of the creative process, the protagonist's revelation points to that unity that Rivera himself searches for in the creative process. The author creates a character who, in turn, is a creator. Upon recreating the experiences of his people, the adolescent creates himself in his own discovery. He arrives at a communion with the *other* which is the collective humanity of his people. The youngster's I grows larger than himself, leaving behind the solitary self and becoming a collective personality. In addition to symbolizing the creative process, the boy represents the *other* for whom Rivera, the author, searches. Upon creating him, Rivera also encounters himself. In the search and encounter of the *other*, both the author and his creation emerge from the labyrinth.

Rivera comments on his protagonist's epiphany and its effect:

> In the final story of my work . . . *y no se lo tragó la tierra*, "Debajo de la casa," the child remembers and discovers. He remembers the child of before. But he also remembers that other years exist. Furthermore, he discovers that existence is, in short, a relationship between memory and constant discovery. But he goes even further. He invents. He invents himself. Arriving home, he climbs a tree. In the horizon he sees a palm tree. He imagines that someone is there

> looking at him, and that is why he greets him moving his arm back
> and forth ... I believe that whoever proposes to discover his own
> life through memory will find the volitive strength to invent himself
> continuously as desiring love for all men on earth.

Volition, here, refers to a will to discovery and self-discovery that affirms a
love for mankind, but in the "literary imaginative process" it refers to the
will to express this love in literature, to give it a form. This last process is
implied in the protagonist's self-invention. Memory has led to discovery,
self-discovery and the encounter of the *other*. Although the structure of
the novel is circular, it is open-ended. At the novel's conclusion, it remains
that this boy give a literary invention to his experience. The boy, thus,
represents an author *en potencia*.

The encounter of one's self, the *other*, and the realization of form give
rise to that exaltation that Rivera calls "The fiesta of the living," and
which is made possible through the literary recreation of the Chicano
experience, which immortalizes *la raza*. Rivera affirms:

> Is it not ... that we sense that we are a part of the same ritual?
> Perhaps this is the case: a bond that comes from a sense of destiny.
> Yes, we sense a prophecy, and we sense a fulfillment of this prophecy.
> We have been alive since time began. We are not just living; we have
> been living for centuries. We must ritualize our existence through
> words. To me there is no greater joy than reading a creative work
> by a Chicano. I like to see my students come to feel this bond and to
> savor moments of immortality, of the total experience.

It is this sensation of immortality that the youth experiences when he
emerges from the darkness beneath the house: "Quisiera ver a toda esa
gente junta. Y luego si tuviera unos brazos bien grandes los podría abrazar
a todos."

Lauro Flores affirms that "Rivera's characters ... predate the Chicano Movement. They inhabit a harsh world in which exploitation and
denial are still the fundamental traits of their existence and which leaves
them with no other exit but to express their anguish through a discourse
of silence."[21] Nonetheless, such a statement has to be tempered by the author's intention of not only documenting the migrant workers' experience
but also as a form of protest against the conditions that permitted such
an existence. Rivera, while portraying in literature a historical reality of
the 1940's and 1950's, is writing at the height of the Chicano Movement.
Rivera saw the migrant workers, with their "spirit of resistance" and will

to endure, as precursors of the struggle of the *movimiento* for social and political justice:

> In ... *Tierra* ... I wrote about the migrant worker in [the] ten year period [1945–1955]. ... I began to see that my role ... would be to document that period of time, but giving it some kind of spiritual strength or spiritual history ... I felt that I had to document the migrant worker para siempre [forever], para que no se olvidara ese espíritu tan fuerte de resistir y continuar under the worst of conditions [so that their spirit of resistance and willingness to endure should not be forgotten], because they were worse than slaves.[22]

The "silence" with which the migrant workers endured their victimization is actually an understated but resounding protest. The struggle for recognition and realization of the self which the unnamed migrant child engages, and the subsequent narratives and the overall fragmentary structure of the novel, are related, then, to those historical events of the late 1960's and early 1970's of the Chicano *movimiento* that struggled, as R. Saldívar affirms, "to fashion out of the instability and fragmentation of social life a utopian vision of collective action" (74).[23]

The sense of orality, "a communal oral history," is one of *Tierra*'s major achievements. Rivera not only artistically captures the speech of his people, but employs it structurally in the form of anonymous dialogues that function as a chorus commenting—often ironically—on the actions and outcome of various episodes. The language reproduced, as Nicolás Kanellos notes:

> helps to bring the reader into a world rarely ever depicted in the written literature of the Spanish language. As the narrative point of view shifts from the impersonal omniscient narrator to dialog, monolog and first-person narration, the Chicano language becomes accordingly more intimate and emotive, opening up new realms of experience with an appropriately new literary vocabulary that is highly endowed with the phonology, neologisms, Anglicisms and idioms of Chicano Spanish. The Chicano language, considered by some as a regional dialect of Spanish, is represented here in its most universal and artistic form, while exhibiting the flexibility and expressiveness to reproduce the argot called for in each social situation ... [24]

Rivera gives a singular literary form to the uniqueness of his people. If, by means of the labyrinth, one searches and encounters one's being and identity, the latter conceived as union with the *other*, with one's people, a singular form is also searched for and realized. ... *y no se lo tragó la tierra* is remarkable for the originality of its literary form. It is original in the true sense; it is an initial work, an inaugural event, of a culture that emerges from folklore. ... *y no se lo tragó la tierra* is characterized by being, at once, novel and story. Rivera's own pronouncements on the hybrid nature of his work confirms the findings of various formal analyses:

> As I read the manuscript for the last time, all the way through, I was satisfied that it had the continuity, compactness, and the sensibility that I had striv[en] for as I wrote-rewrote and read and re-read it. *Tierra* had germinated for several years. I had wanted to write a novel but I so liked the compacted dramatic elements of the short story that I finally decided to structure a work (novel) from which any element (chapter or short story) could be extracted and stand, out of context, on its own, with its own kernel of sensibility and meaning, albeit [with] its ambiguity. As I arranged the short stories and re-read for continuity, I would make changes in vocabulary, sentence structure, etc., to carry out a transitory sense. Finally, I began reducing a number of short stories to the very essence-thought that had provided the stimuli for the urge to write them. These became the anecdotes that I placed between each short story. They are kernels also.[25]

The innovative formal structure of *Tierra* is a reflection of an oral literary heritage based on memory. "Memory," says Rivera, "is a narrative method used by the people. That is, I remember what they remembered and the way they narrated ... in the migratory fields an oral literature was invented. The people sought refuge not only in church or with their brothers, but also sitting in a circle and listening and narrating, and by means of words escaping to other worlds, by inventing themselves as well" ("Remembering ... ").

We have noted that the concepts of labyrinth, *other* and memory, discovery and volition are indispensable in the search and encounter of being, identity and form in Rivera's novel. With regard to form, we add that this search culminates in the realization of three modes of form: 1) the formation of the protagonist; 2) the preservation or documentation of forms of life, the migrant workers, without whose documentation these forms would be lost; and 3) a literary form that, as we shall see in our discussion of "The Searchers," takes its place in the American grain.

La cosecha/The Harvest

The episodes that Rivera excluded from *Tierra*, and which he subsequently published, are "El Pete Fonseca" ("On the Road to Texas: Pete Fonseca") and "Eva y Daniel." The stories that he left unpublished are "La cosecha" ("The Harvest") and "Zoo Island," whose original title was "La vez que se contaron" ("The Time They Took a Census"). While many reasons can be adduced for their exclusion—not including lack of quality—from the novel, the determining factor was the novel's temporal and structural format.[26] The other short stories are "En busca de Borges" ("Looking for Borges"), "Las salamandras" ("The Salamanders") and "La cara en el espejo" ("Inside the Window"). The latter, along with a brief introductory narrative which could not be properly called a short story, are the only recovered installments from *La casa grande del pueblo*.

Like the episodes of *Tierra*, those stories that were excluded from the novel, published and unpublished, unfold within the context of the migratory experience. In the case of "Pete Fonseca" and "Eva y Daniel," this experience provides the setting for the presentation of the themes and the portrayal of the characters. Told from the point-of-view of the narrator-witness, these are tragic love stories, the first dealing with betrayal and the second with fidelity and the despair caused by death.

Central to "Pete Fonseca" is the portrayal of the *pachuco*. The story, narrated by a boy, takes place during the migratory cycle in Iowa. According to some literary critics, towards the end of the 1940's, the pachuco figure had started to disappear and was beginning to take on mythic proportions.[27] This twilight nature of the pachuco is expressed with the appearance of Pete Fonseca at the story's commencement:

> Apenas llegó y ya se quería ir ... Casi estaba oscuro cuando vimos un bulto que venía cruzando la labor (...) Se quitó la cachucha de pelotero y vimos que traía el pelo bien peinado con una onda bien hecha. Traía zapatos derechos, un poco sucios, pero se notaba que eran de buena clase. Y los pantalones casi eran de pachuco. Decía *chale* cada rot y también *nel y simón*, y nosotros por fin decidimos que sí era medio pachuco.
>
> [He'd only just gotten there and he already wanted to leave ... It was almost dark when we saw this shadow crossing the field (...) He took off his baseball cap and we saw that his hair was combed good with a pretty neat wave. He wore those pointed shoes, a little dirty, but you could tell they were expensive ones. And his pants were almost pachuco pants. He kept saying *chale* and also *nel* and *simón*, and we finally decided that he was at least half pachuco.]

The young narrator is taken with Pete, his clothes and manner, and especially with Pete's romance of La Chata, a loser of a woman, abandoned by various men, each of which has left her with at least one child.

With Pete's marriage to La Chata, their hard work and savings, it appears that Pete has gone straight. Implicit in the narration is the potential danger of the narrator's role imitation of the pachuco protagonist, but at this point Pete reveals his parasitic nature. Pete abandons La Chata, taking her money and the car they had saved up to buy. The story closes as it began, this time emphasizing the amoral dimension of the pachuco:

> Nosotros nomás nos acordamos de que apenas había llegado y ya se quería ir. Como quiera, el Pete hizo su ronchita ... Eso pasó allá por el '58.[28] Yo creo que la Chata ya se murió, pero los hijos de ella ya serán hombres. El Pete, recuerdo que llegó como una cosa mala, luego se hizo buena, y luego mala otra vez. Yo creo que por eso se nos pareció como un bulto cuando lo vimos por primera vez.
>
> [All we remembered was how he'd only just gotten there and already he wanted to leave. Anyhow, Pete made his little pile. That all happened around '48. I think La Chata is dead now, but her kids are grown men. I remember that Pete appeared out of nowhere, like the devil himself—bad, then he turned good, then went bad again. I guess that's why we thought he was a shadow when we first saw him.]

In his "Critical Approaches to Chicano Literature and its Dynamic Intimacy," Rivera states that a major reason for the exclusion of "Pete Fonseca" from his novel was an editorial decision concerned with the derogatory presentation of his protagonist:

> I still recall "El Pete Fonseca," a story which I had initially included in *Tierra*, being excluded from it. Both Herminio Ríos and Octavio Romano [publishers of Quinto Sol] were of the opinion that Pete Fonseca, a pachuco-type, was presented in a derogatory manner and negatively sensitive for Chicano literature at the time (1970). I [was] conceded ... but I made and make no pretense at moral judgment and simply wanted to present [him] as [an] amoral type.

In addition to the protagonist's amorality, the story alludes to Pete Fonseca's syphilis, to his past activities as a pimp, and also to the alleged incestuous relationship between La Chata and her uncle. This representation of Pete Fonseca did not conform to the romanticized portrayal of the pachuco as the rebellious Chicano hero that was appearing in this formative period of Chicano literature.

If "Pete Fonseca" is a story of betrayal, "Eva y Daniel" is the contrary; it is a story of love and devotion. Like the previous story, the point-of-view is that of the narrator-witness, but it is uncertain as to who this narrator is. Unlike "Pete Fonseca," however, we sense that the story of Eva and Daniel has become a folk tale known by all the migratory laborers, and it is this oral tradition that frames the story and helps convey its tragic tone. Its source in the oral tradition is made manifest at the beginning of the story: "Todavía recuerda la gente a Eva y Daniel. Eran muy parecidos los dos y la mera verdad daba gusto el verlos juntos" ["The people still remember Eva and Daniel. They were both very good looking, and in all honesty it was a pleasure to see them together"]. That the people retain the story of Eva and Daniel in their collective memory, that the couple is young and handsome—complying with the indispensable criteria of legendary couples—forebodes a tragic ending with the oral formulaic device of creating suspense: "Pero la gente no los recuerda por eso" ["But that's not the reason the people remember them"].

Eva's complicated pregnancy causes Daniel to go AWOL from Army boot camp, during the Korean War, only to arrive too late at her death bed. Bereft and crazed by Eva's death, Daniel does not return to the Army; instead, he orders fireworks from a mail-order catalog and lights up the sky with them as an emotional outlet and as the vision of a splendor that he has lost. Returning to the narrative present that initiated the story, we note that Daniel continues setting off fireworks. It is this action that raises the anecdote of Eva and Daniel into the folk tradition. Every time he illuminates the skies the people are reminded of the tragic story of Eva and Daniel. And for those not aware of the significance of these fireworks, the story is told once again.

Tomás Rivera, in his notes on the construction of the short story, puts emphasis on the conflicts which, for him, a story should address:

> Si no hay conflicto, no hay narración sino mera descripción. El conflicto o el problema de cada cuento es lo que nos interesa en el cuento. Entre más intrigante sea el conflicto, más se interesa el lector en el cuento. Existe en el hombre no sólo la sensibilidad vicaria de sentir a otro hombre en conflicto sino también la tendencia natural de querer saber la resolución de conflictos.[29]

> [If there is no conflict, there is no narration, only mere description. The conflict or problem of each story is what interests us as a story. The more intriguing the conflict, the more the story will

interest the reader. There exists in each of us not only the vicarious sensibility of experiencing the conflict of another person, but also the natural tendency of wanting to know the resolution of conflicts.]

Rivera's discussion of the conflicts follows the three traditional classifications: the physical conflict, between man and nature; the social conflict, between men, which can be ideological, physical or psychological; and the internal conflict which takes place within a character, predominantly psychological but which can manifest aspects of the other conflicts. A short story can contain all three types of conflicts or a combination of two or only one, but it is usually the case that one type will predominate.

By applying these types of conflict to "Pete Fonseca" and to "Eva and Daniel," we will note that the latter is characterized primarily by the third type of conflict: the psychological conflict that Daniel undergoes as a result of Eva's death. In "Pete Fonseca" the social conflict is manifested, but in a twofold manner. First, there is the social conflict between man and woman, as Pete deceives and takes advantage of La Chata; secondly, there is the social conflict between Pete, the pachuco outcast, and the rest of his society which censures his disregard of the society's norms of conduct, and which, likewise, is deceived into believing that Pete has mended his ways. The story's conclusion affirms the society's values and brands Pete as an outcast once again. In the other stories we shall note a more complex combination of conflicts.

"Las salamandras," "La cosecha" and "Zoo Island" bring into the foreground the experience of the migratory cycle. In the first two this cycle is enclosed within the greater cycle of life, death and regeneration. "Zoo Island" depicts the attempt by a group of people to affirm their existence by creating a community.

Like "El Pete Fonseca," the point-of-view in "Las salamandras" is that of an adult remembering a childhood experience; in this case, however, the adolescent is the protagonist: "Lo que más recuerdo de aquella noche es lo oscuro de la noche, el lodo y lo resbaloso de las salamandras. Pero tengo que empezar desde el principio para que puedan comprender todo esto que sentí … " ["What I remember most about that night is the absolute darkness, the mud, and the slime of the salamanders. But I should start from the beginning so you can understand all of this that I felt … "]. The story contains two levels. The first is the narrative level recounting the attempt by a migratory family to find work, during which time the protagonist experiences a profound feeling of alienation, which is overcome when the family unites in the killing of the salamanders that have invaded their tent. The second is the symbolic-allegorical account of a group of dispossessed people—a dispossession experienced in an absolute, metaphysical sense. The Chicano family, pariahs of a majority society, put up their tents on a parcel of land not realizing that they will be invaded by salamanders that seek to reclaim the land. The struggle that ensues with the salamanders can be perceived as a primordial struggle with death, the victory over which achieves their regeneration. "Las salamandras" is probably the most taut, most compelling, most psychologically penetrating story in this collection, ranking among the finest of Rivera's fiction. Taking place in a deluge that causes the migratory family to drift from one farm to another in search of work, framed by a cycle of darkness and dawn, the story takes on a biblical atmosphere, replete with symbolic meaning that culminates in the encounter with the salamanders in a metaphysical struggle with an archetypal death.[30] This story incorporates all of the conflicts as defined by Rivera. There is the physical struggle against nature, the conflict between the migrant farm workers and the dominant society, and the internal, spiritual struggle against death and alienation. This final conflict is, perhaps, the most pervasive one.

"La cosecha" presents a theme that is absent in ... *y no se lo tragó la tierra.* By the novel's very title, we note that the land is seen as the migrant worker's antagonist, the struggle against nature. But within the realm of the social conflict, the land is a political and economic extension of the dominant society. With the land, Anglo agribusiness literally forces the Chicano migrant worker to his knees. Nevertheless, an aspect of Chicano reality is missing in *Tierra*—the campesino's love of the land. In the ideological thrust of the novel, this theme would have been contradictory.

"La cosecha" takes place in *el norte*, up north, where the harvest is about to end and the migrant workers are about to return to Texas. The omniscient narrator's lyrical exposition of the fall harvest places the migrant cycle within the greater cycle of nature:

> Los últimos de septiembre y los primeros de octubre. Ese era el mejor tiempo del año. Primero, porque señalaba que ya se terminaba el trabajo y la vuelta a Texas. También había en el ambiente que creaba la gente un aura de descanso y muerte. La tierra también compartía de esta sensibilidad. El frío se venía más a menudo, las escarchas que mataban por la noche, por la mañana cubrían la tierra de blanco. Parecía que todo se acababa. La gente sentía que todo estaba quedando en descanso.
>
> [The end of September and the beginning of October. That was the best time of the year. First, because it was a sign that the work

was coming to an end and that the return to Texas would start. Also, because there was something in the air that the folks created, an aura of peace and death. The earth also shared that feeling. The cold came more frequently, the frosts that killed by night, in the morning covered the earth in whiteness. It seemed that all was coming to an end. The folks felt that all was coming to rest.]

Through the folk motif of buried treasure, the story's young protagonist discovers not monetary riches but the revelation of belonging to a transcendent cycle of life, death and regeneration. The sense of deracination caused by migrant work is countered by the youngster's awareness of belonging to a world unaffected by external forces. The love and sense of continuity, regeneration, that the earth teaches him awakens him to the love of his people and to the awareness of their continuity.

In "Zoo Island" we note the establishment of community. The action takes place in Iowa where the migrant workers are contracted to clean thistle-covered farm fields. The only lodging afforded them is the landowner's "gallineros," chicken shacks, that have been converted into small living quarters. The protagonist awakens one day with a desire to realize what he has just dreamed: "José tenía apenas los quince años cuando un día despertó con unas ganas tremendas de contarse, de hacer un pueblo y de que todos hicieran lo que el decía" ["José had just turned fifteen when he woke up one day with a great desire of taking a census count, of making a town, and having everybody in it do what he said"].

As in many of the episodes of Rivera's novel, in this story anonymous voices narrate. Thus, while the plot deals with the census and finding a name for the town, the voices express the socio-ideological conflict. The first dialogue registers a complaint against the Anglos, who, filled with curiosity, take Sunday rides by the farm to look at the Chicano field workers, who are made to feel as if they were monkeys in a zoo.[31] The third dialogue, still expressing the social discrepancy between the Chicanos and the Anglos, manifests the desire of the Chicanos to exist as a community. The census makes them feel important, counted; furthermore, they believe themselves to be more than the population of the town down the road:

—Fíjese, en el pueblito donde compramos la comida sólo hay ochenta y tres almas y, ya ve, tienen iglesia, salón de baile, una gasolinera, una tienda de comida y hasta una escuelita. Aquí habemos más de ochenta y tres, le apuesto, y no tenemos nada de eso. Si apenas tenemos la pompa de agua y cuatro excusados, ¿no?"

["See here, in that little town where we buy our food, there're only eighty-three souls, and you know what? They have a church, a dance hall, a filling station, a grocery store and even a little school. Here, we're more than eighty-three, I'll bet, and we don't have any of that. Why, we only have a water pump and four out-houses, right?"]

José and his aids arrive at a census of eighty-seven; actually, there are eighty-six, but, as the narrator explains, "salieron con la cuenta de ochenta y siete porque había dos mujeres que estaban esperando, y a ellas las contaron por tres" ["the boys came up with a figure of eighty-seven because two women were expecting and they counted them for three"].

Then it occurs to José that they forgot to count Don Simón. When they interview him, he leaves them with a revelation: "Bueno, si vieran que me gusta lo que andan haciendo ustedes. Al contarse uno, uno empieza todo. Así sabe uno que no sólo está sino que es" ["Well, you know, I kinda like what ya'll are doing. By counting yourself, you begin everything. That way you know you're not only here but that you're alive"]. Then Don Simón provides the name of their community: "¿Saben cómo deberían ponerle a este rancho? ...Zoo Island" ["Ya'll know what you oughta call this place? ...Zoo Island"]. The next day all the members of the community take their picture next to the sign the boys have put at the farm gate: "Decía: **Zoo Island, Pop. 88**1/2. Ya había parido una de las señoras" ["It said: **Zoo Island, Pop. 88**1/2. One of the women had given birth"].

In this establishment of community, José, who had wanted to found a town where everyone would do what he said, comes to learn that the values of the group prevail over those of the individual. In the story's conclusion, we perceive José's transcendence of his ego, as he experiences the pride and exhilaration of being part of the town.[32]

It is important to note that "Zoo Island" is not a self-deprecatory name; it is a transparent sign through which two societies look at and judge each other. From their perspective outside this new town, the Anglo onlookers will perceive the sign as marking the town's inhabitants as monkeys; but they will fail to note that, with the sign, the Chicanos have ironically marked the Anglos.[33] From within the town, the inhabitants see the spectators as inhumane. "Zoo Island" is a sign both of community and protest. Within the town "almas" ["souls"] abide.

The theme of death, present in much of Rivera's work, appears in two guises, often together. One is the death of a member of the family or Chicano community; the other is death itself, what Rivera calls "la muerte original" ["original death"], as in "Las salamandras." The struggle with death, in the absolute sense, is engaged in order to affirm the existence and continuity of *la raza*, the Chicano people.[34] The death of the individual is part of this struggle, as Rivera's implied author urges his people not to forget the dead.

"La cara en el espejo" ("Inside the Window"), from Rivera's unfinished novel, *La casa grande del pueblo*, deals with the effect that death has on the psyche of the young protagonist, Enrique. As the novel's title suggests, and as the story implies, it appears that Rivera wanted to portray a Chicano community, all of whose members live in one large house.[35] Here the house would be a symbol of that community whose residents number eighty-six, almost the same as "Zoo Island."

In the story, the window is the device through which the reader gains entry into the house and then into the mind of Enrique: "Esa ventana me hace que me sienta como que puedo ver dos veces.... Seguramente, por la noche, si vieran por las ventanas hacia dentro, no podrían distinguir la ventana. Un cuadro gris, que va hacia dentro" ["Surely at night, if you looked in through the window, you would not be aware of the window itself. It's a gray square which looks inside"]. Enrique's narration is an interior monologue that occurs as he lays in bed in the morning, pondering a strange experience. This monologue is interrupted at various points by an anonymous voice telling him to get up: "Ándale, levántate" ["Hurry up, get up"]. This reiterated motif serves as an ironic reversal, when it is Enrique who urges his dead friend Chuy to wake up: "Despierta, Chuy, no estés jugando" ["Wake up, Chuy, stop playing"]. The shocking experience that Enrique reveals at the conclusion not only demonstrates the impact that death has had on him, but also indicates that death is a rite—in Enrique's case, a rite of passage—that solidifies community through the memory of the dead.

The final story, "En busca de Borges" ("Looking for Borges"), is quite unlike the other stories. In it we do not find the migrant experience, nor is it a story based on a concrete reality. In a Borgean style, oneiric and enigmatic, the story concerns a person who, following Borges' advice, seeks the truth in every word, in every book, in every library, a theme familiar to readers of Borges. The story's conclusion leaves no doubt that the story is a parody. By means of his imitation of Borges, Rivera presents an anti-Borgean parable.[36] Although Borges' work insists on the futility of finding an absolute truth in the universe, his stories do exploit philosophical theories on the meaning of existence, not because Borges believes in them but because they appeal to him esthetically, as delicious fictions. Like Borges' libraries, his short stories are enclosed worlds, replete with self-referentiality, without any reference to the world in which we live. With his parable, Rivera sets forth an *ars poetica* which is opposed to Borges' nihilism. Perhaps, Rivera believed (as have others) that Borges "fictions" deal mainly with life in the abstract, without regard to the truth of human problems and social realities.[37] Rivera, through this parody, reveals a philosophy of social commitment.[38]

The Poetry

Searching is a constant theme in the work of Tomás Rivera. We have noted it in his landmark novel, ... *y no se lo tragó la tierra/ ... And the Earth Did Not Devour Him*, where the Chicano migrant workers are constantly searching for work and, spiritually, searching for a sense of community, and where the young protagonist searches for his past and his identity. We have found the same theme in his short fiction, published posthumously in *The Harvest/La cosecha*, and it is also present in his poetry, most notably and appropriately, in the epic "The Searchers."

The theme of searching can be applied to various levels: the search for material gain and economic improvement; the quest for community and a rightful place in society; the search for self-determination and a voice in this country's political establishment; and also the pursuit of meaning which concerns all intellectual endeavors. The figure of the migrant worker is a complex metaphor for all these levels of searching.

Implied in Rivera's discussion of the literary process, we note that the search itself is a figure, in a tropological sense. As we read *Tierra*, for example, its fragmented structure resembles a labyrinth; the successful passage through it entails that we comprehend the search as a figure of writing, as an allegory of the creative process. This fragmented structure is itself a duplication of the mind of the young protagonist who strives to give external form—literature—to the chaos of his experience and unresolved identity. The search, then, involves two complementary goals. One is ontological, the search for meaning and the *other*, and the second is esthetic: the search is "an exact, pure desire to transform what is isolated in the mind into an external form." ("Fiesta"). In Rivera's poetry we shall encounter the theme of searching in its various manifestations and levels.

With his death, Tomás Rivera had published twenty-six poems and had left a slightly larger amount unpublished. Part I of *The Searchers: Collected Poetry* contains those published poems, while Part II presents an equal number of the unpublished poems.[39] In his "Poetics," Rivera states that "poetry should not be explained, categorized, studied, but read and felt and sung." Poetry was for Rivera a very intimate experience. And from his words, I also gather—and this is the sense I get from reading his poetry—that poetry, by and large, was for him a private experience. His fiction he wrote for his people; his poetry he wrote for himself. The exception in this regard is "The Searchers," an epic, which by definition is public poetry. Most of his poetry, however, is intensely lyrical, in which Rivera writes for and to himself. Like many of those Renaissance writers who died keeping their lyrical poetry to themselves, and which editors ferreted out and published after their death, so Rivera left much of his poetry—certainly unintentionally—for this editor to publish posthumously. However, in keeping with Rivera's words and as part of my editorial bargain, I shall keep my discussion of his poetry brief.

The theme of the migrant worker, which permeates Rivera's prose, is found, implicitly and explicitly, in only four of these poems: in "The Rooster Crows en Iowa y en Texas," where the rooster's crows symbolize an unending cycle of work and schooling both in the north and home in Texas; in "The Overalls," which introduces the speaker to the enigma of death; in "Noon-Night," which is notable for its accusatory tone and the shackles of evil; and in "The Searchers," where the migrant workers and their quest are this epic's subject and theme.

"The Searchers" can be considered the *summa* of Rivera's poetic achievement. Incorporating the major themes and motifs of his lyric poetry, this epic is a notable achievement in the American grain. Rivera saw in his people, the migrant workers, that same spiritual nobility and search that brought all immigrants to this country, indeed, to all the Americas:

> I think of the whole American scene—both continents—and the fact that we have transplanted cultures from Europe, and the fact of the indigenous cultures still being here. I wanted to document that, but I also wanted to throw light on the spiritual strength, on the concept of justice so important for the American continents. I wanted to treat the idea of mental and intellectual liberation and where it fits into the spectrum of the Americas. Can it be achieved here, and if so, can it be done? ... creo que aquí tenemos la capacidad y la posibilidad de una emancipación intelectual mucho más fuerte y total [I think that here we have the capacity and possibility of a much stronger and complete intellectual emancipation]. Within those migrants I saw that strength. They may be economically deprived, politically deprived, socially deprived, but they kept moving, never staying in one place to suffer or be subdued, sino siempre buscaban trabajo [but always searching for work]. Siempre andaban buscando [they always kept searching]; that's why they were "migrant" work-

ers. La palabra *trabajador* está muy implícita allí [The word *worker* is very implicit there]; they were travelers. If they stayed where there was no work se morían [they would die], y no se murieron [and they didn't die]. I see that same sense of movement in the Europeans who came here, and that concept of justicia espiritual también [spiritual justice, too]. It was there. And the migrant workers still have that role: to be searchers. I've written a poem called "The Searchers." Para mí era gente que buscaba [To me they were people who searched], and that's an important metaphor in the Americas. My grandfather was a searcher; my father was a searcher; I hope I can also be a searcher. That's the spirit I seek. (Bruce-Novoa, 51)

"The Searchers" has three principal intentions.[40] The first is the affirmation of a spiritual nobility which is manifested in the persistent search for justice and the realization of the Chicano's potential existence. In this regard, the epic, true to its tradition, recounts an odyssey and expresses the collective sentiment of the Chicanos, *la raza*:

> How long
> how long
> have we been searchers?
>
> We have been
> behind the door
> Always
> behind screens and eyes
> of other eyes
> We longed to search
> Always
> longed to search (...)
>
> We searched through
> our own voices
> and through
> our own minds
> We sought with our words

Here we note an allusion to the labyrinth in which the quest for being and identity parallels the search and discovery of form, which constitutes the epic's second intention. While the poem's narrative level sets forth the search for full existence, the Chicano's rightful place in society, the allegorical level expresses the search for form:

From within came
the passions to create
of every clod and stone
a new life
a new dream
each day
In these very things
we searched
as we crumbled
dust, our very own
imaginary beings (...)

A terrón lighted our eyes
and we watered it and made
mud-clay
to create others in

While the lines in English allegorically express the search for form, the poem embeds lines in Spanish that achieved their form centuries ago and which are readily recognizable as *poesía popular* with lines in *arte menor*, octosyllables or less: "naranja dulce / limón partido / dame un abrazo / que yo te pido."[41] Hence, we note in the poem the integration of this traditional form in a search of a more comprehensive form, and one that will express the bicultural and bilingual components of the Chicano artist.

The search and discovery of literary form makes possible the epic's third intention: the search into the past in order to rescue the dead, and, through this resurrection, achieve the salvation of the living:

Death
We searched in Death
We contemplated the original
and searched
and savored it
only to find profound
beckoning
A source that continued the search
beyond creation and death
The mystery
The mystery of our eyes
The eyes we have as
spiritual reflection

and we found we were
not alone

In the search through the zone of death, through the creative space of solitude, the living and the dead are united. Similar to the experience of the young protagonist in *Tierra*, as Rivera affirms, "It is from the past that we are able to perceive, create and give life [to] our ritual; it is from this that we derive strength, that we can recognize our existence as human beings" ("Fiesta," 440). Through memory the Chicanos encounter their salvation, discovering that "We are not alone," but rather carry within themselves the history and collective experience of their people.

The reunification of the dead and the living is formally achieved through the *estribillo* or refrain:

We are not alone ...
when Chona ...
a mythic Chicana,
died in the sugar beet fields ...
or when that truck filled with us
went off the mountain road (...)
We were not alone in Iowa
when we slept in wet ditches
frightened by salamanders (...)
We were not alone
when we created children (...)
We are not alone
after many centuries

Through the modulation of the refrain—"We are not alone/We were not alone"—and its juxtaposition with the past and present, time is eternalized and the dead and the living exist contemporaneously. In their memory and collective conscious, the Chicanos live together. Memory and literary form, thus, make possible the rescue of the dead, the recuperation of the spirit of the search, the salvation of the living and the realization of continuity. Noting again this aspect of Rivera's thought, "Chicano writing," he declares, "is a ritual of immortality ... a ritual of the living ... a fiesta of the living" ("Fiesta," 439). By virtue of literary creation, the Chicano gains his existence and thereby realizes that the living are all Chicanos from the beginning: "We have been alive since time began" ("Fiesta," 440).

Death, in its various masks, is a constant theme in Rivera's works. One of its masks is that death caused by hardship and injustice, as doña

Chona's in "The Searchers" or the children's in some stories of *Tierra*. Another death is the eventual loss of a loved one, such as the father whose empty overalls are "in the garage, hanging." Another of death's masks is what Rivera calls, and as we noted, "original death." This appears to have, for Rivera, two different but experientially similar manifestations. One the one hand, it is an archetypal death, such as that related in "The Searchers" or, most hauntingly, in the short story, "The Salamanders." On the other, "original death" is that experience derived from the esthetic moment, as Rivera implies in his "Poetics": "Poetry gives me pure feelings—time, beauty, man and original death." Whether it be encountered, such as in "The Salamanders," or deliberately sought through memory and the creative act, "original death" is paradoxically the dissolution of the self and its plenitude, a nirvana-like state that tastes of eternity. Through "original death" one is reborn, and Rivera seeks it out in quest of an infinite series of rebirths.

Although a search by definition points to a goal or the object of that search, for Rivera the search is also its own objective, as he states in "Poetics"—"Poetry is finding the search"—and again expresses in "Searching at Leal Middle School" and insinuates in other poems. Thus, while the search leads to discovery, it is the search itself, the act of discovering, the creative act, that Rivera seeks.

In the second section of *The Searchers: Collected Poetry*, among those poems that Rivera left unpublished, the theme and act of searching is repeatedly expressed. Here we encounter the search for the other and the dead: "Las voces del olvido"/"Do Not Forget Me," "Another Day," "Eternity." The search for the past, not only in order to rescue it but also to be free of it is found in "La vida por fin empezó"/"Finally Life Began" and in "Desátate." It is also consistently emphasized as the search for the creative act: "Searching at Leal Middle School," "Nacimiento"/"Birth," "El despertar"/"Awakening," "Palabras," "Soy una palabra."

An important symbol of the search and the act of discovering is the dump. It first appears in *Tierra*, in the story "It's That It Hurts:" " 'if I hurry maybe I can tag along with doña Cuquita. She leaves for the dump about this time ... ' 'Be careful, children ... Look, each of you pick up a long stick and turn over the trash'." The dump reappears in "Searching at Leal Middle School." In an interview, Rivera explained the importance of the dump: "My dad knew I liked to read, so ... We ... used to go to the dump to collect reading materials. I found encyclopedias and different types of books. At home I still have my dump collection gathered from the dumps in northern towns. People threw away a lot of books" (Bruce-Novoa, 143).

The dump is the subject of a poem that appears to be incomplete. Existing only in an autograph state and without a title, and not wanting to just relegate it to an archival box, I reproduce and transcribe this intensely lyrical piece.

[In the Dump]

In the dump
he discovered beautiful flowers
among the cans and broken bottles
and tires worn out.
The sky was blue blue
and even the birds looked at it
and didn't disturb its beauty
with their flight
a sacred blue, pushing toward the earth
encircling his cosmos
pushing his
eyes inward until he would
fall asleep.
He also saw ants
winding slowly toward him
and past him in solitary communion
gasping life through tin can cities
and glass cages among rusty lakes
and giant trees moving their search
among each other when the wind dared.
He wanted to search
to wind slowly with them
and to fly high until he would
touch it.
He reached out and found no search
Only the sky and its blue
suffocating his eyes
until he only heard a white line.

The poem presents a few textual problems; for example, the phrase "when the wind dared" is vague due to the lack of a predicate compliment, that is, what the wind dares *to do* is not expressed nor is it implied. Nor is it clear what the direct object pronoun in "touch it" refers to: is it the "search" of the next line or the sky of line five and of the antepenultimate line?

The poem's textual and semantic incompleteness, and the synesthetic oxymora of the last two lines contribute to the poem's enigmatic quality. However, drawing from those texts in which the dump appears, the poem's subject is presumably an adolescent who discovers in the dump, that which has been thrown away as refuse, objects of beauty. In the dump the subject endeavors to find the search but it appears to elude him. Yet the final line suggests a liminal state, the entrance into that creative solitude that augurs the process of discovery and rebirth. It is clear that the dump, that mountain of refuse into which *la raza* had and has been thrown, is a symbol of search, of discovery and self-discovery which Rivera kept writing about in his fiction, essays and in this poetry he has left us.

The Essays

Upon his death, Tomás Rivera had published eight literary essays, and, except for two, they had all evolved from conference presentations.[42] Another essay, his last,"Richard Rodriquez' *Hunger of Memory* as Humanistic Antithesis," was from its inception written expressly for publication, but appeared posthumously. The present collection contains an additional essay,"Critical Approaches to Chicano Literature and its Dynamic Intimacy," a conference presentation, which I have been able to reconstruct from two drafts.[43]

Rivera's essays are consistent with regard to ideology, to what he perceived, during the period of the 1960's and 1970's, as the mission of Chicano literature. As he states in "Into the Labyrinth: The Chicano in Literature," "Chicano Literature has a triple mission: to represent, to conserve that aspect of life that the Mexican American holds as his own, and at the same time [to] destroy the invention of others of his own life. That is conservation, struggle, and invention." The concepts of the labyrinth and remembering are "rituals" for "capturing a fast-disappearing past" ("Fiesta"), while the struggle, although important socio-politically, is concerned—as he stresses in various of his essays—with achieving "intellectual emancipation" and "decolonizing the mind." Invention is necessary in order to confirm the authenticity of the self and of one's society, as opposed to the false figure of the Chicano fabricated by others.

Rivera notes that the confirmation of the Chicano's forms of existence through literature reveals three themes, which have remained as constants in Chicano literature to this day: *la casa* [the home], *el barrio* [the neighborhood or community] and *la lucha* [the struggle]. For Rivera, *la casa* "is the most beautiful word in the Spanish language. It evokes the constant refuge, the constant father, the constant mother...and the child. It is also beautiful because it demonstrates the strong connection between an image in the mind and an external form." Any symbolic value given to the house in *Tierra* would be confirmed by Rivera's discussion of *la casa*. *El barrio* is that "constant element in the lives of Chicanos" which, while "conserving and cleansing" the writer, "takes him back to primal and basic elements of a specific people." *La lucha* is, again, the struggle to create, to discover one's self and one's *other*, and also the struggle to continue. As such, it is a constant element in the *search*.

It is the failure of *searching* that Rivera notes in Richard Rodriquez' *Hunger of Memory*. What moved Rivera to write about the Chicano experience also compelled him to write a most convincing criticism of this controversial autobiography. In this one essay Rivera synthesizes the themes and ideological thrust of his literary work and essays.

Hunger of Memory confirmed for the Anglo American society their own invention of the Chicano: "it seems so well accepted by the North American public as a key to understanding the Mexican-American."[44] Given that the humanities are a "search for life, a search for form, a search for wisdom," then Rodriguez' *Hunger of Memory* is antihumanistic, because, although the author commences it as a "search for life and form," he eventually disassociates himself from the "basic core of family life" and its culture that are central to autobiography. Essentially, Rivera sees in Rodriguez the antithesis of the child in ...*y no se lo tragó la tierra*. Whereas the child in the novel confirms the self through the encounter of the *other*, his people, Rodriguez forsakes his native culture, and his self, in favor of the *other*, which he perceives—falsely—to be the "public" world. Where the child struggles to discover himself through the reintegration of self and society, Rodriguez' autobiography reveals a schism of the self, as he rejects his native and "private" world, associated with the Spanish language, in order to embrace an "authenticity" bestowed, he believes, by the public, Anglo American world.

Rivera characterizes Rodriguez' disassociation as a split between *Ser* and *Estar*.[45] *Ser* is what one is essentially, while *Estar* is the form that one takes, what one learns to be: "*Ser* is an interior stage, and *Estar* is an exterior one." Thus, "To leave the *Ser* only for the *Estar* is a grievous error," for it entails a rejection of one's being for an inauthentic self.

An ironic dimension of *Hunger of Memory* is that, while its author aspires that he and his work be accepted and confirmed by the Anglo public world, both are in the tradition of Mexican thought. Rivera affirms that Rodriguez adds to that stock of marginated Mexicans the figure of *el pocho*. Where Samuel Ramos wrote of *el pelado* in *El perfil del hombre en la historia de México (Profile of Man and Culture in Mexico)*, and Octavio Paz wrote of *el pachuco* in *El laberinto de la soledad (The Labyrinth of Solitude)*, "with Richard Rodriguez there is a total book on *el pocho*. Instead of achieving intellectual emancipation, *Hunger of Memory* is classic Mexican vintage, clearly seeking approbation of an inferiority complex." Thinking that he has decolonized himself, Richard Rodriguez "will likely enter another colony of despair."

> *I wrote 'Tierra' because I was a Chicano and am a Chicano. This can never be denied, obliterated or reneged from now on. I chose to create and yet I had no idea of the effect of that creation.*[46]

From this succinct but complex statement, we could extrapolate practically all the reasons for the creation of Chicano literature. What Rivera says essentially speaks for all Chicanos. First of all he wrote *Tierra*, the stories of *The Harvest*, his poetry, and even his essays because he was a Chicano. Rivera mentions how in his youth he never found the Chicano in American literature, consequently the Chicano did not exist, *la raza* was invisible. In 1958, however, there occurred a significant event that was fundamental in the determination of Rivera's career as a writer: he discovered and read Américo Paredes' "*With His Pistol in His Hand*," *A Border Ballad and Its Hero*.[47] Paredes' cultural analysis of the folklore hero, Gregorio Cortez, and of the various corridos, ballads, caused Rivera to realize two things: first, that the literature of his people had to be written from the Chicano point of view; it had to be written by a Chicano—who else could write about the Chicano but the Chicano; who else could write about the Chicano experience?; second, that "Chicano" not only designated an ethnic racial group but also a working class. This identification of ethnic group and social class, in turn, determined the ideological posture and the artistic transmission of this Chicano literature. On the one hand, it affirmed the Chicanos' own values and the reparation of injustice caused by Anglo socio-political suppression; and, on the other, it made use of their folklore and oral literary traditions.[48] These are the elements that Rivera saw in the ballads of Gregorio Cortez. What few literary portrayals of the Chicano that existed, written by non-Chicanos, were, thus, incomplete, often untrue and in many cases they presented a distorted view of Chicanos. We can perceive in the cited assertion, then, that Rivera had an ethical obligation to write of his people. In this regard he chose to write of the people with whom he was most ideologically and socially tied: the migrant workers.[49] As a result, his people can read of themselves, and those who are aware of this type of existence can say: "Sí, así era," "Yes, that's the way it was." And those who have little or no knowledge of the migrant experience can find out about that life and vicariously share an experience that is also theirs by virtue of being Chicano. That is, the migrant experience is but one, yet an emblematic one, of the many experiences of the Chicano people. The migrant experience, as Rivera wrote about it, stands in a metonymical relationship to other Chicano experiences. Due to the efforts of Chicano writers like Rivera, the Chicano is now faithfully portrayed in literature. He or she is *invented* in literature, not as a mere figment of the imagination, mind you, but *created* to the extent that this character becomes recognizable, real and true. For Rivera, literature had to *mean* something; it was not just an abstract invention of the mind, a Borgean alphabet soup. Through realistic, literary representation, therefore, Chicanos exist. The Chicano can pick up Rivera's book and say: "Está hablando de nosotros," "He's talking about us." Finally, the rest of the American people, and others, can also gain awareness of the Chicano because *la raza* has become represented in American literature.

I wish to express my gratitude to the National Endowment for the Humanities and to the University of Houston for the travel grants that allowed me do research at the Tomás Rivera Archives, University of California, Riverside, and which made possible this edition of *Tomás Rivera: The Complete Works*. I also acknowledge the assistance of Mr. Armand Martínez-Standifird, archivist of the Tomás Rivera papers, and I especially thank Mrs. Concepción Rivera for her support.

Julián Olivares
University of Houston

... y no se lo tragó la tierra

... y no se lo tragó la tierra.

La primera vez que sintió odio y coraje fue cuando vio llorar a su mamá por su tío y por su tía. A los dos les había dado la tuberculosis y a los dos los habían mandado a distinto sanatorio. Luego entre los tíos hermanos y hermanas se habían repartido los niños y los habían cuidado a como había dado lugar. Luego la tía se había muerto y al poco tiempo habían traído al tío del sanatorio pero venía escupiendo sangre. Fue cuando vio llorar a su mamá llorar cada rato rato. A él le dio coraje por que no podía hacer nada contra nadie. Ahora se sentía lo mismo. Pero ahora era por su papá.

— Se hubieran venido luego, luego, m'ijo. ¿No veían que su tata estaba enfermo? Ustedes sabían muy bien que estaba picado del sol. ¿Por que no se vinieron?

— Pos no sé. Nosotros como andábamos bien mojados de sudor no nos hacía que hacía tanto calor pero yo creo que cuando está picado uno del sol es diferente. Yo como quiera si le dije que se sentara debajo del árbol que está a la orilla de los surcos pero él no quiso. Fue cuando empezó a vomitar y luego vimos que ya no pudo aguantar y casi lo llevamos en rastra y lo pusimos debajo del árbol. El ya no luchó. Nomás se dejó que lo lleváramos. Ni repeló ni nada.

— Pobre viejo, pobre de mi viejo. Anoche casi ni durmió. ¿No lo oyeron ustedes fuera de la casa? Se estuvo retorciendo toda la noche de puros calambres. Dios quiera y se alivie. Le he estado dando para agua de limonada fresca todo el día pero tiene los ojos como de vidrio. Si yo hubiera ido ayer a la labor les aseguro que no se hubiera asoleado. Pobre viejo, le van a durar los calambres por todo el cuerpo a lo menos tres días y tres noches. Ahora

From the autograph manuscript of the original version of . . . *y no se lo tragó la tierra*

El año perdido

Aquel año se le perdió. A veces trataba de recordar y ya para cuando creía que se estaba aclarando todo un poco se le perdían las palabras. Casi siempre empezaba con un sueño donde despertaba de pronto y luego se daba cuenta de que realmente estaba dormido. Luego ya no supo si lo que pensaba había pasado o no.

Siempre empezaba todo cuando oía que alguien le llamaba por su nombre pero cuando volteaba la cabeza a ver quién era el que le llamaba, daba una vuelta entera y así quedaba donde mismo. Por eso nunca podía acertar ni quién le llamaba ni por qué, y luego hasta se le olvidaba el nombre que le habían llamado. Pero sabía que él era a quien llamaban.

Una vez se detuvo antes de dar la vuelta entera y le entró miedo. Se dio cuenta de que él mismo se había llamado. Y así empezó el año perdido.

Trataba de acertar cuándo había empezado aquel tiempo que había llegado a llamar año. Se dio cuenta de que siempre pensaba que pensaba y de allí no podía salir. Luego se ponía a pensar en que nunca pensaba y era cuando se le volvía todo blanco y se quedaba dormido. Pero antes de dormirse veía y oía muchas cosas ...

Lo que nunca supo su madre fue que todas las noches se tomaba el vaso de agua que ella les ponía a los espíritus debajo de la cama. Ella siempre creyó que eran éstos los que se tomaban el agua y así seguía haciendo su deber. Él le iba a decir una vez pero luego pensó que mejor lo haría cuando ya estuviera grande.

Los niños no se aguantaron

Se había venido el calor muy fuerte. Era raro porque apenas eran los primeros de abril y no se esperaba tanto hasta como los últimos del mes. Hacía tanto calor que no les daba abasto el viejo con el bote del agua. Venía solamente dos veces para el mediodía y a veces no se aguantaban. Por eso empezaron a ir a tomar agua a un tanque que estaba en la orilla de los surcos. El viejo lo tenía allí para las vacas y cuando los pescó tomando agua allí se enojó. No le caía muy bien que perdieran tanto tiempo yendo al agua porque no andaban por contrato, andaban por horas. Les dijo que si los pescaba allí otra vez los iba a desocupar del trabajo y no les iba a pagar. Los niños fueron los que no se aguantaron.

—Tengo mucha sed, papá. ¿Ya mero viene el viejo?

—Yo creo que sí. ¿Ya no te aguantas?

—Pos, no sé. Ya siento muy reseca la garganta. ¿Usted cree que ya mero viene? ¿Voy al tanque?

—No, espérate un ratito más. Ya oíste lo que dijo.

—Ya sé, que nos desocupa si nos pesca allí, pero ya me anda.

—Ya, ya, trabájale. Ahorita viene.

—Ni modo. A ver si aguanto. ¿Por qué éste no nos deja traer agua? A nosotros allá en el norte ...

—Porque es muy arrastrado.

—Pero los puede uno esconder debajo del asiento, ¿no? Allá en el norte siempre está mejor ... ¿Y si hace uno como que va para fuera cerca del tanque?

Y así empezaron esa tarde. Todos hacían como que iban para fuera y se pasaban para la orilla del tanque. El viejo se había dado cuenta casi luego, luego. Pero no se descubrió. Quería pescar a un montón y así tendría que pagarles a menos y ya cuando hubieran hecho más trabajo. Notó que un niño iba a tomar agua cada rato y le entró el coraje. Pensó entonces en darle un buen susto y se arrastró por el suelo hasta que consiguió la carabina.

Lo que pensó hacer y lo que hizo fueron dos cosas. Le disparó un tiro para asustarlo; pero ya al apretar el gatillo vio al niño con el agujero en la cabeza. Ni saltó como los venados, sólo se quedó en el agua como un trapo sucio y el agua empezó a empaparse de sangre ...

—Dicen que el viejo casi se volvió loco.

52

—¿Usted cree?

—Sí, ya perdió el rancho. Le entró muy duro a la bebida. Y luego cuando lo juzgaron y que salió libre dicen que se dejó caer de un árbol porque quería matarse.

—Pero no se mató, ¿verdad?

—Pos no.

—Ahí está.

—No crea compadre, a mí se me hace que sí se volvió loco. Usted lo ha visto como anda ahora. Parece limosnero.

—Sí, pero es que ya no tiene dinero.

—Pos sí.

Se había dormido luego, luego, y todos con mucho cuidado de no tener los brazos ni las piernas ni las manos cruzadas, la veían intensamente. Ya estaba el espíritu en su caja.

—A ver ¿en qué les puedo ayudar esta noche, hermanos?

—Pues, mire, no he tenido razón de m'ijo hace ya dos meses. Ayer me cayó una carta del gobierno que me manda decir que está perdido en acción. Yo quisiera saber si vive o no. Ya me estoy volviendo loca nomás a piense y piense en eso.

—No tenga cuidado, hermana. Julianito está bien. Está muy bien. Ya no se preocupe por él. Pronto lo tendrá en sus brazos. Ya va a regresar el mes que entra.

—Muchas gracias, muchas gracias.

Un rezo

Dios, Jesucristo, santo de mi corazón. Este es el tercer domingo que te vengo a suplicar, a rogar, a que me des razón de mi hijo. No he sabido de él. Protéjelo, Dios mío, que una bala no vaya a atravesarle el corazón como al de doña Virginia, que Dios lo tenga en paz. Cuídamelo, Jesucristo, sálvalo de las balas, compadécete de él que es muy bueno. Desde niño cuando lo dormía dándole de mamar era muy bueno, muy agradecido; nunca me mordía. Es muy inocente, protéjelo, él no quiere hacerle mal a nadie, es muy noble, es muy bueno, que no le traspase una bala el corazón.

Por favor, Virgen María, tú también cobíjalo. Cúbrele su cuerpo, tápale la cabeza, tápale los ojos a los comunistas y a los coreanos y a los chinos para que no lo vean, para que no lo maten. Todavía le guardo sus juguetes de cuando era niño, sus carritos, sus troquitas, hasta una güila que me encontré el otro día en el cuartito de la ropa. También las tarjetas y los fonis de ahora que ya ha aprendido a leer. Le tengo todo guardado para cuando regrese.

Protégelo, Jesucristo, que no me lo maten. Ya le tengo prometido a la Virgen de San Juan una visita y a la Virgen de Guadalupe también. El también trae una medallita de la Virgen de San Juan del Valle y él también le prometió algo, quiere vivir. Cuídalo, tápale su corazón con tu mano para que no le entre ninguna bala. Es muy noble. Tenía mucho miedo ir, él me lo dijo. El día que se lo llevaron, al despedirse me abrazó y lloró un rato. Yo sentía su corazón palpitar y me acordaba de cuando era niño y le daba de mamar y de cómo me daba gusto a mí y a él.

Cuídamelo, por favor, te lo ruego. Te prometo mi vida por su vida. Tráemelo bueno y sano de Corea. Tápale el corazón con tus manos. Jesucristo, Dios santo, Virgen de Guadalupe, regrésenme su vida, regrésenme su corazón. ¿Por qué se lo han llevado? El no ha hecho nada. El no sabe nada. Es muy humilde. No quiere quitarle la vida a nadie. Regrésenmelo vivo que no lo quiero muerto.

Aquí está mi corazón por el de él. Aquí lo tienen. Aquí está en mi pecho, palpitante, arránquenmelo si quieren sangre, pero arránquenmelo a mí. Se lo doy por el de mi hijo. Aquí está. ¡Aquí está mi corazón ... Mi corazón tiene su misma sangre ... !

Regrésenmelo vivo y les doy mi corazón.

—Comadre, ¿ustedes piensan ir para Iuta?

—No, compadre, si viera que no le tenemos confianza a ese viejo que anda contratando gente para ... ¿cómo dice?

—Iuta. ¿Por qué, comadre?

—Porque se nos hace que no hay ese estado. A ver, ¿cuándo ha oído decir de ese lugar?

—Es que hay muchos estados. Y ésta es la primera vez que contratan para ese rumbo.

—Pos sí, pero, a ver, ¿dónde queda?

—Pos, nosotros nunca hemos ido pero dicen que queda cerca de Japón.

Es que duele

Es que duele. Por eso le pegué. Y ahora ¿qué hago? A lo mejor no me expulsaron de la escuela. A lo mejor siempre no es cierto. A lo mejor no. *N'ombre sí.* Sí, es cierto, sí me expulsaron. Y ahora ¿qué hago?

Yo creo que empezó todo cuando me dio vergüenza y coraje al mismo tiempo. Ni quisiera llegar a la casa. ¿Qué le voy a decir a mamá? ¿Y luego cuando venga papá de la labor? Me van a fajear de seguro. Pero, también da vergüenza y coraje. Siempre es lo mismo en estas escuelas del norte. Todos nomás mirándote de arriba a abajo. Y luego se ríen de uno y la maestra con el palito de paleta o de ésquimo *pie* buscándote piojos en la cabeza. Da vergüenza. Y luego cuando arriscan las narices. Da coraje. Yo creo que es mejor estarse uno acá en el rancho, aquí en la mota con sus gallineros, o en la labor se siente uno a lo menos más libre, más a gusto.

—Ándale, m'ijo, ya vamos llegando a la escuela.

—¿Me va a llevar usted con la principal?

—N'ombre, a poco no sabes hablar inglés todavía. Mira, allí está la puerta de la entrada. Nomás pregunta si no sabes adónde ir. Pregunta, no seas tímido. No tengas miedo.

—¿Por qué no entra conmigo?

—¿A poco tienes miedo? Mira, ésa debe ser la entrada. Ahí viene un viejo. Bueno, pórtate bien, ¿eh?

—Pero ¿por qué no me ayuda?

—N'ombre, tú puedes bien, no tengas miedo.

Siempre es lo mismo. Lo llevan a uno con la enfermera y lo primero que hace es buscarle los piojos. También aquellas señoras tienen la culpa. Los domingos se sientan enfrente de los gallineros y se espulgan unas a otras. Los gringos a pase y pase en sus carros viéndolas y apuntándoles con el dedo. Bien dice papá que parecen changos del zoológico. Pero no es para tanto.

—Fíjate, mamá, ¿qué crees? Me sacaron del cuarto apenas había entrado y me metieron con una enfermera toda vestida de blanco. Me hicieron que me quitara la ropa y me examinaron hasta la cola. Pero donde se detuvieron más fue en la cabeza. Yo me la había lavado, ¿verdad? Bueno, pues la enfermera trajo un frasco como de vaselina que olía a puro matagusano, ¿todavía huelo así?, y me untó toda la cabeza. Me daba comezón. Luego con un lápiz me estuvo partiendo el pelo. Al rato me dejaron ir pero me dio mucha vergüenza porque me tuve que quitar los pantalones y hasta los calzoncillos enfrente de la enfermera.

Pero, ahora, ¿qué les digo? ¿Que me echaron fuera de la escuela? Pero, si no fue toda la culpa mía. Aquel gringo me cayó mal desde luego, luego. Ese no se reía de mí. Nomás se me quedaba viendo y cuando me pusieron en una esquina aparte de los demás cada rato volteaba la cara y me veía, luego me hacía una seña con el dedo. Me dio coraje pero más vergüenza porque estaba aparte y así me podían ver mejor todos. Luego cuando me tocó leer, no pude. Me oía a mí mismo. Y oía que no salían las palabras... Este camposanto ni asusta. Es lo que me gusta más de la ida y venida de la escuela. ¡Lo verde que está! y bien parejito todo. Puros caminos pavimentados. Hasta parece donde juegan al golf. Ahora no voy a tener tiempo de correr por las lomas y resbalarme echando maromas hacia abajo. Ni de acostarme en el zacate y tratar de oír todas las cosas que pueda. La vez pasada conté hasta veinte y seis... Si me apuro a lo mejor me puedo ir con doña Cuquita al dompe. Sale como a estas horas, ya cuando no está muy caliente el sol.

—Cuidado, muchachos. Nomás tengan cuidado y no vayan a pisar donde hay lumbre por debajo. Donde vean que sale humito es que hay brasas por debajo. Yo sé por qué les digo, yo me di una buena quemada y todavía tengo la cicatriz... Miren, cada quien coja un palo largo y nomás revolteen la basura con ganas. Si viene el dompero a ver qué andamos haciendo, díganle que vinimos a tirar algo. Es buena gente, pero le gusta quedarse con unos libritos de mañas que a veces tira la gente... cuidado con el tren al pasar ese puente. Allí se llevó a un fulano el año pasado... Lo pescó en mero medio del puente y no pudo llegar a la otra orilla... ¿Les dieron permiso de venir conmigo? ... No se coman nada hasta que no lo laven.

Pero si me voy con ella sin avisar me dan otra fajeada. ¿Qué les voy a decir? A lo mejor no me expulsaron. *Sí, hombre, sí.* ¿A lo mejor no? *Sí, hombre.* ¿Qué les voy a decir? Pero, la culpa no fue toda mía. Ya me andaba por ir para fuera. Cuando estaba allí parado en el escusado él fue el que me empezó a hacer la vida pesada.

—Hey, Mex ... I don't like Mexicans because they steal. You hear me?
—Yes.

—I don't like Mexicans. You hear, Mex?
—Yes.
—I don't like Mexicans because they steal. You hear me?
—Yes.

Me acuerdo que la primera vez que me peleé en la escuela tuve mucho miedo porque todo se había arreglado con tiempo. Fue por nada, nomás que unos muchachos ya con bigotes que estaban en el segundo grado todavía nos empezaron a empujar uno hacia el otro. Y así anduvimos hasta que nos peleamos yo creo de puro miedo. Como a una cuadra de la escuela recuerdo que me empezaron a empujar hacia Ramiro. Luego nos pusimos a luchar y a darnos golpes. Salieron unas señoras y nos separaron. Desde entonces me empecé a sentir más grande. Pero lo que fue hasta que me peleé fue puro miedo.

Esta vez fue distinta. Ni me avisó. Nomás sentí un golpe muy fuerte en la oreja y oí como cuando se pone a oír uno las conchas en la playa. Ya no recuerdo cómo ni cuándo le pegué pero sé que sí porque le avisaron a la principal que nos estábamos peleando en el escusado. ¿A lo mejor no me echaron fuera? *N'ombre, sí.* Luego, ¿quién le llamaría a la principal? Y el barrendero todo asustado con la escoba en el aire, listo para aplastarme si trataba de irme.

—The Mexican kid got in a fight and beat up a couple of our boys, ... No, not bad ... but what do I do?
—...
—No, I guess not, they could care less if I expell him ... They need him in the fields.
—...
—Well, I just hope our boys don't make too much about it to their parents. I guess I'll just throw him out.
—...
—Yeah, I guess you are right.
—...
—I know you warned me, I know, I know ... but ... yeah, okay.

Pero cómo me les iba a ir si todos los de la casa querían que fuera a la escuela. Él de todos modos estaba con la escoba en el aire listo para cualquier cosa ... Y luego nomás me dijeron que me fuera.

Ésta es la mitad del camino a la casa. Este camposanto está pero bonito. No se parece nada al de Tejas. Aquél sí asusta, no me gusta para nada. Lo que me da más miedo es cuando vamos saliendo de un entierro y veo para arriba y leo en el arco de la puerta las letras que dicen *no me olvides.* Parece que oigo a todos los muertos que están allí enterrados decir estas palabras y luego se me queda en la cabeza el sonido de las palabras y a veces aunque no mire hacia arriba cuando paso por la puerta, las veo. Pero éste no, éste está pero bonito. Puro zacatito y árboles, yo creo que por eso aquí la gente cuando entierra a alguien ni llora. Me gusta jugar aquí. Que nos dejaran pescar en el arroyito que pasa por aquí, hay muchos pescados. Pero nada, necesitas tener hasta licencia para pescar y luego a nosotros no nos la quieren vender porque somos de fuera del estado.

Ya no voy a poder ir a la escuela. ¿Qué les voy a decir? Me han dicho muchas veces que los maestros de uno son los segundos padres . . . y ¿ahora? Cuando regresemos a Tejas también lo va a saber toda la gente. Mamá y papá se van a enojar; a lo mejor hacen más que fajearme. Y luego se van a dar cuenta mi tío y güelito también. A lo mejor me mandan a una escuela correccional como una de las cuales les he oído platicar. Allí lo hacen a uno bueno si es malo. Son muy fuertes con uno. Lo dejan como un guante de suavecito. Pero, a lo mejor no me expulsaron, *n'ombre, sí* a lo mejor no, *n'ombre, sí.* Podía hacer como que venía a la escuela y me quedaba aquí en este camposanto. Eso sería lo mejor. Pero, ¿y después? Les podía decir que se me perdió la report card. ¿Y luego si me quedo en el mismo año? Lo que me duele más es que ahora no voy a poder ser operador de teléfonos como quiere papá. Se necesita acabar la escuela para eso.

—Vieja, háblale al niño que salga . . . Mire, compadre, pregúntele a su ahijado lo que quiere ser cuando sea grande y que haya acabado ya la escuela.

—¿Qué va a ser, ahijado?

—No sé.

—¡Dile! No tengas vergüenza, es tu padrino.

—¿Qué va a ser, ahijado?

—Operador de teléfonos.

—¿A poco?

—Sí, compadre, está muy empeñado m'ijo en ser eso, si viera. Cada vez que le preguntamos dice que quiere ser operador. Yo creo que les pagan bien. Le dije al viejo el otro día y se rio. Yo creo que cree que m'ijo no puede, pero es que no lo conoce, es más vivo que nada. Nomás le pido a Diosito que le ayude a terminar la escuela y que se haga operador.

Aquella película estuvo buena. El operador era el más importante. Yo creo que por eso papá quiso luego que yo estudiara para eso cuando terminara la escuela. Pero, ... a lo mejor no me echaron fuera. Que no fuera verdad. ¿A lo mejor no? *N'ombre, sí.* ¿Qué les digo? ¿Qué hago? Ya no me van a poder preguntar que qué voy a ser cuando sea grande. A lo mejor no. *N'ombre, sí.* ¿Qué hago? Es que duele y da vergüenza al mismo tiempo. Lo mejor es quedarme aquí. No, pero después se asusta mamá toda como cuando hay relámpago y truenos. Tengo que decirles. Ahora cuando venga mi padrino a visitarnos nomás me escondo. Ya ni para qué me pregunte nada. Ni para qué leerle como me pone papá a hacerlo cada vez que viene a visitarnos. Lo que voy a hacer cuando venga es esconderme detrás de la castaña o debajo de la cama. Así no les dará vergüenza a papá y a mamá. ¿Y que no me hayan expulsado? ¿A lo mejor no? *N'ombre, sí.*

—¿Para qué van tanto a la escuela?

—El jefito dice que para prepararnos. Si algún día hay una oportunidad, dice que a lo mejor nos la dan a nosotros.

—N'ombre. Yo que ustedes ni me preocupara por eso. Que al cabo de jodido no pasa uno. Ya no puede uno estar más jodido, así que ni me preocupo. Los que sí tienen que jugársela chango son los que están arriba y tienen algo que perder. Pueden bajar a donde estamos nosotros. ¿Nosotros qué?

La mano en la bolsa

🌿

¿Te acuerdas de don Laíto y de doña Bone? Así les decían pero se llamaban don Hilario y doña Bonifacia. ¿No te acuerdas? Pues, yo tuve que vivir con ellos por tres semanas mientras se acababan las clases y al principio me gustó pero después ya no. Era verdad lo que decían de ellos cuando no estaban presentes. De cómo hacían el pan, los molletes, de cómo a veces robaban y de que eran bulegas. Yo lo vi todo. De todos modos eran buenas gentes pero ya para terminarse las clases a veces me daba miedo andar con ellos en el moroltí que tenían y hasta de dormir en su casa; y ya al último, pues ni me daban ganas de comer. Así me la pasé hasta que vinieron por mí mi papá, mi mamá y mis hermanos.

Recuerdo que el primer día fueron muy buenos conmigo. Don Laíto se reía cada rato y se le veían los dientes de oro y los podridos. Doña Bone, bien gordota, cada rato me apretaba contra ella y yo nomás la sentía bien gorda. Me dieron de cenar, digo me dieron, porque ellos no comieron. Ahora que recuerdo, pues, nunca los vi comer. La carne que me frio estaba bien verde y olía muy feo cuando la estaba guisando pero al rato ya no olía tanto. Pero no sé si fue que me acostumbré al olor o porque don Laíto abrió la ventana. Solamente partes sabían mal. Me la comí toda porque no quería desagradar. A don Laíto y a doña Bone los quería toda la gente. Hasta los americanos los querían; siempre les daban botes de comida, ropa y juguetes. Y ellos, cuando no podían vendérnoslos a nosotros, nos los daban. También nos visitaban en la labor para vendernos pan de dulce hecho al estilo mexicano, hilo, agujas, botes de comida, y nopalitos, también zapatos, abrigos y otras cosas, a veces muy buenas, a veces muy malas.

—Cómpreme estos zapatos, ándele ... ya sé que están usados pero son de buena clase ... fíjese como todavía no se acaban ... éstos ... le garantizo, duran hasta que se acaban ...

No quise desagradar y por eso me comí todo. Y me hizo mal. Me tuve que pasar buen rato en el escusado. Lo bueno fue cuando me fui a acostar. Me metieron en un cuarto que no tenía luz, olía a pura humedad y estaba repleto de cosas —cajas, botellas, almanaques, bultos de ropa. Solamente había una entrada. No se veían las ventanas de tantas cosas todas amontonadas. La primera noche casi ni pude dormir porque estaba seguro de que del agujero que tenía el cielo del cuarto se bajarían las arañas. Todo olía muy feo. Ya para cuando oscureció no pude ver nada, pero sería medianoche cuando desperté. Yo creo que me había dormido, pero no estoy muy seguro. Lo único que podía ver era el agujero bien oscuro del cielo. Parecía que hasta se veían caras pero era la pura imaginación. De todos modos de allí en adelante me cogió el miedo pero fuerte. Y ya no pude dormir bien. Sólo en la madrugada cuando podía ver el resto de las cosas. A veces me imaginaba a don Laíto y a doña Bone sentados alrededor de mí y hubo veces que hasta estiré la mano para tocarlos, pero nada. Yo creo que desde el primer día quería que vinieran ya por mí. Ya me avisaba mi corazón de lo que pasaría después. No es que no fueran buenas gentes, sí lo eran, pero como dice la gente, tenían sus mañas.

En la escuela las clases iban todas bien. A veces, cuando llegaba por la tarde no se oía ningún ruido en la casita y parecía que no había nadie, pero casi siempre cuando estaba más en paz me asustaba doña Bone. Me apretaba por detrás y se reía y yo hasta saltaba de susto. Ella nomás risa y risa. Las primeras veces yo también terminaba por reírme pero después ya me fastidió eso. Después comenzaron poco a poco a decirme lo que hacían cuando iban al centro. Se robaban muchas cosas —comida, licor, ropa, cigarros y hasta carne. Cuando no podían venderlo a los vecinos, lo daban. Casi repartían todo. También al pasar los días me invitaron a que les viera hacer el pan de dulce. Don Laíto se quitaba la camisa. Se veía bien pellejoso. Empezaba a sudar al amasar la harina. Era cuando se metía las manos en los sobacos y luego seguía amasando la masa cuando me daba más asco. Era verdad lo que decían. Él me miraba a ver si me daba asco y me decía que así lo hacían todos los panaderos. Eso sí, yo nunca volví a comer pan de dulce del que hacía él aunque a veces tenía un montón grandísimo sobre la mesa.

Recuerdo que un día después de la escuela me pusieron a trabajar en el solar. No era que fuera tan duro pero desde ese instante me cogieron de puro contrato. Querían que trabajara a todas horas. Y es que mi papá les había pagado por el abordo. Una vez hasta querían que me calara a robarme un saco de harina de cinco libras. ¿Te imaginas? Yo tenía miedo y además no era justo. Don Laíto nomás se reía y me decía que no tenía *eguis*. De todos modos así siguieron los días, hasta a veces me daban ganas de irme de ahí, pero ni modo, ahí me había puesto papá y había gastado su dinero. La comida empeoró y ya era puro jale todo el tiempo.

Y luego . . . te voy a decir algo . . . pero por favorcito no se lo digas a nadie. Noté que empezó a venir un mojadito a la casa cuando don Laíto no estaba por allí. No sé cómo sabía cuando no estuviera. De todos modos si acaso estaba yo dentro de la casa doña Bone me echaba fuera y si estaba fuera atrancaba las puertas y yo sabía bien que no debía entrar. Una vez me quiso explicar doña Bone todo el mitote pero la mera verdad me dio vergüenza y casi no oí nada de lo que me dijo. Sí supe que le dejaba dinero. Ya estaba viejo el fulano pero cada vez que venía olía a pura loción de rasura y duraba el olor bastante rato después de haberse ido. Una noche oí la conversación entre los dos viejitos.

—Este tiene dinero y además no tiene parientes. Fíjate, viejo, que sería muy fácil. Ni quién se preocupe por él ... n'ombre, ¿tú crees? ... al viejo le importa poco, él sabe bien que es puro mojado y si le pasa algo ¿tú crees que se va a preocupar por él? Nadie sabe que viene aquí ... tú nomás déjamelo a mí ... Uh, eso será muy fácil ...

El día siguiente, después de la escuela, me rayaron en el solar, debajo de unos árboles, un cuadro en la tierra y me dijeron que querían hacer una soterránea y querían que empezara allí poco a poco. La iban a usar para poner todos los frascos de conserva que hacía doña Bone. Duré como tres días para llegarle poco hondo y luego me dijeron que ya no. Que siempre no la iban a hacer. Y luego lo mero bueno.

Me acuerdo muy bien que llegó el mojadito bien hecho de pelo un día y como siempre muy oloroso. Ya al anochecer me llamó doña Bone a que fuera a comer. Ahí estaba don Laíto ya pero no sabía cómo había entrado. Después de la cena me dijeron que me acostara luego, luego.

Llevé un susto pero susto porque al recargarme sobre la cama sentí como una víbora pero en realidad era un brazo del mojadito. Yo creía que estaría borracho porque no despertó. Salté para atrás y salí del cuarto. Los dos viejos se soltaron riendo. Luego noté que parte de la camisa la traía llena de sangre. No hallaba ni qué pensar. Nomás me acuerdo de los dientes de oro y de los podridos de don Laíto.

Cuando ya estaba bien oscuro me hicieron que les ayudara a arrastrarlo y echarlo al pozo que yo mismo había hecho. Yo no quería muy bien pero luego me dijeron que le dirían a la policía que yo lo había matado. Me acordé que mi papá les había pagado por la comida y el cuarto y de que hasta los americanos los querían muy bien. Todo lo que deseaban mis papás era que yo terminara la escuela para poder conseguir un trabajito que no fuera tan duro. Tenía mucho miedo pero como quiera lo eché al pozo. Luego entre los tres le echamos la tierra encima. Nunca le vi la cara. Y todo lo que quería yo era que se acabara la escuela para que vinieran por mí. Las dos semanas que faltaban se me pasaron muy despacio. Yo creía que se me iba a pasar el susto o que me podía olvidar, pero nada. Don Laíto hasta traía ya el reloj de pulsera del mojadito. En el solar quedó un bulto en la tierra.

Cuando por fin vinieron por mí papá y mamá me dijeron que estaba muy flaco y que me veía como que estaba enfermo de susto. Yo les decía que no, que era porque jugaba mucho en la escuela y después de la escuela. Antes de irnos me apretaron don Laíto y doña Bone y me dijeron en voz alta para que oyera papá que no dijera nada o le decían a la policía. Luego se soltaron riendo y noté que papá lo había entendido todo como una broma. Rumbo al rancho hablaron de lo bueno que eran don Laíto y doña Bone y de cómo todos los querían muy bien. Yo nomás seguía viendo para afuera de la ventana del carro y les decía que sí. Después de unos dos meses, ya cuando parecía que se me estaba olvidando todo aquello, vinieron a visitarnos al rancho. Me traían un presente. Un anillo. Me hicieron que me lo pusiera y recordé que era el que traía aquel día el mojadito. Nomás se fueron y traté de tirarlo pero no sé por qué no pude. Se me hacía que alguien se lo hallaba. Y lo peor fue que por mucho tiempo, nomás veía a algún desconocido, me metía la mano a la bolsa. Esa maña me duró mucho tiempo.

Faltaba una hora para que empezara la película de la tarde. Necesitaba cortarse el pelo, así que se metió a la peluquería de enfrente del cine. De primero no comprendió muy bien y se sentó. Pero luego le dijo de nuevo que no podía cortarle el pelo. El creyó que porque no tenía tiempo y se quedó sentado a esperar al otro peluquero. Cuando éste acabó con el cliente él se levantó y se fue al sillón. Pero este peluquero le dijo lo mismo. Que no podía cortarle el pelo. Además le dijo que mejor sería que se fuera. Cruzó la calle y se quedó parado esperando que abrieran el cine, pero luego salió el peluquero y le dijo que se fuera de allí. Entonces comprendió todo y se fue para la casa a traer a su papá.

La noche estaba plateada

La noche que le llamó al diablo estaba plateada. Casi se distinguía todo y hasta olía a día. Durante todo el día había pensado en lo que podría pasarle pero entre más pensaba, más y más era la curiosidad y menos el miedo. Así que para cuando se acostaron todos y apagaron la luz, ya se había decidido salir a la mera medianoche. Tendría que resbalarse por el piso hasta la puerta sin que nadie le sintiera ni le viera.

—Apá. ¿Por qué no deja la puerta abierta? Que al cabo ni hay ni zancudos.

—Sí, pero ¿si se mete un animal? Ya vites cómo se les metió el tejón aquel a los Flores.

—Pero, si eso fue hace dos años. Ándele, déjela abierta. Hace mucho calor. No se mete nada. En esta mota lo único que queda son los cuervos y ésos no buscan las casas. Ándele, fíjese cómo las demás gentes dejan las puertas abiertas.

—Sí, pero siquiera tienen telas.

—No todas, ándele mire qué bonita se ve la luna. Todo en paz.

—Bueno... N'ombre, vieja, no se mete nada. Tú siempre con el miedo.

Lo del diablo le había fascinado desde cuando no se acordaba. Aun ya cuando lo habían llevado a las pastorelas de su tía Pana tenía la curiosidad por lo que podría ser y cómo sería. Recordaba a don Rayos con la máscara de lámina negra y los cuernos rojos y la capa negra. Luego recordaba cuando se había encontrado el ropaje y la máscara debajo de la casa de don Rayos. Se le había ido una canica para debajo de la casa y al sacarla se encontró todo lleno de polvo. Había sacado todo, lo había despolvado, y luego se había puesto la máscara.

—Fíjese, compadre, que con el diablo no se juega. Hay muchos que le han llamado y después les ha pesado. La mayoría casi se vuelve loca. A veces que en grupos le han llamado para no tener tanto miedo. Pero no se les aparece hasta después, de a uno por uno, solitos y de distintas formas. No, no hay que jugar con el diablo. Al hacerlo ya, como quien dice, se le entrega el alma. Hay unos que se mueren de susto, otros no, nomás empiezan a entristecer, y luego ni hablan. Como que se les va el alma del cuerpo.

Desde donde estaba acostado en el piso podía ver el reloj sobre la mesa. Sintió cómo se fueron durmiendo cada uno de sus hermanos y luego los jefitos. Hasta creía oír los ronquidos que venían por la noche desde los otros gallineros. De las once a las once cincuenta y cinco fue lo más despacio. A veces le entraba un poco de miedo pero luego veía hacia fuera y se veía todo tan quieto y tan suave con lo plateado de la luna que se le iba el miedo de pronto.

—Si me voy de aquí a las once cincuenta tendré bastante tiempo para llegar al centro de la mota. De a buena suerte que aquí no hay víboras, si no, sería peligroso andar entre la hierba tan grande que hay en el centro de la mota. A las meras doce le hablo. Más vale llevarme el reloj para saber exactamente cuando son las doce, si no, a lo mejor no viene. Tiene que ser a medianoche, a la mera medianoche, a las meritas doce.

Salió muy despacio sin hacer ruido y levantó el reloj de la mesa. Se lo echó en la bolsa del pantalón y notó que sonaba más fuerte dentro de la bolsa que afuera. Aun ya fuera del gallinero se fue lentamente pisando con cuidado, se detenía de vez en cuando. Sentía que alguien le veía. Siguió cuidadosamente hasta que había pasado el escusado. De allí casi no se podían ver los gallineros y ya empezó a hablarse pero muy quedito.

—Y ¿cómo le llamo? A lo mejor se me aparece. No, no creo. De todos modos si se me aparece no me puede hacer nada. Todavía no me muero. Así que no puede hacerme nada. Nomás quisiera saber si hay o no hay. Si no hay diablo a lo mejor no hay tampoco... No, más vale no decirlo. Me puede caer un castigo. Pero si no hay diablo a lo mejor tampoco hay castigo. No, tiene que haber castigo. Bueno, pero ¿cómo le hablo? Solamente ¿diablo? o ¿pingo? o ¿chamuco? ¿Lucifer? ¿Satanás? ... lo que se me venga primero.

Llegó al centro de la mota y le llamó. Primero no le salían las palabras de puro miedo, pero luego que accidentalmente se le salió el nombre en voz alta y no pasó nada, siguió llamándole de distintas maneras. Y nada. No salió nadie. Todo se veía igual. Todo estaba igual. Todo en paz. Pensó entonces que lo mejor sería maldecir al diablo. Lo hizo. Le echó todas las maldiciones que sabía en distintos tonos de voz. Hasta le echó de la madre. Pero, nada. No se apareció nada ni nadie ni cambió nada. Desilusionado y sintiendo a veces cierta valentía empezó a caminar hacia la casa. El viento que sonaba las hojas de los árboles parecía acompañarle los pasos. No había diablo.

—Pero si no hay diablo tampoco hay . . . No, más vale no decirlo. A lo mejor me cae un castigo. Pero, no hay diablo. A lo mejor se me aparece después. No, se me hubiera aparecido ya. ¿Qué mejor ocasión que en la noche y yo solo? No hay. No hay.

En dos o tres ocasiones sintió que alguien le hablaba pero no quiso voltear, no de miedo sino porque estaba seguro de que no era nadie ni nada. Ya cuando se acostó, con mucho cuidado, sin hacer ruido, y cerciorado de que no había diablo le empezó a entrar un escalofrío y una revoltura en el estómago. Antes de dormirse pensó un buen rato. *No hay diablo, no hay nada.* Lo único que había habido en la mota había sido su propia voz. Pensó que bien decía la gente que no se jugaba con el diablo. Luego comprendió todo. Los que le llamaban al diablo y se volvían locos, no se volvían locos porque se les aparecía sino al contrario, porque no se les aparecía. Y se quedó dormido viendo cómo la luna saltaba entre las nubes y los árboles contentísima de algo.

Una tarde el ministro de una de las iglesias protestantes del pueblo vino al rancho y les avisó que iba a venir un fulano a enseñarles trabajos manuales para que ya no tuvieran que trabajar solamente en la tierra. Casi la mayor parte de los hombres se animaron. Les iba a enseñar a ser carpinteros. El fulano vino como a las dos semanas en una camioneta y con una trailer. Traía de ayudante a la esposa del ministro para que le interpretara. Pero nunca les enseñaron nada. Se pasaban todo el día dentro de la trailer. A la semana se fueron sin decir una palabra. Supieron después que le había quitado la esposa al ministro.

... y no se lo tragó la tierra

La primera vez que sintió odio y coraje fue cuando vio llorar a su mamá por su tío y su tía. A los dos les había dado la tuberculosis y a los dos los habían mandado a distintos sanatorios. Luego entre los otros hermanos y hermanas se habían repartido los niños y los habían cuidado a como había dado lugar. Luego la tía se había muerto y al poco tiempo habían traído al tío del sanatorio, pero ya venía escupiendo sangre. Fue cuando vio llorar a su madre cada rato. A él le dio coraje porque no podía hacer nada contra nadie. Ahora se sentía lo mismo. Pero ahora era por su padre.

—Se hubieran venido luego luego, m'ijo. ¿No veían que su tata estaba enfermo? Ustedes sabían muy bien que estaba picado del sol. ¿Por qué no se vinieron?

—Pos, no sé. Nosotros como andábamos bien mojados de sudor no se nos hacía que hacía mucho calor pero yo creo que cuando está picado uno del sol es diferente. Yo como quiera sí le dije que se sentara debajo del árbol que está a la orilla de los surcos, pero él no quiso. Fue cuando empezó a vomitar. Luego vimos que ya no pudo azadonear y casi lo llevamos en rastra y lo pusimos debajo del árbol. Nomás dejó que lo lleváramos. Ni repeló ni nada.

—Pobre viejo, pobre de mi viejo. Anoche casi ni durmió. ¿No lo oyeron ustedes fuera de la casa? Se estuvo retorciendo toda la noche de puros calambres. Dios quiera y se alivie. Le he estado dando agua de limonada fresca todo el día pero tiene los ojos como de vidrio. Si yo hubiera ido ayer a la labor les aseguro que no se hubiera asoleado. Pobre viejo, le van a durar los calambres por todo el cuerpo a lo menos tres días y tres noches. Ahora ustedes cuídense. No se ataréen tanto. No le hagan caso al viejo si los apura. Aviéntenle con el trabajo. Como él no anda allí empinado, se le hace muy fácil.

Le entraba más coraje cuando oía a su papá gemir fuera del gallinero. No se quedaba adentro porque decía que le entraban muchas ansias. Apenas afuera podía estar, donde le diera el aire. También podía estirarse en el zacate y revolcarse cuando le entraban los calambres. Luego pensaba en que si su padre se iba a morir de la asoleada. Oía a su papá que a veces empezaba a rezar y a pedir ayuda a Dios. Primero había tenido esperanzas de que se aliviara pronto pero al siguiente día sentía que le crecía el odio. Y más cuando su mamá o su papá clamaba por la misericordia de

Dios. También esa noche los habían despertado, ya en la madrugada, los pujidos de su papá. Y su mamá se había levantado y le había quitado los escapularios del cuello y se los había lavado. Luego había prendido unas velitas. Pero, nada. Era lo mismo de cuando su tío y su tía.

—¿Qué se gana, mamá, con andar haciendo eso? ¿A poco cree que le ayudó mucho a mi tío y a mi tía? ¿Por qué es que nosotros estamos aquí como enterrados en la tierra? O los microbios nos comen o el sol nos asolea. Siempre alguna enfermedad. Y todos los días, trabaje y trabaje. ¿Para qué? Pobre papá, él que le entra parejito. Yo creo que nació trabajando. Como dice él, apenas tenía los cinco años y ya andaba con su papá sembrando maíz. Tanto darle de comer a la tierra y al sol y luego, zas, un día cuando menos lo piensa cae asoleado. Y uno sin poder hacer nada. Y luego ellos rogándole a Dios ... si Dios no se acuerda de uno ... yo creo que ni hay ... No, mejor no decirlo, a lo mejor empeora papá. Pobre, siquiera eso le dará esperanzas.

Su mamá le notó lo enfurecido que andaba y le dijo por la mañana que se calmara, que todo estaba en las manos de Dios y que su papá se iba a aliviar con la ayuda de Dios.

—N'ombre, ¿usted cree? A Dios, estoy seguro, no le importa nada de uno. ¿A ver, dígame usted si papá es de mal alma o de mal corazón? ¿Dígame usted si él ha hecho mal a alguien?
—Pos no.
—Ahí está. ¿Luego? ¿Y mi tío y mi tía? Usted dígame. Ahora sus pobres niños sin conocer a sus padres. ¿Por qué se los tuvo que llevar? N'ombre, a Dios le importa poco de uno los pobres. A ver, ¿por qué tenemos que vivir aquí de esta manera? ¿Qué mal le hacemos a nadie? Usted tan buena gente que es y tiene que sufrir tanto.
—Ay, hijo, no hables así. No hables contra la voluntad de Dios. M'ijo, no hables así por favor. Que me das miedo. Hasta parece que llevas el demonio entre las venas ya.
—Pues, a lo mejor. Así, siquiera se me quitaría el coraje. Ya me canso de pensar. ¿Por qué? ¿Por qué usted? ¿Por qué papá? ¿Por qué mi tío? ¿Por qué mi tía? ¿Por qué sus niños? ¿Dígame usted por qué? ¿Por qué nosotros nomás enterrados en la tierra como animales sin ningunas esperanzas de nada? Sabe que las únicas esperanzas son las de venir para acá cada año. Y como usted misma dice, hasta que

se muere uno, descansa. Yo creo que así se sintieron mi tío y mi tía, y así se sentirá papá.

—Así es, m'ijo. Sólo la muerte nos trae el descanso a nosotros.

—Pero, ¿por qué a nosotros?

—Pues dicen que . . .

—No me diga nada. Ya sé lo que me va a decir —que los pobres van al cielo.

Ese día empezó nublado y sentía lo fresco de la mañana rozarle las pestañas mientras empezaban a trabajar él y sus hermanos. La madre había tenido que quedarse en casa a cuidar al viejo. Así que se sentía responsable de apurar a sus hermanos. Por la mañana, a lo menos por las primeras horas, se había aguantado el sol, pero ya para las diez y media limpió el cielo de repente y se aplanó sobre todo el mundo. Empezaron a trabajar más despacio porque se les venía una debilidad y un bochorno si trabajaban muy aprisa. Luego se tenían que limpiar el sudor de los ojos cada rato porque se les oscurecía la vista.

—Cuando vean oscuro, muchachos, párenle de trabajar o denle más despacio. Cuando lleguemos a la orilla descansamos un rato para coger fuerzas. Va a estar caliente hoy. Que se quedara nubladito así como en la mañana, ni quién dijera nada. Pero nada, ya aplanándose el sol ni una nubita se le aparece de puro miedo. Para acabarla de fregar, aquí acabamos para los dos y luego tenemos que irnos a aquella labor que tiene puro lomerío. Arriba está bueno pero cuando estemos en las bajadas se pone bien sofocado. Ahí no ventea nada de aire. Casi ni entra el aire. ¿Se acuerdan?

—Sí.

—Ahí nos va a tocar lo mero bueno del calor. Nomás toman bastante agua cada rato; no le hace que se enoje el viejo. No se vayan a enfermar. Y si ya no aguantan me dicen luego luego ¿eh? Nos vamos para la casa. Ya vieron lo que le pasó a papá por andar aguantando. El sol se lo puede comer a uno.

Así como habían pensado se habían trasladado a otra labor para las primeras horas de la tarde. Ya para las tres andaban todos empapados de sudor. No traían una parte de la ropa seca. Cada rato se detenían. A veces no alcanzaban respiración, luego veían todo oscuro y les entraba el miedo de asolearse, pero seguían.

—¿Cómo se sienten?

—N'ombre, hace mucho calor. Pero tenemos que seguirle. Siquiera hasta las seis. Nomás que esta agua que traemos ya no quita la sed. Cómo quisiera un frasco de agua fresca, fresquecita acabada de sacar de la noria, o una coca bien helada.

—Estás loco, con eso sí que te asoleas. Nomás no le den muy aprisa. A ver si aguantamos hasta las seis. ¿Qué dicen?

A las cuatro se enfermó el más chico. Tenía apenas nueve años pero como ya le pagaban por grande trataba de emparejarse con los demás. Empezó a vomitar y se quedó sentado, luego se acostó. Corrieron todos a verlo atemorizados. Parecía como que se había desmayado y cuando le abrieron los párpados tenía los ojos volteados al revés. El que se le seguía en edad empezó a llorar pero le dijo luego luego que se callara y que ayudara a llevarlo a casa. Parecía que se le venían calambres por todo el cuerpecito. Lo llevó entonces cargado él solo y se empezó a decir otra vez que por qué.

—¿Por qué a papá y luego a mi hermanito? Apenas tiene los nueve años. ¿Por qué? Tiene que trabajar como un burro enterrado en la tierra. Papá, mamá y éste mi hermanito, ¿qué culpa tienen de nada?

Cada paso que daba hacia la casa le retumbaba la pregunta ¿por qué? Como a medio camino se empezó a enfurecer y luego comenzó a llorar de puro coraje. Sus otros hermanitos no sabían qué hacer y empezaron ellos también a llorar, pero de miedo. Luego empezó a echar maldiciones. Y no supo ni cuándo, pero lo que dijo lo había tenido ganas de decir desde hacía mucho tiempo. Maldijo a Dios. Al hacerlo sintió el miedo infundido por los años y por sus padres. Por un segundo vio que se abría la tierra para tragárselo. Luego se sintió andando por la tierra bien apretada, más apretada que nunca. Entonces le entró el coraje de nuevo y se desahogó maldiciendo a Dios. Cuando vio a su hermanito ya no se le hacía tan enfermo. No sabía si habían comprendido sus otros hermanos lo grave que había sido su maldición.

Esa noche no se durmió hasta muy tarde. Tenía una paz que nunca había sentido antes. Le parecía que se había separado de todo. Ya no le preocupaba ni su papá ni su hermano. Todo lo que esperaba era el nuevo día, la frescura de la mañana. Para cuando amaneció su padre estaba mejor. Ya iba de alivio. A su hermanito también casi se le fueron de encima los calambres. Se sorprendía cada rato por lo que había hecho la tarde anterior. Le iba a decir a su mamá pero decidió guardar el secreto. Solamente le dijo que la tierra no se comía a nadie, ni que el sol tampoco.

Salió para el trabajo y se encontró con la mañana bien fresca. Había nubes y por primera vez se sentía capaz de hacer y deshacer cualquier cosa que él quisiera. Vio hacia la tierra y le dio una patada bien fuerte y le dijo:

—Todavía no, todavía no me puedes tragar. Algún día, sí. Pero yo ni sabré.

El abuelo quedó paralizado del cuello para abajo después del ataque al cerebro. Uno de sus nietos vino a platicar con él un día. El abuelo le preguntó que cuántos años tenía y que qué era lo que más deseaba. El nieto le contestó que tenía veinte y que lo que más quería era que se pasaran los siguientes diez años de su vida inmediatamente para saber lo que había pasado con su vida. El abuelo le dijo que estaba bien estúpido y ya ni le siguió hablando. El nieto no comprendió por qué le había llamado estúpido hasta que cumplió los treinta años.

Primera comunión

❦

La primera comunión siempre la hacía el padre a mediados de la primavera. Yo siempre recordaré aquel día en mi vida. Me acuerdo de lo que llevaba puesto, de mi padrino y del chocolate con pan que desayunamos después de la comunión, pero también me acuerdo de lo que vi en la sastrería que estaba a un lado de la iglesia. Yo creo que todo pasó porque me fui muy temprano a la iglesia. Es que no había podido dormir la noche anterior tratando de recordar los pecados que tenía y, peor, tratando de llegar a un número exacto. Además, como mamá me había puesto un cuadro del infierno en la cabecera y como el cuarto estaba empapelado de caricaturas del fantasma y como quería salvarme de todo mal, pensaba sólo en eso.

—Recuerden, niños, quietitos, quietitos. Ya han aprendido bien los rezos, ahora ya saben cuáles son los pecados mortales y los veniales, ahora ya saben lo que es un sacrilegio, ahora ya saben que ustedes son almas de Dios, pero que pueden ser almas del diablo. Pero cuando vayan a confesarse tienen que decir todos los pecados, tienen que tratar de recordar todos los que hayan hecho. Porque si se les olvida uno y van a comulgar entonces eso sería un sacrilegio y si hacen un sacrilegio van al infierno. Diosito sabe todo. A él no le pueden mentir. A mí sí, al padrecito sí, pero Dios sabe todo, así que si no tienen el alma purificada de pecados entonces no deberían de comulgar; sería sacrilegio. Así que a decir todos los pecados. A recordar todos los pecados. ¿No les daría vergüenza venir a comulgar y después acordarse de algún pecado que se les olvidó? A ver, vamos a practicar con los pecados. ¿Quién quiere empezar? Vamos a empezar con los pecados que hacemos con las manos cuando nos tocamos el cuerpo. ¿Quién quiere empezar?

A la monjita le gustaba que dijéramos los pecados del cuerpo. La mera verdad es que ensayábamos mucho sobre los pecados y también la mera verdad era que yo no comprendía muchas cosas. Lo que sí me daba miedo era el infierno porque unos meses antes me había caído en un baño de brasas que usábamos como calentador en el cuartito donde dormíamos. Me había quemado el chamorro. Bien me podía imaginar lo que sería estar en el infierno para siempre. Eso era todo lo que comprendía. Así que esa noche, vísperas de primera comunión, me la pasé repasando todos los pecados que había cometido. Pero lo más difícil era llegar a un número definitivo como lo quería la monjita. Sería ya la madrugada cuando por fin llegué a un punto de conciencia justificada. Había hecho ciento cincuenta pecados pero iba a admitir a doscientos.

—Si digo ciento cincuenta y se me han olvidado algunos me va mal. Mejor digo doscientos y así por muchos que se me pasen no hago ningún sacrilegio. Sí, he hecho doscientos pecados . . . Padrecito, vengo a confesar mis pecados . . . ¿Cuántos? . . . doscientos . . . de todas clases . . . ¿Los mandamientos? Contra todos los diez mandamientos . . . Así no hay sacrilegios. Es mejor así, diciendo de más queda uno más purificado.

Recuerdo que ese día me levanté más temprano aún de lo que esperaba mamá. Mi padrino iba a estar esperándome en la iglesia y no quería llegar ni un segundo tarde.

—Ándele, mamá, arrégleme los pantalones, yo creía que ya lo había hecho anoche.

—Es que no pude ver más anoche. La vista me está fallando ya y por eso lo dejé mejor para esta mañana. Oye, y ¿qué prisa tienes esta mañana? Es muy temprano todavía. No se van a confesar hasta las ocho y apenas son las seis. Tu padrino no va a estar allí hasta las ocho.

—Ya sé, pero no pude dormir. Ándele, mamá, que ya quiero irme.

—Y ¿qué vas a hacer tan temprano?

—Pues quiero irme porque se me hace que se me olvidan los pecados que tengo que decirle al padre. Estando en la iglesia puedo pensar mejor.

—Bueno, ahorita acabo. No creas, si nomás pudiendo ver, puedo hacer bastante.

Me fui repasando los pecados y los sacramentos de la comunión. Ya estaba bien claro el día pero todavía no se veía mucha gente en la calle. La mañana estaba fresca. Cuando llegué a la iglesia la encontré cerrada. Yo creo que el padre se habría quedado dormido o andaba muy ocupado. Por eso me fui andando alrededor de la iglesia y pasé cerca de la sastrería que estaba a un lado de la iglesia. Me sorprendieron unas risotadas y luego unos gemidos porque no creía que hubiera gente por allí. Pensé que sería un perro pero luego ya se oyó como gente otra vez y por eso me asomé por la ventanita que tenía la puerta. Ellos no me vieron pero yo sí. Estaban desnudos y bien abrazados en el piso sobre unas camisas y vestidos. No sé por qué pero no podía quitarme de la ventanita. Luego me vieron ellos y trataron de taparse y me gritaron que me fuera de allí. La mujer se veía toda desgreñada y como que estaba enferma. Yo, la mera verdad, me asusté y me fui corriendo para la iglesia pero ya no me podía quitar de la cabeza lo que había visto. Pensé entonces que esos serían los pecados que hacíamos con las manos en el cuerpo. Pero no se me quitaba de la vista aquella mujer y aquel hombre en el piso. Cuando empezaron a venir los demás compañeros les iba a decir pero pensé mejor decirles después de que comulgaran. Me sentía más y más como que yo había cometido el pecado del cuerpo.

—Ya ni modo. Pero, no puedo decirles a los otros, si no van a pecar como yo. Mejor no voy a comulgar. Mejor no me confieso. No puedo ahora que sé, no puedo. Pero ¿qué dirán mi papá y mi mamá si no comulgo, y mi padrino, ni modo de dejarlo plantado. Tengo que confesar lo que vi. Me dan ganas de ir otra vez. A lo mejor están en el piso todavía. Ni modo, voy a tener que echar mentiras. ¿A lo mejor se me olvida de aquí a cuando me confiese? ¿A lo mejor no vi nada? ¿Y que no hubiera visto nada?

Recuerdo que cuando me fui a confesar y que me preguntó el padre por los pecados, le dije solamente que doscientos y de todos. Me quedé con el pecado de carne. Al regresar a casa con mi padrino se me hacía todo cambiado, como que estaba y no estaba en el mismo lugar. Todo me parecía más pequeño y menos importante. Cuando vi a papá y a mamá me los imaginé en el piso. Empecé a ver a todos los mayores como desnudos y ya se me hacían las caras hasta torcidas y hasta los oía reír o gemir aunque ni se estuvieran riendo. Luego me imaginé al padre y a la monjita por el piso. Casi ni pude comer el pan dulce ni tomarme el chocolate y nomás acabé y recuerdo que salí corriendo de la casa. Parecía sentirme como que me ahogaba.

—Y ¿éste qué tiene? ¡Qué atenciones!
—Ándele, déjelo, compadre, no se apure por mí, yo tengo los míos. Estos chicos, todo lo que piensan es en jugar todo el tiempo. Déjelo, que se divierta, hoy es su primera comunión.
—Sí, sí, compadre, si yo no digo que no jueguen. Pero tienen que aprender a ser más atentos. Tienen que tener más respeto a los grandes, a sus mayores, contimás a su padrino.
—No, pos, eso sí.

Recuerdo que me fui rumbo al monte. Levanté unas piedras y se las tiré a unos nopales. Luego quebré unas botellas. Me trepé en un árbol y allí me quedé mucho rato hasta que me cansé de pensar. Cada rato recordaba la escena de la sastrería y allá solo hasta me entraba gusto al repasar. Hasta se me olvidó que le había echado mentiras al padre. Y luego me sentía lo mismo que cuando había oído hablar al misionero acerca de la gracia de Dios. Tenía ganas de saber más de todo. Y luego pensé que a lo mejor era lo mismo.

La profesora se asombró del niño cuando éste, al oír que necesitaban un botón para poner como seña en el cartelón de la industria botonera, se arrancó uno de su camisa y se lo dio. Se asombró porque sabía que probablemente era la única camisa que tenía. No supo si lo hizo por ayudar, por pertenecer o por amor a ella. Sí sintió la intensidad de las ganas y más que todo por eso se sorprendió.

Los quemaditos

Los García eran cinco. Don Efraín, doña Chona y los tres niños, Raulito, Juan y María, de siete, seis y cinco años respectivamente. El domingo por la noche habían venido muy entusiasmados del cine porque habían visto una película de boxeo. A don Efraín le había gustado más que a todos y luego cuando habían llegado a la casa había sacado los guantes de boxear que les había comprado a los niños y luego les había hecho que se pusieran los guantes a los dos niños. Hasta les quitó la ropa y los dejó en calzoncillos y les untó un poquito de alcohol en el pechito, así como lo habían hecho en la película. A doña Chona no le gustaba que pelearan porque siempre salía alguien disgustado y luego se formaba la llorería por un buen rato.

—Ya, viejo, ¿para qué les haces que se peleen? Nada vale; a Juan siempre le sale sangre de las narices y tú sabes lo difícil que es parársela después. Ya, viejo, déjalos que se duerman.

—Hombre, vieja.

—Si no soy hombre.

—Déjalos que jueguen. Y a lo mejor aprenden siquiera a defenderse.

—Pero es que apenas cabemos parados en este gallinero y tú andas ahí correteando como si tuviéramos tanto lugar.

—Y ¿tú qué crees que hacen cuando nos vamos al trabajo? Ya quisiera que estuvieran más grandes para poder llevarlos con nosotros a la labor. Para que trabajaran o que se quedaran quietos en el carro siquiera.

—Pos sí. Pero ¿tú crees? Entre más grandes más inquietos. A mí no me gusta nada dejarlos aquí solos.

—A lo mejor uno de éstos sale bueno para el guante y entonces sí nos armamos, vieja. Fíjate nomás lo que ganan los campeones. Miles y miles. A ver si les mando traer un punching bag por catálogo la semana que entra nomás que nos paguen.

—Pos sí, ¿cómo sabe uno, verdad?

—Pos sí. Es lo que digo yo.

A los tres niños los dejaban en casa cuando se iban a trabajar porque al viejo no le gustaba que anduvieran los niños en la labor haciendo travesuras o quitándoles el tiempo a los padres. Habían tratado de llevarlos con ellos y mantenerlos en el carro pero se había puesto muy caliente el día y muy bochornoso y hasta se habían puesto enfermos. Desde entonces decidieron dejarlos en casa mejor, aunque eso sí todo el día andaban bien preocupados por ellos. En lugar de echar lonche iban a casa a comer a mediodía y así se daban cuenta de que si estaban bien o no. Ese siguiente lunes se levantaron como siempre de madrugadita y se fueron a trabajar. Los niños se quedaron bien dormiditos.

—Te ves muy contento, viejo.
—Ya sabes por qué.
—No, no solamente por eso, te ves más contento que por eso.
—Es que quiero mucho a mis hijos. Como tú. Y venía pensando en cómo a ellos también les gusta jugar con uno.

Como a las diez de la mañana divisaron, desde la labor donde andaban, una humadera que se levantaba en el rancho. Todos pararon de trabajar y se echaron en corrida a sus propios carros. A toda velocidad partieron para el rancho. Cuando llegaron hallaron al gallinero de los García envuelto en llamas. Solamente el más grande se salvó. Los otros quedaron quemaditos.

—Dicen que el más grandecito les hizo que se pusieran los guantes a Juan y a María. Andaban jugando nomás. Pero luego creo que les untó alcohol y quién sabe qué más mugrero en los cuerpecitos para hacerle igual que en la película que habían visto. Y así anduvieron jugando.
—Pero, ¿cómo se quemaron?
—Pues, nada, que el más grandecito, Raulito, se puso al mismo tiempo a guisar unos huevos y de un modo y otro se encendieron los cuerpecitos y pa' qué quiere.
—Les echaría mucho alcohol.
—Ande, usted sabe cómo tiene uno mugrero en la casa y tan reducido que está todo. Creo que les explotó el tanque de querosín de la estufa y pa' qué quiere. Les llenaría a todos de lumbre y claro que también el gallinero.
—Pos sí.
—Y ¿sabe qué?
—¿Qué?
—Que lo único que no se quemó fueron los guantes. Dicen que a la niñita la hallaron toda quemadita con los guantes puestos.
—Pero, ¿por qué no se quemarían los guantes?
—Es que esta gente sabe hacer las cosas muy bien y no les entra ni la lumbre.

—Y los García, ¿cómo siguen?

—Pues ya se les está pasando la tristeza aunque no creo que se les olvide. Dígame usted qué más puede hacer uno. Si no sabe uno cuándo le toca, ni cómo. Pobrecitos. Pero no sabe uno.

—Pos no.

Fue un día muy bonito el día del casamiento. Toda esa semana había andado el novio y su padre bien atareados componiendo el solar de la casa de la novia y haciendo una carpa de lona dentro de la cual recibirían las felicitaciones los novios. Trajeron unas ramas de nogal y unas flores del campo y arreglaron todo muy bien. Luego alisaron muy bien y con mucho cuidado enfrente de la carpa. Cada rato le echaban agua para que se fuera aplanando la tierra. Así, cuando empezara el baile no se levantaría la polvadera. Después de que se casaron en la iglesia se vinieron andando por toda la calle con todas las madrinas y los padrinos detrás de ellos. Enfrente de ellos venía un montón de niños corriendo y gritando, "Ahí vienen los novios".

La noche que se apagaron las luces

🌿

La noche que se apagaron las luces en el pueblo unos se asustaron y otros no. No había tormenta ni relámpagos, así que unos no supieron hasta después. Los que habían estado en el baile supieron pero los que no, no ... hasta otro día. Los que se habían quedado en casa nomás se dieron cuenta de que poco después de que se apagaron las luces ya no se oyó la música por entre la noche y adivinaron que se había acabado el baile. Pero no se dieron cuenta de nada hasta otro día.

—Este Ramón quería mucho a su novia. Sí, la quería mucho. Yo sé bien porque era amigo mío y, tú sabes que no hablaba mucho, pero como quiera a mí me decía todo. Muchas veces me dijo que la quería mucho. Andaban de novios desde el año pasado y se habían regalado unos anillos muy bonitos que compraron en el Kres. Ella también lo quería, pero quién sabe qué pasaría este verano. Dicen que apenas la había vuelto a ver desde hace cuatro meses ... no se sabe, no se sabe ...

—Mira, te prometo que no voy a andar con nadie. Ni que le voy a hacer borlote a nadie. Te prometo. Quiero casarme contigo ... Nos vamos ahorita mismo si quieres ... pues entonces hasta que acabe la escuela. Pero, mira, te prometo que no voy a andar con nadie ni le voy a hacer borlote a nadie. Te prometo. Si quieres nos vamos ahorita. Yo te puedo mantener. Ya sé, ya sé ... pero se conforman. Vámonos. ¿Te vas conmigo?

—No, es mejor esperarnos. ¿No crees? Es mejor hacerlo bien. Yo también te prometo ... Tú sabes bien que te quiero. Confía en mí. Papá quiere que acabe la escuela. Y, pues tengo que hacer lo que él dice. Pero no porque no me voy contigo no te quiero. Sí te quiero, te quiero mucho. Confía en mí. Yo también no voy a andar con nadie. Te prometo.

—Sí se sabe, sí se sabe, no me digas que no se sabe. A mí me platicaron otra cosa. A mí me dijeron que había andado con un pelado allá en Minesota. Y que como quiera, dicen que siguió escribiéndole a Ramón. Siguió echándole mentiras. Unos amigos de Ramón se lo contaron todo. Ellos estaban en el mismo rancho donde estaba ella. Y luego cuando se encontraron con él por acá le dijeron luego luego.

El sí le fue fiel, pero ella no. Andaba con un pelado de San Antonio. Era puro recargue y se vestía muy moneneque. Dicen que se ponía zapatos anaranjados y unos sacos bien largos, y siempre con el cuello levantado ... Pero a ella yo creo que le gustaba el borlote también, si no, no le hubiera sido infiel. Lo malo es que no haya perdido con Ramón. Cuando él se dio cuenta todavía no llegaba del norte Juanita y se emborrachaba cada rato. Yo lo vi una vez que andaba borracho y todo lo que decía era que traía una astilla. Que era todo lo que dejaban las viejas, puras astillas por dentro de uno.

—Cuando regrese a Tejas me la robo. Ya no me aguanto. Sí, se viene conmigo. Sí, se viene. Se sale conmigo. Cómo la quiero. Cada azadonazo nomás me retumba su nombre. ¿Por qué se sentirá uno así cuando quiere a alguien? Me canso y no me canso de ver su retrato después de cena hasta que oscurece. Y a mediodía durante la hora de la comida también. Pero lo que pasa es que ya no me acuerdo tanto de cómo es de de veras. El retrato ya no se me hace que se parece a ella. O ella ya no se parece al retrato. Cuando me hacen burla los demás mejor me voy al monte. Veo el retrato pero ya no me acuerdo cómo es aunque vea su retrato. Yo creo que mejor sería no verlo tanto. Me prometió serme fiel. Y sí lo es porque sus ojos y su sonrisa me lo siguen diciendo cuando me la imagino. Ya mero se llega el regreso a Tejas. Cada vez que me despiertan los gallos por la madrugada parece que ya estoy allí, y que la miro andando por la calle. Ya mero.

—Pues no es que no quiera a Ramón, pero éste habla muy suave, y es todo, nomás hablo con él. Y fíjate cómo se le quedan viendo todas. Se viste pero suave también. No es que no quiera a Ramón, pero éste es buena gente y su sonrisa, pues la veo todo el día ... No, no voy a perder con Ramón. Además, qué hay de malo con sólo hablar. Yo no quiero hacerle caso a éste, le prometí a Ramón ... pero me sigue, me sigue y me sigue. Yo no quiero hacerle caso ... No necesito perder con Ramón, no voy a andar con éste. Nomás con que me siga para que se queden picadas las demás, las otras. No, no pierdo con Ramón porque de veras lo quiero mucho. Ya no falta mucho para vernos otra vez ... ¿Quién dijo que le había hablado a Petra? ¿Entonces cómo me sigue a mí? Si me manda cartas todos los días con el hijito de don José ...

— ... ya sé que andas con otro pero me gusta hablar contigo. Desde que vine aquí y te vi, quiero más y más estar contigo. El sábado sal a bailar conmigo todo el baile ... Love you, Ramiro.

—Dicen que empezó a bailar todo el baile con Ramiro solamente. Sus amigas creo que se lo advirtieron pero ella no quiso hacerles caso. Eso empezó ya para acabarse los trabajos y luego ya cuando se despedían durante el último baile dicen que se prometieron verse acá. Yo creo que en ese momento ni se acordaba ella de Ramón. Pero Ramón para entonces ya sabía todo. Por eso el mismo día que se vieron después de cuatro meses él le echó todo por la cara. Yo andaba con él ese día, andaba con él cuando la vio y recuerdo muy bien que le dio mucho gusto al verla y se le quitó todo el coraje que traía. Pero después de hablar con ella un rato le empezó a entrar el coraje de nuevo. Allí mismo y en ese mismo instante perdieron.

—Tú sabes lo que haces.

—Claro. Yo sé lo que hago.

—¿Pierdes conmigo?

—Sí, y a la noche si vas al baile más vale que no vayas a bailar con nadie.

—Va, y ¿por qué? Si ya no somos novios. Ya perdimos. Tú no me mandas.

—A mí no me importa si hemos perdido o no. Me la vas a pagar. Ahora vas a hacer lo que yo te diga cuando yo quiero hasta que yo quiera. De mí no se burla nadie. Así que me la vas a pagar por la buena o por la mala.

—Tú no me mandas.

—Vas a hacer lo que yo te diga, y si no bailas conmigo, no bailas con nadie. Y todo el baile.

—Fíjate, dicen que Juanita le pidió permiso a sus papás muy temprano de ir al baile. Fue con unas amigas suyas y todavía no empezaba a tocar la orquesta y ya estaban allí en el salón cerca de la puerta para que las vieran los muchachos que estaban entrando al baile y para que las sacaran a bailar luego luego. Juanita había bailado todo el baile con uno nada más cuando llegó Ramón. Cuando llegó al salón la buscó por todas partes. La vio y cuando se acabó la pieza fue a quitársela al que andaba bailando con ella. Este, un chamacón, no dijo nada, nomás se fue a coger otra bailadora. De todos modos cuando empezó la música de nuevo, Juanita no quiso bailar con Ramón. Estaban en mero medio del salón y todas las parejas pasaban bailando alrededor de ellos. Se dijeron palabras por un rato. Ella le dio una cachetada, él le gritó quién sabe qué y salió casi corriendo del salón. Juanita fue y se sentó en una banca. Todavía no se acababa la pieza cuando se apagaron las luces del salón. Trataron de prenderlas en medio de toda la gritería pero luego se dieron cuenta de que todo el pueblo estaba apagado.

Los trabajadores de la compañía de la luz hallaron a Ramón dentro de la planta de luz que estaba como a una cuadra del salón. Dicen que estaba bien achicharrado y cogido de uno de los transformadores. Por eso se apagaron las luces de todo el pueblo. Los que estaban en el baile casi luego luego supieron. También los que habían estado cerca de Ramón y Juanita oyeron que le dijo que se iba a matar por ella. Los que estaban en casa no supieron hasta otro día, el domingo por la mañana, antes y después de misa.

—Es que se querían mucho ¿no crees?
—No, pos sí.

Poquito antes de las seis, cuando ya mero regresaban los acelgueros, se oyó primero el pitido del tanque del agua, después se oyeron las apagadoras y luego al ratito la ambulancia. Para las seis ya habían regresado unos de los trabajadores y traían la razón de que una de las trocas que traía gente había dado choque con un carro y que todavía se estaba quemando. Era de caja cerrada y cuando le pegó al carro los que no saltaron para fuera de la caja quedaron atrapados. Los que vieron el choque dijeron que se había encendido luego luego y que habían visto a unos pobres correr por el monte con el cabello en llamas. Dicen que la americana que iba en el carro era de un condado seco y que había estado tomando en una cantina de puro pesar que la había dejado su esposo. Fueron diez y seis muertos.

La noche buena

❧

La noche buena se aproxima y la radio igualmente que la bocina de la camioneta que anunciaba las películas del Teatro Ideal parecían empujarla con canción, negocio y bendición. Faltaban tres días para la noche buena cuando doña María se decidió comprarles algo a sus niños. Esta sería la primera vez que les compraría juguetes. Cada año se proponía hacerlo pero siempre terminaba diciéndose que no, que no podían. Su esposo de todas maneras les traía dulces y nueces a cada uno, así que racionalizaba que en realidad no les faltaba nada. Sin embargo cada navidad preguntaban los niños por sus juguetes. Ella siempre los apaciguaba con lo de siempre. Les decía que se esperaran hasta el seis de enero, el día de los reyes magos y así para cuando se llegaba ese día ya hasta se les había olvidado todo a los niños. También había notado que sus hijos apreciaban menos y menos la venida de don Chon la noche de Navidad cuando venía con el costal de naranjas y nueces.

—Pero, ¿por qué a nosotros no nos trae nada Santo Clos?

—¿Cómo que no? ¿Luego cuando viene y les trae naranjas y nueces?

—No, pero ése es don Chon.

—No, yo digo lo que siempre aparece debajo de la máquina de coser.

—Ah, eso lo trae papá, a poco cree que no sabemos. ¿Es que no somos buenos como los demás?

—Sí, sí son buenos, pero ... pues espérense hasta el día de los reyes magos. Ese es el día en que de veras vienen los juguetes y los regalos. Allá en México no viene Santo Clos sino los reyes magos. Y no vienen hasta el seis de enero. Así que ése sí es el mero día.

—Pero, lo que pasa es que se les olvida. Porque a nosotros nunca nos han dado nada ni en la noche buena ni en el día de los reyes magos.

—Bueno, pero a lo mejor esta vez sí.

—Pos sí, ojalá.

Por eso se decidió comprarles algo. Pero no tenían dinero para gastar en juguetes. Su esposo trabajaba casi las diez y ocho horas lavando platos y haciendo de comer en un restaurante. No tenía tiempo de ir al centro para comprar juguetes. Además tenían que alzar cada semana para poder pagar para la ida al norte. Ya les cobraban por los niños aunque fueran parados todo el camino hasta Iowa. Así que les costaba bastante para hacer el viaje. De todas maneras le propuso a su esposo esa noche, cuando llegó bien cansado del trabajo, que les compraran algo.

—Fíjate, viejo, que los niños quieren algo para Crismes.

—¿Y luego las naranjas y las nueces que les traigo?

—Pos sí, pero ellos quieren juguetes. Ya no se conforman con comida. Es que ya están más grandes y ven más.

—No necesitan nada.

—¿A poco tú no tenías juguetes cuando eras niño?

—Sabes que yo mismo los hacía de barro —caballitos, soldaditos . . .

—Pos sí, pero aquí es distinto, como ven muchas cosas . . . ándale vamos a comprarles algo . . . yo misma voy al Kres.

—¿Tú?

—Sí, yo.

—¿No tienes miedo de ir al centro? ¿Te acuerdas allá en Wilmar, Minesora, cómo te perdiste en el centro? ¿'Tas segura que no tienes miedo?

—Sí, sí me acuerdo pero me doy ánimo. Yo voy. Ya me estuve dando ánimo todo el día y estoy segura que no me pierdo aquí. Mira, salgo a la calle. De aquí se ve la hielería. Son cuatro cuadras nomás, según me dijo doña Regina. Luego cuando llegue a la hielería volteo a la derecha y dos cuadras más y estoy en el centro. Allí está el Kres. Luego salgo del Kres, voy hacia la hielería y volteo para esta calle y aquí me tienes.

—De veras que no estaría difícil. Pos sí. Bueno, te voy a dejar dinero sobre la mesa cuando me vaya por la mañana. Pero tienes cuidado, vieja, en estos días hay mucha gente en el centro.

Era que doña María nunca salía de casa sola. La única vez que salía era cuando iba a visitar a su papá y a su hermana quienes vivían en la siguiente cuadra. Sólo iba a la iglesia cuando había difuntito y a veces cuando había boda. Pero iba siempre con su esposo, así que nunca se fijaba por donde iba. También su esposo le traía siempre todo. Él era el que compraba la comida y la ropa. En realidad no conocía el centro aun estando solamente a seis cuadras de su casa. El camposanto quedaba por el lado opuesto al centro, la iglesia también quedaba por ese rumbo. Pasaban por el centro sólo cuando iban de pasada para San Antonio o cuando iban o venían del norte. Casi siempre era de madrugada o de noche. Pero ese día traía ánimo y se preparó para ir al centro.

El siguiente día se levantó, como lo hacía siempre, muy temprano y ya cuando había despachado a su esposo y a los niños recogió el dinero de sobre la mesa y empezó a prepararse para ir al centro. No le llevó mucho tiempo.

—Yo no sé por qué soy tan miedosa yo, Dios mío. Si el centro está solamente a seis cuadras de aquí. Nomás me voy derechito y luego volteo a la derecha al pasar los traques. Luego, dos cuadras, y allí está el Kres. De allá para acá ando las dos cuadras y luego volteo a la izquierda y luego hasta que llegue aquí otra vez. Dios quiera y no me vaya a salir algún perro. Al pasar los traques que no vaya a venir un tren y me pesque en medio ... Ojalá y no me salga un perro ... Ojalá y no venga un tren por los traques.

La distancia de su casa al ferrocarril la anduvo rápidamente. Se fue en medio de la calle todo el trecho. Tenía miedo andar por la banqueta. Se le hacía que la mordían los perros o que alguien la cogía. En realidad solamente había un perro en todo el trecho y la mayor parte de la gente ni se dio cuenta de que iba al centro. Ella, sin embargo, seguía andando por en medio de la calle y tuvo suerte de que no pasara un solo mueble, si no, no hubiera sabido qué hacer. Al llegar al ferrocarril le entró el miedo. Oía el movimiento y el pitido de los trenes y esto la desconcertaba. No se animaba a cruzar los rieles. Parecía que cada vez que se animaba se oía el pitido de un tren y se volvía a su lugar. Por fin venció el miedo, cerró los ojos y pasó sobre las rieles. Al pasar se le fue quitando el miedo. Volteó a la derecha.

Las aceras estaban repletas de gente y se le empezaron a llenar los oídos de ruido, un ruido que después de entrar no quería salir. No reconocía a nadie en la banqueta. Le entraron ganas de regresarse pero alguien la empujó hacia el centro y los oídos se le llenaban más y más de ruido. Sentía miedo y más y más se le olvidaba la razón por la cual estaba allí entre el gentío. En medio de dos tiendas donde había una callejuela se detuvo para recuperar el ánimo un poco y se quedó viendo un rato a la gente que pasaba.

—Dios mío, ¿qué me pasa? Ya me empiezo a sentir como me sentí en Wilmar. Ojalá y no me vaya a sentir mal. A ver. Para allá queda la hielería. No, para allá. No, Dios mío, ¿qué me pasa? A ver. Venía andando de allá para acá. Así que queda para allá. Mejor me hubiera quedado en casa. Oiga, perdone usted, ¿dónde está el Kres, por favor? ... Gracias.

Se fue andando hasta donde le habían indicado y entró. El ruido y la apretura de la gente era peor. Le entró más miedo y ya lo único que quería era salirse de la tienda pero ya no veía la puerta. Sólo veía cosas sobre cosas, gente sobre gente. Hasta oía hablar a las cosas. Se quedó parada un rato viendo vacíamente a lo que estaba enfrente de ella. Era que ya no sabía los nombres de las cosas. Unas personas se le quedaban viendo unos segundos, otras solamente la empujaban para un lado. Permaneció así por un rato y luego empezó a andar de nuevo. Reconoció unos juguetes y los echó en la bolsa. De pronto ya no oía el ruido de la gente aunque sí veía todos los movimientos de sus piernas, de sus brazos, de la boca, de sus ojos. Pero no oía nada. Por fin preguntó que dónde quedaba la puerta, la salida. Le indicaron y empezó a andar hacia aquel rumbo. Empujó y empujó gente hasta que llegó a empujar la puerta y salió.

Apenas había estado unos segundos en la acera tratando de reconocer dónde estaba, cuando sintió que alguien la cogió fuerte del brazo. Hasta la hicieron que diera un gemido.

—Here she is . . . these damn people, always stealing something, stealing. I've been watching you all along. Let's have that bag.
—¿Pero . . . ?

Y ya no oyó nada por mucho tiempo. Sólo vio que el cemento de la acera se vino a sus ojos y que una piedrita se le metió en el ojo y le calaba mucho. Sentía que la estiraban de los brazos y aun cuando la voltearon boca arriba veía a todos muy retirados. Se veía a sí misma. Se sentía hablar pero ni ella sabía lo que decía pero sí se veía mover la boca. También veía puras caras desconocidas. Luego vio al empleado con la pistola en la cartuchera y le entró un miedo terrible. Fue cuando se volvió a acordar de sus hijos. Le empezaron a salir las lágrimas y lloró. Luego ya no supo nada. Sólo se sentía andar en un mar de gente. Los brazos la rozaban como si fueran olas.

—De a buena suerte que mi compadre andaba por allí. Él fue el que me fue a avisar al restaurante. ¿Cómo te sientes?
—Yo creo que estoy loca, viejo.
—Por eso te pregunté que si no te irías a sentir mal como en Wilmar.
—¿Qué va a ser de mis hijos con una mamá loca? Con una loca que ni siquiera sabe hablar ni ir al centro.
—De todos modos, fui a traer al notario público. Y él fue el que fue conmigo a la cárcel. Él le explicó todo al empleado. Que se te

había volado la cabeza. Y que te daban ataques de nervios cuando andabas entre mucha gente.

—¿Y si me mandan a un manicomio? Yo no quiero dejar a mis hijos. Por favor, viejo, no vayas a dejar que me manden, que no me lleven. Mejor no hubiera ido al centro.

—Pos nomás quédate aquí dentro de la casa y no te salgas del solar. Que al cabo no hay necesidad. Yo te traigo todo lo que necesites. Mira, ya no llores, ya no llores. No, mejor, llora para que te desahogues. Les voy a decir a los muchachos que ya no te anden fregando con Santo Clos. Les voy a decir que no hay para que no te molesten con eso ya.

—No, viejo, no seas malo. Diles que si no les trae nada en la noche buena que es porque les van a traer algo los reyes magos.

—Pero ... Bueno, como tú quieras. Yo creo que siempre lo mejor es tener esperanzas.

Los niños que estaban escondidos detrás de la puerta oyeron todo pero no comprendieron muy bien. Y esperaron el día de los reyes magos como todos los años. Cuando llegó y pasó aquel día sin regalos no preguntaron nada.

Antes de que la gente se fuera para al norte, el cura les bendecía los carros y las trocas a cinco dólares el mueble. Una vez hizo lo suficiente hasta para ir a visitar a sus padres y a sus amigos a Barcelona en España. Le trajo a la gente el agradecimiento de su familia y unas tarjetas de una iglesia muy moderna. Estas las puso al entrar a la iglesia para que vieran y anhelaran una iglesia así. Al poco tiempo empezaron a aparecer palabras en las tarjetas, luego cruces, rayas y con safos así como había pasado con las bancas nuevas. El cura nunca pudo comprender el sacrilegio.

El retrato

Nomás esperaban que regresara la gente del norte y venían los vendedores de retratos de San Antonio. Bajaban al agua. Sabían que la gente traía sus dineritos y por eso, como decía papá, se venían en parvadas. Traían sus velices llenos de muestras. Siempre traían camisa blanca y con corbata y así se veían más importantes y la gente les creía todo lo que decían y les ofrecían el pase a la casa sin pensarlo casi. Yo creo que hasta anhelaban, por debajito, que sus hijos llegaran a ser eso algún día. De todos modos venían y pasaban por las calles polvorientas cargados con los velices llenos de muestras.

Una vez, recuerdo, yo estaba en la casa de un amigo de mi papá, cuando llegó uno de estos vendedores. Recuerdo también que éste se veía un poco asustado y tímido. Don Mateo le pidió que entrara porque quería hacer negocio.

—Buenas tardes, marchante, mire, quisiera explicarle algo nuevo que traemos este año.

—A ver. A ver.

—Pues mire, nos da algún retrato, cualquier retrato que tenga, y nosotros no solamente lo amplificamos sino que lo ponemos en madera, así abultadito, como quien dice en tres dimensiones.

—Bueno, ¿y eso para qué?

—Para que se vea como que está vivo. Así, mire, deje mostrarle éste. ¿Qué tal, no se ve como que está vivo? ¿Como que vive?

—Hombre, sí. Mira, vieja. Qué padre se mira éste. Sabe que nosotros queríamos mandar unos retratos para que nos los hicieran grandes. Y esto ha de costar mucho, ¿verdad?

—No, fíjese que casi cuesta lo mismo. Claro que se lleva más tiempo.

—Bueno, pero, a ver. ¿Cuánto cuesta?

—Solamente por treinta pesitos se lo traemos abultadito. Uno de este tamaño.

—Hijo, está caro, oiga. ¿No dijo que no costaba mucho más? ¿Puede uno abonar?

—Fíjese que ahora tenemos otro gerente y éste quiere todo al contado. Es que el trabajo es muy fino. Se lo dejamos como si fuera de de veras. Así abultadito. Mire. ¿Qué tal? Fino trabajo, ¿no? En un mes se lo regresamos, ya todo terminado. Usted nomás nos dice los colores de la ropa y por aquí pasamos con él cuando menos piense, todo acabado, y con todo y marco. No crea, en un mes a lo más. Pero, como le dije, este hombre que es el gerente ahora quiere al contado. Es muy exigente hasta con nosotros.

—Es que está muy caro.

—Pues sí. Pero es que el trabajo es muy fino. ¿A poco ha visto usted estos retratos abultados de madera antes?

—No, pos sí. ¿Qué dices, vieja?

—Pos a mí me gusta mucho. ¿Por qué no mandamos uno? Y si nos sale bien ... el de Chuy. Dios lo tenga en paz. Es el único que tenemos de él. Se lo tomamos antes de que se fuera para Corea. Pobre de m'ijo, ya no lo volvimos a ver. Mire, aquí está su retrato. ¿Usted cree que lo puede hacer bien abultadito para que parezca que está vivo?

—Pero, ¿cómo no? Hemos hecho muchos de vestido de soldado, si viera. Así abultados son más que retratos. Cómo no. Nomás me dice de qué tamaño lo quiere y si quiere marco redondo o cuadrado. ¿Qué dice? ¿Cómo le apuntamos aquí?

—¿Qué dices, vieja? ¿Lo mandamos a hacer así?

—Pos, yo por mi parte ya te dije. Me gustaría tener a m'ijo así abultadito y en color.

—Bueno, pues, póngale ahí. Pero nos cuida bien el retrato porque es el único que tenemos de nuestro hijo ya de grande. Quedó de mandarnos uno de todo vestido de soldado y con las banderas americana y mexicana cruzándose por arriba de la cabeza, pero apenas llegó por allá y nos cayó una carta diciéndonos que estaba perdido en acción. Así que lo cuida bien.

—No tenga cuidado. Sí, somos responsables. Uno sabe muy bien el sacrificio que hace la gente. No tenga cuidado. Hora verá cuando se lo regresemos cómo va a quedar de bonito. ¿Qué dice, le ponemos el traje azul marino?

—Pero si no tiene traje en el retrato.

—Bueno, pero eso es sólo cuestión de acomodárselo con una poca de madera. Mire éstos. Ya ve éste, no tenía traje pero nosotros le pusimos uno. Así que, ¿qué dice? ¿Se lo ponemos azul marino?

—Bueno.

—No se preocupe usted por su retrato.

Y así se fueron ese día cruzando de calle en calle repletando los velices de retratos. En fin, una gran cantidad de gente había encargado ese tipo de amplificaciones.

—Ya mero nos traen los retratos, ¿no cree?

—Yo creo que sí, es que es trabajo muy fino. Se lleva más tiempo. Buen trabajo que hace esa gente. ¿Se fijó cómo parecían que estaban vivos los retratos?

—No, sí, sí hacen muy buen trabajo. Ni quien se lo quite. Pero, fíjese que ya tienen más de un mes que pasaron por aquí.

—Sí, pero de aquí se fueron levantando retratos por todo el pueblerío hasta San Antonio, de seguro. Y se tardarán un poco más.

—Es cierto. Es cierto.

Y pasaron dos semanas más para cuando se descubrió todo. Se vinieron unas aguas muy fuertes y unos niños que andaban jugando en uno de los túneles que salían para el dompe se hallaron un costal lleno de retratos todos carcomidos y mojados. Nomás se notaban que eran retratos porque eran muchos y del mismo tamaño y casi se distinguían las caras. Comprendieron todos luego luego. Don Mateo se enojó tanto que se fue para San Antonio para buscar al fulano que los había engañado.

—Pues fíjese que me quedé en casa de Esteban. Y todos los días salía con él a vender verduras en el mercado. Le ayudaba en todo. Tenía esperanzas de encontrarme con ese fulanito uno de tantos días. Luego a los pocos días de estar por allí me empecé a salir a los distintos barrios, y así fui conociendo muchas cosas. Si no me podía tanto el dinero sino los lloridos de la pobre vieja con eso de que era el único retrato que teníamos de Chuy. Y aunque lo encontramos en el costal con los demás retratos, se había echado a perder, si viera.

—Bueno, pero ¿cómo lo encontró?

—Pues, mire, para no hacérsela tan larga, él vino a parar al puesto un día. Se paró enfrente de nosotros y compró unas verduras. Como que me quiso reconocer. Yo sí, claro que lo reconocí, porque cuando trae uno coraje no se le borran las caras. Y luego luego allí lo cogí. El pobre ni decía nada. Bien asustado. Yo nomás le dije que quería el retrato de m'ijo y abultadito y que me lo hiciera o me lo echaba al pico. Y me fui con él a donde vivía. Y allí mismo le hice que se pusiera a trabajar. El pobre no sabía ni por donde empezar. Tuvo que hacerlo todo de memoria.

—Y, ¿cómo lo hizo?

—No sé. Pero, con miedo, yo creo que uno es capaz de todo. A los tres días me trajo el retrato acabadito así como lo ve cerquita de la virgen en esa tarima. ¿Usted dirá? ¿Cómo se ve m'ijo?

—Pues, yo la mera verdad ya no me acuerdo cómo era Chuy. Pero ya se estaba, entre más y más, pareciéndose a usted, ¿verdad?

—Sí. Yo creo que sí. Es lo que me dice la gente ahora. Que Chuy, entre más y más, se iba a parecer a mí y que se estaba pareciendo a mí. Ahí está el retrato. Como quien dice, somos la misma cosa.

—Ya soltaron a Figueroa. Salió hace una semana.

—Sí, pero ya viene enfermo. Allí en la pinta si les tienen coraje les ponen inyecciones para que se mueran.

—N'ombre. ¿Qué tienes? Bueno, ¿y quién lo entregaría?

—Sería algún gabacho que no le caía verlo en el pueblo con la bolilla que se trajo de Wisconson. Y ni quien lo defendiera. Dicen que la gabachita tenía diez y siete años y es en contra de la ley.

—Te apuesto que no dura el año.

—Pues dicen que tiene una enfermedad muy rara.

Cuando lleguemos

🌿

Como a las cuatro de la mañana se descompuso la troca. Toda la noche les había hipnotizado el chillido de las llantas sobre el pavimento. Cuando se detuvo, despertaron. El silencio les avisaba que algo había pasado. La troca venía calentándose mucho y luego que se pararon y examinaron el motor se dieron cuenta de que casi se les había quemado el motor. Ya no quiso arrancarse. Tendrían que quedarse allí hasta que amaneciera completamente y luego podrían pedir un levantón para el siguiente pueblo. Dentro de la troca la gente de primero se había despertado y luego se cruzaron varias conversaciones. Luego en lo oscuro se habían empezado a cerrar los ojos y se puso todo tan silencio que hasta se oían los grillos. Unos estaban dormidos, otros estaban pensando.

—De buena suerte que se paró aquí la troca. Me dolía mucho el estómago desde hace rato pero cuando hubiera llegado a la ventana para avisarles, hubiera tenido que despertar a una cantidad de gente. Pero, todavía no se ve nada, casi. Bueno, me voy a bajar a ver si encuentro alguna labor o un diche donde pueda ir para fuera. Yo creo que me hizo mal el chile que me comí, tan picoso que estaba, y por no dejarlo. Ojalá y la vieja vaya bien allí con el niño cargado.

—Este chofer que traemos este año sí es de los buenos. Le da parejito. No se para para nada. Nomás echa gasolina y dale. Ya llevamos más de veinte y cuatro horas de camino. Ya debemos de estar cerca de Dimoins. Cómo quisiera sentarme un ratito siquiera. Me abajara y me acostara al lado del camino pero no sabe uno si hay alguna víbora o algún animal. Antes de dormirme parado sentía que se me doblaban las corbas. Pero, yo creo que se acostumbra el cuerpo luego luego porque ya no se me hace tan duro. Los niños sí se han de cansar yendo allí paraditos. Ni de donde cogerse. Uno de grande siquiera puede cogerse del barrote del centro que detiene la lona. Y no vamos tan apretados como en otras. Yo creo que a lo más llevaremos unas cuarenta personas. Recuerdo una vez, cuando vine con aquel montón de mojados, éramos más de sesenta. No podía uno ni fumar.

—Pero que vieja tan más bruta. Cómo se le pone a tirar la mantilla allá adelante de la troca. Se vino resbalando por toda la lona y de abuenas que traía anteojos, si no, hasta los ojos me los hubiera

llenado de cagada. Qué vieja tan bruta. ¿A quién se le pone hacer
eso? ¿Qué no se le alcanzaba que iba a volar todo el mugrero para los
que veníamos parados? ¿Por qué no se esperaba hasta que llegáramos
a alguna estación de gasolina y el no haber dejado allí todo el mugrero?

—Se quedó el negrito asustado cuando le pedí los 54 jamborgues.
A las dos de la mañana. Y como entré solo en el restaurante y muy
seguro no vio que se paró la troca cargada de gente. Nomás se le
saltaron los ojos ... at two o'clock in the morning, hamburgers?
Fifty-four of them? Man, you must eat one hell of a lot. Es que la
gente no había comido y dijo el chofer que, para no parar tanto y
gastar tanto tiempo, que sólo uno se abajara y pidiera para todos. Se
quedó asustado el negrito. No me podía creer lo que le había pedido.
Que quería 54. A las dos de la mañana y con hambre se puede uno
comer muy bien los jamborgues.

—¡Éste es el último pinche año que vengo para acá! Nomás que
lleguemos al rancho y me voy a ir a la chingada. Me voy a ir a buscar
un jale a Mineapolis. ¡Pura madre que vuelvo a Tejas! Acá siquiera
se puede ganar la vida de mejor manera. Voy a buscar a mi tío, a ver
si me consigue una chamba en el hotel donde él trabaja de belboy. A
lo mejor me dan quebrada allí o en otro hotel. Y luego a las bolillas
nomás de conseguírmelas.

—Si nos va bien este año a ver si nos compramos un carrito para
ya no andar así como vacas. Ya están grandes las muchachas y ya
les da pena a las niñas. A veces hay buenas compras por allí en los
garajes. Voy a hablar con mi compadre, él ya conoce algunos de los
viejos que venden carros. Me voy a conseguir uno que me guste
aunque esté viejo y de segunda mano. Ya estoy cansado de venir para
acá en troca. El compadre se llevó buen carro el año pasado. Si nos
va bien en la cebolla, me compro uno que esté a lo menos pasadero.
Enseño a m'ijo a manejar y él se lo puede llevar hasta Tejas. A ver si
no se pierde como mi sobrino, por no preguntar fueron a dar a Nuevo
México en lugar de a Tejas. O, si no, le digo a Mundo que lo maneje
y no le cobro el pasaje. A ver si quiere.

—Con el dinero que me emprestó el señor Tomson tenemos para
comer a lo menos unos dos meses. Para entonces nos llega el dinero
del betabel. A ver si no nos endrogamos mucho. Me emprestó doscientos pesos pero para cuando paga uno los pasajes se le va la mitad

casi, con eso de que ya me cobran por los niños el medio precio. Y luego cuando regrese le tengo que pagar lo doble. Cuatrocientos pesos. Es mucho interés, pero ni modo, cuando uno lo necesita ni para qué buscarle. Me han dicho que lo reporte porque es mucho el interés pero ya tiene hasta los papeles de la casa. Ojalá y nos vaya bien en el betabel, si no, nos vamos a quedar en el aire. Tenemos que juntar para pagarle los cuatrocientos. Luego a ver si nos queda algo. Y éstos ya necesitan ir a la escuela. No sé, ojalá y nos vaya bien, si no, quién sabe cómo le iremos a hacer. Nomás le pido a Diosito que haya trabajo.

—Pinche vida, pinche vida, pinche vida, pinche vida, por pendejos, por pendejos, por pendejos. Somos una bola de pendejos. Chingue a su madre toda la pinche vida. Esta es la última vez que vengo así como una pinche bestia parado todo el camino. Nomás que lleguemos me voy a Mineapolis, a fuerza hallo allí algo que hacer donde no tenga que andar como un pinche buey. Pinche vida, un día de estos me la van a pelar todos. Chinguesumadre por pendejo.

—Pobre viejo, ha de venir bien cansado ya, parado todo el viaje. Hace rato lo vi que iba cabeceando. Y ni cómo ayudarle con estos dos que llevo en los brazos. Ya quisiera que hubiéramos llegado para acostarnos aunque sea en el piso bien duro. Estos niños son puro trabajo. Ojalá y le pueda ayudar con algo en la labor pero se me hace que este año, con estos huerquitos, no voy a poder hacer nada. Les tengo que dar de mamar cada rato y luego que están muy chicos todavía. Qué ya estuvieran más grandecitos. Como quiera le voy a hacer la lucha para ayudarlo. Aunque sea me voy ayudándole en el surco para que no se ataree tanto. Aunque sea en ratitos. A qué mi viejo, apenas están chiquititos y él ya quisiera que fueran a la escuela. Ojalá y le pueda ayudar. Dios quiera y le pueda ayudar.

—De aquí se ven a toda madre las estrellas. Parece que se bajan a tocar la lona de la troca. Bueno, ni parece que hay gente dentro. Casi no hay tráfico a esta hora. De vez en cuando pasa una trailer. Lo silencio de la madrugada hace que todo esté como de seda. Y ahora, ¿con qué me limpio? ¿Por qué no sería mejor todo el tiempo de madrugada? Aquí vamos a estar hasta el mediodía, de seguro. Para cuando consigan ayuda en el pueblo y luego para cuando arreglen el motor. Que se quedara de madrugada ni quien dijera nada. Voy a estar viendo el cielo hasta que se desaparezca la última estrella. ¿Cuántos más estarán viendo la misma estrella? ¿Cuántos más estarán pensando que cuantos más estarán viendo la misma estrella? Está tan silencio que hasta se me parece que los grillos les están hablando a ellas.

—Chingada troca, ya es pura mortificación con esta troca. Cuando lleguemos ahí la gente que se las averigüe como pueda. Yo nomás la voy a repartir a los rancheros y me voy a la chingada. Además no tenemos ningún contrato. Ellos se podrán conseguir con quién regresarse para Tejas. Vendrá alguien de seguro y se los levanta. El betabel ya no deja nada de dinero. Lo mejor es regresarme a Tejas nomás que deje a la gente y a ver cómo me va cargando sandía. Ya mero se llega la sandía. Y ahora falta que en este pinche pueblo no puedan componer la troca. ¿Y entonces qué chingaos hago? Nomás que no me vaya a venir a joder la chota a que me mueva de aquí. Ya ni la jodieron en aquel pueblo. Si ni nos paramos y como quiera vino la chota y nos alcanzó para decirnos que no quería que nos quedáramos allí. Yo creo nomás quería aventarse con los del pueblo. Pero si ni nos paramos en su pinche pueblo. Cuando lleguemos, nomás que los reparta y me devuelvo. Cada quien por su santo.

—Cuando lleguemos a ver si consigo una cama buena para mi vieja, ya le molestan mucho los riñones. Nomás que no nos vaya a tocar un gallinero como el del año pasado con piso de cemento. Aunque le echábamos paja ya nomás que entre el frío y no se aguanta. Por eso me entraron pesado las riumas a mí, estoy seguro.

—Cuando lleguemos, cuando lleguemos, ya, la mera verdad estoy cansado de llegar. Es la misma cosa llegar que partir porque apenas llegamos y . . . la mera verdad estoy cansado de llegar. Mejor debería decir, cuando no lleguemos porque esa es la mera verdad. Nunca llegamos.

—Cuando lleguemos, cuando lleguemos . . .

Los grillos empezaron a dejar de chirriar poco a poco. Parecía como que se estaban cansando y el amanecer también empezó a verificar los objetos con mucho cuidado y lentamente como para que no se diera cuenta nadie de lo que estaba pasando. La gente se volvía gente. Empezaron a bajar de la troca y se amontonaron alrededor y empezaron a platicar de lo que harían cuando llegaran.

Bartolo pasaba por el pueblo por aquello de diciembre cuando tanteaba que la mayor parte de la gente había regresado de los trabajos. Siempre venía vendiendo sus poemas. Se le acababan casi para el primer día porque en los poemas se encontraban los nombres de la gente del pueblo. Y cuando los leía en voz alta era algo emocionante y serio. Recuerdo que una vez le dijo a la raza que leyeran los poemas en voz alta porque la voz era la semilla del amor en la oscuridad.

Debajo de la casa

Las pulgas le hicieron moverse. Se encontraba debajo de una casa. Allí había estado por varias horas, o así le parecía, escondido. Esa mañana al caminar hacia la escuela le dieron ganas de no ir. Pensó que de seguro le iba a pegar la maestra porque no sabía las palabras. Luego pensó meterse debajo de la casa pero no sólo por eso. Tenía ganas de esconderse también pero no sabía en dónde ni por cuánto tiempo, así que se le hizo fácil hacerlo allí. De primero no le habían molestado las pulgas y había estado muy a gusto en lo oscuro. Aunque estaba seguro de que había arañas se había metido sin miedo y allí estaba. De donde estaba nada más se veía una línea blanca de luz todo alrededor como un pie de alto. Estaba boca abajo y al moverse sentía que el piso le rozaba la espalda. Esto le hacía sentirse hasta seguro. Pero ya cuando empezaron a picarle las pulgas cada rato se tenía que mover. Y le comenzó a molestar porque tenía cuidado de que la gente que vivía en esa casa se fuera a dar cuenta de que estaba allí y lo iban a sacar de debajo del piso. Pero, tenía que moverse cada rato.

—¿Cuánto tiempo llevaré aquí ya? Hace rato que salieron los niños a jugar. Ya debo de llevar bastantito tiempo aquí. Nomás que no vayan a asomarse para debajo de la casa porque me descubren y entonces sí. Se ven curiosos los niños, nomás se les ven las puras piernas, y a corre y corre. Aquí no está mal. Me podría venir aquí todos los días. Yo creo que esto es lo que hacen los que corren la venada. Aquí ni quien me diga nada. Puedo pensar a gusto.

Y hasta se le olvidaron las pulgas. Y que estaba debajo de la casa. En lo oscuro podía pensar muy bien. No necesitaba cerrar los ojos. Pensó un rato en su papá de cuando le contaba cuentos de brujas por las noches, de cómo las tumbaba rezándoles y echando los siete nudos.

—Cuando venía del trabajo, entonces teníamos terreno nuestro, de riego, ya en la madrugada, siempre se veían unas bolas de luces, como de lumbre, que iban saltando por los alambres de los teléfonos. Venían rumbo de Morelos, ahí dicen que está la matriz. Yo una vez ya merito tumbaba a una. Don Remigio me enseñó a rezar los siete rezos que van con los siete nudos. Todo lo que tienes que hacer es comenzar a rezar cuando veas las bolas de lumbre. Después de cada rezo echas un nudo. Esta vez llegué hasta el número siete pero si vieras que no pude echarlo, como quiera la bruja casi se cayó a mis pies y luego se levantó ... estaba

114

tan chiquito el niño y no entienden tanto en esa edad. Y no se pudo
aguantar. No le van a hacer nada al viejo, tiene mucha palanca. ¿Te
imaginas lo que harían si uno les mataba a un huerco de ellos? Dicen
que un día el papá del niño se fue con el rifle a buscarlo porque quería
pagárselas, pero no lo encontró . . . la señora casi siempre que entraba a
la iglesia lloraba y luego cuando empezaba a rezar, para cuando menos
lo pensaba, ya estaba hablando en voz alta. Y luego empezaba a gritar,
como que le entraba un ataque . . . yo creo que doña Cuquita todavía
vive. Hace mucho que no la veo. Se cuidaba mucho cuando íbamos al
dompe. A ella sí que la quería yo. Como nunca conocí a las mías. Yo
creo que hasta papá la quería como agüelita porque él tampoco conoció
a las suyas. Lo que más me gustaba era que me abrazara y que me
dijera eres más águila que la luna . . . get out of there, get away from
that goddamn window. Go away. Go away . . . you know, you can't
come home with me anymore. Look, I don't mind playing with you
but some old ladies told mama that mexicans steal and now mama says
not to bring you home anymore. You have to turn back. But we can
still play at school. I'll choose you and you choose me . . . que te digo,
te digo que de jodido no pasa uno. Yo sé por qué te lo digo. Si hay
otra guerra nosotros no vamos a sufrir. No seas pendejo. Los que se
van a joder son los que están arriba, los que tienen algo. Nosotros ya
estamos jodidos. Si hay otra guerra a nosotros hasta nos va a ir bien . . .
¿por qué ya no comes pan dulce? You don't like it anymore? . . . Fíjese
que yo hasta fui al pueblo y me compré un martillo nuevo para estar
preparado para cuando vinieran a enseñarnos. Dicen que el ministro,
cuando se dio cuenta, se fue a la casa e hizo pedazos todos los muebles
con un hacha y luego sacó todo para fuera de la casa y lo prendió. Allí
se estuvo hasta que se volvió todo puras cenizas . . . yo creo que mi viejo
ya no va a poder trabajar en el sol. El viejo no dijo nada cuando le
dijimos que se había asoleado, nomás movió la cabeza. A él lo que le
preocupaba más era que la lluvia se había venido muy seguido y se le
estaba echando a perder la cosecha. Nomás con eso se ponía triste. Ni
cuando le tuvieron que operar a la señora porque tenía cáncer se puso
triste, contimás cuando le contamos lo de mi viejo . . . estos cabrones te
van a cortar el pelo o me los echo el pico . . . no hay diablo, no hay, el
único diablo que hay es don Rayos cuando se viste con los cuernos y con la
capa para ir a la pastorela . . . pendejo, ¿por qué no pones cuidado en lo
que vas haciendo? ¿Estás ciego o qué? . . . ¿por qué lloraría la maestra
cuando vinieron por él? Desde que entró a ese cuarto nomás lo estaba
viendo todo el tiempo. Y estaba tan joven, no era como las de Tejas,
puras viejitas con la tabla en la mano cuidando que no perdiera uno el

lugar en el libro. Y si lo perdía, sácatelas. Nomás te empinaban... ¿tú crees que así se quemarían? Es que es difícil creerlo. Pero, ¿tan pronto? Es que la llama es muy fuerte y pescándose la ropa en fuego, qué tienes, hombre. ¿Te acuerdas de la familia aquella que se quemó durante la navidad? Se quedaron dormiditos para siempre. Luego los bomberos andaban hasta llorando sacando los cuerpos porque se les llenaban las botas de grasa de los niños... soberanos —ese día es de suma y magna importancia. Fue en mil ochocientos sesenta y dos cuando las tropas de Napoleón sufrieron una derrota ante las fuerzas mexicanas que tan valientemente pelearon —así comenzaba yo los discursos, siempre usaba la palabra soberano, cuando yo era joven, hijo, pero ahora desde que me dio el ataque, ya no puedo recordar muy bien lo que le decía a la gente. Luego vino la revolución y perdimos nosotros al último, a Villa le fue bien, pero yo me tuve que venir para acá, aquí nadie sabe en lo que anduve. A veces quiero recordar pero la mera verdad, ya no puedo. Ya se me vuelve todo borrascoso. Ahora, dime, ¿qué es lo que más quisieras en este momento de tu vida? En este mero momentito... ayer juntamos cincuenta libras de cobre. Enrique se halló un imán y con ése es más fácil para encontrar el fierro entre tanto mugrero que tira la gente. A veces nos va bien. Pero más del tiempo es puro perder el tiempo. Siquiera para algo para comer. Bueno, y ¿qué es el precio del estaño ahora? ¿Por qué no se vienen con nosotros la próxima vez? ... ya se está viniendo el frío. Te apuesto que mañana va a amanecer todo el suelo parejito de escarcha. Y fíjate como las grúas ya pasan cada rato... el domingo va a haber casamiento. De seguro nos van a dar cabrito en mole con arroz y luego luego el baile, y el novio bien desesperado porque se venga la noche ... fíjese, comadre, que nos asustamos tanto anoche que se apagaron las luces. Estábamos jugando con los niños cuando de repente todo oscuro. Y luego que no teníamos ni una velita. Pero eso no fue lo que nos dio el susto. El tarugo de Juan se estaba comiendo una naranja y no supimos ni cómo pero se le metió una semilla para adentro de la nariz y en lo oscuro no podíamos sacársela. Y él a chille y chille. Su compadre a prende y prende cerillos. Bueno, y ¿qué pasaría? Si todo el pueblo estaba oscuro... al hijo de doña Amada lo encontraron en una acequia y al hijo de don Tiburcio lo encontraron bien quemadito dentro de la caja de la troca, creo que le van a poner pleito a don Jesús por andar transportando gente en una troca con caja cerrada, dicen que cuando lo quisieron extender, porque lo encontraron acurrucado en una esquina, cuando quisieron extender el cuerpo para echarlo en la carroza, se le cayó una pierna ... ya no vienen para acá los de los retratos. Es que don Mateo les metió buen susto... casi se volvió loca mamá. Siempre se ponía a llorar cuando le platicaba a alguien de lo que le había pasado en el centro.

—*Quisiera ver a toda esa gente junta. Y luego si tuviera unos brazos bien grandes los podría abrazar a todos. Quisiera poder platicar con todos otra vez, pero que todos estuvieran juntos. Pero eso apenas en un sueño. Aquí sí que está suave porque puedo pensar en lo que yo quiera. Apenas estando uno solo puede juntar a todos. Yo creo que es lo que necesitaba más que todo. Necesitaba esconderme para poder comprender muchas cosas. De aquí en adelante todo lo que tengo que hacer es venirme aquí, en lo oscuro, y pensar en ellos. Y tengo tanto en que pensar y me faltan tantos años. Yo creo que hoy quería recordar este año pasado. Y es nomás uno. Tendré que venir aquí para recordar los demás.*

Volvió a la situación del presente cuando oyó que un niño estaba gritando y al mismo tiempo sintió un golpe en la pierna. Le estaba tirando con piedras para debajo del piso.

—Mami, mami, aquí está un viejo debajo de la casa. Mami, mami, mami, pronto, sal, aquí está un viejo, aquí está un viejo.
—¿Dónde? ¿Dónde? ¡Ah! . . . deja traer unas tablas y tú, anda a traer el perro de doña Luz.

Y vio sinnúmero de ojos y caras en lo blanco y luego se puso más oscuro debajo del piso. Los niños le tiraban con piedras, el perro ladraba y la señora trataba de alcanzarlo con unas tablas.

—¿Quién será?

Tuvo que salir. Todos se sorprendieron que fuera él. Al retirarse de ellos no les dijo nada y luego oyó que dijo la señora:
—Pobre familia. Primero la mamá, y ahora éste. Se estará volviendo loco. Yo creo que se le está yendo la mente. Está perdiendo los años.
Se fue sonriente por la calle llena de pozos que conducía a su casa. Se sintió contento de pronto porque, al pensar sobre lo que había dicho la señora, se dio cuenta de que en realidad no había perdido nada. Había encontrado. Encontrar y reencontrar y juntar. Relacionar esto con esto, eso con aquello, todo con todo. Eso era. Eso era todo. Y le dio más gusto. Luego cuando llegó a la casa se fue al árbol que estaba en el solar. Se subió. En el horizonte encontró una palma y se imaginó que ahí estaba alguien trepado viéndolo a él. Y hasta levantó el brazo y lo movió para atrás y para adelante para que viera que él sabía que estaba allí.

La cosecha

La vez que se contaron

Juan tenía sólo apenas los quince años cuando un día se despertó con unas ganas tremendas de contarse, de hacer un pueblo, y de que todos hicieran lo que él decía. Al levantarse primeramente contó a su familia y a sí mismo— cinco. "Somos cinco" pensó. Después pasó a la otra familia que vivía con la de él, la de su tío, —"cinco más." Diez. Luego pasó al gallinero de enfrente. Manuel y su esposa y cuatro —seis, y diez que llevaba. Luego pasó a la casa del tío de Manuel— allí había tres familias. La primera, la de don José tenía siete así que ya iban 23. Cuando pasó a contar la otra le avisaron que se preparara para irse a trabajar. Eran las 5:30 de la mañana, estaba oscuro todavía, pero ese día tenían que ir unas 50 millas para llegar a la labor llena de cardo y luego que acabaran ésa tenían que seguir buscando trabajo. De seguro no regresaban hasta ya noche. En el verano podían trabajar hasta las ocho. Luego una hora de camino de regreso, más la parada en la tiendita para comprar algo que comer. Llegarían tarde al rancho —pensó pero ya tenía algo que hacer ese día— Tendría que sacar cardo pero durante el día podía asegurarse exactamente cuántos eran los que estaban en aquel rancho en Iowa.

— Ahí vienen ya estos sanababiches.
— No digas maldiciones enfrente de los niños viejo, van a aprender. Luego van a andar diciendo cada rato y entonces sí quedan muy bien.
— Les rompo la trompa si le oigo que andan diciendo maldiciones. Pero ahí vienen ya estos bolillos. Nomás se llega

Las salamandras

Lo que más recuerdo de aquella noche es lo oscuro de la noche, el lodo y lo resbaloso de las salamandras. Pero tengo que empezar desde el principio para que puedan comprender todo esto que sentí y también de que, al sentirlo, comprendí algo que traigo todavía conmigo. Y no lo traigo como recuerdo solamente, sino también como algo que siento aún.

Todo empezó porque había estado lloviendo por tres semanas y no teníamos trabajo. Se levantó el campamento, digo campamento porque eso parecíamos. Con ese ranchero de Minesora habíamos estado esperando ya por tres semanas que se parara el agua, y nada. Luego vino y nos dijo que mejor nos fuéramos de sus gallineros porque ya se le había echado a perder el betabel. Luego comprendimos yo y mi 'apá que lo que tenía era miedo de nosotros, de que le fuéramos a robar algo o de que alguien se le enfermara y entonces tendría él que hacerse el responsable. Le dijimos que no teníamos dinero, ni qué comer, y ni cómo regresarnos a Texas; apenas tendríamos con que comprar gasolina para llegarle a Oklahoma. Y él nomás nos dijo que lo sentía pero quería que nos fuéramos, y nos fuimos. Ya para salir se le ablandó el corazón y nos dio dos carpas llenas de telarañas que tenía en la bodega y una lámpara y kerosín. También le dijo a 'apá que, si nos íbamos rumbo a Crystal Lake en Iowa, a lo mejor encontrábamos trabajo en la ranchería que estaba por allí, y que a lo mejor no se les había echado a perder el betabel. Y nos fuimos.[1]

En los ojos de 'apá y 'amá se veía algo original y puro que nunca les había notado. Era como cariño triste. Casi ni hablábamos al ir corriendo los caminos de grava. La lluvia hablaba por nosotros. Ya al faltar algunas cuantas millas de llegar a Crystal Lake, nos entró el remordimiento. La lluvia que seguía cayendo nos continuaba avisando que seguramente no podríamos hallar trabajo, y así fue. En cada rancho que llegamos, nomás nos movían la cabeza desde adentro de la casa, ni nos abrían la puerta para decirnos que no. Entonces me sentía que no era parte ni de 'apá ni de 'amá, y lo único que sentía que existía era el siguiente rancho.

El primer día que estuvimos en el pueblito de Crystal Lake nos fue mal. En un charco se le mojó el alambrado al carro y papá le gastó la batería al carro. Por fin un garage nos hizo el favor de cargarla. Pedimos trabajo en varias partes del pueblito pero luego nos echó la chota.[2] Papá le explicó que sólo andábamos buscando trabajo pero él nos dijo que no quería húngaros[3] en el pueblo y que nos saliéramos. El dinero ya casi se nos había acabado, y nos fuimos.[4] Nos fuimos al oscurecer y paramos el carro a unas tres millas del pueblo, y allí vimos el anochecer.[5]

La lluvia se venía de vez en cuando. Sentados todos en el carro a la orilla del camino, hablábamos un poco.[6] Estábamos cansados. Estábamos solos.[7] En los ojos de 'apá y 'amá veía algo original. Ese día no habíamos comido casi nada para dejar dinero para el siguiente día. Ya 'apá se veía más triste, agüitado. Creía que no íbamos a encontrar trabajo. Y nos quedamos dormidos sentados en el carro esperando el siguiente día. Casi ni pasaron carros por ese camino de grava durante la noche.[8]

En la madrugada desperté y todos estaban dormidos, y podía verles los cuerpos y las caras a mi 'apá, a mi 'amá y a mis hermanos, y no hacían ruido. Eran caras y cuerpos de cera. Me recordaron a la cara de 'buelito el día que lo sepultamos. Pero no me entró miedo como cuando lo encontré muerto a él en la troca. Yo creo porque sabía que estaban vivos. Y por fin amaneció completamente.

Ese día buscamos trabajo todo el día, y nada. Dormimos en la orilla del camino y volví a despertar en la madrugada y volví a ver a mi gente dormida.[9] Pero esa madrugada me entró un poco de miedo. No porque se veían como que estaban muertos, sino porque ya me empezaba a sentir que no era de ellos.

El día siguiente buscamos trabajo todo el día, y nada. Dormimos en la orilla del camino y volví a despertar en la madrugada y volví a ver a mi gente dormida.[10] Y esa madrugada, la tercera, me dieron ganas de dejarlos a todos porque ya no me sentía que era de ellos.

A mediodía paró de llover y nos entró ánimo. Dos horas más tarde encontramos a un ranchero que tenía betabel y a quien, según creía él, no se le había echado a perder la cosecha. Pero no tenía casas ni nada. Nos enseñó los acres de betabel que tenía y todo estaba por debajo del agua, todo enlagunado. Nos dijo que, si nos esperábamos hasta que se bajara[11] el agua para ver si no estaba echado a perder, y si estaba bien el betabel, nos pagaría bonos por cada acre que le preparáramos.[12] Pero no tenía casas ni nada. Nosotros le dijimos que teníamos unas carpas y que, si nos dejaba, podríamos sentarlas en su yarda. Pero no quiso. Nos tenía miedo. Nosotros lo que queríamos era estar cerca del agua de beber que era lo necesario, y también ya estábamos cansados de dormir sentados, todos entullidos, y claro que queríamos estar debajo de la luz que tenía en la yarda. Pero no quiso, y nos dijo que, si queríamos trabajar allí, que pusiéramos las carpas al pie de la labor de betabel y que esperáramos allí hasta que se bajara el agua. Y pusimos las carpas al pie de la labor de betabel, y nos pusimos a esperar.[13]

Al osurecer prendimos la lámpara de kerosín en una de las carpas y luego decidimos dormir todos en una sola carpa. Recuerdo que todos nos sentíamos a gusto al poder estirar las piernas, y el dormirnos fue fácil. Luego lo primero que recuerdo de esa noche y lo que me despertó fue el sentir lo que yo creía que era la mano de uno de mis hermanos, y mis propios gritos. Me quité la mano de encima y luego vi que lo que tenía en la mano yo era una salamandra.[14] Estábamos cubiertos de salamandras que habían salido de lo húmedo de las labores, y seguimos gritando y quitándonos las salamandras del cuerpo. Con la ayuda de la luz de kerosín, empezamos a matar las salamandras. De primero nos daba asco porque al aplastarles les salía como leche del cuerpo, y el piso de la carpa se empezó a ver negro y blanco. Se habían metido en todo, dentro de los zapatos, en las colchas...[15] Al ver fuera de la carpa con la ayuda de la lámpara, se veía todo negro el suelo. Yo realmente sólo las veía como bultitos negros que al aplastarlos les salía leche. Luego parecía que nos estaban invadiendo la carpa, como que querían reclamar el pie de la labor. No sé por qué matamos tantas salamandras esa noche. Lo fácil hubiera sido subirnos al carro. Ahora que recuerdo, creo que sentíamos nosotros también el deseo de recobrar el pie de la labor, no sé. Sí recuerdo que hasta empezamos a buscar más salamandras, para matarlas. Queríamos encontrar más para matar más. Y luego recuerdo me gustaba aluzar con la lámpara y matar despacio a cada una. Sería que les tenía coraje por el susto. Sí, me empecé a sentir como que volvía a ser parte de mi 'apá y de mi 'amá y de mis hermanos.

Lo que más recuerdo de aquella noche fue lo oscuro de la noche, el zoquete, lo resbaloso de las salamandras y lo duro que a veces se ponían antes de que las aplastara. Lo que traigo conmigo todavía es lo que vi y sentí al matar la última. Y yo creo que por eso recuerdo esa noche de las salamandras. Pesqué a una y la examiné bien con la lámpara, luego le estuve viendo los ojos antes de matarla. Lo que vi y sentí es algo que traigo todavía conmigo, algo puro —la muerte original.

El Pete Fonseca

Apenas llegó y ya se quería ir. Había llegado un domingo por la tarde, a pie. Venía del pueblito donde comprábamos la comida los sábados y donde no nos hacían mala cara cuando llegábamos todos mugrientos del trabajo por las tardes. Casi estaba oscuro cuando vimos un bulto que venía cruzando la labor. Nosotros habíamos andado jugando entre los árboles, y cuando lo vimos nos dio miedo, pero luego recordamos que éramos varios y casi no nos entró miedo. Nos habló cuando se acercó. Quería saber si había trabajo. Le dijimos que sí pero que no. Sí había, pero no había hasta que saliera la hierba. Como había estado muy seco el tiempo, no quería salir la hierba y todas las labores estaban bien limpiecitas. El viejo del rancho desde luego estaba contentísimo porque no tenía que pagar porque estuvieran limpias las labores de cebolla. Nuestros papases renegaban[1] porque lloviera para que se viniera la hierba y nosotros también teníamos que hacernos los desanimados, pero en realidad nos gustaba levantarnos tarde y andar por entre los árboles y por el arroyo matando pájaros con huleras. Por eso le dijimos que sí pero que no. Que sí había trabajo, pero que no para el día siguiente.

—Me lleva la chingada.

A nosotros no nos pareció mal que hablara así. Yo creo que vimos cómo le quedaban las palabras a su cuerpo y a sus ropas.

—No hay trabajo en ninguna pinche parte. Oigan, ¿me pueden dar un lonchecito? Me lleva la chingada de hambre. Mañana me voy pa' Illinois. Allá sí hay jale.

Se quitó la cachucha de pelotero y vimos que traía el pelo bien peinado con una onda bien hecha. Traía zapatos derechos, un poco sucios, pero se notaba que eran de buena clase. Y los pantalones casi eran de pachuco. Decía *chale* cada rato y también *nel* y *simón*,[2] y nosotros por fin decidimos que sí era medio pachuco. Nos fuimos con él hacia nuestro gallinero. Le decíamos así porque en realidad era una casa de guajolotes. El viejo del rancho le había comprado diez casitas de guajolotes a otro viejo que vendía guajolotes y se las había traído para su rancho. Allí vivíamos; estaban bien chicas para dos familias pero estaban bien hechas. No les entraba el agua cuando llovía —eso sí, aunque las lavamos muy bien por dentro, les duró mucho el olor de caca de gallina.

Se llamaba Pete Fonseca y papá conocía muy bien un amigo de él. Decía papá que era muy recargue[3] porque siempre andaba diciendo que tenía catorce camisas de gabardina y en realidad así le llamaba la palomilla —el Catorce Camisas. Hablaron de Catorce Camisas un rato y luego que fuimos a cenar frijolitos con trozos de espem[4] y tortillitas de harina bien calientitas, le invitó papá que comiera con nosotros. Se lavó muy bien la cara y las manos y luego se peinó con mucho cuidado; nos pidió brillantina y se volvió a peinar. Le gustó mucho la cena y notamos que mientras estaba mamá cerca, no decía palabras de pachuco. Después de cenar habló otro rato y luego se acostó en el zacate, en lo oscuro, donde no le diera la luz de la casa. Al rato se levantó y fue al excusado y luego se volvió a acostar y a quedarse dormido. Antes de dormirnos, oí a mamá que le dijo a papá que no le tenía confianza a ese fulano.

—Yo tampoco. Es puro buscón. Hay que tener cuidado con él. A mí me han hablado de él. El Catorce Camisas se las recarga mucho pero creo que éste fue el que se echó a un mojadito en Colorado y lo desterraron de allá o se le escapó a la chota. Creo que él es. También le entra a la mariguana. Creo que él es. No estoy muy seguro...

El día siguiente amaneció lloviendo y cuando vimos para fuera de la ventana vimos que Pete se había metido a nuestro carro. Estaba sentado pero parecía que estaba dormido porque no se movía para nada. El agua le había despertado y se había tenido que meter al carro. Para las nueve había dejado de llover, así que salimos y le invitamos a desayunar. Mamá le hizo unos huevos y luego él preguntó que si había alguna casa libre o algún lugar donde meterse. Y que cuándo iba a empezar el trabajo, y que cuánto se podía ganar allí por día y que cuántos de nosotros trabajábamos. Papá le dijo que todos nosotros trabajábamos, los cinco, y que a veces ganábamos hasta setenta dólares al día si acaso trabajábamos unas catorce horas. Después de desayunar se salieron papá y Pete y oímos que le preguntó a papá que si había algunas chamaconas en el rancho. Le contestó riéndose que solamente había una dejada. La Chata. Y se fueron hablando por el camino que rodeaba a las casitas y que iba a dar a la pompa de agua.

Le decían la Chata porque cuando muy pequeña le había pegado una enfermedad como roña en la cara y el hueso de la nariz se le había infectado. Luego se alivió pero la nariz le quedó chiquita. Era muy bonita menos la nariz y todos hablaban mal de ella. Decían que desde muy chica le habían gustado mucho los hombres y el borlote. Cuando tenía apenas quince años dio luz a un niño. Le echaban la culpa a uno de sus tíos pero ella nunca descubrió de quién era. Sus papases creo que no se enojaron con ella. Eran muy buenas gentes. Todavía lo son. Después, cada rato

se juntaba con diferentes, y cada uno le hacía al menos uno. Unos los
daba, otros los cuidaban los padres, pero los dos más grandes los traía con
ella. Ya trabajaban. Para entonces, para cuando llegó el Pete, tenía dos
semanas de dejada. Su último esposo se había ido; ni se enojó con ella, ni
nada. Se fue nomás. Por eso papá le había dicho a Pete que solamente
había una dejada. Hasta nos pareció que le había puesto cuidado, pero
nos pareció curioso porque la Chata ya tendría sus treinta y cinco años y
el Pete, pues, tendría unos veinte y cinco a lo más.

De todos modos, sí le había hecho caso a lo que le había dicho papá
porque después, cuando andábamos jugando cerca de la pompa, nos preguntó por la Chata. Que dónde vivía, que cuántos años tenía, que si estaba
buena. En eso estábamos cuando bajó la Chata a llevar agua y le dijimos
que ésa era. Nosotros le saludamos y ella nos saludó, pero notamos que
se fijó en el Pete. Le echó el ojo, como dice la gente. Y más cuando éste
le preguntó cómo se llamaba.

> —Chavela.
> —Así se llamaba mi madre.
> —Mira, mira.
> —A lo macho, y mi abuela también.
> —Anda, chocante.
> —Pero si no me conoces todavía.

Se retiró la Chata de la pompa y ya cuando iba lejecitos, suspiró Pete
y dijo en voz alta:

> —Mamacita, 'sota linda.

Para que oyera, después nos dijo. Porque, según él, a las viejas les
gustaba que les dijeras así. Desde ese momento notamos que cada vez
que estaba cerca de Pete la Chata, aquél le decía siempre en voz alta *mi
chavelona*. Lo decía fuerte para que oyera y yo creo que a la Chata le
gustaba que le dijera así porque, ya cuando empezó el trabajo, siempre
cogía surcos cerca de Pete, y si él se adelantaba ella también lo hacía. Y
luego cuando nos traía agua el viejo, Pete siempre la dejaba tomar agua
a ella primero. O le ayudaba a subirse a la troca o a bajarse. El primer
sábado que nos pagaron después de que había llegado Pete, les compró
unos paquetes de fritos a los niños de la Chata. Y así empezó.

A mí me gustaba más cuando le cantaba canciones. Pete se había
quedado a trabajar, decía él, hasta que se acabara todo. Se metió a vivir
con otros dos muchachos en una trailer[5] vieja que estaba por allí. Nosotros
íbamos después de la cena a platicar con ellos y nos poníamos a cantar. El

se salía de la trailer, se encuadraba hacia la casa de la Chata y le cantaba con todo lo que podía. En la labor también nomás nos acercábamos a ella o ella se acercaba a nosotros y el Pete se soltaba con sus canciones. A veces hasta en inglés: *sha bum, sha bum* o *lemi go, lemi go, lober* y luego en español: *Ella quiso quedarse, cuando vio mi tristeza . . . Cuando te hablen de amor y de ilusiones . . .* A veces hasta le paraba de trabajar y se levantaba del surco, si el viejo no estaba por allí, y movía las manos y todo el cuerpo. La Chata lo veía de reojo, como que le caía mal, pero siempre seguía cogiendo surcos cerca de Pete, o encontrándose con él, o emparejándose. Como a las dos semanas se iban los dos juntos a tomar agua a la troca cuando el viejo no la traía y luego se iban por detrás de la troca y luego salía la Chata componiéndose la blusa.

El Pete nos platicaba todo después. Un día nos dijo que, si queríamos ver algo, que nos escondiéramos detrás de la trailer esa noche y él trataría de meterla a la trailer.

—Ya sabes pa' qué . . . pa' darle pa' los dulces . . .

Los muchachos que vivían con él y nosotros nos escondimos detrás de la trailer[6] esa noche y ya después de mucho rato vimos que venía la Chata rumbo a la trailer. El Pete la estaba esperando y apenas se acercó un poco y la cogió de la mano y la estiró hacia él. Le metió la mano debajo de la falda y la comenzó a besar. La Chata no decía nada. Luego la rejuntó contra la trailer, pero ella se le salió de donde la tenía cogida y le dijo que, no cabrón, que no tan pronto. El Pete le estuvo invitando a que se metiera a la trailer, pero no quiso y así estuvieron. Que si me quieres, que si te casas conmigo, que sí, que cuándo, que ahora mismo, que el otro vato. Por fin se fue. Salimos de lo oscuro y nos platicó todo. Luego nos estuvo platicando de otras viejas que se había echado. Hasta gabachas. Se había traído una de Chicago y luego había puesto su negocio en Osten.[7] Allí, según él, hacían línea los cabrones, a cinco dólares el palo. Pero decía que la vieja que sí había querido era la primera con quien se había casado por la buena y por la iglesia, pero se había muerto con el primer niño.

—Que si lloré por esa vieja, y desde entonces, ni madre. Esta pinche vida . . . ahora con esta chavelona, ya empiezo a sentir algo por ella . . . es buena gente, si vieran . . .

Y notamos que a veces se ponía a pensar. Luego decía con cierta sinceridad:

—A qué mi chavelona . . . es muy caliente . . . pero no se deja . . . hasta que me case con ella, dice.

Al tercer día de cuando nos habíamos escondido, Pete ya había decidido casarse. Y por eso toda esa semana era todo lo que platicaba. No podía perder nada. Entre él y la Chata y los dos muchachos podrían juntar bastante. También tendría quien le hiciera sus gorditas y el cafecito bien calientito, y quien le lavara la ropa y, según Pete, cada noche a lo menos un palito. Se ponía a hacer cuentas: a cuatro dólares el palo, a lo menos, por siete noches eran veintiocho dólares por semana. Aunque no hubiera trabajo, le iba bien. También decía que le caían bien los niños de la Chata. Se podían comprar una ranfla y luego los domingos se podían ir a pasear, al mono, a pescar, al dompe[8] a juntar alambre de cobre para vender. En fin, decía que le convenía casarse con la chavelona. Y entre más pronto, mejor.

Al poco tiempo vino a hablar con papá una noche. Se salieron al camino donde nadie les pudiera oír y estuvieron hablando por un buen rato. Esa noche oímos lo que le decía papá a mamá en lo oscuro de la noche.

—Fíjate que éste se quiere casar con la Chata. Se la quería robar pero en qué. Así que mejor se quiere casar bien. Pero, fíjate que está enfermo de la sangre, así que no quiere ir al pueblo a sacar los papeles. Entonces lo que quiere es que yo le vaya a pedir la mano de la Chata a su papá, Chon. Quiere que vaya mañana mismo ... 'Señor don Chon, vengo aquí, hoy, con la comisión de pedir la mano de su hija, Isabel, para comunión de matrimonio con el joven Pedro Fonseca ... ' ¿Qué tal, eh? ... ¿Cómo se oye, vieja? ... Mañana mismo después del trabajo, antes de cenar.

El siguiente día todo lo que se oía era de que iban a pedir a la Chata. Ese día Pete y Chavela ni se hablaron. Anduvo muy quieto todo el día trabajando, pero pesado el Pete, como para mostrar que era hombre serio. Ni nos dijo chistes como lo hacía siempre. Y la Chata también se veía muy seria. No se rio en todo el día y cada rato andaba regañando a los muchachos para que le trabajaran más aprisa. Por fin se terminó el día de trabajo y antes de cenar papá se lavó bien, se hizo el partido cuatro o cinco veces y se fue derechito a la casa de don Chon. Pete lo encontró en medio del patio y los dos sonaron la puerta.

Entraron. *Les dieron el pase ya.*[9] Como a la media hora salieron todos riéndose de la casa. *La dieron.* El Pete traía a la Chata bien abrazada. Al rato entraron a la casa de Chavela y ya al oscurecer se cerraron las puertas de la casa y los trapos de las ventanas también. Esa noche nos contó papá como diez veces cómo le había ido con el pedir de la mano.

—N'ombre, nomás le hablé así con mucha política y no puso ningún pero ...

El siguiente día llovió. Era sábado y fue cuando en realidad se celebró la boda. Casi todos se emborracharon. Hubo un poco de baile. Se pelearon unos, pero al rato se apaciguó todo.

Fueron felices. Se vino el trabajo con fuerza. El Pete, la Chata y los niños trabajaban siempre. Se compraron un carro. Los domingos iban muy seguido de paseo. Fueron a Meison Sidi[10] a visitar a unos familiares de la Chata. Esta parecía que andaba bien buchona de puro orgullo. Los niños andaban más limpios que nunca. El Pete se compró bastante ropa y también andaba muy limpio. Trabajaban juntos, se ayudaban, se cuidaban muy bien, cantaban juntos en la labor. En fin, a todos nosotros nos gustaba verlos, porque a veces hasta se besaban en la labor. Iban entre los surcos cogidos de la mano ... *Aquí vienen los mil amores*. Los sábados iban al mandado, se metían a una cantinita que estaba allí y se tomaban unas cuantas después de comprar la comida. Regresaban al rancho y a veces hasta iban al mono por la noche. La pasaban muy bien.

—Quién hubiera dicho que este carajo se fuera a casar con la Chata y que le cumpliera tan bonito. Fíjate que parece que la quiere mucho. Nomás diciéndole "mi chavelona" cada rato. Y fíjate cómo quiere a los niños. Te digo que es de buen corazón. Pero quién iba a decir que lo era. Se parece puro pachuco. Fíjate cómo la quiere. Y no se ve descarado tampoco. Y ella, pos, lo trae más arreglado que al otro que tenía antes, ¿no crees? ... Y a los niños, nomás jugando con ellos. Ellos también lo quieren mucho. Y ni quien se lo quite, es muy jalador. Y la Chata, tú sabes que ella también le entra parejito. Se van a llevar sus buenos centavitos, ¿no crees? ... Hasta que le fue bien a la Chata ... N'ombre, yo no sé por qué eres tan desconfiada tú, vieja ...

Seis semanas después del casamiento se acababa ya la pisca de papa. Faltarían unos dos días a lo más para que se acabara el trabajo. Nosotros tanteábamos que se acababa todo para el martes y por eso arreglamos el carro ese fin de semana, porque ya teníamos las narices apuntando para Texas. El lunes recuerdo que nos levantamos temprano y papá, como siempre, nos ganó el excusado. Pero yo creo que ni llegó, porque volvió casi luego luego con la noticia de que el Pete se había ido del rancho.

—Pero ¿cómo viejo?

—Sí, se fue. Se llevó el carro y todo el dinero que habían juntado
entre él y la Chata y los niños. La dejó sin un centavo. Se llevó todo
lo que habían ganado ... ¿Qué te dije? ... Se fue ... ¿Qué te dije?

La Chata no fue a trabajar ese día. En la labor nadie hablaba más que
de eso. Le avisaron al viejo, pero dijeron que el nomás había movido la
cabeza. Los papases de la Chata bien enojados y nosotros, pues, casi no.
Yo creo que porque no nos había pasado nada a nosotros.

El día siguiente se acabó el trabajo. Ya no volvimos a ver a la Chata
ese año. Nos vinimos para Texas y acá, unos dos meses más tarde, papá
habló con don Chon, quien acababa de llegar de Iowa. Papá le preguntó
por Pete y le dijo que no sabía en realidad, pero que creo que lo habían
cortado en una cantina en Minesora, que creo que andaba diciendo que
la chota[11] le había quitado todo el dinero y hasta el carro, que creo que
el viejo del rancho siempre sí le había avisado a la chota y que lo habían
pescado en Aberlí.[12] De todos modos, ni a don Chon ni a la Chata les
regresaron nada. Nosotros nomás nos acordamos de que apenas había
llegado y ya se quería ir. Comoquiera, el Pete hizo su ronchita.[13] Pero,
como dicen, nadie sabe pa' quién trabaja. Eso pasó allá por el '58.[14] Yo
creo que la Chata ya se murió, pero los hijos de ella ya serán hombres. El
Pete, recuerdo que llegó como la cosa mala, luego se hizo buena, y luego
mala otra vez. Yo creo que por eso se nos pareció como un bulto cuando
lo vimos por primera vez.

Eva y Daniel

Todavía recuerda la gente a Eva y Daniel. Eran muy bien parecidos los dos y, la mera verdad, daba gusto el verlos juntos. Pero la gente no los recuerda por eso. Estaban muy jóvenes cuando se casaron, mejor decir cuando se salieron. A los padres de ella casi ni les dio coraje o, si les dio, les duró muy poco, y era que casi todos los que conocían a Daniel lo querían muy bien y por muchas razones. Fue en el norte cuando se fueron, durante la feria del condado que hacían cada año en Bird Island.

Las dos familias vivían en el mismo rancho. Trabajaban juntas y en las mismas labores, iban al pueblo en la misma troca y casi comían juntas. Por eso no extrañó nada que se hicieran novios. Y aunque todos sabían, aparentaban no saber, y hasta ellos en lugar de hablarse se mandaban cartas a veces. El sábado que se fueron recuerdo muy bien que iban muy contentos a la feria en la troca. El viento les llevaba todos despeinados, pero cuando llegaron a la feria ni se acordaron de peinarse. Se subieron en todos los juegos, se separaron del resto del grupo y ya no los vieron hasta en dos días.

—No tengas miedo. Nos podemos ir en un taxi al rancho. Hazte para acá, arrímate, déjame tocarte. ¿O es que no me quieres?

—Sí, sí.

—No tengas miedo. Nos casamos. A mí no me importa nada. Nomás tú. Si nos deja la troca, nos vamos en un taxi.

—Pero me van a regañar.

—No te apures. Si te regañan, yo mismo te defiendo. Además, quiero casarme contigo. Le pido el pase ya a tu papá, si quieres. ¿Qué dices? ¿Nos casamos?

A la media noche se cerraron todos los juegos y se apagaron las luces del carnaval y ya no se oyeron los tronidos de los cohetes, pero nada que aparecían Eva y Daniel. Entonces les empezó a dar cuidado a los padres, pero no avisaron a la ley. Ya para la una y media de la mañana la demás gente empezó a impacientarse. Se bajaban y subían de la troca cada rato y por fin el padre de Eva le dijo al chofer que se fueran. Pero iban con cuidado las dos familias. Ya les daba por las patas que se habían huido y estaban seguros de que se casarían, pero comoquiera les daba cuidado. Y estarían con cuidado hasta que no los volvieran a ver. Lo que no sabían era que Eva y Daniel ya estaban en el rancho. Pero estaban escondidos en la bodega, en lo más alto donde guardaba el viejo la paja para el invierno.

Por eso, aunque los anduvieron buscando en los pueblos cercanos, no los encontraron hasta dos días después cuando bajaron de la bodega bien hambreados.

Hubo algunas discusiones bastante calurosas, pero por fin consintieron los padres de Eva que se casaran. Al día siguiente les llevaron a que se sacaran la sangre,[1] luego a la semana los llevaron con el juez civil y tuvieron que firmar los padres porque estaban muy jóvenes.

—Ya ves cómo todo salió bien.

—Sí, pero me dio miedo cuando se enojó papá todo. Hasta creí que te iba a pegar cuando nos vio de primero.

—A mí también. Ya estamos casados. Ya podemos tener hijos.

—Sí.

—Que crezcan bien grandotes y que se parezcan a ti y a mí.

—¿Cómo irán a ser?

—Que se parezcan a mí y a ti.

—Si es mujer, que se parezca a ti; si es hombre, que se parezca a mí.

—¿Y si no tenemos?

—¿Cómo que no? Mi familia y tu familia son muy familiares.

—Eso sí.

—¿Entonces?

—Pos, yo nomás decía.

Realmente, después de casarse las cosas empezaron a cambiar. Primeramente, porque ya para el mes de casados Eva andaba de vasca cada rato y luego también le cayó una carta del gobierno a Daniel diciéndole que estuviera en tal pueblo para que tomara los exámenes físicos para el ejército. Al ver la carta sintió mucho miedo, no tanto por sí mismo, sino que sintió inmediatamente la separación que vendría para siempre.

—Ves, m'ijo, si no hubieras ido a la escuela, no hubieras pasado el examen.

—A qué mamá. Pero no es porque pasa uno el examen que se lo llevan.[2] Además, ya estoy casado, así que a lo mejor no me llevan por eso. Y también Eva ya está esperando.

—Ya no hallo qué hacer, m'ijo, estoy rezando todas las noches porque no te lleven. Eva también. Les hubieras mentido. Te hubieras hecho tonto para no pasar.

—A qué mamá.

Para noviembre, en lugar de regresarse a Texas con su familia, se quedó Daniel en el norte y en unos cuantos días ya estaba en el ejército. Los días le parecían no tener razón —ni para qué hubiera noche ni mañana ni día. No le importaba nada de nada a veces. Varias veces pensó en huirse y regresar a su pueblo para estar con Eva. Cuando pensaba era en lo que pensaba —Eva. Yo creo que hasta se puso enfermo alguna vez, o varias veces serían, al pensar tanto en ella. La primera carta del gobierno le había traído la separación y ahora la separación se ensanchaba más y más.

—¿Por qué será que no puedo pensar en otra cosa más que en Eva? Si no la hubiera conocido ¿en qué pensaría? Y creo que en mí mismo, pero ahora . . .

Pero así como son las cosas, nada se detuvo. El entrenamiento de Daniel siguió al compás del embarazo de Eva. Luego mandaron a Daniel para California, pero antes tuvo la oportunidad de estar con Eva en Texas. La primera noche durmieron besándose. Estuvieron felices otra vez por un par de semanas, pero luego llegó la separación de nuevo. Le daban ganas de quedarse a Daniel, pero luego decidió seguir su camino a California. Le preparaban más y más para mandarlo a Corea. Luego empezó a enfermarse Eva. El niño le daba complicaciones. Entre más cerca el alumbramiento, más complicaciones.

—Si vieras, viejo, que este niño va mal.

—¿Por qué crees?

—Esta tiene algo. Por las noches se le vienen unas fiebres pero fiebres. Ojalá y salga todo bien, pero hasta el doctor se ve bastante preocupado. ¿No te has fijado?

—No.

—Ayer me dijo que teníamos que tener mucho cuidado con Eva. Nos dio un montón de instrucciones, pero con eso de que uno no entiende. ¿Te imaginas? Cómo quisiera que estuviera Daniel aquí. Te apuesto que hasta se aliviaba Eva. Ya le mandé decir que está muy enferma para que venga a verla, pero no le creerán sus superiores y no lo dejarán venir.

—Pues, escríbele otra vez. Quien quita puede hacer algo si habla.

—Ya, ya le he escrito muchas cartas mandándole decir lo mismo. Fíjate que ya ni me preocupa tanto él. Ahora es Eva. Tan jovencitos los dos.

—Sí, verdad.

Eva empeoró y, cuando recibió una carta de su madre donde le suplicaba que viniera a ver a su esposa, Daniel no supo explicar o no le creyeron sus superiores. No lo dejaron venir. Pero él se huyó ya en vísperas de que lo mandaran a Corea. Duró tres días para llegar a Texas en el autobús. Pero ya no la alcanzó.

Yo recuerdo muy bien que lo trajo un carro de sitio a la casa. Cuando se abajó y oyó el llanto dentro de la casa, entró corriendo. Luego se volvió como loco y echó a todos para fuera de la casa y allí estuvo él solo encerrado casi todo un día. Salía nada más para ir al excusado, pero aún allí dentro se le oía sollozar.

Ya no volvió al ejército ni nadie vino a buscarlo alguna vez. Yo lo vi muchas veces llorar de repente. Yo creo que se acordaba. Luego perdió todo interés en sí mismo. Casi ni hablaba.

Se empeñó una vez en comprar cohetes para vender durante la Navidad. Le costó bastante el paquete de cohetes que mandó traer por medio de una dirección de una revista. Pero cuando los recibió, en lugar de venderlos, no descansó hasta que no los había tronado todos él mismo.[3] Y desde entonces es todo lo que hace con lo poquito que gana para mantenerse. Casi todas las noches truena cohetes. Yo creo que por eso, por estos rumbos del mundo, la gente todavía recuerda a Eva y a Daniel. No sé.

La cosecha

Los últimos de septiembre y los primeros de octubre. Ese era el mejor tiempo del año. Primero, porque señalaba que ya se terminaba el trabajo y la vuelta a Texas. También había en el ambiente que creaba la gente un aura de descanso y muerte. La tierra también compartía de esta sensibilidad. El frío se venía más a menudo, las escarchas que mataban por la noche, por la mañana cubrían la tierra de blanco. Parecía que todo se acababa. La gente sentía que todo estaba quedando en descanso. Se ponían todos más pensativos. Se hablaba más del regreso a Texas, de las cosechas, de que si les fue bien o mal,[1] de que si regresarían al mismo lugar el año próximo o no. Unos empezaban a dar largos paseos alrededor de la mota. En fin, parecía que había en los últimos días de trabajo un velorio sobre la tierra. Hacía pensar.

Por eso no les extrañaba mucho que don Trine se fuera solo por la mota después del trabajo y que se paseara por las labores todas las tardes. Esto fue al principio pero, cuando una vez unos jóvenes le pidieron permiso de ir con él, hasta se enojó. Les dijo que no quería que se le anduviera pegando nadie.

—¿Por qué quedrá[2] andar solo?

—Allá él, es negocio suyo.

—Pero, fíjate, que no le falla. Todas las tardes, a veces yo creo que ni cena, se va a andar. ¿No crees que hay algo raro en esto?

—Pos sí. Pero ya vites cómo se enojó cuando le dijimos que si íbamos con él. No era para que se enojara. Este terreno no es de él. Nosotros podemos ir adonde nos dé la gana. El no nos manda.

—Por eso digo ¿por qué quedrá andar solo? ¿A lo mejor encontró algo por ahí? Esto no lo hacía hasta hace poco. Y luego . . . no sé, es algo raro. Tú dirás si lo seguimos a escondidas un día de estos para ver qué es lo que hace cuando se desaparece en la mota o en la labor.

Y así empezaron los díceres sobre los paseos de don Trine. No podían saber en qué o por qué se podría divertir saliendo todas las tardes. Cuando salía y alguien le iba a espiar, siempre se daba cuenta de alguna manera u otra y solamente daba una vuelta corta y regresaba a su gallinero. De todas maneras, ya empezaban a decir que iba a esconder dinero que había ganado ese año, o que se había hallado un dinero enterrado y que cada día se traía de a poquito a poquito algo para la casa. Luego empezaron a decir que, cuando había sido joven, había andado con una pandilla en México y que tenía mucho dinero que todo el tiempo traía con él. Hablaban también de cómo, aunque hiciera mucha calor, el comoquiera traía una faja llena de dinero debajo de la camiseta. Casi toda la especulación se centraba alrededor de la idea de que tenía dinero.

—A ver ¿a quién mantiene? Es solterón. Nunca ha tenido mujer ni familia. Así, tantos años de trabajar ... ¿tú crees que no ha de tener dinero? Y luego, ¿en qué gasta ese hombre su dinero? Lo único que compra es su comidita cada sábado. De vez en cuando, una cervecita, pero es todo.

—Sí, muy seguro tiene sus dineritos. Pero, ¿tú crees que los va a enterrar por aquí?

—¿Quién dijo que enterraba nada? Mira, él siempre va a la comida el sábado. Vamos a espiar bien por donde se va esta semana y el sábado cuando ande en el mandado, vamos a ver qué se carga. ¿Qué dices?

—Está bien. A ver si no nos descubre.

Esa semana estuvieron observando con mucho cuidado los paseos de don Trine. Notaron que se desaparecía en la mota y que luego salía por el norte, cruzaba el camino y luego cruzaba una labor hasta llegar a la acequia. Allí se perdía por un rato pero luego aparecía en la labor del oeste. Era allí donde se desaparecía y se detenía más. Notaron también que para despistar a veces cogía otra ruta, pero siempre se detenía más tiempo en la acequia que atravesaba la labor del oeste. Decidieron entonces investigar la acequia y aquella labor el sábado próximo.

Cuando llegó aquel día, la anticipación fue grande, y apenas había salido la troca y ya iban en camino a aquella labor. Todavía no se desaparecía la troca y ya habían cruzado la mota. Lo que hallaron casi lo esperaban. En la acequia no había nada, pero en la labor, la cual habían rastreado con mucho cuidado después de haberle sacado toda la papa, se encontraron con una cantidad de pozos.

—Aquí hay como pozos, ¿te fijas? Estos no los hizo la rastra. Mira, aquí hay huellas de zapatos y fíjate que [los pozos] tienen a lo menos un pie de hondo. Cabe bien el brazo hasta el codo. Estos no los hace algún animal. ¿Qué crees?

—Pos, entonces será don Trine. ¿Pero qué esconderá? ¿Por qué hará tantos pozos? ¿Tú crees que el viejo ya se dio cuenta?

—N'ombre. Fíjate que desde el camino no se ven. Necesita uno entrarle un poco a la labor para darse cuenta de que aquí están. ¿Para

qué los hará? ¿En qué los usará? Y, mira, casi todos están del mismo
ancho. ¿Qué crees?

—Pos, no sé. Apenas escondiéndose uno en la acequia y ver lo
que hace cuando viene aquí.

—Mira, aquí está un bote de café. Te apuesto que con éste es
con que escarba.

—Yo creo que sí.

[Los muchachos] tuvieron que esperar hasta el lunes ya tarde para
tratar de descubrir lo de los pozos. La palabra se pasó de boca en boca
y ya todos sabían que don Trine tenía una cantidad de pozos en aquella
labor. Trataban de despistar pero eran muy obvias las alusiones que hacían
durante el día en la labor hacia los pozos. Les parecía que seguramente
había una gran explicación. Así, [los muchachos] se pusieron a espiar con
más cuidado y con más esmero.

Esa misma tarde lograron engañar a don Trine y pudieron observar lo
que hacía. Vieron que con el bote de café, como lo habían deducido, don
Trine sacaba y sacaba tierra. Cada rato medía con su brazo lo hondo que
iba el pozo. Cuando ya daba hasta el codo, metía el brazo izquierdo y luego
con la mano derecha se tapaba de tierra todo el brazo hasta el codo. Así se
quedaba por mucho rato. Se veía muy satisfecho y hasta trató de encender
un cigarro con una mano. Como no pudo, se lo dejó entre los labios.
Después hacía otro pozo y repetía el proceso. No pudieron comprender
por qué hacía eso. Esto fue lo que les sorprendió más. Creían que, al
descubrir lo que hacía [don Trine], iban a comprender todo. Pero no fue
así. Trajeron la razón al resto de la mota y allí nadie comprendió tampoco.
En realidad, cuando supieron que no se trataba de dinero escondido, lo
juzgaron de loco y hasta perdieron interés. Pero no todos.

Al día siguiente, uno de los muchachos que habían descubierto lo de
don Trine se fue solo a una labor. Allí imitó el mismo proceso que había
presenciado el día anterior. Lo que sintió y lo que nunca olvidó fue el
sentir que la tierra se movía, que parecía que le cogía los dedos y hasta los
acariciaba. También sintió el calor de la tierra. Sintió que estaba dentro
de alguien. Entonces comprendió lo que hacía don Trine. No estaba loco,
solamente le gustaba sentir la tierra cuando se estaba durmiendo.

Por eso siguió yendo todas las tardes a la labor, hasta que una noche
cayó una helada muy fuerte y ya no pudo hacer pozos en la tierra. Estaba
ya bien dormida. Luego pensó en el año entrante, en octubre, durante la
cosecha cuando podría otra vez hacer lo mismo que don Trine. Era como
cuando se moría un querido. Siempre se culpaba por no haberlo querido
más antes de la muerte.

Zoo Island

José tenía apenas los quince años cuando un día despertó con unas ganas tremendas[1] de contarse, de hacer un pueblo y de que todos hicieran lo que él decía. Todo había ocurrido porque durante la noche había soñado que estaba lloviendo y, como no podrían trabajar el día siguiente, había soñado con hacer varias cosas. Pero cuando despertó no había nada de lluvia. De todas manera ya traía las ganas.

Al levantarse primeramente contó a su familia y a sí mismo —cinco. "Somos cinco", pensó. Después pasó a la otra familia que vivía con la de él, la de su tío —"cinco más, diez". De ahí pasó al gallinero de enfrente. "Manuel y su esposa y cuatro, seis". Y diez que llevaba —"diez y seis". Luego pasó al gallinero del tío Manuel. Allí había tres familias. La primera, la de don José, tenía siete, así que ya iban veinte y tres. Cuando pasó a contar la otra le avisaron que se preparara para irse a trabajar.

Eran las cinco y media de la mañana, estaba oscuro todavía, pero ese día tendrían que ir casi las cincuenta millas para llegar a la labor llena de cardo donde andaban trabajando. Y luego que acabaran ésa, tendrían que seguir buscando trabajo. De seguro no regresaban hasta ya noche. En el verano podían trabajar hasta casi las ocho. Luego una hora de camino de regreso, más la parada en la tiendita para comprar algo para comer. "Llegaremos tarde al rancho", pensó. Pero ya tenía algo que hacer durante el día mientras arrancaba cardo. Durante el día podría asegurarse exactamente de cuántos eran los que estaban en aquel rancho en Iowa.

—Ahí vienen ya estos sanababiches.[2]

—No digas maldiciones enfrente de los niños, viejo. Van a aprender. Luego van a andar diciéndo[las] ellos también cada rato. Entonces sí quedan muy bien, ¿no?

—Les rompo todo el hocico si les oigo que andan diciendo maldiciones. Pero ahí vienen ya estos bolillos. No lo dejan a uno en paz. Nomás se llega el domingo y se vienen a pasear por acá a vernos, a ver cómo vivimos. Hasta se paran para tratar de ver para dentro de los gallineros. El domingo pasado ya vites la ristra de carros que vino y pasó por aquí. Todos risa y risa y apuntando con el dedo. Nada vale la polvadera que levantan. Ellos qué ... con la ventana cerrada, pues, se la pasan pero suave. Y uno acá haciéndola de chango como en el parque en San Antonio, el Parquenrich.[3]

—Déjalos, que al cabo no nos hacen nada, no nos hacen mal, ni que jueran húngaros. ¿Para qué te da coraje?

—Pues a mí, sí me da coraje. ¿Por qué no van a ver a su abuela? Le voy a decir al viejo que le ponga un candado a la puerta para que, cuando vengan, no puedan entrar.

—Mira, mira, no es pa' tanto.

—Sí es pa' tanto.

* * *

—Ya mero llegamos a la labor. 'Apá, ¿cree que encontramos trabajo después de acabar aquí?

—Sí, hombre, hay mucho. A nosotros no nos conocen por maderistas.[4] Ya vites cómo se quedó picado el viejo cuando empecé a arrancar el cardo en la labor sin guantes. Ellos para todo tienen que usar guantes. Así que de seguro nos recomiendan con otros rancheros. Ya verás que luego nos vienen a decir que si queremos otra labor.

* * *

—Lo primero que voy a hacer es apuntar los nombres en una lista. Voy a usar una hoja para cada familia, así no hay pierde. A cada soltero también, uso una hoja para cada uno. Voy también a apuntar la edad de cada quien. ¿Cuántos hombres y cuántas mujeres habrá en el rancho? Somos cuarenta y nueve manos de trabajo, contando los de ocho y los de nueve años. Y luego hay un montón de güerquitos,[5] luego las dos agüelitas que ya no pueden trabajar. Lo mejor sería repartir el trabajo de contar también entre la Chira y la Jenca.[6] Ellos podrían ir a cada gallinero y coger toda la información. Luego podríamos juntar toda la información. Sería bueno también ponerle número a cada gallinero. Yo podría pintar los números arriba de cada puerta. Hasta podríamos recoger la correspondencia del cajón y repartirla, y así hasta la gente podría poner el número del gallinero en las cartas que hacen. Te apuesto que se sentirían mejor. Luego podríamos también poner un marcador al entrar al rancho que dijera el número de personas que viven aquí, pero ... ¿cómo llamaríamos al rancho,[7] no tiene nombre. Esto se tendrá que pensar.

El siguiente día llovió y el que siguió también. Y así tuvo José tiempo y la oportunidad de pensar bien su plan. A sus ayudantes, la Chira y la Jenca, les hizo que se pusieran un lápiz detrás de la oreja, reloj de pulsera, que consiguieron con facilidad, y también que se limpiaran bien los zapatos. También repasaron todo un medio día sobre las preguntas que iban a hacer a cada jefe de familia o a cada solterón. La demás gente se dio cuenta de lo que se proponían a hacer y al rato ya andaban diciendo que los iban a contar.

—Estos niños no hallan qué hacer. Son puras ideas que se les vienen a la cabeza o que les enseñan en la escuela. A ver, ¿para qué? ¿Qué van a hacer contándonos? Es puro juego, pura jugadera.

—No crea, no crea, comadre. Estos niños de hoy en día siquiera se preocupan con algo o de algo. Y a mí me da gusto, si viera que hasta me da gusto que pongan mi nombre en un hoja de papel, como dicen que lo van a hacer. A ver ¿cuándo le ha preguntado alguien su nombre y que cuántos tiene de familia y luego que lo haya apuntado en una hoja? No crea, no crea. Déjelos. Siquiera que hagan algo mientras no podemos trabajar por la lluvia.

—Sí, pero, ¿para qué? ¿Por qué tanta pregunta? Luego hay unas cosas que no se dicen.

—Bueno, si no quiere, no les diga nada, pero, mire, yo creo que sólo es que quieren saber cuántos hay aquí en la mota. Pero también yo creo que quieren sentirse que somos muchos. Fíjese, en el pueblito donde compramos la comida sólo hay ochenta y tres almas y, ya ve, tienen iglesia, salón de baile, una gasolinera, una tienda de comida y hasta una escuelita. Aquí habemos más de ochenta y tres, le apuesto, y no tenemos nada de eso. Si apenas tenemos la pompa de agua y cuatro excusados, ¿no?

* * *

—Ustedes son los que van a recoger los nombres y la información. Van juntos para que no haya nada de pleitos. Después de cada gallinero me traen luego, luego toda la información. Lo apuntan todo en la hoja y me la traen. Luego yo apunto todo en este cuaderno. Vamos a empezar con la familia mía. Tú, Jenca, pregúntame y apunta todo. Luego me das lo que has apuntado para apuntarlo yo. ¿Comprenden bien lo que vamos a hacer? No tengan miedo. Nomás suenan la puerta y pregunten. No tengan miedo.

Les llevó toda la tarde para recoger y apuntar detalles, y luego a la luz de la lámpara de petróleo estuvieron apuntando. Sí, el poblado del rancho pasaba de los ochenta y tres que tenía el pueblito donde compraban la comida. Realmente eran ochenta y seis pero salieron con la cuenta de ochenta y siete porque había dos mujeres que estaban esperando, y a ellas las contaron por tres. Avisaron inmediatamente el número exacto, explicando lo de las mujeres preñadas y a todos les dio gusto saber que el rancho era en realidad un pueblo. Y que era más grande que aquél donde compraban la comida los sábados.

Al repasar todo la tercera vez, se dieron cuenta de que se les había olvidado ir al tecurucho de don Simón. Sencillamente se les olvidó porque estaba al otro lado de la mota. Cuando don Simón se había disgustado y peleado con el mocho, aquél le había pedido al viejo que arrastrara su gallinero con el tractor para el otro lado de la mota donde no lo molestara nadie. El viejo lo había hecho luego, luego. Don Simón tenía algo en la mirada que hacía a la gente hacer las cosas luego, luego. No era solamente la mirada sino que también casi nunca hablaba. Así que, cuando hablaba, todos ponían cuidado, bastante cuidado para no perder ni una palabra.

Ya era tarde y [los muchachos] se decidieron no ir hasta otro día, pero de todos modos les entraba un poco de miedo el sólo pensar que tenían que ir a preguntarle algo. Recordaban muy bien la escena de la labor cuando el mocho le había colmado el plato[8] a don Simón y éste se le había echado encima, y luego él lo había perseguido por la labor con el cuchillo de la cebolla. Luego el mocho, aunque joven, se había tropezado y se había caído enredado en unos costales. Don Simón le cayó encima dándole tajadas por todas partes y por todos lados. Lo que le salvó al mocho fueron los costales. De a buena suerte que sólo le hizo una herida en una pierna y no fue muy grave, aunque sí sangró mucho. Le avisaron al viejo y éste corrió al mocho, pero don Simón le explicó cómo había estado todo muy despacito y el viejo le dejó que se quedara, pero movió el gallinero de don Simón al otro lado de la mota como quería él. Así que por eso era que le tenían un poco de miedo. Pero como ellos mismos se dijeron, nomás no colmándole el plato, era buena gente. El mocho le había atormentado por mucho tiempo con eso de que su mujer lo había dejado por otro.

    —Don Simón, perdone usted, pero es que andamos levantando el censo del rancho y quisiéramos preguntarle algunas preguntas. No necesita contestarnos si no quiere.

    —Está bien.

    —¿Cuántos años tiene?

    —Muchos.

    —Cuándo nació?

    —Cuando me parió mi madre.

    —¿Dónde nació?

    —En el mundo.

—¿Tiene usted familia?
—No.
—¿Por qué no habla usted mucho don Simón?
—Esto es para el censo ¿verdad que no?
—No.
—¿Para qué? ¿Apoco creen ustedes que hablan mucho? Bueno, no solamente ustedes sino toda la gente. Lo que hace la mayor parte de la gente es mover la boca y hacer ruido. Les gusta hablarse a sí mismos, es todo. Yo también lo hago. Yo lo hago en silencio, los demás lo hacen en voz alta.
—Bueno, don Simón, yo creo que es todo. Muchas gracias por su cooperación. Fíjese, aquí en el [rancho] habemos ochenta y ocho almas. Somos bastantes ¿no?
—Bueno, si vieran que me gusta lo que andan haciendo ustedes. Al contarse uno, uno empieza todo. Así sabe uno que no sólo está sino que es. ¿Saben cómo deberían ponerle a este rancho?
—No.
—Zoo Island.[9]

El siguiente domingo casi toda la gente del rancho se retrató junto al marcador que habían construido el sábado por la tarde y que habían puesto al entrar al rancho. Decía: **Zoo Island, Pop. 88**1/2.[10] Ya había parido una de las señoras.

Y José todas las mañanas nomás se levantaba e iba a ver el marcador. El era parte del número, él estaba en Zoo Island, en Iowa y, como decía don Simón, en el mundo. No sabía por qué pero le entraba un gusto calientito por los pies y se le subía por el cuerpo hasta que lo sentía en la garganta y por dentro de los sentidos. Luego este mismo gusto le hacía hablar, le abría la boca. Hasta lo hacía echar un grito a veces. Esto de echar el grito nunca lo comprendió el viejo cuando llegaba todo dormido por la mañana y lo oía gritar. Varias veces le iba a preguntar, pero luego se preocupaba de otras cosas.

La cara en el espejo

¿Por qué ese sueño constante? Constante.

Es casi imposible oír con toda la gritería de los huercos y sus chillidos. Pero qué ocurrencia de la gente de arriba. Es que son solteros, y tantos. Pero, comoquiera, qué puntadas de emborracharse hasta la madrugada. Como si no supieran que hay más gente y con niños chicos. Nada vale, y luego la gritería. También constante. Como el sueño. No sé por qué sigo con el mismo sueño. El olor de las colchas a veces me hace olvidar el ruido, así como la ventana que siempre tengo a la cabecera. Esa ventana me hace que me sienta como que puedo ver dos veces, pero lo de afuera sé que no está en dos. Ya cuando se apagan las luces por la noche y sólo entra luz por las rendijas de la puerta o por el techo, que es piso para los de arriba, se distingue bien la ventana. Al principio le poníamos unas colchas para que por la noche la gente que estuviera afuera no pudiera ver para dentro, pero yo creo que les empezó a importar eso menos y menos a mamá y güelito. De día no importaba que no tuviera algunas garras tapándola porque no se podía ver para dentro, pero por la noche, sí. Como que las cosas se aluzaran para dentro. De todos modos, fue güelito[1] quien dijo que ya no le importaba si lo veían por la noche, que al cabo comoquiera eran muchos dentro de la casa —ochenta y seis. Ochenta y seis almas, como dice, en una casa por grande que sea, se hacen más. Seguramente, por la noche, si vieran por las ventanas hacia dentro, no podrían distinguir la ventana. Un cuadro gris, que ve hacia dentro, desde el piso de donde me acuesto se ve extraña, de distintos tamaños. A veces empiezo a ver la cara en la ventana, la cara que vi en el espejo el otro día cuando me encontré con aquella cara en mis hombros.

—Ándale, Enrique, que se hace tarde pa' la escuela. ¿No sé cómo puedes estar acostado ahí tan tarde con toda esa gente pasando por arriba de ti desde tan temprano? Ándale, levántate. Hasta parece que no duermes. ¿Qué estás haciendo ahí echado, tapado hasta la cabeza? Ándale, vas a llegar tarde. Ya desde cuando que se fueron los hombres al trabajo, Dios los cuide, y ya pasaron todos los gringos a la escuela ... nomás van siempre bobeando para acá, para la casa, con eso de que la casa tiene ventanas tan grandes y se puede ver todo pa' dentro. Ándale, levántate ...

¿A quién le digo? ¿A quién le digo lo de la cara en el espejo? Desde que se ahogó Chuy no tengo con quién platicar a gusto ...

—Ándale, levántate . . .

Pero, ¿por qué se ahogó? *Yo no traigo pistola ni cuchillo, sólo traigo muy grande el corazón, arriba el norte a ver quién tira el grito, que les traigo todita la razón.*[2] Qué si le gustaba cantar. En la tarde que salíamos de la escuela nos buscábamos y luego nos veníamos corriendo por las lomitas y las arboleras. Descansábamos en ratos y era cuando gritaba Chuy, como los mariachis, y luego le metía a la canciones: *Yo soy de León Guanajuato, no vengo a pedir favores, yo no le temo a la muerte, tengo fama de bravero.*[3] Ya párale, Chuy, ¿no te cansas? Tú no te cansas, ¿verdad? Ya sé que te gusta cantar pero cuando te veo así, cantando, pareces otra persona, y ya no haces caso de nada. ¿Todavía te subes a los árboles a cantar? No, cabrón, desde que te agarraron a pedradas los gabachos por estar allá cantando arriba del palo. Y ni cómo defenderte, a mí ya me habían amarrado al mismo árbol. Un día nos los encontramos, Chuy, son puros domperos que viven por acá por las afueras del pueblo y nos tienen coraje porque vivimos en la casa grande del pueblo. Un día nos los encontramos, no van a la escuela pero, un día nos los encontramos en el dompe o en el swimming pool. Un día se nos aparecen otra vez. Ya párale, Chuy. Párale de cantar, ya estás muerto. Los ojos de Chuy son los que no olvido, lo demás ya casi no recuerdo. Los ojos, sí. Lo redondo. Ventanas grises, verdes, negras.

Me vine corriendo desde el swimming pool hasta la casa grande. Me encontré la ambulancia que iba para allá, tan lejos, se me hace, de donde yo venía.[4] Parece que fue entonces cuando empecé ese sueño constante. Constante.

—Ándale, levántate, se te va a hacer tarde.

Venía corriendo por páginas de libros, parecía que me volteaban las hojas, como que todo estaba ya sólo pintado. Cuando pasaba la gente, al pasarla, eran ya como una hoja, con dos lados nada más. Cuando me iba acercando a la casa, vi que las mujeres que estaban en los portales se levantaron casi al mismo tiempo todas, y luego cuando me acerqué más se les empezó a retorcer la cara y una de ellas tiró un chillido —era la mamá de Chuy. Ni pude decirle nada; ella comprendió todo en mi cara, yo creo.

—Ándale, levántate . . .

Chuy se veía tan pálido en el cajón. Dicen que les sacan la sangre para que no apesten. Pero, tanto que les rogábamos que tuvieran cuidado . . . ¿Qué pasó? No sé. Andábamos con más ánimo que nada porque por fin nos habíamos encontrado con los domperos y les dimos en toda la torre.[5] Después, más tarde, andaban en el swimming pool también, pero ya no se nos acercaban; nomás nos andaban rodeando, con miedo. Yo le dije a Chuy que ya no les hiciera borlote, que ya nos la habíamos pagado, pero él comoquiera les siguió haciendo la vida pesada. Les quitó un tubo que traían y se metió a lo hondo. Ya no lo vi hasta que lo sacaron y se juntó un montón de gente alrededor de él.

— ¿No te vas a levantar, o qué?

Despierta, Chuy, no estés jugando, cabrón. No te hagas. Abre los ojos, cabrón. Levántate. Ándale. Se nos va a hacer tarde. Ándale, hombre. ¿No me oyes o qué? Nos van a regañar si llegamos tarde a la casa. Ya se está haciendo tarde, hombre. ¿Para qué te metías en lo hondo? *Yo no traigo pistola ni cuchillo, sólo traigo muy grande el corazón, arriba el norte* ... Ándale, levántate, abre los ojos, no seas ... no te hagas ... Hace días, que por las mañanas, después de levantarme ... lo primero que hago es ver para fuera de la ventana ... A lo mejor lo encuentro allí, por fuera, por fuera del vidrio. O a lo mejor lo encuentro adentro, aquí en el baño, dentro del espejo donde yo y él nos peinábamos antes de ir al cine los sábados. Así como en el sueño. No lo esperaba esa mañana, y desde entonce allí ha estado sobre mis hombros. No se me olvida, esa mañana. La noche anterior había soñado mucho. Desperté cansado de andar y de hablar. Al levantarme me sentí muy extraño, algo me molestaba. Cuando hablaba me oía yo mismo, clara y finamente bien. Luego, cuando entré al baño y me cambié de ropa y me empecé a peinar, algo me seguía molestando. Me dije que a lo mejor traía puesto algo mal. Me fijé en los zapatos, luego en los pantalones, luego en la camisa y luego me vi la cara en el espejo y sentí algo fuera de sí, algo que estaba mal, algo que no quedaba. Empecé a verme en los ojos y me acerqué más y más al espejo hasta que casi lo toqué con la cara. Luego me di cuenta de algo horroroso y no oí ningún ruido más. La cara en el espejo era la de Chuy. Todo era yo, menos la cara, la cara era de Chuy.[6]

—Levántate, ándale, ¿cuántas veces quieres que te diga que te levantes?

Ya párale de sonreír Chuy, ya estás muerto. *Yo no traigo pistola ni cuchillo, sólo traigo muy grande el corazón, arriba el norte, a ver quién pega un grito* ... El olor de las colchas a veces me hace olvidar el ruido, así como la ventana que siempre tengo en la cabecera. Un cuadro gris, que ve hacia dentro, como los ojos de Chuy —grises, verdes, negros ... que están allí en la cara en el espejo. Constantes.

En busca de Borges

—¿Por qué mé sentiré así?

—Porque cuando eres todo, no eres nada. No me crees, ¿verdad? Pregúntale a Borges, pregúntale; no temas. Lo encontrarás en la biblioteca debajo de cada palabra. Aún se afana, a tal edad, por encontrar o decifrar la manzana ¿o pera?, lo que representó la revista *Life* cómo fuese el mundo ... o mejor, cómo se ve la tierra desde el espacio. Sus palabras, las de Borges, y también sus planos, y los globos terrestres y, además, aún más palabras.

Ciertamente. Lo encontré, lo encontré y me entró un sentimiento de seguridad, como que el encuentro había pasado antes, pero no fue nostalgia, eso lo sé. Me dijeron que sería humorístico, laberintoso, oscuro, que me daría su oscuridad, que me diría dónde buscar, y que me indicaría también la manera de buscar. No me mencionaron encontrar o hallar, eso lo recuerdo bien. Lo encontré delirantemente triste, como si hubiera o acabara de encontrar alguna verdad. Y me dijo, "Lee toda palabra, toda palabra en toda biblioteca, en esta biblioteca y entonces te vas a otra y a otra y a otra, y así le sigues". El había venido así por las palabras, trabajándolas, desde la Argentina. Lo sé porque me enseñó su trayectoria en el mapa. No en el plano que trae en sus manos bien apretadas o el que está en la pared, sino el que trae en los ojos. Y le creí. Y empecé a leer. Y lo hice porque me dijo que era mi turno. Que me tocaba a mí.

—Ahora soy una palabra. Y al leer me hago más palabra.

—Te ves un poco pálido, un poco gastado, un poco maltratado.

—Pero, y eso, ¿por qué? ¿Por qué será?

—Pues, ¿cuánto tiempo tienes de estar aquí ya?

—Desde que empecé.

—Y eso, ¿cuándo fue?

—No sé, ¿quién sabe de esas cosas?

—Alguien deberá saber, alguien sabrá.

—Es por eso que continúo leyendo.

—Pero, ¿es que no sabes? Eso no te dirá nada. Lo hubiera dicho desde hace tanto tiempo. Y, en realidad, eso ya se ha pronunciado.

—Tienes razón.

—Te ves un poco pálido. ¿Te sientes mal?

—Un poco. Náusea. Tengo una *w* boca abajo en el estómago. Creo que eso será.

146

—¿Qué harás ahora? ¿Qué vas a hacer?

—No sé, ya me cansé de leer y de ver mapas. Los viejos, los nuevos, son lo mismo. Me encuentro al mismo hombre siglo tras siglo. Pero sigo con la esperanza de encontrar a Borges otra vez. Recuerdo muy bien, tan bien, que me dijo que era mi turno, que me tocaba a mí.

—Y él, ¿ya dejó de buscar? ¿A lo mejor te busca a ti?

—¿Eh? No. Nunca se detiene, sigue, irá por allá, muy adelante de mí... no sé.

—No lo encontrarás, entonces.

—Borges encontró algo una vez, debajo de una palabra.

—Y eso, ¿qué fue?

—Algo, dije. He soñado de ello muchas veces.

—¿De lo que halló?

—No... pues, sí, de todo. De toda la cosa.

—¿Qué cosa... toda?

—Las palabras. Lo que son.

—Y, ¿eso?

—La biblioteca, donde primero lo encontré. Toda palabra lo estaba mirando todo el rato que estuvo hablando conmigo. Eso lo sé porque lo sentí.

—Y, ¿qué te dijo?

—Que me tocaba a mí.

—Te ves enfermo. Más de lo que hace un año.

—Siento el estómago más revuelto. Tendré gusanos en el estómago. Mira lo grande que se me ha puesto. Lleno de gusanos, me imagino. Anoche tuve la pesadilla otra vez.

—¿Qué fue?

—No tengo muchas, en realidad... las mismas. Esta es, de veras, solamente la segunda. La primera me duró muchos años. Siempre iba subiendo una loma muy inclinada y luego, al caer al otro lado, sentía que caía hacia otra loma, más profunda, donde no había ruido. Sólo la arena que tenía vida. Y me caía así, y me iba penetrando en la loma sin poder detenerme ni cogerme de nada. Siempre la loma infeliz.

—Y, esta segunda pesadilla, ¿qué es?

—Te la voy a contar en el tiempo pasado porque está en el futuro.

Estaba yo dentro de una biblioteca donde toda persona me estaba observando. Donde todos apuntaban con las manos, y los ojos, y las cabezas, y con el cuerpo hacia mí. A mí no me molestaba porque andaba buscando a Borges. Me parecía que todos sabían lo que yo buscaba. A cada minuto esperaban que les dijera algo, que les revelara algo. Luego empezaron todos a rodearme, se pusieron en círculo y yo sólo les decía que andaba en busca de Borges. Me trajeron más y más libros. A cada segundo esperaban que les dijera algo. Les pedí que me ayudaran pero me dijeron que no, que me tocaba a mí. Luego me empezó a molestar algo. Me empezó a molestar la esperanza que mostraban los ojos. La esperanza que tenían. Como si yo estuviera por revelarles algo. Como si yo supiese algo y se los fuera a decir. Algunos me empezaron a voltear las páginas, a tirar de los mapas que traía en los bolsillos, a voltearme la cara para que viera en cierta dirección. Me quedé allí muchos años. Eso lo sé porque se empezaron a envejecer hasta los libros. La gente empezó a quedarse inmóvil, casi, viéndome, cerrando los ojos, a veces para no abrirlos jamás. Me seguían con los ojos cada vez que levantaba la cabeza del libro. Los libros que tenía allí y los más que seguían trayendo. Y luego me enfermé. Me sentí como si fuese a vomitar. Me sentía avergonzado. Más que todo porque se pusieron tristes. Me cubrí la boca, pero demasiado tarde. Me cubrí la boca con las manos y empecé a correr fuera de la biblioteca. Todos me siguieron, traté de empujarme el vómito para dentro de la boca pero fue inútil. Vomité por varias horas. Entre todas las letras que vomité en montones de distintos diseños, creo que vi cierta palabra o a lo mejor fue simplemente una combinación de letras. Me retiré ya descansado. Desde la distancia pude observar a la gente con palos volteando los montones con una cara de esperanza que a veces me parecía imbécil.[1]

And the Earth Did Not Devour Him

The Lost Year

🌿

That year was lost to him. At times he tried to remember and, just about when he thought everything was clearing up some, he would be at a loss for words. It almost always began with a dream in which he would suddenly awaken and then realize that he was really asleep. Then he wouldn't know whether what he was thinking had happened or not.

It always began when he would hear someone calling him by his name but when he turned his head to see who was calling, he would make a complete turn and there he would end up—in the same place. This was why he never could discover who was calling him nor why. And then he even forgot the name he had been called.

One time he stopped at mid-turn and fear suddenly set in. He realized that he had called himself. And thus the lost year began.

He tried to figure out when that time he had come to call "year" had started. He became aware that he was always thinking and thinking and from this there was no way out. Then he started thinking about how he never thought and this was when his mind would go blank and he would fall asleep. But before falling asleep he saw and heard many things . . .

What his mother never knew was that every night he would drink the glass of water that she left under the bed for the spirits. She always believed that they drank the water and so she continued doing her duty. Once he was going to tell her but then he thought that he'd wait and tell her when he was grown up.

The Children Couldn't Wait

The heat had set in with severity. This was unusual because it was only the beginning of April and this kind of heat was not expected until the end of the month. It was so hot that the bucket of water the boss brought them was not enough. He would come only two times for the midday and sometimes they couldn't hold out. That was why they took to drinking water from a tank at the edge of the furrow. The boss had it there for the cattle and when he caught them drinking water there he got angry. He didn't much like the idea of their losing time going to drink water because they weren't on contract, but by the hour. He told them that if he caught them there again he was going to fire them and not pay them. The children were the ones who couldn't wait.

"I'm very thirsty, Dad. Is the boss gonna be here soon?"

"I think so. You can't wait any longer?"

"Well, I don't know. My throat already feels real dry. Do you think he's almost gonna be here? Should I go to the tank?"

"No, wait just a little longer. You already heard what he said."

"I know, that he'll fire us if he catches us there, but I can't wait."

"Come on now, come on, work. He'll be here real soon."

"Well ... I'll try to wait. Why doesn't this one let us bring water? Up north ... "

"Because he's no good, that's why."

"But we could hide it under the seat, couldn't we? It was always better up north ... And what if I make like I'm gonna go relieve myself by the tank?"

And this was what they started doing that afternoon. They pretended they were going to relieve themselves and they would go on to the edge of the tank. The boss became aware of this almost right away. But he didn't let on. He wanted to catch a bunch of them and that way he could pay fewer of them and only after they had done more work. He noticed that one of the children kept going to drink water every little while and he became more and more furious. He thought then of giving him a scare and he crawled on the ground to get his rifle.

What he set out to do and what he did were two different things. He shot at him once to scare him but when he pulled the trigger he saw the boy with a hole in his head. And the child didn't even jump like a deer does. He just stayed in the water like a dirty rag and the water began to turn bloody ...

"They say that the old man almost went crazy."

"You think so?"

"Yes, he's already lost the ranch. He hit the bottle pretty hard. And then after they tried him and he got off free, they say he jumped off a tree 'cause he wanted to kill himself."

"But he didn't kill himself, did he?"

"Well, no."

"Well, there you have it."

"Well, I'll tell you, compadre, I think he did go crazy. You've seen the likes of him nowadays. He looks like a beggar."

"Sure, but that's 'cause he doesn't have any more money."

"Well ... that's true."

She had fallen asleep right away and everyone, very mindful of not crossing their arms nor their legs nor their hands, watched her intensely. The spirit was already present in her body.

"Let's see, how may I help you this evening, brothers and sisters?"

"Well, you see, I haven't heard from my boy in two months. Yesterday a letter from the government arrived telling me that he's lost in action. I'd like to know whether or not he's alive. I feel like I'm losing my mind just thinking and thinking about it."

"Have no fear, sister. Julianito is fine. He's just fine. Don't worry about him anymore. Very soon he'll be in your arms. He'll be returning already next month."

"Thank you, thank you."

A Prayer

🌿

Dear God, Jesus Christ, keeper of my soul. This is the third Sunday that I come to implore you, beg you, to give me word of my son. I have not heard from him. Protect him, my God, that no bullet may pierce his heart like it happened to Doña Virginia's son, may he rest in God's peace. Take care of him for me, Dear Jesus, save him from the gunfire, have pity on him who is so good. Since he was a baby, when I would nurse him to sleep, he was so gentle, very grateful, never biting me. He's very innocent, protect him, he does not wish to harm anyone, he is very noble, he is very kind, may no bullet pierce his heart.

Please, Virgin Mary, you, too, shelter him. Shield his body, cover his head, cover the eyes of the Communists and the Koreans and the Chinese so that they cannot see him, so they won't kill him. I still keep his toys from when he was a child, his little cars, little trucks, even a kite that I found the other day in the closet. Also his cards and the funnies that he has learned to read. I have put everything away until his return.

Protect him, Jesus, that they may not kill him. I have made a promise to the Virgen de San Juan to pay her homage at her shrine and to the Virgen de Guadalupe, too. He also wears a little medallion of the Virgen de San Juan del Valle and he, too, has made a promise to her; he wants to live. Take care of him, cover his heart with your hand, that no bullet may enter it. He's very noble. He was very afraid to go, he told me so. The day they took him, when he said his farewell he embraced me and he cried for a while. I could feel his heart beating and I remembered when he was little and I would nurse him and the happiness that I felt and he felt.

Take care of him for me, please, I beseech you. I promise you my life for his. Bring him back from Korea safe and sound. Cover his heart with your hands. Jesus Christ, Holy God, Virgen de Guadalupe, bring him back alive, bring me back his heart. Why have they taken him? He has done no harm. He knows nothing. He is very humble. He doesn't want to take away anybody's life. Bring him back alive, I don't want him to die.

Here is my heart for his. Here is my heart. Here, in my chest, palpitating. Tear it out if blood is what you want, but tear it out of *me*. I sacrifice my heart for his. Here it is. Here is my heart! Through it runs his very own blood . . .

Bring him back alive and I will give you my very own heart.

"Comadre, do you all plan to go to Utah?"

"No, compadre. I'll tell you, we don't trust the man that's contracting people to go work in—how do you say it?"

"Utah. Why, comadre?"

"Because we don't think there's such a state. You tell me, when've you ever heard of that place?"

"Well, there's so many states. And this is the first time that they've contracted for work in those parts."

"Yeah, but tell me, where is it?"

"Well, we've never been there but I hear it's somewhere close to Japan."

It's That It Hurts

🌾

It hurts a lot. That's why I hit him. And now what do I do? Maybe
they didn't expel me from school. Maybe it ain't so, after all. Maybe it's
not. *Sure it is!* It is so, they did expel me. And now what do I do?

I think it all started when I got so embarrassed and angry at the same
time. I dread getting home. What am I going to tell Mother? And then
when Dad gets home from the fields? They'll whip me for sure. But it's
embarrassing and angering. It's always the same in these schools in the
north. Everybody just stares at you up and down. And then they make
fun of you and the teacher with her popsicle stick, poking your head for
lice. It's embarrassing. And then when they turn up their noses. It makes
you angry. I think it's better staying out here on the ranch, here in the
quiet of this knoll, with its chicken coops, or out in the fields where you
at least feel more free, more at ease.

"Come on, son, we're almost there."

"You gonna take me to the principal?"

"Of course not. Don't tell me you don't know how to speak
English yet. Look, that's the entrance over there. Just ask if you
don't know where to go. Don't be shy, ask someone. Don't be
afraid."

"Why can't you go in with me?"

"Don't tell me you're scared. Look, that's probably the entrance
there. Here comes someone. Now, you behave, you hear me?"

"But why don't you help me?"

"No. You'll do just fine, don't be afraid."

It's always the same. They take you to the nurse and the first thing she
does is check you for lice. And, too, those ladies are to blame. On Sundays
they sit out in front of the chicken coops picking lice from each other's
heads. And the gringos, passing by in their cars, looking and pointing at
them. Dad is right when he says that they look like monkeys in the zoo.
But it's not all that bad.

"Mother, you won't believe it. They took me out of the room.
I had just walked in, and they put me in with a nurse all dressed in
white. And they made me take off my clothes and they even examined
my behind. But where they took the longest was on my head. I had
washed it, right? Well, the nurse brought out a jar of, like vaseline,

160

it smelled like worm-killer, do I still smell? And she smeared it all over my head. It itched. And then she started parting my hair with a pencil. After a while they let me go but I was so ashamed because I had to take off my pants, even my underwear, in front of the nurse."

But now what do I tell them? That they threw me out of school? But it wasn't all my fault. I didn't like that gringo, right off. This one didn't laugh at me. He'd just stare and when they put me in the corner apart from everyone he kept turning to look at me, and then he'd make a gesture with his finger. I was mad but mostly I felt embarrassed because I was sitting away from everyone where they could see me better. Then when it was my turn to read, I couldn't. I could hear myself. And I could hear that no words were coming out ... This cemetery isn't scarey at all. That's what I like best about the walk to school and back. The greenness! And everything so even. The roads all paved. It even looks like where they play golf. Today I won't have time to run up the hills and slide down tumbling. Nor to lie down on the grass and try to hear all the sounds. Last time I counted to 26 ... If I hurry maybe I can go to the dump with Doña Cuquita. She heads out about this time when the sun's not so hot.

"Careful, children. Just be careful and don't step where there's fire burning underneath. Wherever you see smoke coming out, there's coals underneath. I know what I'm telling you, I once got a bad burn and I still have the scar ... Look, each of you get a long stick and just turn the trash over briskly. If the dump man comes to see what we're doing, tell him we came to throw away some stuff. He's a kind man, but he likes to keep those little books with nasty pictures that people sometimes throw away ... watch out for the train as you cross that bridge. It ran over a man last year ... caught him right in middle of the bridge and he wasn't able to make it to the other side ... Did they give you permission to come with me? ... Don't eat anything until after you've washed it."

But if I go with her without permission they'll whip me even more. What am I going to tell them? Maybe they didn't expel me. *Sure, they did!* Maybe not. *Yeah, they did!* What am I going to tell them? But it wasn't all my fault. I couldn't wait anymore. While I was standing there in the restroom he's the one that started picking on me.

"Hey, Mex ... I don't like Mexicans because they steal. You hear me?"
"Yes."

"I don't like Mexicans. You hear, Mex?"
"Yes."
"I don't like Mexicans because they steal. You hear me?"
"Yes."

I remember the first fight I had at school, I got real scared because everything happened so slow. There wasn't any reason, it's just that some of the older boys who already had mustaches and who were still in the second grade started pushing us against each other. And they kept it up until we started fighting, I think, 'cause we were plain scared. It was about a block from school, I remember, when they started pushing me towards Ramiro. Then we began to scuffle and hit at each other. Some ladies came out and broke us up. Since then I got to feeling bigger. But all it was, up until I fought, was plain fear.

This time it was different. He didn't warn me. I just felt a real hard blow on my ear and I heard something like when you put a conch to your ear at the beach. I don't remember anymore how or when I hit him but I know I did because someone told the principal that we were fighting in the restroom. Maybe they didn't throw me out? *Sure they did!* And then, I wonder who called the principal? And the janitor all scared and with his broom up in the air, ready to swat me if I tried to leave.

"The Mexican kid got into a fight and beat up a couple of our boys ... No, not bad ... but what do I do?"
" ... "
"No, I guess not, they could care less if I expel him ... They need him in the fields."
" ... "
"Well, I just hope our boys don't make too much out about it to their parents. I guess I'll just throw him out."
" ... "
"Yeah, I guess you're right."
" ... "
"I know you warned me, I know, I know ... but ... yeah, ok."

But how could I even think of leaving knowing that everyone at home wanted me to go to school. Anyways, the janitor stood with his broom up in the air, ready for anything ... And then they just told me to leave.

I'm halfway home. This cemetery is real pretty. It doesn't look anything like the one in Texas. That one *is* scarey, I don't like it at all. What scares me the most is when we're leaving after a burial and I look up and I read the letters on the arch over the gate that say, *Don't forget me*. It's like I can hear all the dead people buried there saying these words and then the sound of these words stays in my mind and sometimes even if I don't look up when I pass through the gate, I still see them. But not this one, this one is real pretty. Just lots of soft grass and trees, I guess that's why here when people bury somebody they don't even cry. I like playing here. If only they would let us fish in the little creek that runs through here, there's lots of fish. But no, you even need a license to fish and then they don't even sell us one 'cause we're from out of state.

I won't be able to go to school anymore. What am I going to tell them? They've told me over and over that our teachers are like our second parents ... and now? And when we get back to Texas everyone will find out too. Mother and Dad will be angry; I might get more than just a whipping. And then my Uncle will find out and Grandpa. Maybe they might even send me to a reform school like the ones I've heard them talk about. There they turn you into a good person if you're bad. They're real hard on you. They leave you soft as a glove. But maybe they didn't expel me, *sure they did*, maybe not, *sure they did*. I could make like I'm going to school and stay here in the cemetery. That would be better. But then what? I could tell them that I lost my report card. And then what if I stay in the same grade? What hurt me the most is that now I won't be able to be a telephone operator like Dad wants me to. You need to finish school for that.

> "Vieja, call m'ijo out here ... look, compadre, ask your godson what he wants to be when he grows up and finishes school."
> "What will you be, godson?"
> "I don't know."
> "Tell him! Don't be embarrassed. He's your godfather."
> "What will you be, son?"
> "A telephone operator."
> "Is that so?"
> "Yes, compadre, he's very determined, you know that? Every time we ask him he says he wants to be an operator. I think they pay well. I told the boss the other day and he laughed. I don't think he believes that my son can do it, but that's 'cause he doesn't know him. He's smarter than anything. I just pray God helps him finish school so he can become an operator."

That movie was good. The operator was the most important one. Ever since then I suppose that's why Dad has wanted me to study for that after I finish school. But ... maybe they didn't throw me out. What if it's not true? Maybe not. *Sure, it is*. What do I tell them? What do

I do? Now they won't be able to ask me what I'm going to be when I grow up. Maybe not. *No, yeah.* What do I do? It's that it hurts and it's embarrassing at the same time. I better just stay here. No, but then Mother will get scared like she does when there's lightning and thunder. I've gotta tell them. And when my padrino comes to visit us I'll just hide. No need for him to find out. Nor for me to read to him like Dad has me do every time he comes to visit us. What I'll do when he comes is hide behind the chest or under the bed. That way Dad and Mother won't feel embarrassed. And what if I really wasn't expelled? Maybe I wasn't? *No, yeah.*

"Why do y'all go to school so much?"

"My Dad says it's to prepare us. He says that if someday there's an opportunity, maybe they'll give it to us."

"Sure! If I were you I wouldn't worry about that. The poor can't get poorer. We can't get worst off than we already are. That's why I don't worry. The ones who have to be on their toes are the ones who are higher up. They've got something to lose. They can end up where we're at. But for us what does it matter?"

Hand in His Pocket

Remember Don Laíto and Doña Bone? That's what everyone called them but their names were Don Hilario and Doña Bonifacia. Don't you remember? Well, I had to live with them for three weeks until school ended. At first I liked it but then later on I didn't.

Everything that people used to say about them behind their backs was true. About how they baked the bread, the pastries, how they would sometimes steal and that they were bootleggers. I saw it all. Anyways, they were good people but by the time school was about to end I was afraid of being with them in that Model-T that they had and even of sleeping in their house. And towards the end I didn't even feel like eating. That's why I'd go to the little neighborhood store to buy me some candy. And that's how I got along until my Dad, my Mother and my brothers and sisters came to get me.

I remember they were very nice to me on the first day. Don Laíto laughed a lot and you could see his gold teeth and the rotten ones, too. And every little while Doña Bone, fat as could be, would grab me and squeeze me against her and I could feel her, real fat. They fed me dinner—I say *fed* me because *they* didn't eat. Now that I'm remembering, you know, I never saw them eat. The meat that she fried for me was green and it smelled really bad when she was cooking it. But after a while it didn't smell as much. But I don't know whether this was because I got used to the smell or because Don Laíto opened the window. Just parts of it tasted bad. I ate it all because I didn't want to hurt their feelings. Everybody liked Don Laíto and Doña Bone. Even the Anglos were fond of them. They gave them canned foods, clothes, toys. And when Don Laíto and Doña bone weren't able to sell these to us, they'd give them to us. They would also pay us visits out in the fields to sell us Mexican sweetbread, thread and needles, canned food and nopalitos, and also shoes, coats and other things that sometimes were good, sometimes pretty bad.

> "Won't you buy these shoes ... oh, come on ... I know they're used, but they're the expensive kind ... look how they're not worn out yet ... these ... I guarantee you, they last until they wear out ..."

I didn't want to seem ungrateful, so I ate it all. It made me sick. I had to spend a long time in the restroom. The worst of it was when I went to bed. They put me in a room with no light and that smelled musty and

166

was crowded with things: boxes, bottles, almanacs, bundles of clothing. There was only one entrance. You couldn't even see the windows with so many things all piled up. The first night I hardly slept because I was sure that spiders would be crawling down from the hole in the ceiling. Everything smelled so awful. By the time it grew dark I couldn't see anything, but it must have been around midnight when I woke up. I think I had fallen asleep, but I'm not too sure. The only thing I could see was that real dark hole in the ceiling. It seemed I could see faces but it was just my imagination. In any case, fear got the best of me. And I wasn't able to sleep anymore. Only at dawn when I could see the rest of the things in the room. Sometimes I would imagine Don Laíto and Doña Bone seated around me and there were times when I would even reach my hand out to touch them, but there was nothing. I think that from that very first day I wanted them to come get me. Something in my heart told me that something would happen. It's not that they weren't good people, they were, but like they say, they had their bad side.

At school, classes were going well. Sometimes when I came back from school in the afternoon not a sound could be heard in the small house and it seemed like no one was around. But always, when I was feeling most at peace, Doña Bone would scare me. She'd grab me from behind and laugh, and me, I'd jump, I was so scared. And she would just laugh and laugh. The first few times I'd end up laughing too, but later I got tired of it. Then later on they told me bit by bit what they would do when they went downtown. They stole lots of things: food, liquor, clothes, cigarettes, even meat. When they weren't able to sell it to the neighbors, they gave it away. They would get rid of almost everything. Another thing, after a few days they invited me to see how they made sweet bread. Don Laíto would take off his shirt. He looked very hairy. He would start sweating as he kneaded the dough. But it was when he would stick his hands under his arms and then keep on kneading the dough that made me the sickest. It was true what people said. He would look at me to see if I was getting nauseous and he would tell me that this was what all the bakers did. One thing for sure, I never again ate any of the sweet bread that he baked, even though they sometimes had a bunch of it on the table.

I remember one day after school they put me to work in the yard. Not that it was so hard, but since that moment they had me working all the time. They wanted me to work at all hours. It's that my Dad had paid them for my board! One time they even wanted me to try to steal a five-pound sack of flour. Can you imagine? I was scared, and besides, it wasn't right. Don Laíto would just laugh and tell me that I didn't have any balls. Anyway, the days went on this way until, sometimes, I even felt like leaving, but how could I? My Dad had left me there and he had spent his money. The food got worse, and it got to be all work all the time.

And then ... I'll tell you something ... but please don't tell anyone. I noticed that this wetback started coming to the house while Don Laíto was away. I don't know how he knew when he wasn't there. Anyway, if I happened to be inside the house, Doña Bone would throw me out, and if I wasn't inside she would latch the doors and I knew I wasn't supposed to enter. One time Doña Bone tried to explain the whole thing to me but, to be very honest, I felt embarrassed and I hardly heard anything she told me. I did know that he left her money. Whoever he was, he was old and every time he came he smelled of shaving lotion and the smell would linger for a good while after he left. One night I overheard a conversation between the old couple.

"This guy has money and, besides that, he doesn't have any rel-atives. Look, viejo, it would be so easy. Not even anyone to worry about him ... I don't think so, do you? ... That boss could care less, he darn sure knows that he's a wetback and if something happens to him, you think he'll be concerned about him? Nobody knows that he comes here ... you just leave it up to me ... Oh, that'll be so easy ... "

The next day, after school, they marked a square on the ground in the yard under some trees, and they told me that they wanted to build a cellar and that they wanted me to start digging there, little by little. They were going to use it to store the jars of preserves that Doña Bone made. It took me three days to dig somewhat deep and then they told me to stop digging, that they weren't going to build it after all. And then came the good part.

I remember well that the wetback arrived, his hair combed real good and fragrant, like always. At dusk Doña Bone called me to come eat. There was Don Laíto, already, but I didn't know how he had entered. After dinner they told me to go to bed right away.

I got the scare of my life when I stretched out on the bed and I touched what felt like a snake but what was in reality the wetback's arm. I thought he must be drunk because he didn't wake up. I jumped back and got out of the room. The old couple burst into laughter. Then I noticed that part of my shirt was full of blood. I didn't know what to think. I just remember Don Laíto's gold teeth and his rotten ones.

When it got real dark they made me help them drag him out and throw him into the hole that I myself had dug. As for me, I didn't really want to but then they told me that they would tell the police that I had killed him. I thought of how my Dad had paid them for my room and board and how even the Anglos liked them so much. All that my parents wanted was for me to finish school so I could find me some job that wasn't so hard. I was real scared but I went ahead and threw him in the hole. Then the three of us threw dirt over him. I never saw his face. All I wanted was for school to end so they would come for me. The two weeks left went by very slowly. I thought that I'd get over my fright or that I'd be able to forget about it, but no. Don Laíto was even wearing the wetback's wrist watch. In the yard you could see the mound of dirt.

When my Dad and my Mother finally came for me they told me that I was very thin and that I looked like I was sick from fright. I told them no, that it was because I played so much at school and after school. Before we left, Don Laíto and Doña Bone squeezed me and told me in loud voices, so that Dad could hear, not to say anything or they would tell the police. Then they started laughing and I noticed that Dad had taken it as a joke. On the way to the farm they talked about how kind Don Laíto and Doña Bone were and how everyone liked them so much. I just kept looking out the car window and telling them yes. After about two months or so, just about when it seemed that I was forgetting all about it, they came to visit us at the farm. They had a present for me. A ring. They made me put it on and I remembered that it was the one the wetback had on that day. As soon as they left I tried to throw it away but I don't know why I couldn't. I thought that someone might find it. And the worst was that for a long time, as soon as I would see a stranger, I'd slip my hand into my pocket. That habit stayed with me for a long time.

It was an hour before the afternoon movie started. He needed a haircut, so he went into the barber shop across the street from the theater. At first he didn't quite understand, so he sat down and waited. But then the barber told him again that he couldn't cut his hair. He thought the barber didn't have time, so he remained seated waiting for the other barber. When he was finished with the client, he got up and walked to the barber's chair. But this barber told him the same thing. That he couldn't cut his hair. Furthermore, he told him that it would be better if he left. He crossed the street and stood there waiting for the theater to open, but then the barber came out and told him to leave. Then it all became clear to him and he went home to get his father.

A Silvery Night

❦

It was a silvery night when he called the devil. Everything was almost clear and it even smelled like day. The whole day he thought about what could happen to him, but the more he thought about it the more curious he became and the less fearful. So that by the time everybody went to bed and turned off the lights, he had already decided to go out right at midnight. He would have to slide across the floor to the door without anyone hearing or seeing him.

"Dad. Why don't you leave the door open. There aren't any mosquitos, anyway."

"Yes, but what if some animal gets in. You remember that badger that got into the Flores' home."

"But that was two years ago. Come on, leave it open. It's real hot. Nothing's gonna get in. All that's left around here are crows, and those don't get into people's houses. Come on. See how all the other people leave their doors open."

"Yes, but at least they've got screens."

"Not all of them. Please. See how pretty the moon looks. Everything is so peaceful."

"All right ... No, Vieja, no animal is going to crawl in. You and your fears."

The devil had fascinated him as far back as he could remember. Even when they had taken him to the shepherds plays at his Aunt Pana's, he was already curious about how it might look. He thought about Don Rayos, with his black metal mask, with his red horns and black cape. Then he remembered how he found the costume and the mask under Don Rayos' house. One of his marbles had rolled under the house and when he reached for it he found everything all full of dust. He pulled everything out, dusted it off and then he put on the mask.

"I tell you, compadre, you don't fool around with the devil. There are many who have summoned him and have regretted it afterwards. Most of them go insane. Sometimes they get together in groups to summon him, so they won't be afraid. But he doesn't appear before them until later, when each of them is alone, and he appears in different shapes. No, nobody should fool with the devil. If you do, as they say, you give up your soul. Some die of fright, others don't.

They just start looking real somber and then they don't even talk anymore. It's like their spirits have left their bodies."

From where he was lying on the floor he could see the clock on the table. He sensed each of his brothers and sisters falling asleep, one by one, and then his parents. He thought he could even make out the sound of snores coming from the other chicken shacks. Eleven to eleven-fifty went by the slowest. Occasionally, he felt somewhat fearful, but then he would look outside where everything was so still and serene under the silvery light of the moon and his fears quickly passed.

"If I leave here at eleven-fifty I'll have enough time to get to the center of the knoll. Good thing there's no snakes here, otherwise it'd be dangerous walking through the weeds that grow so tall at the center of the knoll. I'll call him right at twelve. I better take the clock so I'll know when it's exactly twelve. Otherwise, he might not come. It has to be right at midnight, exactly midnight."

Very slowly, without making a sound, he left, picking up the clock from the table. He put it in his pants' pocket and he noticed that it ticked louder inside the pocket than outside. Even once he was past the chicken coops he walked very slowly, stepping carefully and stopping every now and then. He felt someone was watching him. He proceeded cautiously until he had passed the outhouse. From there the chicken coops were barely visible and he began talking to himself but very softly.

"And how do I call him? Maybe he'll appear. No, I don't think so. In any case, if he does appear he can't do anything to me. I haven't died yet. So he can't do anything to me. I'd just like to know whether there is or isn't ... If there isn't a devil, maybe there also isn't ... No, I better not say it. I might get punished. But if there's no devil maybe there's no punishment. No, there has to be punishment. Well, how do I call him? Just, devil? Or, imp? Or, demon? Lucifer? Satan? ... Whatever comes first."

He got to the center of the knoll and summoned him. At first no words came out, from pure fright, but then his name slipped out in a loud voice and nothing happened. He kept calling him by different names. And nothing. No one came out. Everything looked the same. Everything was the same. All peaceful. Then he thought it would be better to curse the devil instead. So he did. He swore at him using all the cuss words that he knew and in different tones of voice. He even cursed the devil's mother. But nothing. Nothing nor no one appeared, nor did anything change. Disillusioned and feeling at moments a little brave, he headed back for the house. The sound of the wind rustling the leaves of the trees seemed to accompany his every step. There was no devil.

"But if there's no devil neither is there ... No, I better not say it. I might get punished. But there's no devil. Maybe he'll appear before me later. No, he would've appeared already. What better time than at night and me, alone? No, there's no devil. There isn't."

Two or three different times he sensed someone calling him but he didn't want to turn around. He didn't get scared because he felt sure that it wasn't anyone nor anything. After he laid down, very careful not to make a sound, certain that there was no devil, he began to feel chills and his stomach became upset. Before falling asleep he thought for a good while. *There is no devil, there is nothing.* The only thing that had been present in the woods was his own voice. No wonder, he thought, people said you shouldn't fool around with the devil. Now he understood everything. Those who summoned the devil went crazy, not because the devil appeared, but just the opposite, because he didn't appear. He fell asleep gazing at the moon as it jumped through the clouds and the trees, as if it were extremely content about something.

One afternoon a minister from one of the protestant churches in the town came to the farm and informed them that some man would be coming to teach them manual skills so that they would no longer have to work just in the fields. Practically all of the men got excited. He was going to teach them carpentry. A man came about two weeks later in a station wagon hauling a trailer. He brought with him the minister's wife to assist him as interpreter. But they never taught them anything. They would spend the entire day inside the trailer. A week later they left without a word. They later learned that the man had run off with the minister's wife.

And the Earth Did Not Devour Him

🌾

The first time he felt hate and anger was when he saw his mother crying for his uncle and his aunt. They both had caught tuberculosis and had been sent to different sanitariums. So, between the brothers and sisters, they had split up the children among themselves and had taken care of them as best they could. Then the aunt died, and soon thereafter they brought the uncle back from the sanitarium, but he was already spitting blood. That was when he saw his mother crying every little while. He became angry because he was unable to do anything against anyone. Today he felt the same. Only today it was for his father.

"You all should've come home right away, m'ijo. Couldn't you see that your Daddy was sick? You should have known that he'd suffered a sunstroke. Why didn't you come home?"

"I don't know. Us being so soaked with sweat, we didn't feel so hot, but I guess that when you're sunstruck it's different. But I did tell him to sit down under the tree that's at the edge of the rows, but he didn't want to. And that was when he started throwing up. Then we saw he couldn't hoe anymore and we dragged him and put him under a tree. He didn't put up a fuss at that point. He just let us take him. He didn't even say a word."

"Poor viejo, my poor viejo. Last night he hardly slept. Didn't you hear him outside the house. He squirmed in bed all night with cramps. God willing, he'll get well. I've been giving him cool lemonade all day, but his eyes still look glassy. If I'd gone to the fields yesterday, I tell you, he wouldn't have gotten sick. My poor viejo, he's going to have cramps all over his body for three days and three nights at the least. Now, you all take care of yourselves. Don't overwork yourselves so much. Don't pay any mind to that boss if he tries to rush you. Just don't do it. He thinks its so easy since he's not the one who's out there stooped."

He became even angrier when he heard his father moan outside the chicken coop. He wouldn't stay inside because he said it made him feel very anxious. Outside where he could feel the fresh air was where he got some relief. And also when the cramps came he could roll over on the grass. Then he thought about whether his father might die from the sunstroke. At times he heard his father start to pray and ask for God's help. At first he had faith that he would get well soon but by the next day he felt the anger growing inside of him. And all the more when he heard his mother and his father clamoring for God's mercy. That night, well past midnight, he had been awakened by his father's groans. His mother got up and removed the scapularies from around his neck and washed them. Then she lit some candles. But nothing happened. It was like his aunt and uncle all over again.

"What's to be gained from doing all that, Mother? Don't tell me you think it helped my aunt and uncle any. How come we're like this, like we're buried alive? Either the germs eat us alive or the sun burns us up. Always some kind of sickness. And every day we work and work. For what? Poor Dad, always working so hard. I think he was born working. Like he says, barely five years old and already helping his father plant corn. All the time feeding the earth and the sun, only to one day, just like that, get struck down by the sun. And there you are, helpless. And them, begging for God's help . . . why, God doesn't care about us . . . I don't think there even is . . . No, better not say it, what if Dad gets worse. Poor Dad, I guess that at least gives him some hope."

His mother noticed how furious he was, and that morning she told him to calm down, that everything was in God's hands and that with God's help his father was going to get well.

"Oh, Mother, do you really believe that? I am certain that God has no concern for us. Now you tell me, is Dad evil or mean-hearted? You tell me if he has ever done any harm to anyone."

"Of course not."

"So there you have it. You see? And my aunt and uncle? You explain. And the poor kids, now orphans, never having known their parents. Why did God have to take them away? I tell you, God could care less about the poor. Tell me, why must we live here like this? What have we done to deserve this? You're so good and yet you have to suffer so much."

"Oh, please, m'ijo, don't talk that way. Don't speak against the will of God. Don't talk that way, please, m'ijo. You scare me. It's as if already the blood of Satan runs through your veins."

"Well, maybe. That way at least, I could get rid of this anger. I'm so tired of thinking about it. Why? Why you? Why Dad? Why my uncle? Why my aunt? Why their kids? Tell me, Mother, why? Why us, burrowed in the dirt like animals with no hope for anything? You know the only hope we have is coming out here every year. And like you yourself say, only death brings rest. I think that's the way my aunt and uncle felt and that's how Dad must feel too."

"That's how it is, m'ijo. Only death brings us rest."

"But why us?"

"Well, they say that ... "

"Don't say it. I know what you're going to tell me—that the poor go to heaven."

That day started out cloudy and he could feel the morning coolness brushing his eyelashes as he and his brothers and sisters began the day's labor. Their mother had to stay home to care for her husband. Thus, he felt responsible for hurrying on his brothers and sisters. During the morning, at least for the first few hours, they endured the heat but by ten-thirty the sun had suddenly cleared the skies and pressed down against the world. They began working more slowly because of the weakness, dizziness and suffocation they felt when they worked too fast. Then they had to wipe the sweat from their eyes every little while because their vision would get blurred.

"If you start blacking out, stop working, you hear me? Or go a little slower. When we reach the edge we'll rest a bit to get our strength back. It's gonna be hot today. If only it'd stay just a bit cloudy like this morning, then nobody would complain. But no, once the sun bears down like this not even one little cloud dares to appear out of fear. And the worst of it is we'll finish up here by two and then we have to go over to that other field that's nothing but hills. It's okay at the top of the hill but down in the lower part of the slopes it gets to be real suffocating. There's no breeze there. Hardly any air goes through. Remember?"

"Yeah."

"That's where the hottest part of the day will catch us. Just drink plenty of water every little while. It don't matter if the boss gets mad. Just don't get sick. And if you can't go on, tell me right away, all right? We'll go home. Y'all saw what happened to Dad when he pushed himself too hard. The sun has no mercy, it can eat you alive."

Just as they had figured, they had moved on to the other field by early afternoon. By three o'clock they were all soaked with sweat. Not one part of their clothing was dry. Every little while they would stop. At times they could barely breath, then they would black out and they would become fearful of getting sunstruck, but they kept on working.

"How do y'all feel?"

"Man, it's so hot! But we've got to keep on. 'Til six, at least. Except this water don't help our thirst any. Sure wish I had a bottle of cool water, real cool, fresh from the well, or a coke ice-cold."

"Are you crazy? That'd sure make you sunsick right now. Just don't work so fast. Let's see if we can make it until six. What do you think?"

At four o'clock the youngest became ill. He was only nine years old, but since he was paid the same as a grown up he tried to keep up with the rest. He began vomiting. He sat down, then he laid down. Terrified, the other children ran to where he lay and looked at him. It appeared that he had fainted and when they opened his eyelids they saw his eyes were rolled back. The next youngest child started crying but right away he told him to stop and help him carry his brother home. It seemed he was having cramps all over his little body. He lifted him and carried him by himself and, again, he began asking himself *why?*

"Why Dad and then my little brother? He's only nine years old. Why? He has to work like a mule buried in the earth. Dad, Mom, and my little brother here, what are they guilty of?"

Each step that he took towards the house resounded with the question, *why?* About halfway to the house he began to get furious. Then he started crying out of rage. His little brothers and sisters did not know what to do, and they, too, started crying, but out of fear. Then he started cursing. And without even realizing it, he said what he had been wanting to say for a long time. He cursed God. Upon doing this he felt that fear instilled in him by the years and by his parents. For a second he saw the earth opening up to devour him. Then he felt his footsteps against the earth, compact, more solid than ever. Then his anger swelled up again and he vented it by cursing God. He looked at his brother, he no longer looked sick. He didn't know whether his brothers and sisters had understood the graveness of his curse.

That night he did not fall asleep until very late. He felt at peace as never before. He felt as though he had become detached from everything. He no longer worried about his father nor his brother. All that he awaited was the new day, the freshness of the morning. By daybreak his father was doing better. He was on his way to recovery. And his little brother, too; the cramps had almost completely subsided. Frequently he felt a sense of surprise upon recalling what he had done the previous afternoon. He thought of telling his mother, but he decided to keep it secret. All he told her was that the earth did not devour anyone, nor did the sun.

He left for work and encountered a very cool morning. There were clouds in the sky and for the first time he felt capable of doing and undoing anything that he pleased. He looked down at the earth and kicked it hard and said.

"Not yet, you can't swallow me up yet. Someday, yes. But I'll never know it."

A stroke left the grandfather paralyzed from the neck down. One day one of his grandsons came by to visit with him. The grandfather asked him how old he was and what he most desired in life. The grandson replied that what he most wanted was for the next ten years to pass by immediately so that he would know what had happened in his life. The grandfather told him he was very stupid and cut off the conversation. The grandson did not understand why he had called him stupid until he turned thirty.

First Communion

❈

The priest always held First Communion during mid-spring. I'll always remember that day in my life. I remember what I was wearing and I remember my godfather and the pastries and chocolate that we had after mass, but I also remember what I saw at the cleaners that was next to the church. I think it all happened because I left so early for church. It's that I hadn't been able to sleep the night before, trying to remember all of my sins, and worse yet, trying to arrive at an exact number. Furthermore, since Mother had placed a picture of hell at the head of the bed and since the walls of the room were papered with images of the of the devil and since I wanted salvation from all evil, that was all I could think of.

"Remember, children, very quiet, very very quiet. You have learned your prayers well, and now you know which are the mortal sins and which are the venial sins, now you know what sacrilege is, now you know that you are God's children, but you can also be children of the devil. When you go to confession you must tell all of your sins, you must try to remember all of the sins you have committed. Because if you forget one and receive Holy Communion then that would be a sacrilege and if you commit sacrilege you will go to hell. God knows all. You cannot lie to God. You can lie to me and to the priest, but God knows everything; so if your soul is not pure of sin, then you should not receive Holy Communion. That would be a sacrilege. So everyone confess all of your sins. Recall all of your sins. Wouldn't you be ashamed if you received Holy Communion and then later remembered a sin that you had forgotten to confess? Now, let's see, let us practice confessing our sins. Who would like to start off? Let us begin with the sins that we commit with our hands when we touch our bodies. Who would like to start?"

The nun liked for us to talk about the sins of the flesh. The real truth was that we practiced a lot telling our sins, but the real truth was that I didn't understand a lot of things. What did scare me was the idea of going to hell because some months earlier I had fallen against a small basin filled with hot coals which we used as a heater in the little room where we slept. I had burned my calf. I could well imagine how it might be to burn in hell forever. That was all that I understood. So I spent that night, the eve of my First Communion, going over all the sins I had committed. But what was real hard was coming up with the exact number like the nun wanted us to. It must have been dawn by the time I finally satisfied my conscience. I had committed one hundred and fifty sins, but I was going to admit to two-hundred.

> "If I say one-hundred and fifty and I've forgotten some, that would be bad. I'll just say two-hundred and that way even if I forget lots of them I won't commit any kind of sacrilege. Yes, I have committed two-hundred sins ... Father, I have come to confess my sins ... How many? ... Two-hundred ... of all kinds ... The Commandments? Against all of the Ten Commandments ... This way there will be no sacrilege. It's better this way. By confessing more sins you'll be purer."

I remember I got up much earlier that morning than Mother had expected. My godfather would be waiting for me at the church and I didn't want to be even one second late.

> "Hurry, Mother, get my pants ready, I thought you already ironed them last night."
> "It's just that I couldn't see anymore last night. My eyesight is failing me now and that's why I had to leave them for this morning. But tell me, what's your hurry now? It's still very early. Confession isn't until eight o'clock and it's only six. Your padrino won't be there until eight."
> "I know, but I couldn't sleep. Hurry, Mother, I want to leave now."
> "And what are you going to do there so early?"
> "Well, I want to leave because I'm afraid I'll forget the sins I have to confess to the priest. I can think better at the church."
> "All right, I'll be through in just a minute. Believe me, as long as I can see I'm able to do a lot."

I headed for church repeating my sins and reciting the Holy Sacraments. The morning was already bright and clear but there weren't many people out in the street yet. The morning was cool. When I got to the church I found that it was closed. I think the priest might have overslept or was very busy. That was why I walked around the church and passed by the cleaners that was next to the church. The sound of loud laughter and moans surprised me because I didn't expect anybody to be in there. I thought it might be a dog but then it sounded like people again and that's why I peeked in through the little window in the door. They didn't see me but I saw them. They were naked and embracing each other, lying on some shirts and dresses on the floor. I don't know why but I couldn't move away from the window. Then they saw me and tried to cover themselves, and they yelled at me to get out of there. The woman's hair looked all messed up and she looked like she was sick. And me, to tell the truth, I got scared and ran to the church but I couldn't get my mind off of what I had seen. I realized then that maybe those were the sins that we committed with our hands. But I couldn't forget the sight of that woman and that man lying on the floor. When my friends started arriving I was going to tell them but then I thought it would be better to tell them after communion. More and more I was feeling like I was the one who had committed a sin of the flesh.

> "There's nothing I can do now. But I can't tell the others 'cause they'll sin like me. I better not go to communion. Better that I don't go to confession. I can't, now that I know, I can't. But what will Mom and Dad say if I don't go to communion? And my padrino, I can't leave him there waiting. I have to confess what I saw. I feel like going back. Maybe they're still there on the floor. No choice, I'm gonna have to lie. What if I forget it between now and confession? Maybe I didn't see anything? And if I hadn't seen anything?"

I remember that when I went in to confess and the priest asked for my sins, all I told him was two-hundred and of all kinds. I did not confess the sin of the flesh. On returning to the house with my godfather, everything seemed changed, like I was and yet wasn't in the same place. Everything seemed smaller and less important. When I saw my Dad and my Mother, I imagined them on the floor. I started seeing all of the grown-ups naked and their faces even looked distorted, and I could even hear them laughing and moaning, even though they weren't even laughing. Then I started imagining the priest and the nun on the floor. I couldn't hardly eat any of the sweet bread or drink the chocolate. As soon as I finished, I recall running out of the house. It felt like I couldn't breath.

> "So, what's the matter with him? Such manners!"
>
> "Ah, compadre, let him be. You don't have to be concerned on my account. I have my own. These young ones, all they can think about is playing. Let him have a good time, it's the day of his First Communion."
>
> "Sure, compadre, I'm not saying they shouldn't play. But they have to learn to be more courteous. They have to show more respect toward adults, their elders, and all the more for their padrino."
>
> "No, well, that's true."

I remember I headed toward the thicket. I picked up some rocks and threw them at the cactus. Then I broke some bottles. I climbed a tree and stayed there for a long time until I got tired of thinking. I kept remembering the scene at the cleaners, and there, alone, I even liked recalling it. I even forgot that I had lied to the priest. And then I felt the same as I once had when I had heard a missionary speak about the grace of God. I felt like knowing more about everything. And then it occurred to me that maybe everything was the same.

The teacher was surprised when, hearing that they needed a button on the poster to represent the button industry, the child tore one off his shirt and offered it to her. She was surprised because she knew that this was probably the only shirt the child had. She didn't know whether he did this to be helpful, to feel like he belonged or out of love for her. She did feel the intensity of the child's desire and this was what surprised her most of all.

The Little Burnt Victims

🌿

There were five in the García family. Don Efraín, Doña Chona and their three children: Raulito, Juan and María—seven, six and five years old, respectively. On Sunday evening they arrived from the theater excited over the movie about boxing that they had seen. Don Efraín was the most excited. When they arrived, he brought out the boxing gloves he had bought for the children and then he made them put them on. He even stripped them down to their shorts and rubbed a bit of alcohol on their little chests, just like they had seen done in the movie. Doña Chona didn't like for them to box because someone would always end up getting mad and then the wailing would start and last for a long time.

"That's enough, viejo. Why do you make them fight? Remember how Juan's nose always starts to bleed and you know how hard it is to make the bleeding stop. Come on, viejo, let them go to bed."

"Man, vieja!"

"I'm not a man."

"Oh, let them fight. Maybe they'll at least learn how to defend themselves."

"But can't you see that we barely have enough room to stand up in this chicken shack and there you are running around like we had so much space."

"And what do you think they do when we go to work? I wish they were older so we could take them with us to the fields. They could work or at least sit quietly in the car."

"Yeah, but do you really think so? The older they get, the more restless they become. I don't like it at all leaving them here by themselves."

"Maybe one of them will turn out good with the glove, and then we'll be set vieja. Just think how much money champions win. Thousands and thousands. I'm gonna see if I can order them a punching bag through the catalog next week, as soon as we get paid."

"Well, true. You never know, right?"

"Right. That's what I'm telling you."

The three children were left to themselves in the house when they went to work because the owner didn't like children in the fields doing mischief and distracting their parents from their work. Once they took them along and kept them in the car, but the day had gotten very hot

188

and suffocating and the children had even gotten sick. From then on they decided to leave them at home instead, although, sure enough, they worried about them all day long. Instead of packing a lunch, they would go home at noon to eat and that way they could check on them to see if they were all right. That following Monday they got up before dawn as usual and left for work. They left the children fast asleep.

"You look real happy, viejo."

"You know why."

"No, it's not just that. You look like you're happier than just because of that."

"It's just that I love my children so much, like you. And on the way I was thinking about how they also like to play with us."

At about ten o'clock that morning, from where they were working in the fields they noticed smoke rising from the direction of the farm. Everyone stopped working and ran to their cars. They sped toward the farm. When they arrived they found the García's shack engulfed in flames. Only the eldest child was saved. The bodies of the other children were charred in the blaze.

"They say that the oldest child made little Juan and María put on the gloves. They were just playing. But then I think he rubbed some alcohol on their chests and who knows what other stuff on their little bodies like they had seen done in the movie. That's how they were playing."

"But how did the fire get started?"

"Well, poor things, the oldest, Raulito, started to fry some eggs while they were playing and somehow or other their little bodies caught on fire, and you can imagine."

"He must have rubbed lots of alcohol on them."

"You know all the junk that piles up in the house, so cramped for space and all. I believe the kerosene tank on the stove exploded and ...that was it. The explosion must have covered them with flames and, of course, the shack, too."

"Why, sure."

"And you know what?"

"What?"

"The only thing that didn't get burnt up was the pair of gloves. They say they found the little girl all burnt up and with the gloves on."

"But I wonder why the gloves didn't get burned up?"

"Well, you know how those people can make things so good. Not even fire can destroy them."

"And the García's, how are they getting along?"

"Well, they're getting over their grief, although I don't believe they'll ever be able to forget it. What else can you do? I tell you, you never know when your turn's up. My heart goes out to them. But you never know."

"So true."

It was a beautiful wedding day. Throughout the entire week prior the groom and his father had been busy fixing up the yard at the bride's house and setting up a canvass tent where the couple would receive the congratulations of family and friends. For decorations they used the limbs of pecan trees and wild flowers and everything was arranged very nicely. Then they smoothed down the ground in front of the tent very neatly. Every little while they sprinkled water on it to pack down the soil. This way the dust wouldn't get stirred up so much once the dancing got started. After they were married in the church the couple strolled down the street followed by a procession of godmothers and godfathers and ahead of them a bunch of children running and shouting, "Here come the newlyweds!"

The Night the Lights Went Out

The night the lights of the town went out some became frightened and others did not. It wasn't storming nor was there any lightning, so some didn't find out until later. Those who were at the dance had found out but those who weren't hadn't ... until the next day. Those who stayed home just noticed that right after the lights went out the music was no longer heard through the night and they figured that the dance had ended. But they didn't find out anything until the next day.

"That Ramón, he loved his girlfriend a lot. Yes, he loved her a lot. I know so because he was my friend and, well, you know he wasn't one who talked much, but anyway, he would tell me everything. Many times he'd say how much he loved her. They'd been going together since last year and they had given each other real pretty rings that they bought at Kress. And she loved him too but who knows what had happened this summer. They say it was the first time in four months that he had seen her ... no one knows, no one really knows ... "

"Look, I promise you I'm not gonna see anybody else or flirt with anyone. I promise you. I want to marry you ... Look, we can go away together right now if you want to ... Well, we'll wait then, until we finish school. But, look, I promise you I won't go around with anyone else nor flirt with anyone. I promise you. We can leave right now if you want to. I can support you. I know, I know ... but they'll get over it. Let's go. Will you go with me?"

"No, it's better to wait, don't you think? It's better if we do it right. I promise you too ... You know that I love you. Trust me. Dad wants me to finish school. And, well, I have to do what he says. But that doesn't mean I don't love you just 'cause I can't go away with you. I do love you, I love you very much. I won't go around with anybody else either. I promise you."

"Oh, come on. You know everybody knows. I heard something else. Somebody told me that she'd been going around with some dude out there in Minnesota. And that she still kept on writing to Ramón. Kept on lying to him. Some of Ramón's friends told him everything. They were working at the same farm where she was.

And then when they saw him out here they told him right off. He was faithful to her but she wasn't. She was going around with some guy from San Antonio. He was nothing but a show-off and he was always all duded up. They say he wore orange shoes and real long coats and always had his collar turned up ... But her, I think she liked to mess around, otherwise she wouldn't have been unfaithful. What was bad was her not breaking up with him. When he found out, Juanita hadn't returned yet from up north and he took to drinking a lot. I saw him once when he was drunk and all he would say was that he was hurting. That that was all that women left behind, nothing but pain inside."

"When I get back to Texas I'll take her away with me. I can't go on like this anymore. She'll come with me. She will. She's done me wrong. How I love her. With each swing of this hoe I hear her name. How come you feel this way when you're in love? I no sooner finish supper and I'm staring at her picture until dark. And at noon, during the lunch hour, too. But the thing is, I don't really remember how she looks. The picture doesn't seem to look like her anymore. Or she doesn't look like the picture. When the others make fun of me, I just go off to the woods. I see the picture but I just don't remember anymore how she looks, even if I see her picture. Maybe it's best to not look at it so much. She promised she'd be faithful. And she is, because her eyes and her smile keep telling me so when I picture her in my mind. Soon it'll be time to return to Texas. Each time I wake to the early crow of the roosters I feel like I'm already there and that I'm watching her walk down the street. It won't be long now."

"Well, it's not that I don't love Ramón, but this guy, he's a real smooth talker and we just talk, that's all. And all the girls just stare at him. He dresses really fine, too. It's not that I don't love Ramón, but this guy is real nice and his smile, I see it all day long ... No, I'm not breaking up with Ramón. And, anyway, what's wrong with just talking? I don't want to get serious with this guy, I promised Ramón ... but he just keeps on following and following me around. I don't want to get serious with him ... I don't want to lose Ramón, I'm not getting involved with this guy. I just want him around to make the other girls jealous. No, I can't break up with Ramón because I really do love him a lot. It won't be long before we'll see each other again ... Who said he was talking to Petra? Well, then, why is he always following me around? I'll have you know he even sends me letters every day with Don José's little boy."

" ... I know you're going with someone else but I like talking to you. Since I got here and saw you I want to be with you more and more. Go to the dance Saturday and dance with me all night ... Love you, Ramiro."

"They say she danced the whole night with Ramiro. I think her friends told her something about it but she just ignored them. This happened about the time when the work season was almost over and at the last dance, when they were saying good-bye, they promised to see each other back here. I don't think she even remembered Ramón at that moment. But by then Ramón already knew everything. That's why on that day, after not seeing each other in four months, he threw it all in her face. I was with him that day, I was with him when he saw her and I remember well that he was so happy to see her that he wasn't mad anymore. But then, after talking to her for a while he started getting mad all over again. They broke up right then and there."

"You do whatever you want."

"You can be sure of that."

"You're breaking up with me?"

"Yeah, and if you go to the dance tonight you better not dance with anyone else."

"And why shouldn't I? We're not going around anymore. We broke up. You can't tell me what to do."

"I don't care if we broke up or not. You're gonna pay for this. You're gonna do what I say, when I say and for as long as I say. Nobody makes a fool out of me. You're gonna pay for this one, one way or another."

"You can't tell me what to do."

"You're gonna do what I say and if you don't dance with me, you don't dance with anyone. And I mean for the entire dance."

"Well, they say that Juanita asked her parents for permission to leave early for the dance. She went with some of her friends and the orchestra hadn't even started playing yet and there they were already at the dance hall, standing by the door so the guys would see them and ask them to dance right away. Juanita had been dancing with only one guy when Ramón got there. He walked in and looked all around for her. He saw her dancing and when the song ended he went over and grabbed her away from the guy. This guy, just a kid, didn't say anything, he just walked away and asked someone else to dance. Anyway, when the music started again Juanita refused to dance with Ramón. They were standing right in the middle of the dance floor and all the other couples were dancing around them. They stood there arguing and then she slapped him, and he yelled something at her and charged out of the dance hall. Juanita walked over to a bench and sat down. The song hadn't even ended when all the lights went out. There was a bunch of yelling and screaming and they tried to turn them back on but then they saw that the whole town had blacked out."

The workers from the light company found Ramón inside the power plant that was about a block away from the dance hall. They say that his body was burnt to a crisp and that he was holding on to one of the transformers. That's why all the lights of the town went out. The people at the dance found out almost right away. And the ones who were close to Ramón and Juanita heard him tell her that he was going to kill himself because of her. The people at home didn't find out until the next day, that Sunday morning before and after mass.

"They just loved each other so much, don't you think?"
"No doubt."

A little before six, just before the spinach pickers would be getting home, there was the high-pitched signal of the horn at the water tank, then the sound of fire trucks, and then some moments later the ambulance sirens. By six o'clock some of the workers arrived with the news of how one of the trucks transporting workers had collided with a car and was still burning. When the car hit it, those who were not thrown out of the van on impact were trapped. Those who witnessed the crash said that the truck had immediately burst into flames and that they had seen some victims, poor souls, running from the wreckage toward the thicket with their hair aflame. They say the Anglo woman driving the car was from a dry county and that she'd been at a bar drinking, upset because her husband had left her. There were sixteen dead.

The Night Before Christmas

𝕐

Christmas Eve was approaching and the barrage of commercials, music and Christmas cheer over the radio and the blare of announcements over the loud speakers on top of the stationwagon advertising movies at the Teatro Ideal resounded and seemed to draw it closer. It was three days before Christmas when Doña María decided to buy something for her children. This was the first time she would buy them toys. Every year she intended to do it but she always ended up facing up to the fact that, no, they couldn't afford it. She knew that her husband would be bringing each of the children candies and nuts anyway and, so she would rationalize that they didn't need to get them anything else. Nevertheless, every Christmas the children asked for toys. She always appeased them with the same promise. She would tell them to wait until the sixth of January, the day of the Magi, and by the time that day arrived the children had already forgotten all about it. But now she was noticing that each year the children seemed less and less taken with Don Chon's visit on Christmas Eve when he came bearing a sack of oranges and nuts.

"But why doesn't Santa Claus bring us anything?"

"What do you mean? What about the oranges and nuts he brings you?"

"No, that's Don Chon."

"No, I'm talking about what you always find under the sewing machine."

"What, Dad's the one who brings that, don't think we don't know that. Aren't we good like the other kids?"

"Of course, you're good children. Why don't you wait until the day of the Reyes Magos. That's when toys and gifts really arrive. In Mexico, it's not Santa Claus who brings gifts, but the Three Wisemen. And they don't come until the sixth of January. That's the real date."

"Yeah, but they always forget. They've never brought us anything, not on Christmas Eve, not on the day of the Three Kings."

"Well, maybe this time they will."

"Yeah, well, I sure hope so."

That was why she made up her mind to buy them something. But they didn't have the money to spend on toys. Her husband worked almost eighteen hours a day washing dishes and cooking at a restaurant. He didn't have time to go downtown and buy toys. Besides, they had to save money every week to pay for the trip up north. Now they even charged for children too, even if they rode standing up the whole way to Iowa. So it cost them a lot to make the trip. In any case, that night when her husband arrived, tired from work, she talked to him about getting something for the children.

"Look, viejo, the children want something for Christmas."

"What about the oranges and nuts I bring them."

"Well, they want toys. They're not content anymore with just fruits and nuts. They're a little older now and more aware of things."

"They don't need anything."

"Now, you can't tell me you didn't have toys when you were a kid."

"I used to *make* my own toys, out of clay . . . little horses and little soldiers . . . "

"Yes, but it's different here. They see so many things . . . come on, let's go get them something . . . I'll go to Kress myself."

"You?"

"Yes, me."

"Aren't you afraid to go downtown? You remember that time in Wilmar, out in Minnesota, how you got lost downtown. Are you sure you're not afraid?"

"Yes, yes, I remember, but I'll just have to get my courage up. I've thought about it all day long and I've set my mind to it. I'm sure I won't get lost here. Look, I go out to the street. From here you can see the ice house. It's only four blocks away, so Doña Regina tells me. When I get to the ice house I turn to the right and go two blocks and there's downtown. Kress is right there. Then, I come out of Kress, walk back towards the ice house and turn back on this street, and here I am."

"I guess it really won't be difficult. Yeah. Fine. I'll leave you some money on top of the table when I go to work in the morning. But be careful, vieja, there's a lot of people downtown these days."

The fact was that Doña María very rarely left the house. The only time she did was when she visited her father and her sister who lived on the next block. And she only went to church whenever someone died and, occasionally, when there was a wedding. But she went with her husband, so she never took notice of where she was going. And her husband always brought her everything. He was the one who bought the groceries and clothing. In reality she was unfamiliar with downtown even though it was only six blocks away. The cemetery was on the other side of downtown and the church was also in that direction. The only time that they passed through downtown was whenever they were on their way to San Antonio or whenever they were returning from up north. And this would usually be during the wee hours of the morning or at night. But that day she was determined and she started making preparations.

The next day she got up early as usual, and after seeing her husband and children off, she took the money from the table and began getting ready to go downtown. This didn't take her long.

> "My God, I don't know why I'm so fearful. Why, downtown is only six blocks from here. I just go straight and then after I cross the tracks turn right. Then go two blocks and there's Kress. On the way back, I walk two blocks back and then I turn to the left and keep walking until I'm home again. God willing, there won't be any dogs on the way. And I just pray that the train doesn't come while I'm crossing the tracks and catches me right in the middle ... I just hope there's no dogs ... I hope there's no train coming down the tracks."

She walked the distance from the house to the railroad tracks rapidly. She walked down the middle of the street all the way. She was afraid to walk on the sidewalk. She feared she might get bitten by a dog or that someone might grab her. In actuality there was only one dog along the entire stretch and most of the people didn't even notice her walking toward downtown. She nevertheless kept walking down the middle of the street and, luckily, not a single car passed by, otherwise she would not have known what to do. Upon arriving at the crossing she was suddenly struck by intense fear. She could hear the sound of moving trains and their whistles blowing and this was unnerving her. She was too scared to cross. Each time she mustered enough courage to cross she heard the whistle of the train and, frightened, she retreated and ended up at the same place. Finally, overcoming her fear, she shut her eyes and crossed the tracks. Once she got past the tracks, her fear began to subside. She got to the corner and turned to the right.

The sidewalks were crowded with people and her ears started to fill up with a ringing sound, the kind that, once it started, it wouldn't stop. She didn't recognize any of the people around her. She wanted to turn back but she was caught in the flow of the crowd which shoved her onward toward downtown and the sound kept ringing louder and louder in her ears. She became frightened and more and more she was finding herself unable to remember why she was there amidst the crowd of people. She stopped in an alley way between two stores to regain her composure a bit. She stood there for a while watching the passing crowd.

"My God, what is happening to me? I'm starting to feel the same way I did in Wilmar. I hope I don't get worse. Let me see ... the ice house is in that direction—no it's that way. No, my God, what's happening to me? Let me see ... I came from over there to here. So it's in that direction. I should have just stayed home. Uh, can you tell me where Kress is, please? ... Thank you."

She walked to where they had pointed and entered the store. The noise and pushing of the crowd was worse inside. Her anxiety soared. All she wanted was to leave the store but she couldn't find the doors anywhere, only stacks and stacks of merchandise and people crowded against one another. She even started hearing voices coming from the merchandise. For a while she stood, gazing blankly at what was in front of her. She couldn't even remember the names of the things. Some people stared at her for a few seconds, others just pushed her aside. She remained in this state for a while, then she started walking again. She finally made out some toys and put them in her bag. Then she saw a wallet and also put that in her bag. Suddenly she no longer heard the noise of the crowd. She only saw the people moving about—their legs, their arms, their mouths, their eyes. She finally asked where the door, the exit was. They told her and she started in that direction. She pressed through the crowd, pushing her way until she pushed open the door and exited.

She had been standing on the sidewalk for only a few seconds, trying to figure out where she was, when she felt someone grab her roughly by the arm. She was grabbed so tightly that she gave out a cry.

"Here she is ... these damn people, always stealing something, stealing. I've been watching you all along. Let's have that bag."

"But ... "

Then she heard nothing for a long time. All she saw was the pavement moving swiftly toward her face and a small pebble that bounced into her eye and was hurting a lot. She felt someone pulling her arms and when they turned her, face up, all she saw were faces far away. Then she saw a security guard with a gun in his holster and she was terrified. In that instant she thought about her children and her eyes filled with tears. She started crying. Then she lost consciousness of what was happening around her, only feeling herself drifting in a sea of people, their arms brushing against her like waves.

"It's a good thing my compadre happened to be there. He's the one who ran to the restaurant to tell me. How do you feel?"

"I think I must be insane, viejo."

"That's why I asked you if you weren't afraid you might get sick like in Wilmar."

"What will become of my children with a mother who's insane? A crazy woman who can't even talk, can't even go downtown."

"Anyway, I went and got the notary public. He's the one who went with me to the jail. He explained everything to the official. That you got dizzy and that you get nervous attacks whenever you're in a crowd of people."

"And if they send me to the insane asylum? I don't want to leave my children. Please, viejo, don't let them take me, don't let them. I shouldn't have gone downtown."

"Just stay here inside the house and don't leave the yard. There's no need for it anyway. I'll bring you everything you need. Look, don't cry anymore, don't cry. No, go ahead and cry, it'll make you feel better. I'm gonna talk to the kids and tell them to stop bothering you about Santa Claus. I'm gonna tell them there's no Santa Claus, that way they won't trouble you with that anymore."

"No, viejo, don't be mean. Tell them that if he doesn't bring them anything on Christmas Eve, it's because the Reyes Magos will be bringing them something."

"But ... well, all right, whatever you say. I suppose it's always best to have hope."

The children, who were hiding behind the door, heard everything, but they didn't quite understand it all. They awaited the day of the Reyes Magos as they did every year. When that day came and went with no arrival of gifts, they didn't ask for explanations.

Before people left for up north the priest would bless their cars and trucks at five dollars each. One time he made enough money to take a trip to Barcelona, in Spain, to visit his parents and friends. He brought back words of gratitude from his family and some postcards of a very modern church. These he placed by the entrance of the church for the people to see, that they might desire a church such as that one. It wasn't long before words began to appear on the cards, then crosses, lines, and con safos symbols, just as had happened to the new church pews. The priest was never able to understand the sacrilege.

The Portrait

As soon as the people returned from up north the portrait salesmen began arriving from San Antonio. They would come to rake in. They knew that the workers had money and that was why, as Dad used to say, they would flock in. They carried suitcases packed with samples and always wore white shirts and ties. That way they looked more important and the people believed everything they would tell them and invite them into their homes without giving it much thought. I think that down deep they even longed for their children to one day be like them. In any event, they would arrive and make their way down the dusty streets, going house to house carrying suitcases full of samples.

I remember once I was at the house of one of my father's friends when one of these salesmen arrived. I also remember that that particular one seemed a little frightened and timid. Don Mateo asked him to come in because he wanted to do business.

"Good afternoon, traveler. I would like to tell you about something new that we're offering this year."

"Well, let's see, let's see ... "

"Well, sir, see, you give us a picture, any picture you may have, and we will not only enlarge it for you but we'll also set it in a wooden frame like this one and with inlays, like this—three dimensional, as they say."

"And what for?"

"So that it will look real. That way ... look, let me show you ... see? Doesn't he look real, like he's alive?"

"Man, he sure does. Look, vieja. This looks great. Well, you know, we wanted to send some pictures to be enlarged ... but now, this must cost a lot, right?"

"No, I'll tell you, it costs about the same. Of course, it takes more time."

"Well, tell me, how much?"

"For as little as thirty dollars we'll deliver it to you done with inlays just like this, one this size."

"Boy, that's expensive! Didn't you say it didn't cost a lot more? Do you take installments?"

"Well, I'll tell you, we have a new manager and he wants everything in cash. It's very fine work. We'll make it look like real.

Done like that, with inlays ... take a look. What do you think? Some fine work, wouldn't you say? We can have it all finished for you in a month. You just tell us what color you want the clothes to be and we'll come by with it all finished one day when you least expect, framed and all. Yes, sir, a month at the longest. But like I say, this man who's the new manager, he wants the full payment in cash. He's very demanding, even with us."

"Yes, but it's much too expensive."

"Well, yes. But the thing is, this is very fine work. You can't say you've ever seen portraits done like this, with wood inlays."

"No, well, that's true. What do you think, vieja?"

"Well, I like it a lot. Why don't we order one? And if it turns out good ... my Chuy ... may he rest in peace. It's the only picture we have of him. We took it right before he left for Korea. Poor m'ijo, we never saw him again. See ... this is his picture. Do you think you can make it like that, make it look like he's alive?"

"Sure, we can. You know, we've done a lot of them in soldier's uniforms and shaped it, like you see in this sample, with inlays. Why, it's more than just a portrait. Sure. You just tell me what size you want and whether you want a round or square frame. What do you say? How should I write it down?"

"What do you say, vieja, should we have it done like this one?"

"Well, I've already told you what I think. I would like to have m'ijo's picture fixed up like that and in color."

"All right, go ahead and write it down. But you take good care of that picture for us because it's the only one we have of our son grown up. He was going to send us one all dressed up in uniform with the American and Mexican flags crossed over his head, but he no sooner got there when a letter arrived telling us that he was lost in action. So you take good care of it."

"Don't you worry. We're responsible people. And we understand the sacrifices that you people make. Don't worry. And you just wait and see. When we bring it to you'll see how pretty it's gonna look. What do you say, should we make the uniform navy blue?"

"But he's not wearing a uniform in that picture."

"No, but that's just a matter of fixing it up with some wood fiber overlays. Look at these. This one, he didn't have a uniform on but we put one on him. So what do you say? Should we make it navy blue?"

"All right."

"Don't you worry about the picture."

And that was how they spent the entire day going house to house, street by street, their suitcases stuffed with pictures. As it turned out, a whole lot of people had ordered enlargements of that kind.

"They should be delivering those portraits soon, don't you think?"

"I think so, it's delicate work and takes more time. That's some fine work those people do. Did you see how real those pictures looked?"

"Yeah, sure. They do some fine work. You can't deny that. But it's already been over a month since they passed by here."

"Yes, but from here they went on through all the towns picking up pictures . . . all the way to San Antonio for sure. So it'll probably take a little longer."

"That's true, that's true."

And two more weeks had passed by the time they made the discovery. Some very heavy rains had come and some children who were playing in one of the tunnels leading to the dump found a sack full of pictures, all worm-eaten and soaking wet. The only reason they could tell that these were pictures was because there were a lot of them and most of them the same size and with faces that could just barely be made out. Everybody caught on right away. Don Mateo was so angry that he took off to San Antonio to find the so and so who had swindled them.

"Well, you know, I stayed at Esteban's house. And every day I went with him to the market to sell produce. I helped him with everything. I had faith that I would run into that son of a gun some day soon. Then, after I'd been there for a few days, I started going out to the different barrios and I found out a lot that way. It wasn't so much the money that upset me. It was my poor vieja, crying and all because we'd lost the only picture we had of Chuy. We found it in the sack with all the other pictures but it was already ruined, you know."

"I see, but tell me, how did you find him?"

"Well, you see, to make a long story short, he came by the stand at the market one day. He stood right in front of us and bought some vegetables. It was like he was trying to remember who I was. Of course, I recognized him right off. Because when you're angry enough, you don't forget a face. I just grabbed him right then and there. Poor guy couldn't even talk. He was all scared. And I told him that I wanted that portrait of my son and that I wanted it three dimensional and that he'd best get it for me or I'd let him have it.

And I went with him to where he lived. And I put him to work right then and there. The poor guy didn't know where to begin. He had to do it all from memory."

"And how did he do it?"

"I don't know. I suppose if you're scared enough, you're capable of doing anything. Three days later he brought me the portrait all finished, just like you see it there on that table by the Virgin Mary. Now tell me, how do you like the way my boy looks?"

"Well, to be honest, I don't remember too well how Chuy looked. But he was beginning to look more and more like you, isn't that so?"

"Yes, I would say so. That's what everybody tells me now. That Chuy's a chip off the old block and that he was already looking like me. There's the portrait. Like they say, one and the same."

"They let Figueroa out. He's been out a week."

"Yeah, but he's not well. There in the pen, if they don't like someone, they'll give them injections so they'll die."

"Damn right. Who do you think turned him in?"

"Probably some gringo who couldn't stand seeing him in town with that white girl he brought back with him from Wisconsin. And no one to defend him. They say the little gringa was seventeen and it's against the law."

"I'll bet you he won't last a year."

"Well, they say he has a very strange disease."

When We Arrive

❧

At about four o'clock in the morning the truck broke down. All night they stood hypnotized by the high-pitched whir of the tires turning against the pavement. When the truck stopped they awakened. The silence alone told them something was wrong. All along the way the truck had been overheating and then when they stopped and checked the motor they saw that it had practically burned up. It just wouldn't go anymore. They would have to wait there until daybreak and then ask for a lift to the next town. Inside the trailer the people awakened and then struck up several conversations. Then in the darkness their eyes had gradually begun to close and all became so silent that all that could be heard was the chirping of the crickets. Some were sleeping, others were thinking.

"Good thing the truck stopped here. My stomach's been hurting a lot for some time but I would've had to wake up a lot of people to get to the window and ask them to stop. But you still can't hardly see anything. Well, I'm getting off, see if I can find a field or a ditch. Must've been that chile I ate, it was so hot but I hated to let it go to waste. I hope my vieja is doing all right in there, carrying the baby and all."

"This driver that we have this year is a good one. He keeps on going. He doesn't stop for anything. Just gases up and let's go. We've been on the road over twenty-four hours. We should be close to Des Moines. Sure wish I could sit down for just a little while at least. I'd get out and lie down on the side of the road but there's no telling if there's snakes or some other kind of animal. Just before I fell asleep on my feet it felt like my knees were going to buckle. But I guess your body gets used to it right away 'cause it doesn't seem so hard anymore. But the kids must feel real tired standing like this all the way and with nothing to hold on to. Us grownups can at least hold on to this center bar that supports the canvas. And to think we're not as crowded as other times. I think there must be forty of us at the most. I remember that one time I traveled with that bunch of wetbacks, there were more than sixty of us. We couldn't even smoke."

"What a stupid woman! How could she be so dumb as to throw that diaper out the front of the truck. It came sliding along the canvas and good thing I had glasses on or I would even have gotten the shit in my eyes! What a stupid woman! How could she do that? She should've known that crap would be blown towards all of us standing up back here. Why the hell couldn't she just wait until we got to a gas station and dump the shit there!"

"El Negrito just stood there in disbelief when I ordered the fifty-four hamburgers. At two in the morning. And since I walked into the restaurant alone and I'm sure he didn't see the truck pull up loaded with people. His eyes just popped wide open ... 'at two o'clock in the morning, hamburgers? Fifty-four of them? Man, you must eat one hell of a lot.' It's that the people hadn't eaten and the driver asked for just one of us to get out and order for everyone. El Negrito was astounded. He couldn't believe what I ordered, that I wanted fifty-four hamburgers. At two o'clock in the morning you can eat that many hamburgers very easily, especially when you're starving."

"This is the last fuckin' year I come out here. As soon as we get to the farm I'm getting the hell out. I'll go look for a job in Minneapolis. I'll be damned if I go back to Texas. Out here you can at least make a living at a decent job. I'll look for my uncle, see if he can find me a job at the hotel where he works as a bellboy. Who knows, maybe they'll give me a break there or at some other hotel. And then the gringas, that's just a matter of finding them."

"If things go well this year, maybe we'll buy us a car so we won't have to travel this way, like cattle. The girls are pretty big now and I know they feel embarrassed. Sometimes they have some good buys at the gas stations out there. I'll talk to my compadre, he knows some of the car salesmen. I'll get one I like, even if it's old. I'm tired of coming out here in a truck like this. My compadre drove back a good little car last year. If we do well with the onion crop, I'll buy me one that's at least half-way decent. I'll teach my boy how to drive and he can take it all the way to Texas. As long as he doesn't get lost like my nephew. They didn't stop to ask for directions and ended up in New Mexico instead of Texas. Or I'll get Mundo to drive it and I won't charge him for gas. I'll see if he wants to."

"With the money Mr. Thompson loaned me we have enough to buy food for at least two months. By then we should have the money from the beet crop. Just hope we don't get too much in debt. He loaned me two-hundred dollars but by the time you pay for the trip practically half of it is gone, and now that they've started charging me half-fare for the children . . . And then when we return, I have to pay him back double. Four-hundred dollars. That's too much interest, but what can you do? When you need it, you need it. Some people have told me to report him because that's way too much interest but now he's even got the deed to the house. I'm just hoping that things go okay for us with the beet crop or else we'll be left to the wind, homeless. We have to save enough to pay him back the four-hundred. And then we'll see if we have something left. And these kids, they need to start going to school. I don't know. I hope it goes okay for us, if not I don't know how we're going to do it. I just pray to God that there's work."

"Fuckin' life, this goddamn fuckin' life! This fuckin' sonofa-bitchin' life for being pendejo! pendejo! pendejo! We're nothing but a bunch of stupid, goddamn asses! To hell with this goddamn motherfuckin' life! This is the last time I go through this, standing up all the way like a goddamn animal. As soon as we get there I'm headed for Minneapolis. Somehow I'll find me something to do where I don't have to work like a fuckin' mule. Fuckin' life! One of these days they'll fuckin' pay for this. Sonofabitch! I'll be goddamn for being such a fuckin' pendejo!"

"Poor viejo. He must be real tired now, standing up the whole trip. I saw him nodding off a little while ago. And with no way to help him, what with these two in my arms. How I wish we were there already so we could lie down, even if it's on the hard floor. These children are nothing but trouble. I hope I'll be able to help him out in the fields, but I'm afraid that this year, what with these kids, I won't be able to do anything. I have to breastfeed them every little while and then they're still so little. If only they were just a bit older. I'm still going to try my best to help him out. At least along his row so he won't feel so overworked. Even if it's just for short whiles. My poor viejo . . . the children are still so little and already he wishes they could start school. I just hope I'll be able to help him. God willing, I'll be able to help him."

"What a great view of the stars from here! It looks like they're coming down and touching the tarp of the truck. It's almost like there aren't any people inside. There's hardly any traffic at this hour. Every now and then a trailer passes by. The silence of the morning twilight makes everything look like it's made of satin. And now, what do I wipe myself with? Why couldn't it always be early dawn like this? We're going to be here till midday for sure. By the time they find help in the town and then by the time they fix the motor ... If only it could stay like early dawn, then nobody would complain. I'm going to keep my eyes on the stars till the last one disappears. I wonder how many more people are watching the same star? And how many more might there be wondering how many are looking at the same star? It's so silent it looks like it's the stars the crickets are calling to."

"Goddamn truck. It's nothing but trouble. When we get there Everybody will just have to look out for themselves. All I'm doing is dropping them off with the growers and I'm getting the hell out. Besides, we don't have a contract. They'll find themselves somebody to take them back to Texas. Somebody's bound to come by and pick them up. You can't make money off beets anymore. My best bet is to head back to Texas just as soon as I drop these people off and then see how things go hauling watermelons. The melon season's almost here. All I need now is for there not to be anyone in this goddamn town who can fix the truck. What the hell will I do then? So long as the cops don't come by and start hassling me about moving the truck from here. Boy, that town had to be the worst. We didn't even stop and still the cop caught up with us just to tell us that he didn't want us staying there. I guess he just wanted to show off in front of the town people. But we didn't even stop in their goddamn town. When we get there, as soon as I drop them off, I'll turn back. Each one to fend for himself."

"When we get there I'm gonna see about getting a good bed for my vieja. Her kidneys are really bothering her a lot nowadays. Just hope we don't end up in a chicken coop like last year, with that cement floor. Even though you cover it with straw, once the cold season sets in you just can't stand it. That was why my rheumatism got so bad, I'm sure of that."

"When we arrive, when we arrive, the real truth is that I'm tired of arriving. Arriving and leaving, it's the same thing because we no sooner arrive and ... the real truth of the matter ... I'm tired of arriving. I really should say when we don't arrive because that's the real truth. We never arrive."

"When we arrive, when we arrive ... "

Little by little the crickets ceased their chirping. It seemed as though they were becoming tired and the dawn gradually affirmed the presence of objects, ever so carefully and very slowly, so that no one would take notice of what was happening. And the people were becoming people. They began getting out of the trailer and they huddled around and commenced to talk about what they would do when they arrived.

.

Bartolo passed through town every December when he knew that most of the people had returned from work up north. He always came by selling his poems. By the end of the first day, they were almost sold out because the names of the people of the town appeared in the poems. And when he read them aloud it was something emotional and serious. I recall that one time he told the people to read the poems out loud because the spoken word was the seed of love in the darkness.

Under the House

※

The fleas made him move. He was under a house. He had been there for several hours, or so it seemed to him, hiding. That morning on his way to school he felt the urge not to go. He thought of how the teacher would spank him for sure because he didn't know the words. Then he thought of crawling under the house but not just because of that. He felt like hiding, too, but he didn't know where nor for how long, so he just went ahead and hid there. At first the fleas didn't bother him and he felt very comfortable in the dark. Although he was sure there were spiders, he had crawled in unafraid and there he remained. From where he was all he could make out was a white strip of daylight, about a foot high, lining the house all around. He was lying face down and whenever he moved he could feel his back brush against the floor of the house. This even gave him a feeling of security. But once the fleas started biting him he had to move constantly. And he started to worry that the people who lived there might find out that he was there and make him get out. But he had to keep moving constantly.

> *I wonder how long I've been here now. The kids came out of the house to play some time ago. It seems I've been here for a good while. As long as they don't look under the house 'cause they'll see me for sure, and then what? The children look funny, all I can see are their legs running. It's not bad here. I could come here every day. I think that must be what the others do when they play hooky. No one to bother me here. I can think in peace.*

He had even forgotten all about the fleas and even that he was under the house. He could think very clearly in the dark. He didn't need to close his eyes. He thought about his father for a while, about how he used to tell him stories at night about witches and how he would make them fall from the sky by praying and tying the seven knots.

> *When I'd be coming back from work, at that time we had our own land with irrigation, in the early morning twilight, I'd always see these globes of light, like fireballs, bouncing off the telephone lines. They would come from the direction of Morelos, they say that's where they originate. One time I nearly made one fall down. Don Remigio taught me how to say the seven prayers that go with the seven knots. All you have to do is start praying when you see those balls of fire. After each*

prayer you tie a knot. This one time I got to the seventh prayer but you know, I wasn't able to tie that last knot, but the witch fell anyway, practically landing at my feet, and then she got up ... The boy was so young and children don't understand too much at that age. And he couldn't hold out. They're not going to do anything to the boss, he's got too much pull. Can you imagine what they'd do if one of us killed one of their kids? They say that one day the boy's father took a rifle and went looking for him because he wanted to pay him back but he didn't find him ... The woman would almost always start crying when she entered the church, and then she'd start praying. But before she was even aware of it, she would start talking in a loud voice. Then she'd start yelling, like she was having some kind of attack ... I think Doña Cuquita is still living. I haven't seen her in a long time. She used to be very careful whenever we went to the dump. Now her I really loved. And since I never knew my grandparents. I think even Dad loved her like a grandmother because he, too, never knew his grandparents. What I liked best was for her to embrace me and tell me, "You're smarter than an eagle and more watchful than the moon" ... Get out of there! Get away from that goddamn window! Go away! Go away ... You know, you can't come home with me anymore. Look, I don't mind playing with you but some old ladies told mama that Mexicans steal and now mama says not to bring you home anymore. You have to turn back. But we can still play at school. I'll choose you and you choose me ... What can I tell you! I know what I'm telling you, I'm saying that we can't get any more screwed than we already are. I know why I'm telling you. If there's another war, we won't be the ones to suffer. Don't be a damn fool. The ones who will pay for it are the ones on top, the ones who have something. Us, we're already screwed. If there's another war, hell, things might even get better for us ... Why don't you eat sweetbread anymore? You don't like it, anymore? ... Well, I tell you, I even went downtown and bought me a new hammer so I could be ready for when they'd come to teach us. They say that the minister, when he found out, he went straight home, took a hatchet and broke all the furniture to pieces and than he took everything outside and set it on fire. He stood there and watched everything burn to ashes ... I don't think my viejo is going to be able to work out in the sun anymore. The boss didn't say a thing when we told him that he had gotten sick from the heat. He just shook his head. What worried him the most was that it was raining too much and the crop was getting ruined. That was the only thing he was sad about. He wasn't even sad when they had to operate on his wife because she had cancer, much less when we told

*him about my viejo ... These sonofabitches are gonna cut your hair,
I'll see to that, if I have to bust their noses ... There is no devil, there
isn't. The only devil is Don Rayos when he dresses up with horns and
with the cape to go to the shepherds' play ... Goddamn fool! Why don't
you pay attention to what you're doing? You almost crashed with that
truck! Didn't you see it? Are you blind, or what? ... Why did the
teacher cry when they came for him? Ever since he was put in her class
she always just kept looking at him. And she was so young, she wasn't
like the ones in Texas, little old ladies holding a paddle in their hands
making sure you didn't lose your place in the book. And if you did,
pow! They'd just bend you over ... You think that was how they were
burned? It's just hard to believe. But so fast? It's that fire spreads fast
and once your clothes catch on fire, that's it. You remember that family
that died in that fire around Christmas time? They fell asleep, never to
wake up again. And then the firemen crying as they removed the bodies,
the grease from the children's little burned up bodies dripping all over
their boots ... Free citizens, this is a day of magnificent and profound
importance. It was in the year eighteen-hundred and seventy-two that
Napoleon's troops suffered a defeat against Mexican soldiers who fought
so valiantly—that was how I would begin my discourse. I always used
the words "free citizens" when I was young, son, but now ever since I
had the attack I can't remember too well anymore what I would say to
the people. Then came the Revolution and in the end we lost. Villa
made out well but I had to come out here. No one here knows what I
went through. Sometimes I want to remember but, truth is, I'm not
able to anymore. All my thoughts become hazy. Now, tell me, what is it
that you most desire at this moment of your life? At this very moment
... Yesterday we collected fifty pounds of copper in all. Enrique found
a magnet and that makes it much easier to find the iron buried under so
much junk that people throw away. Sometimes we do well but usually
it's a waste of time. But at least enough to buy something to eat. And
tell me, what's the price of tin these days? Why don't you all come with
us next time we go? ... The cold weather is setting in. I'll bet you
that tomorrow morning the ground will be all covered with frost. And
notice how often the cranes fly by ... There's going to be a wedding
Sunday. For sure they'll serve us cabrito in mole sauce, with rice, and
then the dance, and the groom, anxious for night to arrive ... I tell you,
comadre, we got so frightened last night when the lights went out. We
were there playing with the children when all of a sudden it was pitch
dark. And we didn't even have one candle. But that wasn't why we
got frightened. That knucklehead, Juan, was eating an orange and we*

don't know how but he got a seed in his nose and we couldn't get it out in the dark. And he was just crying and crying. And your compadre, lighting match after match. I wonder what happened. Why, all the lights of the town went out ... They found Doña Amada's son in a ditch and Don Tiburcio's son inside the trailer. I think they're going to sue Don Jesús for transporting people in an closed van. They say that when they tried to stretch out his body, because they found him all curled up in a corner, when they tried to stretch him out to put him in the hearse, one of his legs fell off ... Those people who sell those portraits don't come around here anymore. Don Mateo gave them a good scare ... Mom nearly lost her mind. She always started crying whenever she talked with anyone about what happened to her downtown.

I would like to see all of the people together. And then, if I had great big arms, I could embrace them all. I wish I could talk to all of them again, but all of them together. But that, only in a dream. I like it right here because I can think about anything I please. Only by being alone can you bring everybody together. That's what I needed to do, hide, so that I could come to understand a lot of things. From now on, all I have to do is to come here, in the dark, and think about them. And I have so much to think about and I'm missing so many years. I think today what I wanted to do was recall this past year. And that's just one year. I'll have to come here to recall all of the other years.

He became aware of the present when he heard one of the children yelling and at the same time felt a blow to his leg. They were throwing rocks at him under the house.

"Mami, mami, there's a man under the house! Mami, mami, mami, hurry, come here, there's a man here, there's a man here!"

"Where? Where? Ah! ... Let me get some boards and you run and get Doña Luz's dog."

And he saw countless faces and eyes looking at him. Then it grew darker under the house. The children kept throwing rocks at him and the dog kept barking while the woman was trying to poke him with some boards.

"Who could it be?"

He had to come out. Everyone was surprised that it was him. He didn't say anything to them, just walked away. And then he heard the woman say:

"That poor family. First the mother and now him. He must be losing his mind. He's losing track of the years."

Smiling, he walked down the chuckhole-ridden street leading to his house. He immediately felt happy because, as he thought over what the woman had said, he realized that in reality he hadn't lost anything. He had made a discovery. To discover and rediscover and piece things together. This to this, that to that, all with all. That was it. That was everything. He was thrilled. When he got home he went straight to the tree that was in the yard. He climbed it. He saw a palm tree on the horizon. He imagined someone perched on top, gazing across at him. He even raised one arm and waved it back and forth so that the other could see that he knew he was there.

The Harvest

What I remember most about that night was the absolute blackness, the mud, and the ~~slippery~~ ~~slime~~ sliminess of the salamanders. But I should really begin from the beginning so that you can understand ~~and if this that~~ ~~everything~~ I felt and perhaps, also, ~~so~~ you will understand that when I felt all this I understood something that I still have with me. And I don't have it with me as something ~~I could~~ ~~remember~~ but as something I still ~~feel~~ sense.

It all began because it had been raining for three weeks and we had no work. The ~~military~~ ~~camps~~ lifted up, I say military camp, not because we were, but rather resembled it one. We had been waiting with that certain farmer in Minnesota for three ~~weeks~~, waiting for the rain to stop. Uselessly. Then he came and ~~told us~~ that the best thing for us to do was to leave ~~his~~ Quonset huts because the rain had already rotted away his sugar beets. But my dad and I understood that he was really afraid of us, afraid that we might start stealing from him, ~~or~~ afraid that one of us might get sick and then it would be ~~his~~ responsibility to ~~respond~~ seek help for us. We told him that we had no money, nor anything to eat, and no way how to return to Texas, we barely had enough to buy gasoline to get us to Oklahoma. And he just told us that he was very sorry but that he wanted us to leave and we left. We were about to leave when his heart softened and he came to us

From the autograph manuscript of Rivera's translation of "The Salamanders."

The Salamanders

W hat I remember most about that night is the darkness, the mud and the slime of the salamanders. But I should start from the beginning so you can understand all of this, and how, upon feeling this, I understood something that I still have with me. But I don't have this with me only as something I remember, but as something that I still feel.

It all began because it had been raining for three weeks and we had no work. We began to gather our things and made ready to leave. We had been with that farmer in Minnesota waiting for the rain to stop but it never did. Then he came and told us that the best thing for us to do was to leave his shacks because, after all, the beets had begun to rot away already. We understood, my father and I, that he was in fact afraid of us. He was afraid that we would begin to steal from him or perhaps that one of us would get sick, and then he would have to take the responsibility because we had no money. We told him we had no money, neither did we have anything to eat and no way of making it all the way back to Texas. We had enough money, perhaps, to buy gasoline to get as far south as Oklahoma. He just told us that he was very sorry, but he wanted us to leave. So we began to pick up our things. We were leaving when he softened up somewhat and gave us two tents, full of spider webs, that he had in the loft in one of his barns. He also gave us a lamp and some kerosene. He told my dad that, if we went by way of Crystal Lake in northern Iowa, perhaps we would find work among the farmers and perhaps it had not been raining there so much and the beets had not rotted away. And we left.

In my father's eyes and in my mother's eyes, I saw something original and pure that I had never seen before. It was a sad type of love, it seemed. We barely talked as we went riding over the gravel roads. The rain seemed to talk for us. A few miles before reaching Crystal Lake, we began to get remorseful. The rain that continued to fall kept on telling us monotonously that we would surely not find work there. And so it was. At every farm that we came to, the farmers would only shake their heads from inside the house. They would not even open the door to tell us there was no work. It was when they shook their heads in this way that I began to feel that I was not part of my father and my mother. The only thing in my mind that existed was the following farm.

The first day we were in the little town of Crystal Lake everything went bad. Going through a puddle, the car's wiring got wet and my father drained the battery trying to get the car started. Finally, a garage did us the favor of recharging the battery. We asked for work in various parts of that little town, but then they got the police after us. My father explained that we were only looking for work, but the policeman told us that he did not want any gypsies in town and told us to leave. The money was almost gone, but we had to leave. We left at twilight and we stopped the car some three miles from town and there we saw the night fall.

The rain would come and go. Seated in the car near the ditch, we spoke little. We were tired. We were hungry. We were alone. We sensed that we were totally alone. In my father's eyes and in my mother's eyes, I saw something original. That day we had hardly eaten anything in order to have money left for the following day. My father looked sadder, weakened. He believed we would find no work, and we stayed seated in the car waiting for the following day. Almost no cars passed by on that gravel road during the night. At dawn I awoke and everybody was asleep, and I could see their bodies and their faces. I could see the bodies of my mother and my father and my brothers and sisters, and they were silent. They were faces and bodies made of wax. They reminded me of my grandfather's face the day we buried him. But I didn't get as afraid as that day when I found him inside the truck, dead. I guess it was because I knew they were not dead and that they were alive. Finally, the day came completely.

That day we looked for work all day, and we didn't find any work. We slept at the edge of the ditch and again I awoke in the early morning hours. Again I saw my people asleep. And that morning I felt somewhat afraid, not because they looked as if they were dead, but because I began to feel again that I no longer belonged to them.

The following day we looked for work all day again, and nothing. We slept at the edge of the ditch. Again I awoke in the morning, and again I saw my people asleep. But that morning, the third one, I felt like leaving them because I truly felt that I was no longer a part of them.

On that day, by noon, the rain stopped and the sun came out and we were filled with hope. Two hours later we found a farmer that had some beets which, according to him, probably had not been spoiled by the rain. But he had no houses or anything to live in. He showed us the acres of beets which were still under water, and he told us that, if we cared to wait until the water went down to see if the beets had not rotted, and if they had not, he would pay us a large bonus per acre that we helped him cultivate. But he didn't have any houses, he told us. We told him we had some tents with us and, if he would let us, we would set them up in his yard. But he didn't want that. We noticed that he was afraid of us. The only thing that we wanted was to be near the drinking water, which was necessary, and also we were so tired of sleeping seated in the car, and, of course, we wanted to be under the light that he had in his yard. But he did not want us, and he told us, if we wanted to work there, we had to put our tents at the foot of the field and wait there for the water to go down. And so we placed our tents at the foot of the field and we began to wait. At nightfall we lit up the lamp in one of the tents, and then we decided for all of us to sleep in one tent only. I remember that we all felt so comfortable being able to stretch our legs, our arms, and falling asleep was easy. The thing that I remember so clearly that night was what awakened me. I felt what I thought was the hand of one of my little brothers, and then I heard my own screaming. I pulled his hand away, and, when I awoke, I found myself holding a salamander. Then I screamed and I saw that we were all covered with salamanders that had come out from the flooded fields. And all of us continued screaming and throwing salamanders off our bodies. With the light of the lamp, we began to kill them. At first we felt nauseated because, when we stepped on them, they would ooze milk. It seemed they were invading us, that they were invading the tent as if they wanted to reclaim the foot of the field. I don't know why we killed so many salamanders that night. The easiest thing to do would have been to climb quickly into our car. Now that I remember, I think that we also felt the desire to recover and to reclaim the foot of the field. I do remember that we began to look for more salamanders to kill. We wanted to find more to kill more. I remember that I liked to take the lamp, to seek them out, to kill them very slowly. It may be that I was angry at them for having frightened me. Then I began to feel that I was becoming part of my father and my mother and my brothers and sisters again.

What I remember most about that night was the darkness, the mud and the slime of the salamanders, and how hard they would get when I tried to squeeze the life out of them. What I have with me still is what I saw and felt when I killed the last one, and I guess that is why I remember the night of the salamanders. I caught one and examined it very carefully under the lamp. Then I looked at its eyes for a long time before I killed it. What I saw and what I felt is something I still have with me, something that is very pure—original death.

On the Road to Texas: Pete Fonseca

🌿

He'd only just gotten there and he already wanted to leave. He arrived one Sunday afternoon walking from the little town where we bought our food on Saturdays and where they didn't mind that we came in the afternoon all dirty from work. It was almost dark when we saw this shadow crossing the field. We'd been fooling around in the trees and when we saw him we were almost scared, but then we remembered there was more of us so we weren't so scared. He spoke to us when he got near. He wanted to know if there was any work. We told him that there was and there wasn't. There was, but there wasn't till the weeds grew. It'd been pretty dry and the weeds didn't grow and all the fields were real clean. The landowner was pretty happy about it since he didn't have to pay for weeding the onion fields. Our parents cursed the weather and prayed for rain so the weeds'd grow and we had to make like we cared too, but, really, we liked getting up late, wandering around among the trees and along the stream killing crows with our slingshots. That's why we said there was but there wasn't. There was work but not tomorrow.

"Aw, fuck it all."

We didn't mind him talking like that. I think we realized how good his words went with his body and clothes.

"There's no goddamned work no fuckin' place. Hey, can you give me something to eat? I'm fuckin' hungry. Tomorrow I'm going to Illinois. There's work there for sure ... "

He took off his baseball cap and we saw that his hair was combed good with a pretty neat wave. He wore those pointed shoes, a little dirty, but you could tell they were expensive ones. And his pants were almost pachuco pants. He kept saying *chale* and also *nel* and *simón*** and we finally decided that he was at least half pachuco. We went with him to our chicken coop. That's what we called it because it really was a turkey coop. The owner had bought ten turkey coops from a guy who sold turkeys and brought them to his farm. We lived in them, though they were pretty small for two families, but pretty sturdy. They didn't leak when it rained, but, even though we cleaned them out pretty good inside, they never really lost that stink of chicken shit.

---

* *Caló*: "chale"—no, cool it; "nel"—no; "simón"—yes.

226

His name was Pete Fonseca and Dad knew a friend of his pretty good. Dad said he was a big mouth since he was always talking about how he had fourteen gabardine shirts and that's why the folks called him *El Catorce Camisas*. They talked about Fourteen Shirts a while, and, when we went to eat beans with slices of Spam and hot flour-tortillas, Dad invited him to eat with us. He washed his face good and his hands too, and then he combed his hair real careful, asked us for Brilliantine and combed his hair again. He liked the supper a lot and we noticed that when Mom was there he didn't use pachuco words. After supper he talked a little more and then laid down on the grass, in the shade where the light from the house wouldn't hit him. A little while later he got up and went to the outhouse and then he laid down again and fell asleep. Before we went to sleep, I heard Mom say to Dad that she didn't trust that guy.

"Me neither. He's a real con man. Gotta be careful with him. I've heard about him. Catorce Camisas is a big mouth, but I think it's him who stabbed that wetback in Colorado and they kicked him out of there or he got away from the cops. I think it's him. He also likes to smoke marijuana. I think it's him. I'm not too sure ... "

Next morning it was raining and when we looked out the window we saw that Pete had gotten in our car. He was sitting up but it looked like he was sleeping because he wasn't moving at all. I guess the rain waked him up and that's how come he got in the car. Around nine it stopped raining so we went out and told him to come have breakfast. Mom made him some eggs and then he asked if there was any empty house or some place he could live. And when was work going to start? And how much did they pay? And how much could you get a day? And how many of us worked? Dad told him that we all worked, all five of us, and that sometimes we made almost seventy bucks a day if we worked about fourteen hours. After breakfast Dad and Pete went out and we heard him ask Dad if there were any broads on the farm. Dad answered laughing that there was only one and she was sort of a loser. La Chata, snub-nose. And they went on talking along the path that went around the huts and to the water pump.

They called her *La Chata* because when she was little she got sick with something like mange on her face and the nose bone had gotten infected. Then she got better but her nose stayed small. She was real pretty except for her nose and everyone spoke bad about her. They said that even when she was little she liked men a lot and everything about them. When she was fifteen she had her first kid. Everyone blamed one of her uncles but she never told who it was. Her Mom and Dad didn't even get angry. They were pretty nice. Still are. After that, she'd shack up with one guy and then another, and each one left her with at least one kid. She gave some away, her parents took care of others, but the two oldest stayed with her. They were big enough to work now. When Pete arrived, it was just two weeks after she'd lost again. Her last husband had left; he didn't even get mad at her or anything. Just left. La Chata lived in one of the biggest chicken coops with her two sons. That's why Dad told Pete there was only one and she was sort of a loser. We figured Pete was pretty interested in what Dad said, and it seemed pretty funny since La Chata must've been about thirty-five and Pete, well, he couldn't have been more than twenty-five.

Anyhow, it turned out he was interested in what Dad said, because later, when we were fooling around near the pump, he asked us about La Chata. Where did she live, how old was she, was she any good? We were just talking about that when La Chata came down to get water and we told him that was her. We said hello to her and she said hello to us, but we noticed that she kept on looking at Pete. Like the people say, she gave him the eye. And even more when he asked her her name.

> "Chavela."
> "Hey, that's my mother's name."
> "No kidding."
> "Honest, and my grandmother's too."
> "You son-of-a-bitch."
> "You don't know me yet."

La Chata left the pump, and when she was pretty far away, Pete sighed and said real loud:

> "Hey, mamasita, mamasota linda!"

Just to make sure she heard—he told us afterwards. Because, according to him, broads like to be called that. From then on we noticed that everytime La Chata was near Pete he would always call her *mi chavelona* real loud. He said it loud so she'd hear and I think La Chata liked it because, when work started, she always chose the rows nearest Pete and, if he got ahead of her, she'd try and catch up. And then when the boss brought us water, Pete always let her drink first. Or he helped her get on and off the truck. The first Saturday they paid us after Pete got there, he bought some fritos for La Chata's kids. That's how it began.

I liked it best when he sang her songs. Pete was going to stay and work, he'd say, until everything was over. He went to live with two other guys in an old trailer they had there. We used to go after supper to talk to them, and sometimes we'd sing. He'd go outside, turn towards La Chata's house and sing with all his might. In the fields, too, we'd just get close to her or she'd come along and Pete would let go with one of his songs. Sometimes he even sang in English: *sha bum sha bum* or *lemi go, lemi go lober*, and then in Spanish: *Ella quiso quedarse, cuando vio mi tristeza ... Cuando te hablen de amor y de ilusiones ...* Sometimes he'd even stop working and stand up in the row, if the boss wasn't there, and he'd sort of move his hands and his body. La Chata'd look out of the corner of her eye, like it bothered her, but she always went on taking the rows next to Pete, or meeting him, or catching up to him. About two weeks later they both started going to get water at the truck together, when the boss didn't bring it, and then they'd go behind the truck a while and then La Chata would come out fixing her blouse.

Pete would tell us everything afterwards. One day he told us that, if we wanted to see something, we should hide behind the trailer that night and he'd try and get her to go in the trailer.

"You know what for ... to give her candy ... "

Us and the guys who lived with him hid behind the trailer that night and then after a long time we saw La Chata coming towards the trailer. Pete was waiting for her and she'd just got there and he took her hand and pulled her towards him. He put his hand up under her skirt and started kissing her. La Chata didn't say anything. Then he leaned her up against the trailer, but she got away and told him you son-of-a-bitch, not so fast. Pete was inviting her to come into the trailer but she didn't want to and so they stayed outside. Do you love me, will you marry me, yes I will, when, right now, what about the other cat. Finally she left. We came out of the dark and he told us all about it. Then he started telling us all about other broads he'd made. Even white ones. He'd brought one from Chicago and set up his business in Austin. There, according to him, the Johns would line up at five bucks a throw. But he said that the broad he'd really loved was the first one he married, the right way, in the Church. But she'd died with the first kid.

"I sure cried for that woman, and since then nothing. This fuckin' life ... now with this *chavelona*, I'm beginning to feel something for her ... she's a good person, if you know what I mean."

And sometimes he'd start thinking. Then he'd say real sincere like:

"Ay, mi chavelona ... man, she's a hot one ... but she won't let me ... until I marry her, she says."

Three days after we'd hid, Pete decided to get married. That's why all that week that's all he talked about. He had nothing to lose. Why, him and La Chata and the two boys could save a lot. He'd also have someone to cook his gorditas for him and his nice hot coffee, and someone to wash his clothes, and according to Pete, she could handle at least one John a night. He'd start calculating: at four dollars a throw, at least, times seven nights, that was twenty-eight dollars a week. Even if *he* couldn't work, things'd be pretty good. He also said he liked La Chata's boys. They could buy a jalopy and then Sundays they could take rides, go to a show, go fishing or to the dump and collect copper wire to sell. In fact, he said, him marrying La Chavelona was good for all of them. And the sooner the better.

A little while later he came to talk to Dad one night. They went out on the road where no one could hear them and they talked a pretty long time. That night we heard what Dad and Mom were saying in the dark:

"Get this: he wants to marry La Chata! He wants to elope with her, but what in? So it's better to get married for real. But—get this—he's got some sickness in his blood so he doesn't want to go into town to get the papers. So what he wants is for me to go and ask La Chata's father, Don Chon, for her hand. He wants me to go right away, tomorrow ... 'Don Chon, I've come today commissioned to ask for the hand of your daughter, Isabel, in matrimony with young Pedro Fonseca.' How's that eh? ... How's it sound, honey? ... Tomorrow after work, right before supper ... "

Next day all you heard about was how they were going to ask for La Chata's hand. That day Pete and Chavela didn't even talk to each other. Pete went around all day real quiet and sort of glum, like he wanted to show us how serious he was. He didn't even tell us any jokes like he always did. And La Chata also looked real serious. She didn't laugh any all day and every now and then she'd yell at her kids to work faster. Finally the work day finished and before supper Dad washed up, parted his hair four or five times, and went straight to Don Chon's house. Pete met him in the front yard and they both knocked at the door. They went in. *It was okay—they'd asked them to come in.* About half an hour later they all came out of the house laughing. *They'd agreed.* Pete was hugging La Chata real tight. Pretty soon they went into Chavela's house and when it got dark they closed the doors and pulled down the shade on the windows, too. That night Dad told us about ten times what had happened when he went to ask for her hand.

"Man, I just spoke real diplomatic and he couldn't say no ... "

Next day it rained. It was Saturday and that was when we really celebrated the wedding. Almost everyone got drunk. There was a little dancing. Some guys got into fights but pretty soon everything calmed down.

They were real happy. There started to be more and more work. Pete, La Chata and the boys always had work. They bought a car. Sundays they'd go driving a lot. They went to Mason City to visit some of La Chata's relatives. She was sort of strutting around real proud. The boys were cleaner now than ever. Pete bought a lot of clothes and was also pretty clean. They worked together, they helped each other, they took real good care of each other, they even sang together in the fields. We all really liked to see them because sometimes they'd even kiss in the fields. They'd go up and down the rows holding hands ... *Here come the young lovers.* Saturday they'd go shopping, and go into some little bar and have a couple after buying the groceries. They'd come back to the farm and sometimes even go to a show at night. They really had it good.

"Who would of said that that son-of-a-gun would marry La Chata and do her so right? It looks like he really loves her a lot. Always calling her *mi chavelona.* And can you beat how much he loves those kids? I tell you he's got a good heart. But who was to say that he did? Boy, he looks like a real pachuco. He really loves her, and he doesn't act at all high and mighty. And she sure takes better care of him than the other guy she had before, don't you think? And the kids, all he does is play with them. They like him a lot too. And you gotta say this about him, he's a real hard worker. And La Chata, too, she works just as hard. Boy, they're gonna pick up a pretty penny, no? ... La Chata finally has it pretty good ... Man, I don't know why you're so mistrusting, honey ... "

Six weeks after the wedding the potato picking ended. There were only a couple of days more work. We figured by Tuesday everything would be over and so we fixed up the car that weekend since our heads were already in Texas. Monday I remember we got up early and Dad, like always, beat us to the outhouse. But I don't even think he got there because he came right back with the news that Pete had left the farm.

"But what do you mean, Dad?"

"Yeah, he left. He took the car and all the money they'd saved between him and La Chata and the boys. He left her without a cent. He took everything they'd made ... What did I tell You? ... He left ... What did I tell you?"

La Chata didn't go to work that day. In the fields that's all people talked about. They told the boss about it but he just shook his head, they said. La Chata's folks were good and mad, but I guess we weren't too much. I guess because nothing had happened to us.

Next day work ended. We didn't see La Chata again that year. We came to Texas and a couple of months later, during Christmas, Dad talked to Don Chon who'd just come down from Iowa. Dad asked him about Pete and he said he didn't know, that he heard he'd been cut up in a bar in Minnesota and was going around saying the cops had taken all his money and the car, and that the boss had told the cops after all, and they'd caught him in Albert Lea. Anyhow, no one had given any money to Don Chon or La Chata. All we remembered was how he'd only just gotten there and he already wanted to leave. Anyhow, Pete made his little pile. That all happened around '48. I think La Chata is dead now, but her kids must be grown men. I remember that Pete appeared out of nowhere, like the devil himself—bad, then he turned good, then went bad again. I guess that's why we thought he was a shadow when we first saw him.

Eva and Daniel

※

People still remember Eva and Daniel. They were both very good looking, and in all honesty it was a pleasure to see them together. But that's not the reason people remember them. They were very young when they got married or, rather, when they eloped. Her parents hardly got angry at all, and, if they did, it was for a very short time and that was because everyone who knew Daniel liked him very much and had many good reasons to like him. They eloped up north during the County Fair that was held every year in Bird Island.

Both families lived on the same ranch. They worked together in the same fields, they went to town in the same truck and they just about had their meals together; they were that close. That's why no one was surprised when they started going together. And, even though everyone knew about it, no one let on, and even Eva and Daniel, instead of talking with one another, would write letters to each other once in a while. I remember very clearly that that Saturday when they eloped they were going happily to the fair in the truck. Their hair was all messed up by the wind, but when they got to the fair they didn't even remember to comb it.

They got on every ride, then they separated from the group and no one saw them again until two days later.

"Don't be afraid. We can take a taxi to the ranch. Move over this way, come closer, let me touch you. Don't you love me?"

"Yes, yes."

"Don't be afraid. We'll get married. I don't care about anything else. Just you. If the truck leaves us behind, we'll go back in a taxi."

"But they're going to get after me."

"Don't worry. If they do, I'll protect you myself. Anyway, I want to marry you. I'll ask your father for permission to court you if you want me to. What do you say? Shall we get married?"

At midnight, when all the games were closed and the lights of the fair were turned off and the explosions of the fireworks were no longer heard, Eva and Daniel still hadn't shown up. Their parents started to worry then, but they didn't notify the police. By one-thirty in the morning the other people became impatient. They got on and off the truck every few minutes and, finally, Eva's father told the driver to drive off. Both families were worried. They had a feeling that Eva and Daniel had eloped and they were sure they would get married, but they were worried anyway. And they would keep on worrying until they saw them again. What they didn't know was that Eva and Daniel were already at the ranch. They were hiding in the barn, up in the loft where the boss stored hay for the winter. That's why, even though they looked for them in the nearby towns, they didn't find them until two days later when they came down from the loft very hungry.

There were some very heated discussions but, finally, Eva's parents consented to their marriage. The following day they took Eva and Daniel to get their blood test, then a week later they took them before the judge and the parents had to sign because they were too young.

"You see how everything turned out all right."

"Yes, but I was afraid when father got all angry. I even thought he was going to hit you when he saw us for the first time."

"I was afraid too. We're married now. We can have children."

"Yes."

"I hope that they grow real tall and that they look like you and me. I wonder how they will be?"

"Just let them be like you and me."

"If it's a girl I hope she looks like you; if it's a boy I hope he looks like me." ·

"What if we don't have any?"

"Why not? My family and your family are very large."

"I'll say."

"Well, then?"

"I was just talking."

Things really began to change after they were married. First of all because, by the end of the first month of their marriage, Eva was vomiting often, and then also Daniel received a letter from the government telling him to be in such and such town so that he could take his physical for the army. He was afraid when he saw the letter, not so much for himself, but he immediately sensed the separation that would come forever.

"You see, son, if you hadn't gone to school you wouldn't have passed the examination."

"Oh, mama. They don't take you just because you passed the examination. Anyway I'm already married, so they probably won't take me. And another thing, Eva is already expecting."

"I don't know what to do, son, every night I pray that they won't take you. So does Eva. You should have lied to them. You should have played dumb so you wouldn't pass."

"Oh, come on, mama."

By November, instead of returning to Texas with his family, Daniel stayed up north, and a few days he was in the army. The days didn't seem to have any meaning for him—why should there be night, morning or day. Sometimes he didn't care anything about anything. Many times he thought about escaping and returning to his own town so that he could be with Eva. When he thought at all, that was what he thought about—Eva. I think he even became sick, once or maybe it was several times, thinking so much about her. The first letter from the government had meant their separation, and now the separation became longer and longer.

"I wonder why I can't think of anything else other than Eva? If I hadn't known her, I wonder what I would think about. Probably about myself, but now ... "

Things being what they were, everything marched on. Daniel's training continued at the same pace as Eva's pregnancy. They transferred Daniel to California, but before going he had the chance to be with Eva in Texas. The first night they went to sleep kissing. They were happy once again for a couple of weeks but then right away they were separated again. Daniel wanted to stay but then he decided to go on to California. He was being trained to go to Korea. Later Eva started getting sick. The baby was bringing complications. The closer she came to the day of delivery, the greater the complications.

"You know, viejo, something is wrong with that baby."

"Why do you say that?"

"Something is wrong with her. She gets very high fevers at night. I hope everything turns out all right, but even the doctor looks quite worried. Have you noticed?"

"No."

"Yesterday he told me that we had to be very careful with Eva. He gave us a whole bunch of instructions, but it's difficult when you can't understand him. Can you imagine? How I wish Daniel were here. I'll bet you Eva would even get well. I already wrote to him saying that she is very sick, hoping that he'll come to see her, but maybe his superiors won't believe him and won't let him come."

"Well, write to him again. Maybe he can arrange something, if he speaks out."

"Maybe, but I've already written him a number of letters saying the same thing. You know, I'm not too worried about him anymore. Now I worry about Eva. They're both so young."

"Yes they are, aren't they."

Eva's condition became worse and, when he received a letter from his mother in which she begged him to come see his wife, either Daniel didn't make himself understood or his superiors didn't believe him. They didn't let him go. He went AWOL just before he was to be sent to Korea. It took him three days to get to Texas on the bus. But he was too late.

I remember very well that he came home in a taxi. When he got down and heard the cries coming from inside the house he rushed in. He went into a rage and threw everyone out of the house and locked himself in for almost the rest of the day. He only went out when he had to go to the toilet, but even in there he could be heard sobbing.

He didn't go back to the army and no one ever bothered to come looking for him. Many times I saw him burst into tears. I think he was remembering. Then he lost all interest in himself. He hardly spoke to anyone.

One time he decided to buy fireworks to sell during Christmas time. The package of fireworks which he sent for through a magazine advertisement cost him plenty. When he got them, instead of selling them, he didn't stop until he had set them all off himself. Since that time that's all he does with what little money he earns to support himself. He sets off fireworks just about every night. I think that's why around this part of the country people still remember Eva and Daniel. Maybe that's it.

The Harvest

🌿

The end of September and the beginning of October. That was the best time of the year. First, because it was a sign that the work was coming to an end and that the return to Texas would start. Also, because there was something in the air that the folks created, an aura of peace and death. The earth also shared that feeling. The cold came more frequently, the frosts that killed by night, in the morning covered the earth in whiteness. It seemed that all was coming to an end. The folks felt that all was coming to rest. Everyone took to thinking more. And they talked more about the trip back to Texas, about the harvests, if it had gone well or bad for them, if they would return or not to the same place next year. Some began to take long walks around the grove. It seemed like in these last days of work there was a wake over the earth. It made you think.

That's why it wasn't very surprising to see Don Trine take a walk by himself through the grove and to walk along the fields every afternoon. This was at the beginning, but when some youngsters asked him if they could tag along, he even got angry. He told them he didn't want anybody sticking behind him.

"Why would he want to be all by hisself, anyway?"

"To heck with him; it's his business."

"But, you notice, it never fails. Every time, why, sometimes I don't even think he eats supper, he takes his walk. Don't you think that's a bit strange?"

"Well, I reckon. But you saw how he got real mad when we told him we'd go along with him. It wasn't anything to make a fuss over. This ain't his land. We can go wherever we take a liking to. He can't tell us what to do."

"That's why I wonder, why'd he want to walk by himself?"

And that's how all the rumors about Don Trine's walks got started. The folks couldn't figure out why or what he got out of taking off by himself every afternoon. When he would leave, and somebody would spy on him, somehow or other he would catch on, then take a little walk, turn around and head right back to his chicken coop. The fact of the matter is that everybody began to say he was hiding the money he had earned that year or that he had found some buried treasure and every day, little by little, he was bringing it back to his coop. Then they began to say that when he was young he had run around with a gang in Mexico and that he always carried around a lot of money with him. They said, too, that even if it was real hot, he carried a belt full of money beneath his undershirt. Practically all the speculation centered on the idea that he had money.

"Let's see, who's he got to take care of? He's an old bachelor. He ain't never married or had a family. So, with him working so many years ... Don't you think he's bound to have money? And then, what's that man spend his money on? The only thing he buys is his bit of food every Saturday. Once in a while, a beer, but that's all."

"Yeah, he's gotta have a pile of money, for sure. But, you think he's going to bury it around here?"

"Who said he's burying anything? Look, he always goes for his food on Saturday. Let's check close where he goes this week, and on Saturday, when he's on his errand, we'll see what he's hiding. Whadda you say?"

"Good 'nuff. Let's hope he doesn't catch on to us."

That week the youngsters closely watched Don Trine's walks. They noticed that he would disappear into the grove, then come out on the north side, cross the road then cross the field until he got to the irrigation ditch. There he dropped from sight for a while, then he reappeared in the west field. It was there where he would disappear and linger the most. They noticed also that, so as to throw people off his track, he would take a different route, but he always spent more time around the ditch that crossed the west field. They decided to investigate the ditch and that field the following Saturday.

When that day arrived, the boys were filled with anticipation. The truck had scarcely left and they were on their way to the west field. The truck had not yet disappeared and they had already crossed the grove. What they found they almost expected. There was nothing in the ditch, but in the field that had been harrowed after pulling the potatoes they found a number of holes.

"You notice all the holes here? The harrow didn't make these. Look, here's some foot prints, and notice that the holes are at least a foot deep. You can stick your arm in them up to your elbow. No animal makes these kind of holes. Whadda you think?"

"Well, it's bound to be Don Trine. But, what's he hiding? Why's he making so many holes? You think the landowner knows what he's up to?"

"Naw, man. Why, look, you can't see them from the road. You gotta come in a ways to notice they're here. What's he making them for? What's he using them for? And, look, they're all about the same width. Whadda you think?"

"Well, you got me. Maybe we'll know if we hide in the ditch and see what he does when he comes here."

"Look, here's a coffee can. I bet you this is what he digs with."

"I think you're right."

The boys had to wait until late the following Monday to discover the reason for the holes. But the word had spread around so that everybody already knew that Don Trine had a bunch of holes in that field. They tried not to let on but the allusions they made to the holes while they were out in the fields during the day were very obvious. Everybody thought there had to be a big explanation. So, the youngsters spied more carefully and astutely.

That afternoon they managed to fool Don Trine and saw what he was doing. They saw, and as they had suspected, Don Trine used the coffee can to dig a hole. Every so often, he would measure with his arm the depth of the hole. When it went up to his elbow, he stuck in his left arm, then filled dirt in around it with his right hand, all the way up to the elbow. Then he stayed like that for some time. He seemed very satisfied and even tried to light a cigarette with one hand. Not being able to, he just let it hang from his lips. Then he dug another hole and repeated the process. The boys could not understand why he did this. That was what puzzled them the most. They had believed that, with finding out what it was he did, they would understand everything. But it didn't turn out that way at all. The boys brought the news to the rest of the folks in the grove and nobody there understood either. In reality, when they found out that the holes didn't have anything to do with money, they thought Don Trine was crazy and even lost interest in the whole matter. But not everybody.

The next day one of the boys who discovered what Don Trine had been up to went by himself to a field. There he went through the same procedure that he had witnessed the day before. What he experienced and what he never forgot was feeling the earth move, feeling the earth grasp his fingers and even caressing them. He also felt the warmth of the earth. He sensed he was inside someone. Then he understood what Don Trine was doing. He was not crazy, he simply liked to feel the earth when it was sleeping.

That's why the boy kept going to the field every afternoon, until one night a hard freeze came on so that he could no longer dig any holes in the ground. The earth was fast asleep. Then he thought of next year, in October at harvest time, when once again he could repeat what Don Trine did. It was like when someone died. You always blamed yourself for not loving him more before he died.

Zoo Island

Jose had just turned fifteen when he woke up one day with a great desire of taking a census count, of making a town and making everybody in it do what he said. All this happened because during the night he had dreamed that it was raining and, since they would not be working in the fields the next day, he dreamed about doing various things. But when he awoke, it hadn't rained at all. Anyway, he still had the desire.

The first thing he did when he got up was to count his family and himself—five. "We're five," he thought. Then he went on to the other family that lived with his, his uncle's—"Five more, and that's ten." Next he counted the people living in the chicken coop across the way. "Manuel and his wife and four more—that's six." And, with the ten he already had—"that's sixteen." Then he took into account the coop where Manuel's uncle lived, where there were three families. The first one, Don Jose's family, had seven, so now there were twenty-three. He was about to count the second family, when they told him to get ready to go to the fields.

It was still dark at five-thirty in the morning, and that day they would have to travel some fifty miles to reach the field overgrown with thistle that they had been working on. And as soon as they finished it, they would have to continue searching for more work. It would be way after dark by the time they got back. In the summertime, they could work up to eight o'clock. Then add an hour on the road back, plus the stop at the little store to buy something to eat ... "We won't get back to the farm till late," he thought. But now he had something to do during the day while they were pulling up thistle. During the day, he could figure out exactly how many there were on that farm in Iowa.

"Here come those sonsabitches."

"Don't say bad words in front of the kids, Pa. They'll go around saying 'em all the time. That'd really be something, then, wouldn't it?"

"I'll bust them in the mouth if I hear them swearing. But here come those Whities. They don't leave a person in peace, do they? Soon as Sunday comes, and they come riding over to see us, to see how we live. They even stop and try to peek inside our chicken coops. You saw last Sunday how that row of cars passed by here. Them all laughing and laughing, and pointing at us. And you think they care about the dust they raise? Hell no. With their windows closed, why,

241

they go on by just as fine as you please. And here we are, just like a bunch of monkeys in that park in San Antonio—Parkenrich."*

"Aw, let 'em be, Pa. They're not doing nothing to us, they're not doing any harm—not even if they was gypsies. Why you get all heated up for?"

"Well, it sets my blood a boiling, that's all. Why don't they mind their own business? I'm going to tell the owner to put a lock on the gate, so when they come they can't drive inside."

"Aw, let it go, it's nothing to make a fuss over."

"It sure is."

*   *   *

"We're almost to the field. Pa, you think we'll find work after we finish here?"

"Sure, son, there's always a lot of work. They don't take us for a bunch of lazy-bones. You saw how the boss' eyes popped out when I started pulling out all that thistle without any gloves on. Huh, they have to use gloves for everything. So, they're bound to recommend us to the other landowners. You'll see how they'll come and ask us if we want another field to work."

*   *   *

"The first thing I'll do is jot down the names on a list. Then, I'll use a page for each family, and that way I won't lose anybody. And for each bachelor, too, I'll use a page for each one, yeah. I'll also write down everybody's age. I wonder how many men and women there are on this farm, any way? We're forty-nine field hands, counting the eight and nine-year-olds. Then, there's a bunch of kids, and then there's the two grandmothers that can't work anymore. The best thing to do is to get Jitter and Hank to help me with the counting. They could go to each coop and get the information, then we could gather up all the numbers. Too, it would be a good idea to put a number on each coop. Then, I could paint the number above each door. We could even pick up the mail from the box and distribute it, and that way the folks could even put the number of their coop on the letters they write. Sure, I bet that would make them feel better. Then we could even put up a sign at the farm gate that'll tell the number of people that live here, but ... what would we call the farm? It doesn't have a name. I gotta think about that."

---

*Brackenridge Park Zoo.

It rained the next day, and the following day as well. Therefore, Jose had the time and the opportunity to think over his plan. He made his helpers, Jitter and Hank, stick a pencil behind their ear, strap on a wrist watch—which they acquired easily enough—and shine their shoes. They also spent a half day reviewing the questions they would put to each household head and to each bachelor. The folks became aware of what the youngsters were up to and were soon talking about how they were going to be counted.

"These kids are always coming up with something ... just ideas that pop into their heads or that they learn in school. Now, what for? What're they going to get out of counting us? Why, it's just a game, plain tomfoolery."

"Don't think that, comadre, no, no. These kids nowadays are on the ball, always inquiring about something or other. And you know, I like what they're doing. I like having my name put on a piece of paper, like they say they're gonna do. Tell me, when's anybody ever asked you your name and how many you got in the family and then write it all down on paper. You better believe it! Let them boys be, let 'em be, leastways while the rain keeps us from working."

"Yeah, but, what's it good for? I mean, how come so many questions? And then there's some things a person just doesn't say."

"Well, if you don't want to, don't tell 'em nothin.' But, look, all they want to know is how many of us there are in this grove. But, too, I think they want to feel like we're a whole lot of people. See here, in that little town where we buy our food there're only eighty-three souls, and you know what? They have a church, a dance hall, a filling station, a grocery store and even a little school. Here, we're more than eighty-three, I'll bet, and we don't have any of that. Why, we only have a water pump and four out-houses, right?"

* * *

"Now, you two are going to gather the names and the information. Ya'll go together so there won't be any problems. After each coop, you'll bring me the information right back. Ya'll jot it down on a sheet of paper and bring it to me, then I'll make a note of it in this notebook I got here. Let's start out with my family. You, Hank, ask me questions and jot down everything. Then you give me what you wrote down so that I can make a note of it. Do ya'll understand what we're going to do? Don't be afraid. Just knock on the door and ask. Don't be afraid."

It took them all afternoon to gather and jot down the details, then they compiled all the figures by the light of an oil lamp. Yes, it turned out that there were more fieldhands on the farm than there were people in the town where they bought their food. Actually, there were eighty-six on the farm, but the boys came up with a figure of eighty-seven because two women were expecting and they counted them for three. They gave the exact number to the rest of the folks, explaining the part about the pregnant women. Everyone was pleased to know that the farm settlement was really a town and bigger than the one where they bought their groceries every Saturday.

The third time the boys went over the figures they realized that they had forgotten to go over to Don Simon's shack. They had simply overlooked it because it was on the other side of the grove. When old Don Simon had gotten upset and fought with Stumpy, he asked the owner to take the tractor and drag his coop to the other side of the grove, where no one would bother him. The owner did this right away. There was something in Don Simon's eyes that made people jump. It wasn't just his gaze but also the fact that he hardly ever spoke. So, when he did talk everybody listened up so as not to lose a single word.

It was already late and the boys decided not to go see him until the next day, but the fact of the matter was they were a little afraid just thinking that they would have to go and ask him something. They remembered the to-do in the field when Don Simon got fed up with Stumpy's needling him and chased Stumpy all over the field with his onion knife. Then Stumpy, even though he was much younger, tripped and fell, tangling himself in the tow-sacks. Right then, Don Simon threw himself on Stumpy, slicing at him with his knife. What saved Stumpy were the tow-sacks. Luckily, Stumpy came out of it with only a slight wound in his leg; nonetheless, it did bleed quite a bit. When the owner was told what had happened, he ran Stumpy off. But Don Simon explained that it wasn't much to make a fuss over, so he let Stumpy stay but the owner did move Don Simon's coop to the other side of the grove, just like Don Simon wanted. So, that's why the boys were a little afraid of him. But, like they told themselves, just not riling him, he was good folk. Stumpy had been riling Don Simon for some time about his wife leaving him for somebody else.

"Excuse us, Don Simon, but we're taking up the farm census, and we'd like to ask you a few questions. You don't have to answer them if you don't want to."

"All right."

"How old are you?"

"Old enough."

"When were you born?"

"When my mother born me."

"Where were you born?"

"In the world."

"Do you have a family?"

"No."

"How come you don't talk much?"

"This is for the census, right?"

"No."

"What for, then? I reckon ya'll think you talk a lot. Well, not only ya'll but all the folks here. What ya'll do most of the time is open your mouth and make noise. Ya'll just like to talk to yourselves, that's all. I do the same, but I do it silently, the rest of you do it out loud."

"Well, Don Simon, I believe that's all. Thanks for your cooperation. You know, we're eighty-eight souls here on this farm. We're plenty, right?"

"Well, you know, I kinda like what ya'll are doing. By counting yourself, you begin everything. That way you know you're not only here but that you're alive. Ya'll know what you oughta call this place?"

"No."

"Zoo Island."*

The following Sunday just about all the people on the farm had their picture taken next to the sign the boys had made on Saturday afternoon and which they had put up at the farm gate. It said: **Zoo Island, Pop. 88 1/2.** One of the women had given birth.

And every morning Jose would no sooner get up than he would go see the sign. He was part of that number, he was in Zoo Island, in Iowa, and like Don Simon said, in the world. He didn't know why, but there was a warm feeling that started in his feet and rose through his body until he felt it in his throat and in all his senses. Then this same feeling made him talk, made him open his mouth. At times it even made him shout. The shouting was something the owner never managed to understand. By the time he arrived sleepy-eyed in the morning, the boy would be shouting. Sometimes he thought about asking him why he shouted, but then he'd get busy with other things and forget all about it.

---

*Reference to "Monkey Island," Brackenridge Park Zoo.

Inside the Window

꧁

Why the constant dream? That constant dream. It's almost impossible to hear anything with all the crying and screaming of the children.

But how thoughtless of the people upstairs. The fact they're single is no excuse. So many of them. Still, what a pain for them to get drunk and keep the rest of us awake into the morning hours. Don't they realize that there are families here with children? Then the crying and screaming. Also constantly. As the dream. Why do I keep on with the same dream? The smell of urine on the blankets sometimes makes me forget the noise. So does the window that I have at the head of my bed. The window makes me believe that I can see twice, but really I know that what's outside is not double. When the lights are finally out in our room and the only light that enters comes from under the door or from the cracks in the ceiling, the window is distinctly etched. It's a large window. When we first arrived here, we used to place some bed sheets or blankets over it, especially at night, so people outside could not see in. But I guess that began to matter less and less to my father and mother and grandfather. During the day it didn't matter that it had no rags covering it because you couldn't see inside, but at night it was different. It was as if all things had an inward light at night. It was my grandfather who finally said that it didn't really matter to him if people outside could see him at night. There were so many people living in *la casa grande*—eighty-six. Eighty-six souls, no matter how large the house, became more than eighty-six. Surely at night, if you look in, you even forget the window itself. It's a gray square that looks inside. From where I lie to sleep, it looks strange, different sizes at different times. Sometimes I begin to see the face in the window, the face I saw in the mirror the other day when I found it on my shoulders.

> "Hurry up Enrique, you're going to be late for school. How can you lie there so late with all these people walking all over you? Hurry up, damn it, get up! Don't you sleep or what? What are you doing there all covered up to your face? Do you like to smell the blankets? Hurry up, you're going to be late. The men, God take care of them, left for work some time ago, and all the gringos passed by here already on the way to school ... they're always gaping over here, trying to see ... Hurry up, get up."

Who should I tell? Who should I tell about the face? Since Chuy drowned I've had no one to talk with for a long time.

"Hurry up, get up ... "

But why did he drown? He's singing his song now. *Yo no traigo pistola ni cuchillo, sólo traigo muy grande el corazón, arriba el norte, que aquí les traigo todita la razón.* He really liked to sing. After school we would look for each other and then we would race through the hilly cemetery and run around the trees. Once in a while we would sit down to rest. As we rested, Chuy would begin to scream-sing, like the mariachis, and then ... he's singing now: *Yo soy de León, Guanajuato, no vengo a pedir favores, yo no le temo a la muerte, tengo fama de bravero.* Hey stop it now Chuy! Don't you get tired? You don't get tired, do you? I know you like to sing a lot but, when I see you like that, singing the way you sing, you seem to become another person, you no longer pay attention to anything. Do you still climb trees and hang there and sing? What's the matter, goddamnit? You haven't done it since those gringos caught you up in the tree singing and they stoned the shit out of you. And I couldn't help you. Remember, they tied me up to the same tree. We'll get even with them bastards. We'll see them again, Chuy, don't worry. They take care of the dump yards. They live out there on the outskirts of town. We'll run across them again and we'll be ready. Maybe we should go to the dump and look for them. One day we'll jump on them when they least expect it. It will be our turn. Our turn will come. Stop it, Chuy! Stop singing! You're dead! I can't forget Chuy's eyes, the rest of him, yes. His eyes, no. The roundness. Gray windows, green, black.

I ran all the way from the swimming pool to *la casa grande*. The screaming ambulance passed me in the opposite direction, it seemed to be going so far away in all its agony and speed. It seems that it was then that I began that constant dream.

"Hurry up, get up, you're going to be late."

I ran through the pages of books. Someone was turning the pages. Everything was pictured so clearly. When I passed people, I noticed they were flat, like a leaf, two dimensional. As I approached *la casa grande*, I saw the women sitting on the porch arise in unison, and as I got closer the faces began to twist out of shape. One of them screamed. It was Chuy's mother. I couldn't even speak to her, no matter how hard I tried, but she understood my face.

"Hurry up, get up ... "

Chuy looks very pale, so pale in the coffin. They take all the blood out of your body and put in some other stuff. But we begged you so much to be careful. Why weren't you careful? What happened? We were feeling good. About everything. Real good. We ran across the guys that stoned us and beat the hell out of them. Later, they were in the swimming pool also, but they didn't come near us. They seemed scared. I told Chuy not to bother them anymore, we had already gotten even. But he wouldn't stop, he kept bothering them. He took a tire tube away from them, and then he jumped into deep water. I didn't see him again until they brought him out and a bunch of people gathered around him.

"Aren't you going to get up today?"

Wake up Chuy, stop playing, you son-of-a-bitch. Stop acting! Open your eyes, damn it! Get up, hurry up! It's getting late. Hurry up, man! Can't you hear me? We're going to get it at home, if we get home late. Stop acting, man! It's getting late. Why in the hell did you jump into the deep? Chuy is singing again: *Yo no traigo pistola ni cuchillo, sólo traigo muy grande el corazón, arriba el norte* ... Hurry up, get up, open your eyes, don't be ... For some time now, in the morning, after I get up, the first thing I do is look out the window. I think maybe I'll find him there, outside, on the outside of the glass. Or perhaps I'll find him in the bathroom, inside the mirror, where he and I used to comb our hair before going to the movies on Saturdays. As in the dream. I didn't expect him that morning and since then he has been there on my shoulders. Unforgettable morning. The night before I had dreamed so much. I awoke exhausted from talking and walking such long distances in search of water. I felt very strange as I got up, something bothered me. I kept hearing myself speak, clearly and with fine and delicate sounds. Later in the bathroom after I changed my clothing and I began to comb my hair, something continued to bother me. I thought for a moment that I was wearing something out of place. I looked at my shoes, pants, my shirt, and then I looked at my face in the mirror, and I sensed something out of place, something didn't fit. I began to concentrate on my eyes and got closer to the mirror, almost touched it. Then I found out something, and my world became soundless. The face in the mirror was Chuy's. Everything was me, except the face. The face was Chuy's.

"Get up! How many times do you want me to tell you to get up?"

Stop smiling, Chuy. You're dead. *Yo no traigo pistola ni cuchillo, sólo traigo muy grande el corazón, arriba el norte, a ver quién pega un grito* ...

The smell of urine in the blankets sometimes makes me forget the shrill screaming and the crying of the children. Sometimes the window at the head of my bed helps if I begin to imagine myself looking out through the monotonous glass. The window. A gray square looking inside me, like Chuy's eyes—gray, green, black ... there on the face in the mirror. Constantly.

Looking for Borges

"Why do I feel this way?"

"Because when you are everything, you are nothing. You don't believe me? Ask Borges. You'll find him in the library under every word, still trying at such an old age to decipher the whole apple or is it pear that *Life* showed the earth to be like? His own words and maps and globes and again more words."

For sure. To be sure, to be sure, I found him. I was told that he would be humorous, labyrinthine, dark, that he would give me his darkness, that he would tell me where to look and how to look—didn't say find—to look, to search. I found him deliriously sad, almost as if he had found some truth. Read every word he said, every word in every library, in this library, then go on to the next and the next. He had worked himself through all those words all the way from Argentina. He showed me on the map. Not the one on the wall, not the one under his armpit, but the one he has in his eyes. And I believed him and I began to read and I did so because he told me it was my turn.

"I am a word. And as I read I become more word."

"You look rather pale."

"How could that be?"

"Well, how long have you been here?"

"Since I began."

"When was that?"

"Who knows?"

"Somebody must."

"That's why I read."

"But that won't tell you anything. It would have told you something long ago. Because it's been told."

"You're right."

"You look rather pale. Do you feel sick?"

"A bit of nausea. Got an upside down w in my stomach."

"What will you do now?"

"I don't know. I'm tired of reading and looking at maps. Old or new they're all the same. The same guy, century after century after century. But I keep thinking I'll find Borges again. He did say it was my turn."

"Did he stop looking?"

"No. He never stops, he's way ahead of me, I know."

"You won't find him again then."

"Borges found something once underneath a word."

"What was that?"

"Something I said, I've dreamed about it many times."

"About what he found?"

"No, well, yes, about the whole thing."

"What whole thing?"

"The words."

"What was that?"

"The library, where I first saw him. Every word was looking at him when he spoke to me."

"What did he say?"

"That it was my turn."

"You look sick, more than a year ago."

"I do feel more nauseous. Must have worms in my stomach. See how big it is? Full of worms probably. Last night I had the nightmare again."

"What was it?"

"I don't have many, really, just the same ones. This is really the second one. The first one lasted many years. I was always falling over a hill into a bigger hill of nothing. Always that damn hill."

"What's the new one, what happens?"

"I'll tell it to you in the past tense because it's in the future."

I was in a library where everyone looked at me. Where everyone talked of me. Where everyone pointed at me. I didn't mind because I was looking for Borges. Everyone seemed to know what I was doing, or so it appeared. Every minute they expected me to tell them something, to reveal something to them. Then they began to encircle me but I could only tell them that I was looking for Borges. They brought me more and more books. Every second they expected me to tell them something. I asked them to help look but they only said it was my turn. What bothered me most was the hope they had. As if I were about to reveal something to them. As if I were supposed to know and tell. Some even tugged at the map I had under my arm. I recall staying there for years, the people almost immobile, looking at me, following my every move with their eyes when I would lift my head from the books. The books there, the books they brought. And then I got sick and felt as if I were about to throw up. It was embarrassing, very embarrassing because they looked hurt. I covered my mouth but it was too late. I covered my mouth with both hands and began to run out of the library. But everyone followed, I tried to push the puke in. My cheeks kept bulging until I could hold it no longer. I let myself go for several hours and among all the letters which I vomited in neat piles I believe I saw a certain word or perhaps it was just a combination of letters. From a distance I saw them turning over the piles with long sticks, with a look of hope on their faces which at times seemed idiotic.

The Searchers:
Collected Poetry

In the dump
he discovered beautiful flowers
among the cans and broken bottles
and ~~wa~~ tires worn out.
The sky was blue blue
and even the birds looked at it
and didn't disturb its beauty
with their flight
A ~~sacred~~ blue, pushing toward the earth
encircling his cosmos pushing his
eyes inward until he would
fall asleep.

He also saw ants
winding slowly toward him
and past him in solitary communion
gasping ~~of~~ life through tin can cities
and glass cages among rusty lakes
and giant trees ~~swaying standing~~
reviving their search
among each other when the wind died.
He wanted to search
& wind slowly with them
and to fly high until he would
touch. #
He reached out and found no search
~~The~~ Only the sky and its blue
suffocating ~~putting~~ his eyes, ~~suffocating them~~
until he ~~saw only~~ heard ~~only~~ a white line.

Original manuscript of "In the Dump."

I

noon-night

To hate him, anyone
a white face, why
everyone.
You see this sore, on my knee
and on his
and on hers
on all of us
we will never be cured.
but I guarantee
you will not do it to my son
nor to my daughter
they will not kneel, not kneel.

I'll remind them,
I'll tell them of the old times
when dust choked this throat
and when I was hit and laughed at
when I was made to eat shit
in a taco — laughing, all laughing

To hate him, anyone.

I'm silent. I keep quiet quiet
I am, not so
I'm knowing evil ~~with you~~,

Original manuscript of "Noon-Night."

Poetics

Poetry is one of the most human of experiences because it begins with nothing. It is the birth and death of the word and the poet, as he freezes abstractions, severs relationships with his utterances. Poetry is finding the search, finding the word. It is not inventing, but finding, starting the invention. Yet poetry should not be explained, categorized, studied, but read and felt and sung. Poetry denies the poet but not his expression and utterance. Poetry, then, is a way of becoming nothing and everything. In a way, poetry is and is not what Octavio Paz says: "knowledge, salvation, power, abandonment." Poetry gives me pure feelings—time, beauty, man and original death.

The Rooster Crows en Iowa y en Texas

The rooster crows.
The alarm rings.
They eat and go to work.

"Aladín y su lámpara maravillosa"

The snow falls.
The truck runs full of people.
And we return . . . . home.

"Once upon a time there were three little pigs"

To spend money.
And to walk in the holes
full of street
of my town.

The street calls and
extends itself
to the house of the door
and the fence of the gate
and . . .

I look . . .
It looks at me . . .
yawns and shakes its dust.

And I yawn and sleep
until the rooster crows.

De niño   De joven   De viejo

El vidrio que brilla
en el césped, azul,
la boca que habla
con sonora sonrisa.

El sol que calienta
las sienes repletas
de ganas de risas
de juegos de grandes.

La mañana refresca
los sueños soñados.
Las ventanas que se abren
a paredes de vida.

Las puertas abiertas.
Los pasos contentos.
Los tientos de carne
que dan calor.

Los cuentos contados
son los sueños soñados
de pasos contentos
de sienes repletas.

Cada mañana
la frescura
le limpia la cara,
le abre los ojos,
le da una sonrisa,
le mueve los pies.
Y el ñino
se mueve en un mundo
y empieza a soñar

* * *

La casa que huele
a sol apagado

que a veces alumbra
sin saber por qué.

La puerta cerrada
que no quiere abrirse.
Los pasos cauteles,
las sonrisas fingidas,
los pesares pesando
la noche sin fin.

La ventana cerrada.
La mañana caliente
que hace sudar.
El día sin fin
con odios y amores
y sordos temores.

Las miradas abajo,
pensadas sentencias.
Los dientes cerrados
detrás labios hambrientos
en noches de días
tan largos.

La vida sin rumbo
como sueños de sed,
las vidas y vida
sin saber por qué.

Cada mañana
el calor
le suda la cara,
le cierra los ojos,
para despertarlo
a un nuevo soñar.

* * *

Los sueños pasados,
los viejos amigos,
las tardes sueñosas,

las manos cerradas.

Las mañanas oscuras,
sin seña de vida.
La puerta entreabierta
a otro nuevo soñar.

El sol penetrante
por cabellos resecos
sin vida y color.
Un ruido secreto
de otro vivir.

La boca, los ojos,
los dientes que tragan,
la lengua hecha nudo.
Garganta reseca
de palabras ya muertas
por tanto vividas.

La ventana entreabierta
al recuerdo pasado
de paredes de vida
y vidrio que brilla.

La noche sin fin,
la boca que habla
con sonora risa
de labios hambrientos.

La vida,
la vida, sin rumbo,
le limpia la cara,
le cierra los ojos,
le dice un secreto,
uno de tantos
secretos ruidosos.

De niño, de joven, de viejo,
todo,
todo fue un soñar.

Hide the Old People
or
American Idearium

"A la víbora, víbora de la mar,
de la mar,
por aquí pueden pasar.
Los de adelante corren mucho y
los de atrás se quedarán."

Escóndanlos.
Escóndanlos bien.
Escóndanlos en la casona grande y lujosa,
Escóndanlos.

¡Que nadie los vea, ya están muy viejos!
¡Son puro trabajo,
no valen la pena ya!
¡Que no nos miren!
si ya no nos conocen.

Ellos ya se gastaron.

Escóndanlos.

"Los de adelante corren mucho y
los de atrás se quedarán."

Siempre el domingo

Vayan a la iglesia el domingo
y rueguen por yo pecador,
mientras

yo veo la ametralladora japonesa
y las paracaídas alemanas
y las banderas italianas
y los retratos de tantos hombres muertos
en *Veteran's Place.*

¡Que me hallen allí en la cantina!
¡Que miren las bayonetas
y las banderas
y a Villa
y a Pershing
y a Obregón
y a Ike
y a Carranza
y a mi cuate
y a todos esos hombres muertos
en las guerras!

¡Que nos miren bailar!
¡Que miren que vivimos
como ellos lo quisieran!

Vayan a la iglesia y recen por su salvación.
Yo me voy
a la cantina
a bailarles y
a divertirles
a tantos hombres muertos
mientras
las botellas regurgitan.

Odio

Weeds rupture the marble
and I laugh at the whiteness.
Alone,
daggers,
knifing,
soundless,
unloved through death.
Torn from the earth,
left to dry,
to die.

Future in the seed.

Stone upon stone
of despair.
Stone from which
come the weeds
who blade each other
without love
        to be torn from the earth
        and thrown to the earth.

The seed is here
on the stone
on my forehead.

M'ijo no mira nada

—Mira, m'ijo, qué rascacielo.
"Does it reach the sky and heaven?"
—Mira, m'ijo, qué carrazo.
"Can it get to the end of the world?"
—Mira, m'ijo, ese soldado.
"¿Por qué pelea?"
—Mira, m'ijo, qué bonita fuente.
"Yes, but I want to go to the restrooom."
—Mira, m'ijo, qué tiendota de J. C. Penney,
allí trabajarás un día.
"Do you know the people there, daddy?"
—No,
vámonos a casa,
tú no miras nada.

Me lo enterraron

Yo no, ellos,
ellos me lo enterraron.
Ellos no sabían
que traía su anillote con su M bien grabada,
que siempre nos traía pan dulce por las noches,
que nunca iba a la iglesia pero sabía amar,
que amaba mucho a mi madre pero tenía su "vieja."

Ellos no sabían
que me enseñó a llorar y a amar,
que me pateaba por un quinto y después lloraba,
que siempre trabajaba,
y que cantaba, y que amaba.

Ellos no lo sabían.
Y por eso me lo enterraron.
Yo no quería.
Yo no lo enterré.

Seeds in the Hour of Seeds

Dawn light
fractured by profiles
Touches of life breathing

Anticipated death
prevails
in exhaling essence
Dawn light
separating your profile

The seed,
mine,
yours,
is here, alive
We
One

Have we liberated light?

Full ... now
Profiles ...
You triumph
as light
totally prevails

You,
our son, and me
isolated by light

You,
our son,
seeds we are
in prime light
in dawn light
in the hour of seeds

Young Voices

Young voices,
fresh, loved by the wind
Grasped
delighted
held by the wind

New voices
young voices
who soften the wind
eternally loved
carved forever
into the wind

In the night
the wind is a lover
of young voices
of love seeds
scattered
pollen
eternal

For the voice
is the love seed
in the dark

Perfection of Perfections

Hands entwined
through arms and waists

perfection of perfections
the young bodies

Beauty,
no more beauty than this
there is

in the night
in the night
in the night

to never wait for the light
to savor love
the crystallization of their beauty

Do they know?

Yes

Always

You have seen yourself
for you have been looking
out the door

Always

You never sleep
        never dream
You wait for yourself

Always

You have seen yourself
You were here before
many
yesterday
today
ever
behind the door

Always

Another Me

There must be
there has to be
another me

For how would I know,
why would I want to know?

There must be
there has to be
another me

Our children
am I in them or
they in me?

I was the leaf
that I know

This Solitude

solitude, dark, blackness
through powers of the body
grasping of me
puzzlement
through eyes
unwanting

grasping tightly
images of despair
bits of light, rays
contemplation of sorrows

dull upon dullness
sitting on every dream
so distant now
so distant
so damning to this life
to this darkness
to this solitude
to this dark
      waning
          nodding
              smile

The Overalls

Frightening
as the attic hole
the overalls in the garage, hanging
and the vapor from the train
swung to my face
as the cross that
shouted the lump
in the cemetery
and the sounds of clods
of earth hitting the coffin
reminded me of something
I knew nothing about
the glancing of tearful eyes
embracing
as I sensed
that I had been born
the crushing vapor
and the overalls, hanging
in the garage
never to be filled again

Soundless words

Words without sound
how terribly deaf

What if I were to remain
here
in the words
forever?

A Most Tired Word

Love
a most tired word
replacement needed
overused
abused
love
a most tired word
beyond hollowness
seeking itself
it is

Past Possessions

A piece of string
A broken top
A crooked kite
A wooden gun
A mop ...

Quiet ... noise

A long thin weed a lance
A few large cans a dance
   Boxes
For car and houses

Such trivial things

Run, Puff, Run, Run

We look and see
We come and go

An arm, legs, a head
to be filled
to be filled

Not to think
Not to love
Not to move

To be filled
To be filled

not to be

Jump, jump

Run, puff, run, run

Ennui

desk	pencil	voices
people	words	faces
cars	windows	clothes
paper	war	children
towns	houses	cities
nations	presidents	laws
joy	death	sorrow
religion		
man		
stars		
dirt		
flowers		
animals		
birth		
world		
worlds		

Autumn and Winter

The wind
The beauty
The cold air

humbles the people

The sun
The leaves
The broken twigs

they bow their humility

Reminders

to bend the head
in chest, and
to suck in a
death-smelling air
while the wind and cold
circle the sun

One last gaze at the warm beauty

When Love To Be

When love to be?
when
leaves warmly cover
protectingly from
sun and snow and wind
and feet
everyone will walk toward me
not away
when
love to be
comes
now, no one listens

I've been ready for so long

since many times
of leaves covering
warmly to protect
yet dying
from sun and snow and wind
and feet

I've been ready for so long

when love to be
will everyone walk toward me
and stay?

The Child

The child spoke
as the man spoke
as the child spoke
to understand
each other's
death.

The Eyes of a Child

First, the color,
then the comprehension
of a limitless love.

The eyes of a child
must surely touch.
Its color

Unknown comprehension
open to be shut
open to create.

Color, form, limitless eyes
of a limitless love.

The eyes of a child can touch
The eyes of a child can feel
The eyes of a child can be.

Do they know that we know?

Alone

I am alone
because of the street
and the faces.

I almost spoke to one
once.
Starting is difficult.

I am alone
and the street is long
and the faces

Can't stop.

Shouldn't follow it.

Now, I am really alone
Can't stop.

Perhaps
if I walk backwards with the faces.

A Blas de Otero

La cicatriz del pecado original:
Anonadada la justicia y
el pecado original sobre
las tumbas
encuentran el delirio
de una acción asesinada.

Vuelve a ver al niño
mírale la frente
que allí está el diente
del odio
hundido.

Y por los ojos
sedientos y proféticos
y los brazos añorando
de la madre
que estira la mano
en sueños de pesetas
cayendo por los cielos

sin pan,
sin pan haber nacido
la cicatriz del pecado original
con hambre y sed.

The Searchers

I

How long
how long
have we been searchers?

We have been
behind the door
Always
behind screens and eyes
of other eyes
We longed to search
Always
longed to search

naranja dulce
limón partido
dame un abrazo
que yo te pido

We searched through
our own voices
and through
our own minds
We sought with our words

A la víbora, víbora
de la mar
de la mar
por aquí pueden pasar

How those words
lighted our eyes
From within came
the passions to create
of every clod and stone
a new life
a new dream
each day

In these very things
we searched
as we crumbled
dust, our very own
imaginary beings

Hey, ese vato, chíngate

A terrón lighted our eyes
and we watered it and made
mud-clay
to create others in

II

The search begun
so many years ago only
to feel the loneliness
of centuries
Hollow—soundless centuries
without earth

How can we be alone
How can we be alone
if we are so close to the earth?

Tierra eres
Tierra serás
Tierra te volverás

Una noche caminando
una sombra negra vi
Yo me separaba de ella
y ella se acercaba a mí.

¿Qué anda haciendo, caballero?
¿Qué anda haciendo por aquí?
Ando en busca de mi esposa
que se separó de mí.

Su esposa ya no está aquí
su esposa ya se murió

Cuatro candeleros blancos
son los que alumbran allí.

III

Death
We searched in Death
We contemplated the original
and searched
and savored it
only to find profound
beckoning
A source that continued the search
beyond creation and death
The mystery
The mystery of our eyes
The eyes we have as
spiritual reflection
and we found we were
not alone

In our solitude
we found our very being
We moved into each other's
almost carefully, deliberately

Had we been here before?
What do we have, you and I?
Only our touch, our feeling
shared, that is all that we have
life in such ways, way
again, again, again
We found ourselves in ourselves
and while touching
we found other mysteries
that lay beneath
every layer of truth
unwinding each finding
another lonely vigil
another want, desire
to find
to find what?

What we always had?
Did anyone know that we
were searching?
That every look toward the earth
was a penetrating search that
had lasted for years
the mystery of time halted
and unkown without
itself discovery

IV

At night we searched each other
Somewhere was the soul
Somewhere in there was the heart
Somewhere in the night
was the lonely eye of the soul
Motionless
Waiting

Sometimes we found it
and slept with our lips
on it till the light fractured
everything

Can we find something every day
and every night?
We believed
yes, we had been finding
for centuries

Other beings?
We,
one,
the very same flavor
the very same
We looked behind heads
at the back of heads
The back of white heads
was less dangerous
Sometimes we turned the
heads around only to find

eyes that didn't see
who dared not see
who dared not be
within our own

No estamos solos.

V

We are not alone
if we remember and
recollect our passions
through the years
the giving of hands and backs
"dale los hombros a tus hijos"
We are not alone
Our eyes still meet with the passion
of continuity and prophecy

We are not alone
when we were whipped
in school for losing
the place in the book
or for speaking Spanish
on the school grounds
or
when Chona,
dear Chona,
a mythic Chicana,
died in the sugar beet fields
with her eight-month
child
buried deep within her
still
or
when that truck
filled with us
went off the mountain road
in Utah
with screams
eternally etched among
the mountain snows

We were not alone in death

VI

We were not alone in Iowa
When we slept in wet ditches
frightened by salamanders
at night
reclaiming their territory
and we
killing them
to maintain it as our—
then, our only—possession
or
in San Angelo
when we visited the desiccated
tubercular bodies of
aunts and uncles
friends and lovers

We were not alone
when we created children
and looked into their eyes
and searched for perfection
We were not alone
when taught
the magic of a smile, a kiss
an embrace each morning
and to feel the warmth
and quiver of a human
being

We were not alone
murmuring the novenas,
los rosarios, each night,
los rosarios we hoped
would bring joy and lasting peace
for Kiko
killed and buried in Italy in 1943
or
when we gathered each night
before bed

and waited
for the nightly sound
of the familiar cough
and the sweet/pan dulce
that it brought
Warm milk/pan dulce
opened the evening door
or
when we walked
all over Minnesota
looking for work
No one seemed to care
we did not expect them to care

VII

We were not alone
after many centuries
How could we be alone
We searched together
We were seekers
We are searchers
and we will continue
to search
because our eyes
still have
the passion of prophecy.

Estoy como estás.
Confusión, claridad por instantes
alegría fugaz
y eterna
amargo adiós odiado que sale.

Estoy como estás
un sordo que grita
su llanto sordo
que cae en cabezas
sin oídos y sin ojos.

La voz sale por los ojos
y la mano oye y suelta gritos
y los dedos se hablan y se acarician
y ríen.

Sin ojos, sin oídos,
La boca arrugada
cerrada sin moverse
firme.
nunca se abrirá
no siente, no ve, no oye,
Solos los dedos, los dedos
y las manos,
las manos.
Y el estómago que mastica

Original manuscript of "Estoy como estás."

II

la luz
y el viento se elevan
a una altura y así levantan
cada vez más una etapa de conocimiento
cada vez más ajeno, más distante, más aspero
y mientras
yo no puedo meterme
en esa luz en ese viento, en ese conocimiento
porque solo puedo hablar desde
este nivel
desde este espacio
que es respiro
que vivo
y que soy
a lo menos hoy
Yadamás

Original manuscript of "La luz."

Searching at Leal Middle School

December 11,
Thursday,
foggy day,
morning,
a good day for searching.
I discovered children through the fog
bundles, bultos,
manos en la bolsa turning
bultos in serenity
Leal
Apellido hispano
Who was Leal?
What had he/she done to deserve
his/her name as household word
known by hundreds of students
year after year.

"Yo voy a la Leal"

At first I saw only
the backs of black hair heads
Cabezas de pelo negro, negro era
Cabezas de pelo negro
brillante, de brillo, brillo era
and as
I went to the front of the room
to face them
I saw their limitless eyes
ojos sin límites
ojos oscuros
ojos sonrientes,
juguetones

— ¿Y éste?

We talked of thinking
        of inventing ourselves
        of love for others

        of love to be
        of searching
for ourselves

It was a good day for searching
Yet I became lost in my past
I saw myself and became
each one for an instant
and grasped for a second
the curious blink.
In split instances I became
the student, silent, staring
beyond myself, backwards
to joys so long forgotten of long
roads,
dusty roads
that went forever,
and friends
running toward me
from far away.
Away in the dump yards
where smoke curled and
with long sticks we turned and turned and
found half-rotten fruit
to be washed and eaten
and books—
Livingston's exploration of Africa,
the maps,
the blacks,
I became Henry L. in the forest—
and other books
of diseases and red, blue,
brown and purple organs
and more books discarded by
the rich
(the strange word)
and magazines
I searched for words in the dump
I saw doña Cuquita again:

"Cuidado con la lumbre.

Donde hay humito, hay lumbre por debajo."

And her apron
long apron rolled up
heavy with sweet-smoked fruit
sitting down to eat and listen
cobwebbed eyelashes could not
hide her dark eyes
ojos oscuros que fascinan
Did she know about Livingston?
Through the smoke.

I saw bultos
I discovered bundles of
manos en la bolsa,
children
Monday 11,
Thursday,
foggy day,
a good day for finding at
Leal Middle School.
And now, in the future,
I will search for it also
and for a few
cabezas de pelo negro
de ojos oscuros.

En la hora de las semillas

Albor ...
fracturado por los perfiles.
Tientos
de vida ... respiración.
La muerte prevalece,
anticipada exacta
en la aspiración.

Albor
que separa los perfiles.

La semilla,
tuya,
mía,
está aquí, viva,
entre nosotros.

¿Hemos liberado luz?

Llenos ahora,
los perfiles
triunfan, se construyen
al imponerse la luz.

Tú,
nuestro hijo,
volvemos a las primas semillas.

En la luz prima,
en el albor,
en la hora de las semillas.

Noon-Night

To hate him, anyone,
a white face, why
everyone.
You see this sore, on my knee
and on his
and on hers
on all of us?
We will never be cured.
But I guarantee
you will not do it to my son
nor to my daughter.
They will not kneel, not bend.
I'll remind them,
I'll tell them of the old times
when dust choked this throat
and when I was hit and laughed at,
when I was made to eat shit
in a taco—laughing, all laughing.
To hate him, anyone.
I'm silent. I am quiet.
I am not free.
I'm discovering evil.

Las voces del olvido

Las voces del olvido
me hablaron del presente
y me dijeron
"no me olvides."

Recuerdos
de siglos durmientes
de tantos despertar
de anochecer
de amanecer.

Las voces del olvido
me despiertan al futuro
Recuerdos
de siglos venideros
de tantos despertar
de amanecer
de anochecer.

Y oigo que me dice
mi otro
"no me olvides."

Do Not Forget Me

When I am silent
I always hear dark voices
far away
in me.
They always say,
"Do not forget me."

I must have known them
centuries
ago,
sleeping.
At times, then,
when some being of mine
was awakened,
I also felt the desire to leave
through that pulsating tunnel.

One day,
I was awakened
and I walked out
into the brilliance.

It was then that
I heard for the first time,
all my beings,
"Do not forget me."

Nacimiento

Los colores nacen
a cada instante.

¿Entra o se despega de la luz?

El instante forma las líneas,
forma los colores
y abre luz
y abre luz.

Los colores nacen,
engrandecimiento,
amplificación exacta
en cada forma.

Verificar, verificar.

Los colores nacen
para crear.

El despertar

Cuando todo es nada
y nada está en todo
me ciego en el instante.

Nada está en todo.

Los sentidos me matan.

Muero,
muero al despertar
en el mundo.

Y espero
Y espero

Cuando nada esté en todo
para siempre
y lo perfectamente blanco
me circunde.

Awakening

When everything is nothing
and nothing is in everything
I blind myself in the instant.

Nothing is in everything.

My senses execute me.

I die
I die upon awakening
in the world.

And I wait
and I must wait
until nothing will be in everything

forever
and the perfectly white surrounds me.

Palabras

En esta hoja blanca
dejo caer pedazos vivos de sesos
Aquí me quedo para siempre
Ahora ya me conocen
Detrás de cada letra mis ojos les siguen
Los veo, yo los veo, a ustedes
No quiero salir de aquí
Aquí estoy para siempre
Qué fácil fue romper
el secreto eterno.
¿Por qué no me siguen?
Métanse conmigo entre las palabras.
Juguemos entre ellas, dejemos que
caigan sobre nuestro cuerpo
Amontonémoslas sobre nuestro ombligo
Echémoslas al aire
Leámoslas, amémoslas
que están sedientas de amor
Engendrémoslas, repletémoslas
hasta que salgan de nuestra boca
con ganas.
Por eso en esta hoja blanca
he dejado caer pedazos de sesos
manchados de sangre que
huelen a vida y que sabrán vivir.
Y el secreto ¿qué fue?
Soy una palabra.

Estoy como estás

Estoy como estás.
Confusión, claridad por instantes,
alegría fugaz
y eterna,
amargo odio odiado que sale.

Estoy como estás.
Un sordo que grita
su llanto sordo
que cae en cabezas
sin oídos y sin ojos.

La voz sale por los ojos
y la mano oye y suelta gritos
y los dedos se hablan y se acarician
y ríen.

Sin ojos, sin oídos,
la boca arrugada
cerrada sin moverse,
firme.
Nunca se abrirá,
no siente, no ve, no oye.
Solos los dedos, los dedos
y las manos,
las manos,
y el estómago que se mastica.

La vida por fin empezó

La vida por fin empezó
Salió del pasado, muerta.
La busqué años
    en sueños de esperanzas
    en vida eterna
    en muerte viva.

La encontré, la comprendo ya
    ahora nos vemos alegres
    ahora me sonríe cuando quiero
    ahora la cojo y la suelto, juego con ella
    ahora sé lo que es.

La puedo masticar y escupirla
    o comérmela
    o desearla
    o soñarla.

La vida la tengo en mis manos
    se mueve, se quiere saltar
    ahora me teme, la hice que saltara
    del pasado y por eso no me quiere a veces
    ahora me río de ella, ¡qué incapacitada
    está! Ahora es mi juguete.

Ahora que he encontrado mi vida buscaré otras.
Ahora puedo despegarme de ella, pegarme a otras.
Salió del pasado muerta, y por estar muerta
La comprendo, no la temo, no puede hacerme nada.

Finally Life Began

Finally life began
It came out of the past. Dead.
I searched years
    in dreams of hope
    in eternal life
    in living death.

Now I see and understand it
    now we see each other gladly at times
    now it laughs with me when I want it
    now I grab it and I play with it
    I know what it is.

I can chew it and spit it out
    or I can eat it
    or desire it
    or dream it.

I truly have life in my palms
    it moves, and wants to go free
    now it fears me
    I made it burst out of the past.
    How powerless it is. My toy.

Now I can detach myself from it
and attach myself to others.
It came out of the past. Dead.
Because it's dead I understand it.
I do not fear it.
It can do nothing to me.

To Walk Beyond the Door

To walk beyond the door
each day
out the door of eyes
To the right. To the left.
Straight ahead
directly in front
understood by everyone
out of the many
millions
waiting behind the door
yet unrecognized.
To walk beyond the reach
of eyes
beyond the door of doors
the ultimate one
the one at the very end
which encloses nothing
beyond here and there.

Another Day

Another day
yet not
for faces are the same
always
to be blind
would it matter?
Another day
feeling another day

I can see the sky moving
and the clouds turn
from purple
to red
to white
to blue
constantly colors

Left myself yesterday
encounter myself today
as I step into my face
and into my eyes

I see myself
yet in another day
really another yesterday

Not Unlike the Wind

Not unlike the wind
breathing eternally
into itself.

Not unlike the wind
who swallows
forever.

Moving
everything

You are through
the wind
a mystery.

A Flower

A flower
twitching
between lives
no, not of quiet desperation
between lives
unruly
to twitch
living
thinking
a flower
having captured time
and color
sure of itself
yet trembling
at the onlooker
will he kill
a flower
having captured the warm sun
also
and the many waves of
heat and sound
and my eyes.

Soy una palabra

Soy una palabra
Seré una palabra

En esta hoja,
aquí.

Te sigo desde aquí.

Espero,
siempre espero

el secreto eterno
contigo.

Soy una palabra.

Fake or Fink

I know this jovial man
Who stomps the ground and shouts "hurray"
When there are people in sight

I know this happy man
Who says "hello" and dresses well
When there are people in sight.

I know this Christian man
Who goes to church and pays his tithe
When there are people in sight.

I know this educated man
Who speaks so well and listens light
When there are people in sight

I know this wealthy man
Who shows his generosity and glistens his teeth
When there are people in sight.

I know this wealthy, educated, jovial, happy,
Christian man
Who cries and fears at night
Because he cannot do it
When there are people in sight.

Eternity

The living
live because of the dead,
and the dead lived
because of the dead.

And the living
will live dead
for the living.

The living will always be dead
and the dead will
always be living.

I Go to Church at 'Veteran's Place'

Go to church on Sunday and be saved,
Pray for us sinners.

I'll see you at one at *Veteran's Place.*
Where the German parachute and the machine gun
Will be looking at me.
The pictures on the wall
All those men in uniform will be looking at me.

And so will the luger and the Japanese flag
And so will the saber and the pliers with which
He handles hot checks.
Even Eisenhower will look at me,
Even General Pershing and his horse will be there.

The one-eyed empty beer bottles
Will look into my eyes and burp.

All those young men in uniform,
All those memories,
We must let them see us.

"... for they have not died in vain"

Pray "for us sinners" on Sunday,
While we dance for the pictures
And the sorrowful jukebox.

Desátate

Soy del otro mundo y de éste.
¿De dónde eres tú?
¿Acaso eres de aquel nudo
que no pudo desatarse,
que dejó matarse?

Soy del otro mundo y de éste
porque me desaté.

¿Qué te cuesta? Piensa hombre ...
desátate, que eres inmortal mientras vives,
¿o es que no vives?

Eres el mundo, no eres mudo ... piensa
agita, haz, muévete, que estás vivo.
Desátate de ese nudo
o queda mudo y mortal viviente.

Soy del otro mundo y de éste
porque me desaté.

From the Past

From the past
from the past,
dead.
Search, search, in
the past.
Search, search, in
the future.
Yet, lingering in their presence.
Thread, upon thread, upon thread
mucus membrane
Is this all?
From the past
in the future
yet lingering
thread, upon thread, upon thread.

Through the Window

Alive,
swaying,
clinging,

drops.

Verge
transparently transparent
in concave
convex forms.

Life drops,
swaying drops,
drying.

Dry ring.

We Didn't Bury Him

We didn't bury him, they did.
They didn't know
That he had a ring with an M nor did they know
That he always brought pan dulce home.
That he never went to church but believed in God.
That he loved mother but had a mistress.
That he loved us but never touched us.
That he gave and worked but was avaricious.
That he cursed in English but not in Spanish.
That he drank and smoked once.

They didn't know that he kicked me once when I lost 10
    cents.
And that he cried when his father died.

They didn't know that he taught me to cry.
And that he told me I was stupid when I cut my foot.

They didn't know that he baked the turkey at the wedding.
And that he winked his eye when we left on our honeymoon.
Nor did they know that he kissed our little girl when we
Were not looking.

They didn't know him, they buried him when he died.

We didn't. (I, my mother and brothers.)

My Life

A learned man spoke last night
Of the wonders and terrors of the world
Of how to live right
Of how not to live wrong
He talked and talked and made me happy for a while.

And then he was gone,
And I was alone
In the wonders of terrors of the world
And I was sadly happy.

And I understood
That I was truly alone, forever more alone,
That I had my own terrrors and wonders.
He had seen and known.

Now
I have to see and know the wonders and terrors of my life.

La luz

La luz
y el viento se elevan
a una altura y así levantan
cada vez más una etapa de conocimiento
cada vez más ajeno, más distante, más áspero
y mientras
yo no puedo meterme
en esa luz en ese viento, en ese conocimiento
porque sólo puedo hablar desde
este nivel
desde este espacio
que respiro
y que soy
a lo menos hoy
nadamás

Critical Essays

Into the Labyrinth:
The Chicano in Literature

🌿

Fiction and reality—it is difficult to distinguish general lines of differences between these two concepts. It is even difficult to define each concept, and perhaps herein lies the basic problem of perceiving the differences if we care to. It can be generally stated that reality is actual existence, a true state of affairs, while fiction is that which is imagined or made up, that which is an imaginary account or statement. But why is it so difficult to distinguish reality from fiction if they are in a sense so different? Is it not because fiction draws from reality? Because it draws from another type of reality—an imagined, invented one. One prototype is the labyrinth.

Why a labyrinth? We must remember to make the analogy between the Greek myth of Daedalus and Minos and our own lives. For this was the intention of Greek myth. The labyrinth was and is a man-made structure full of intricate passageways that make it difficult to find the way from the interior to the entrance or from the entrance to the center. In essence, the important element here is that the labyrinth provided a setting for a search toward the exterior or toward the interior. In either case, the setting provided not only a setting for search but also a setting for tension.

Literature and fiction provide tension. Literature represents man's life; it also reflects his inner and his outward search. It is, in a sense, an intricate maze to provide either exteriorization or internalization of the human involvement and evolvement [evolution]. However, whether it is internal or external, there exists a search. And the search can only exist if there is an impulse into the labyrinth of the human totality of conditions. Thus, the search and the labyrinth complement each other to bring forth a vicarious sensibility to the perceiver.

What does a labyrinth represent? As such, a labyrinth is a man-made maze for the purpose of testing and for the purpose of observing. Mainly, it is to observe if someone is capable of searching and finding his way to the center or the entrance, whatever may be the case. For it is a vicarious notion of humanity, or man, to attempt to search for the other, "alter ego," in order to comprehend himself better. Again, the labyrinth represents to

From *New Voices in Literature: The Mexican American*, Edward Simmen, Ed. Edinburg TX: Pan American University, 1971: 18–25.

man a structure into which his life can and does fit. It is a mold wherein he can place his life. In essence, is it not life in search of form—a conquest, a labyrinth in which to reflect his human condition? This brings us to the Chicano, for he is a complete man, a complete human, who also wishes to create a labyrinth, who wishes to invent himself in the labyrinth where he can vicariously live his total human condition. However, since he has perceived continually the development of two others, the North American and the Mexican literatures, literatures which have reached great heights of intricateness and sophistication for their counterparts, more stress is given to his finding form or forms for expression. So we find Chicano literature and Chicanos in fiction as simply life in search of form.

Let us identify life here (with the use of a *Petite Larrouse*) as the result of the play of the organs, which concurs with development and the conservation of the subject. How can we identify the search? Let us allow here that it is an investigation, a disquisition—reasoned analysis and exposition. But, a search for what? An exterior figure? A labyrinth of sorts? It is a figure, a structure, a language, all this that reveals life. One recognizes that the literary form is as significant as the very life that it tries to capture. There exists, therefore, a complement of base and form, just as there exists a complement of search and labyrinth. The Chicano and Chicano literature is now in the search, into the labyrinth, life in search of form.

It will not be necessary to emphasize here any statistics concerning those lives that denominate themselves as Chicanos. A renaissance has been developing, perhaps since the years after the second World War, perhaps as late as the years after the Korean War. (You'll have to pardon me for the use of wars as a reference point in pointing out a renaissance and the evolution of a people.) There is, regardless, this renaissance which is attempting to occur, and which is trying and succeeding. I may add, in verifying life for the Chicano. Parallel to this intent and an integral part is the anxiety to conserve this life. Twenty years ago these very lives attempted to disengage themselves from anything which was not Anglosaxon. However, now the intent is different. These lives are coming to know themselves as Chicano lives; better, they are inventing themselves as such. And I question Octavio Paz when he says that to invent is to lie. For if that is true, then life, yes, and love itself is a lie. It is the opinion of this writer that the invention of ourselves by ourselves is in actuality an extension of our will—really an exteriorization of our will. Thus, as the Chicano invents himself, he is complementing his will. Another complement. This is of great importance because these lives are trying to find form. This development is becoming a unifying consciousness. The thoughts of the Chicano are beginning to gyrate constantly over his own life, over his own development, over his identity, and as such over his own conservation. This, of necessity, encases the political field, the economic field, the social field, and of course—the creative impulse. In literature life is submitted into the labyrinth of finding form—since the word, as a symbol, can verify, can search, can identify, can conserve. In short, the literary intent is but one, a very important one at least, of the many reflections of the intellectual development and of the very own characteristics of the people or *raza*. It will not be necessary to underline the fact that there now exists a Chicano literature because it already exists. It is out of the oral or latent states.[1] We can observe the Chicano's frenetic intent in getting into the labyrinth and searching for forms. We can sense that here is life in search of form.

What have been the vehicles through which Chicano literature has been expressing itself? As all literatures of all times, the genesis manifests itself orally. It begins in the *corridos*, the ballads. Dr. Américo Paredes, University of Texas professor of anthropology and English, in his work *With a Pistol in his Hand*,[2] published in 1957, gives us what can be recognized as one of the first major works of Chicano literature. Of course, those lexical, dialectical or pedagogical studies which have been carried out by Mexican-Americans in the United States are herewith excluded since we are dealing primarily with literature. Dr. Paredes' work, although in its great part presents to us a formal study of the *corrido*, reflected already a renaissance in the intent of presenting a Chicano life in a more complete form. That is, the hero is revealed to us totally from the Mexican-American perspective. And this is of great importance for the Chicano being, as it is the corrido, a popular form, a form of the people, which is the primary vehicle through which a more spiritual totality is explained for this being.

However, the corrido is not the only form through which the Chicano has been explaining himself. Between the years 1848 and 1958 there have existed more than five hundred Chicano newspapers. The press has been a constant vehicle for the expression of the Mexican-American. The newspapers which have existed so prolifically through all these years are to engender what today is manifested as the Chicano Press Association. A study of great merit would be one which would very meticulously and profoundly research the Mexican-American journalism. Today, Chicano journalism is perhaps the strongest impulse which has resolved to present the present condition, human condition, of la raza. Although the press tends to be at times propagandist (what news vehicle isn't) and although at times it lacks a serious objectivity, its intent is of great value. It is without doubt the most aggressive arm of the Chicano. The language of the newspapers is at times in Spanish, at times in English. At times the newspapers are in bilingual editions. Those newspapers of major care use a universal Spanish. What is of literary interest is the fact that all have in some form a literary input. An invention of sorts of the Chicano—be it poetry, short stories, legends. The poetry most of the time has an ideological intent. It does follow diverse forms which are capable at times of reaching a strong and valid denunciation of the system in which Chicano life has to exist.

At the same time that journalism begins to flourish with a greater emphasis, because, as it has been noted, it is a vehicle which has always existed and which in reality negates the complete illiteracy of the Chicano, *El grito*,[3] a completely independent Mexican-American quarterly is begun. This journal of contemporary Mexican-American thought published in Berkeley, California, by a group of Mexican-American university students, as early as 1967, began to flourish, and it evolved into the publishing house *El Quinto Sol*. A year and a half later *Quinto Sol* published the Mexican-American anthology of literature which has had the greatest success, *El espejo/The Mirror*.[4] This anthology reflects distinct forms of formulation in its literary intents: essay, poetry, short story, etc., and it achieves an indicative impulse, an indicative push which reveals the Mexican-American condition. The literary impulse of La Raza is a frenetic surge to ensnare and to conserve that which is Chicano in all literary forms. In so doing one is able to sense that the important element here is not so much the form or forms but life itself.

Quinto Sol has converted itself into a funnel for the Chicano writer. Through its pages more than one hundred and forty Chicano writers have been published—all of this during the last four years. The plan of action that *Quinto Sol* follows is to provide a completely independent vehicle for the Chicano writer, and to permit that he manifest himself in all forms. (We can truthfully say that Octavio Romano, Herminio Ríos, and others who have aided *Quinto Sol* are the labyrinth providers for the myth makers which will be the Chicano writers.) This is the reason that on any occasion *El grito*, journal by *Quinto Sol*, will provide us an erudite essay in English over some Chicano ideological perspective next to a short story in which the Pachuco dialect is crystallized in an artistic sensibility which gives it literary quality. There is no doubt that *Quinto Sol* has given the strongest thrust to the substance and form of Chicano literature. It also provided an impulse for there to be established a Chicano editorial house in Texas—La Casa Jacinto Treviño.

It is interesting to note that the first work which was to be presented by this house, *Semillas de liberación*,[5] has in it, according to pre-publication data, a little of everything (drama, poetry, jokes, lies, etc.). There exists this same persistence to present all forms and different literary styles, and this is not due to the simple fact that it is an anthology, I believe.

I question. Is this persistence a desire to represent that there exists an amplitude of Chicano Literature? Or is this persistence underlying a search and so it is in all forms? Or does this persistence reflect the variety of thrust of an ethnic group that is in itself pluralistic? Or is it because this new literature—this Chicano literature—has, in a sense, germinated, latently, between two flourishing and great literatures—the North American and the Mexican—and suddenly feels that its thrust be just as great? I certainly feel this last statement is possible.

There should also be mentioned the propension [*sic*] of other editorial houses such as the Ventura Press through which Raymond Barrio published his novel *The Plum Plum Pickers*,[6] the North American publisher of *Pocho*,[7] a novel by [José Antonio] Villareal, and *Chicano*,[8] a novel by Richard Vasquez. In the field of sociology and history, other studies by Mexican Americans have been published. Many studies follow a trajectory implicated by the North American stereotype. Such is the case also when we delve into literature which concerns the Mexican American not written by him. For we must remember that Chicano literature must reflect, as Herminio Ríos states,

> the multiple experiences of the Mexican American and explore a multiplicity of Mexican American themes. The reflection of these experiences and the exploration of their related themes must be from the point of view of an inside participant. In the artistic world that is created, the literary characters must move, speak, and feel as true and complex creations, not in the predetermined mold of the stock character of a sociological or historical model.[9]

Luis Valdez and Stan Steiner, [the former] director of *El Teatro Campesino*, of Fresno, California, and [the latter] author of *La Raza, The Mexican Americans*,[10] [are collaborating on an anthology] which will be published by Knopf during the spring of 1972.[11] It will be published totally in English. This brings us to a deep-rooted problem—language and form. Let us perceive this problem through the different genres.

The novel.

The novel that has been written to this day has been one in English. Cannot the Chicano experience be written in any other form? Or is it a fact that everything gyrates around the commercial aspect in publishing? Notwithstanding, the intention of Barrio in *The Plum Plum Pickers* transcends the problem of language. It is more than a mere description of a family of migrant workers. It reflects justly the torn spirit of the Chicano. The novel *Chicano* by Richard Vasquez, on the contrary, is to a high degree the reflection of a false interpretation of the Chicano, sociologically and anthropologically. There is an abundance of stereotyped characters which have been in reality created by various other North American authors—O'Henry, Bret Harte, Steinbeck and others. I do not believe that Vasquez lacks the feeling and the sensibility for the Chicano, but his work must have suffered a tremendous editing for its commercial fomentation. In short, to where does the Chicano novel thrust? Can there be written a Chicano novel in Spanish, in bilingual effort, or a dialectal one, or does there always exist in the writer's mind the commercial aspect? Can Chicano life search its ultimate and best labyrinth in the novel? One would have to submit Chicano literature to other questions: Is Chicano Literature written for self-concept, self-development, or is it written to verify itself as a complete life, totally human, in the eyes of another?

The short story.

The short story, as well as poetry, is quite prolific and uses different forms of language. It is written in Spanish, in English, in a bilingual form, in the Pachuco dialect. It manifests itself in all the dialectal and universal forms which Spanish and English frame within—from the sensitive, transcendent, *"English Short Story"* by Rudy Espinosa[12] and the incisive story by Philip Ortego[13] to the dialectal efforts of Jesús Maldonado, *"El Flaco,"*[14] who is able to render the Pachuco dialect as artistically sound. The environment which is represented by the short story is also fully complete—from the rural to the suburb and the city barrio. The language used, as has been noted, is realistic, and at times both English and Spanish are used, at times English totally, at times Spanish only, sometimes only the Pachuco dialect. It is in the short story, as well as in the poetry, that there exists an earnest desire to represent more realistically the language forms of the Chicano. The different linguistic thrust in reality say, "We are all this and more."

Poetry.

This is the genre which represents the fullest precipitation of life because it is in poetry where the Chicano sensibility can be compressed. The Chicano newspapers and anthologies are soaked with poetry. Alurista in

Floricanto en Aztlán[15] gives an excellent collection of literature of today and how they have brought about their own cultural renaissance. According to Octavio I. Romano, editor of *Quinto Sol,* poetry is what *la raza,* the people, write most. It is almost impossible to note the great poetic precipitation—different forms, different dialects, languages, mixtures, etc. [The following are two examples: a bilingual work, "Mis ojos hinchados," by Alurista,[1] and another, "Mi cuento," in modified Chicano idiom, by Sergio Elizondo.[2]

Mis ojos hinchados

Mis ojos hinchados
    flooded with lágrimas
de bronce
melting on the cheek bones
of my concern
    razgos indígenas
the scars of history on my face
    and the veins of my body
that aches
    vomito sangre
y lloro libertad
    I do not ask for freedom
I *am* freedom
    no one
not even Yahweh
    and his thunder
can pronounce
    and on a stone
la ley del hombre esculpir
    no puede
mi libertad
and the round tables
    of ice cream
        hot dogs
    meat ball lovers meet
to rap
    and rap
and I hunger
    y mi boca está seca
el agua cristalina
    y la verdad

transparente
in a cup
   is never poured
dust gathers on the shoulders
   of dignitaries
y de dignidad
   no saben nada
muertos en el polvo
   They bite the earth
and return
   to dust

Mi Cuento

Paso ahora
al agosto de grandes guerras,
que retiemblan mi pecho
y bailan mi corazón.
En un establo de Francia,
chante de piedra
y vino de botellas pardas,
celebré mi libertad.
Parche de hombros otro cuento,
fusiles,
pan.

Canto mi épica Chicana,
Chingueasumadre el mundo
y viva la llamada democracia americana!
En cien escaramuzas me metí donde mis primos no podían,
contra otros pobres que nada me debían,
Fiel, nuevo lustre en mi bronce,
me aventé en inglés.
Refinaba en gringo,
mucho *down*, mucho *up*,
plenty of money,
I rode cars;
La banda de Miller me llevó,
en trombones, saxofones,
hasta los brazos de la primera
y dije: "Aquí chingo".

Desfilaban a toda madre por New York.
Yo y mi cuerpo, solos.

Esperando sepultura.
Me la negaron en Tejas.
El Aguila de las aceitunas y flechas
me enterró en sagrado.
Y yo y mi espíritu viejo
en la tierra de mis padres.

Mano, presta la lira,
tú con el bajo sexto.
No tengo himno de gloria
a ver qué sacamos de esto.
Yo:

Soldado me fui, hombre vine.
Moreno por las alas de la pasión de mis padres,
prieto por el sol de los trabajos,
blanco por los ojos de la Virgen,
picante como el chile colorado.
Ella:

Se mece en las curvas de sus pasos.
Canta cuando habla.
En su morena piel
el sol fundió la miel,
y en sus ojos,
el calor de las abejas
que pausan bajo rosales.

Amigo: tengo todo.
De aquí pa'lante,
las uvas que me esperan en los campos
amigas de mi armonía,
con tiernos dedos acaricio hermanas.
Adán y Eva, dos en uno, en todos estos años
que llaman historia,
soy israelí de mis viñedos.
Guardo mi cuchillo
p'al panzón con gafas

que mi espalda guacha,
mientras que yo callado,
trabajo,
y de reojo miro a mi muchacha.
Uvas de amor siento que me dejas;
prefiero hoy mi ser valioso
y jamás tener quejas.
Adiós, adiós, patrón
tengo un asunto,
Chicana el alma,
gringos los bolsillos,
carro al lado,
águila cuando brinco.
¡Ora sí! ¡Chingueasumadre! amigo.
En las paredes de mi barrio escribo,
a grandes letras,
que miren mis ojazos,
vivo, gozo, chingo,
quiero,
tomo,
y en las esquinas
de Juana un frajo.
No me alcanzan,
vuelo;
y por si acaso,
la placa con otras pistolas,
allá la dejo
yo le digo que ya sabe,

mientras que me pinto con safos.][16]

Theatre.

The Chicano theatre is experimental, *engagé*, and it certainly reveals many of the aspects of the *juegos de escarnio* [burlesque and satire] which started the Hispanic theatrical tradition during the 13th and 14th centuries. Its sarcasm, bitter irony cannot help but give it a didactic sense. The Chicano student theatre overflows with sarcasm and its combating reality. One must mention the theatre which Luis Valdez directs in Fresno, California, and the one which Guadalupe Saavedra directs here in the Valley under the Colegio Jacinto Treviño. The Chicano theatre is created with the full intention of taking the people's reality to the people.

But, can it transcend? It can be noted that this is without doubt the most committed. Its language is Spanish bilingual (Spanish, English), Chicano, and realistic. Also, one must note that it has a very traditional Hispanic trait—the bitter humor of self condemnation.

Essay.

The essay is written totally in English. It has thus the most powerful thrust, and it is the major way of tearing down the negative social stereotypes which are constantly being attributed to the Chicano. This genre represents the most intellectual and incisive aspect of the Mexican American Renaissance. The essay appears to have a double mission: to create a proper image, one which is true and constructive, and at the same time destroy those stereotypes which have developed and evolved over so many years of non-invention by the Chicano. Octavio Romano, Herminio Ríos, Nick Vaca, Philip Ortego, Américo Paredes, George Sánchez, are at the fore-front. Perhaps it is Romano and Vaca who have taken the challenge to decipher and to strengthen the Chicano's own image with greatest independence and who have had the greatest success.[17]

Upon briefly reviewing the different genres one can make several general observations:

1. The novel and the essay are written or have been written in English. The intent hence seems to be to reach the total North American public. As such, the language and form verify an intellectual development for that person who is not a Chicano.

2. The short story is the genre which has the most forms. It represents itself in all forms or in combinations. There is a pulsating life which searches for form.

3. Poetry is the strongest thrust, the most frenetic and the most prolific and in all its forms it underlines, most of all, a spiritual totality.

4. Drama manifests itself as didactic and *engagé*. It follows the great literary tradition of Hispanic drama in verifying the popular spirit of the Chicano.

Also, one can note that those forms that are most capable of changing stereotypes and of giving forth an intellectual emancipation are written in English. These forms most capable of reaching the raza are written in the popular language or in Spanish.

What is, then, the principal intent of Chicano Literature: to change one stereotype for another? To destroy stereotypes? To verify that which is Chicano and to conserve it? To commit the Chicano to social change? To provide a vehicle for self-reflection, a proper mirror, a proper labyrinth? Why not all of this? All of this has value. All of these encompass the totality of the Chicano being.

Chicano Literature has a triple mission: to represent, to conserve that aspect of life that the Mexican American holds as his own, and at the same time destroy the invention of others of his own life. That is—conservation, struggle, and invention. It is not surprising that Chicano literature is life. In a sense all the organs of the Chicano are in play; he concurs with his development and proper conservation. It is also a disquisition, a reasoned investigation in an attempt to find and use the forms that can manifest him as a totally human individual. This is why he has to search in himself, out of himself; this is why he wants to conserve himself and in so doing also invent himself in all forms. He is searching for the labyrinth. The Chicano invents himself in all forms immediately. The spontaneous vitality of Chicano Literature expresses itself as a life which not only exists but also wants to be (*ser* and *estar*). *El ser* is life, *el estar* is the form.

Again it is difficult to distinguish general lines of difference between these two concepts although grammatically this is not true. Somehow through vicarious feeling one is able to comprehend the reality of both beings, the actual and the invented. The labyrinth that is literature provides a setting where differences disappear and one gains an insight into the human condition—our human condition.

Allow me to conclude by saying that as the Chicano invents himself as a total human being, he not only gains complete psychological control over his world and gives thrust to his will but also, and perhaps most important, he condemns himself to liberty and in so doing joins the twentieth-century family of man. Into the labyrinth goes the Chicano, condemned by himself to search for intellectual emancipation, and to internalize his life and to externalize his life to make it more complete. The labyrinth is not a provider of great truths but a reflector of great questions. This is what the Chicano will find. He could not find these if he himself had not gotten into the labyrinth. And thus Chicano Literature is an actuality.

Notes

[1]At the time of this writing, Tomás Rivera was referring to the Chicano

literature that was being produced in part as a corollary of the Chicano Movement that began in the 1960s, a literary movement called, for better or worse, the "Chicano Renaissance." Rivera was aware that Chicano or Mexican American literature had been produced long before this period, as he affirms in his reference to the period between 1848 and 1958. However, literary production—oral and written—in what is now the United States began with the advent of the first Spanish-speaking settlers, predominately in the West and Southwest, towards the end of the sixteenth century, and has continued unabated to the present.

This article was reproduced in a briefer form, that omits the first part of the present essay with regard to the concept of the labyrinth in Chicano literature, as "Literatura chicana: Vida en busca de forma" (ERIC Document 058 808, 1971); and was translated by Martha Cotera as "Chicano Literature: Life in Search of Form" in Martha Cotera & Larry Hufford, Eds., *Bridging Two Cultures: Multidisciplinary Readings in Bilingual, Bicultural Education* (Austin: National Educational Laboratory Publishers, 1980): 333–41. I have omitted this essay, and its translation, from this collection, but I have inserted within brackets a portion of the translation, which will be indicated with a note. The editor's notes are designated within brackets.

[2]*"With His Pistol in His Hand," A Border Ballad and Its Hero* (Austin: University of Texas Press, 1958).

[3]*El grito* 1.1, a publication of Quinto Sol Publications, Inc., and whose first editor was Nick C. Vaca, had its inaugural publication in the Fall of 1967.

[4]*El espejo/The Mirror: Selected Mexican-American Literature*, Ed. Octavio I. Romano-V. (Berkeley, CA: Quinto Sol, 1969).

[5]The Casa Jacinto Treviño was the publishing outlet of the Colegio Jacinto Treviño established in Mercedes, Texas. The *Semillas de liberación* was an anthology whose projected publication was never realized.

[6]*The Plum Plum Pickers* (Sunnyvale, CA: Ventura Press, 1969).

[7]*Pocho* (Garden City, NY: Doubleday and Company, 1959).

[8]*Chicano* (Garden City, NY: Doubleday and Company, 1970).

[9]There is no identification of the source of this citation.

[10]*La Raza: The Mexican Americans* (New York: Harper, 1970).

[11]*Aztlan: An Anthology of Mexican American Literature* (New York: Vintage Books [Alfred A. Knopf], 1972).

[12]A frequent contributor to *El grito* (e.g. "Little Eagle and the Rainbow," *El grito* 2.2 (1969): 78–80; "Mi casa es su casa," *El grito* 3.2 (1970): 19–27; the editor encounters no documentation for Rudy Espinoza's "English Short Story."

[13]Perhaps "The Coming of Zamora, a Story," *El grito* 1.3 (1968): 12–17.

[14]"Capirocita Roja," [sic] *El grito* 3.4 (1970): 12–16.

[15]*Floricanto en Aztlán* (Los Angeles: Chicano Cultural Center, UCLA, 1971).

[1]*El grito* 2.1 (1968): 6.

[2]*El grito* 3.4 (1970): 9–11 [See "Chicano Literature: Fiesta of the Living" for the translation of this poem].

[16]Tomás Rivera, "Chicano Literature: Life in Search of Form," 336–39.

[17]Editors of *El grito*.

Chicano Literature:
Fiesta of the Living

🌾

> Every poem we read is a recreation, that is,
> a ceremonial ritual, a fiesta.
>
> Octavio Paz, *The Labyrinth of Solitude*

I have been involved with Chicano literature for over six years. I have lived its roots all my life, a life that for the most part has known no literature to represent it. For me the literary experience is one of total communion, an awesome awareness of the "other,"[1] of one's potential self. I have come to recognize my "other" in Chicano literature, but by this I do not mean to say that I find or reflect or faithfully render the Chicano experience. As a matter of fact, I would hope that what I write goes further. To claim that my own writing is representative of the Chicano experience is not my intention. Rather, I should like to focus on Chicano writing as a ritual of immortality, of awe in the face of the "other"—a ritual of the living, in a sense, a fiesta of the living.

To write is a total experience, like life itself. It is an original experience, like that of the complete and splendid act of sexual union, of birth, of death, of the joy one has in loving mankind, because of the feelings involved—compassion and brotherhood. Chicano writers are no different from other men who enter this total experience. I have known and have come to feel a bond with many of them. The majority I have met in person, and the others I have come to know through their works. I have felt their humanity. None has deceived me. I have found them to be truthful, ritualistic, in love with the "other" which each of them has found. Why do I feel this bond? Because I expect to do so? Or is it because they write of what I know? Not what I have learned, but what I know. Still, I have felt this same bond with other writers, although, I must confess, not as strongly and completely. I think we must return to the direct experience of life and to our need for ritual. When I began my formal education and learned to read, I saw man manifested in so many words and with such evocative imagery that I came to expect that miracles, heroics, love and all human experience could be contained in

From *Books Abroad* 49.3 (1975): 439–52. Copyright 1975 by the University of Oklahoma Press.

words. I have found this to be the case in Walt Whitman, Hemingway, Shakespeare, Azuela, Cela, in Sábato, Machado, Guillén, Lorca. Even in the worst writings I have found an exact, pure desire to transform what is isolated in the mind into an external form. To perceive what people have done through this process and to come to realize that one's own family group or clan is not represented in literature is a serious and saddening realization. At twelve, I looked for books by my people, by my immediate people, and found very few. Very few accounts in fact existed. When I met Bartolo, our town's itinerant poet, and when on a visit to the Mexican side of the border, I also heard of him—for he would wander on both sides of the border to sell his poetry—I was engulfed with *alegría*. It was an exaltation brought on by the sudden sensation that my own life had relationships, that my own family had relationships, that the people I lived with had connections beyond those at the conscious level. It was Bartolo's poetry—or was it simply those papers that looked like his poetry—that gave me this awareness. I have previously mentioned his preoccupation with words, with their sound and with their relationship to communication in ... *y no se lo tragó la tierra*:

> Bartolo pasaba por el pueblo por aquello de diciembre cuando tanteaba que la mayor parte de la gente había regresado de los trabajos. Siempre venía vendiendo sus poemas. Se le acababan casi para el primer día porque en los poemas se encontraban los nombres de la gente del pueblo. Y cuando los leía en voz alta era algo emocionante y serio. Recuerdo que una vez le dijo a la raza que leyeran los poemas en voz alta porque la voz era la semilla del amor en la oscuridad.

> Bartolo passed through the town every December when he knew that most of the people had returned from work up north. He always came by selling his poems. By the end of the first day, they were almost sold out because the names of the people of the town appeared in the poems. And when he read them aloud it was something emotional and serious. I recall that one time he told the people to read the poems out loud because the spoken word was the seed of love in the darkness.[2]

Bartolo's poetry was my first contact with literature by my own people. It was to be my only contact for a long time. The bond that I felt with him and that I feel with other Chicano writers is the same. It is not pure nationality, Mexican, Chicano, Pocho, or otherwise; it is not because we take part in the same struggle against the same injustices; it is not because we come from the same environment or social class, although all these do manifest a *vigencia* of sorts. Is it not, rather, that we sense that we are part of the same ritual? Perhaps this is the case: a bond that comes from a feeling of uniqueness, from a common set of beliefs, from a sense of destiny. Yes, we sense a prophecy, and we sense a fulfillment of this prophecy. We have been alive since time began. We are not just living; we have been living for centuries. We must ritualize our existence through words. To me there is no greater joy than reading a creative work by a Chicano. I like to see my students come to feel this bond and to savor moments of immortality, of the total experience.

Yet, what is this bond? What brings it about? Is it just a sense of awareness? The creative act itself? Its product? One has to go beyond prophecy and ritual and seek the nature of this bond in the act of remembering. Remembering, because the past is what we have and it is all that we have. It is from the past that we are able to perceive, create and give life of our ritual; it is from this that we derive strength, that we can recognize our existence as human beings. I think we also come to the realization that life is perhaps not simply a relationship between the world, ourselves, and others, but in addition, the discovery and recollection of the relationship and these things. All societies have rituals of remembering. The Chicano is no different. The folklore traditions are based on remembering, retelling and reliving.

La literatura Chicana es un esfuerzo en darle forma, armonía y unidad a la vida Chicana porque se manifiesta ésta como vida que vale mientras esté sobre la tierra. Y así florecen el arte Chicano, la literatura Chicana, el drama—en fin se inventa y se futuriza el Chicano como un ser humanamente total. Esto es de gran importancia para el suroeste, ya que es inconcebible la humanización de esta región sin la actuación propia de este segmento de la población de esta región. Pero, ¿por cuáles procesos se lleva a cabo la invención y la futurización?

En mi obra, ... *tierra*, hice hincapié en los procesos del recuerdo, del desubrimiento y de la voluntad. Primeramente esto del recuerdo. Me refiero al método de narrar que usaba la gente. Es decir, recuerdo lo que ellos recordaban y la manera en que narraban. Siempre existía una manera de comprimir y exaltar una sensibilitdad con mínimas palabras. También, existía constantemente el inventarle nuevas ocurrencias. Esto, claro está, es lo que elabora la tradición oral. Aunque muchos de aquellos padres que andaban en los trabajos eran analfabetos, el sistema narrativo predominaba. Siempre había alguien que sabía los cuentos viejos—del gigante moro, del negrito güerín, etc. Luego, había siempre aquellas personas que interpretaban películas, que narraban sobre partes distintas del mundo, y siempre los cuentos de Aladín y su lámpara maravillosa. De esta manera, en los campos migratorios, se desarrolló una literatura oral. La gente buscaba refugio no solamente en la iglesia, o con sus hermanos, sino también al sentarse en ruedo y escuchar y narrar, y por medio de palabras escaparse a otros mundos, e inventarse también. Desde luego en los niños se desarrolló también una especie de mundo narrativo y en el tedio trabajo de cada día se cristalizaron mundos.

Las narraciones orales se formulaban también sobre México, o sobre las costumbres, sobre la revolución de 1910. También desde luego, se formulaban sobre lo fantasmagórico—los espantos, las ánimas, la llorona, el diablo, Juan sin miedo, las apariciones de mujeres con caras de caballo, los tesoros escondidos y las llamas que los anunciaban o las ánimas que los protegían. El pasado y el futuro se concretaban no como intrahistoria, que se conoce casi siempre por medio del estudio, sino como intrasensibilidad que se conoce por medio de la sensibilidad creada e imaginada. El recuerdo cada vez untado de imaginación fue capaz de proyectar esta intrasensibilidad.

Al recordar y al contar, el elemento imaginativo y la sensibilidad se elaboraron, se prepararon y se inventaron. Así, fue esto no solamente intrasensibilidad sino intrainventividad. [Esta capacidad se le pasó a los niños. La capacidad inventiva se volvió realidad y de esta manera se fertilizó para el descubrimiento.] El recuerdo revela una vida, revela una imaginación, y así es una especie de incubación.[3]

What I should like to discuss here is the ritual of remembering as a basis for a living culture for the Chicano of today. Chicano literature has many currents and facets, and within its complexity are contained distinct strata and orientations. In my perception, what Chicano writers strive for most is the capturing of a fast-disappearing past—the conserving of past experiences, real or imagined, through articulation. But to me the past is now, as well. There exists in Chicano literature both an external and an internal preoccupation with the past. I might add that it is not mere nostalgia brought about through a disillusionment with what has happened, nor a disorientation within a value system nor the exploding of the myth or a moral government; but, rather, it is a ritual from which to derive and maintain a sense of humanity—a ritual of cleansing and a prophecy.

As stated before, I have known and have come to feel a bond with most Chicano writers. The poets cited below are personal acquaintances of mine, and whenever I read from their works, I participate fully in their intentions. For me they evoke my people. One comes to realize that we must love those with whom we live, those with whom we share.

La casa, el barrio and *la lucha* are constant elements in the ritual of Chicano literature. I shall start with *la casa* as one of three parts in this ritual. *La casa* is to me the most beautiful word in the Spanish language. It evokes the constant refuge, the constant father, the constant mother. It contains the father, the mother and the child. It is also beautiful because it demonstrates the strong connection between an image in the mind and an external form. The following poems recall for me those constant presences and this connection. The first is by Alurista, the most prolific of Chicano poets and one who has manifested and captured the binary spirit of the Chicano experience in his bilingual poetry.

la casa de mi padre

la casa de mi padre
    la de las alcobas mil
my people will sleep
    cama de piedra
tierra mojada—our floor
    y palmas verdes—our roof
the cantos
    corridos y jaranas
    boleros
    baladas tristes
and the melancholia of our passion
    to announce our arrival
la hacienda
    y sus portones abiertos
open and waiting for La Raza
    to swell
    in space
to draw from
    and shape
    dimensions three
en la casa de mi padre[4]

Continuing with the constant theme of *la casa*, the following is a poem by Ricardo Sánchez, a poet from El Paso, Texas. He begins his poem with the word "recuerdo." It is a poem dedicated to his father.

Recuerdo . . .

recuerdo un viejo fuerte,
con hombros anchos, alma llena,
y palabras que iluminaban mi vida

y tal hombre era
padre mío,
fuerte y cariñoso
como lamento cantado/llorado
su consejo amoroso declamado . . .
hombre maduro y macho,
sin temor al mundo él vivía;
padre mío
puro hombre
un chicano orgulloso . . .
en aquellos tiempos . . .
cuando
los militantes presentes
eran aún conservadores.
él ya era protestador . . .

east el paso lo respetaba,
barelas albuquerque lo conoció
    él entonces era asote,
    chicano que no se cuarteaba,

era Pedro Lucero Sánchez
    su madre era Gurulé por apellido,
y él fue
casi padre del barrio del diablo en el paso;

era yonquero de los mejores,
    a nadie se le postraba,
su mundo lo admiraba . . .
    ese hombre fue mi padre

lo que hoy me puede, carnales,
es tristeza del corazón—
el día que lo entierraron [sic]
yo estaba hundido en prisión . . . [5]

"La jefita" by José Montoya is representative of the many poems written about the Chicano mother, *abnegada*, whose great warmth and strength have contributed to the solidarity of the family. In the following poem, the poet also remembers that one person who provided strength—*la jefita*, the dear one, the dear little mother.

La jefita

When I remember the campos
    Y las noches and the sounds
Of those nights en carpas o
Vagones I remember my jefita's
    Palote
    Clik-clok; clik-clak-clok
    Y su tocesita.
(I swear, she never slept!)
Reluctant awakenings a la media
Noche y la luz prendida.
    PRRRRRRINNNNGGGGGG!
A noisy chorro missing the
    Basín.
¿Qué horas son, 'amá?
Es tarde mi hijito. Cover up
Your little brothers.
Y yo con pena but too sleepy,
    Go to bed little mother!
A maternal reply mingled with
The hissing of hot planchas
Y los frijoles de la hoya
boiling musically dando segunda
a los ruidos nocturnos and
The snores of the old man
    Lulling sounds y los perros
Ladrando—then the familiar
Hallucinations just before sleep.
    And my jefita was no more.
But by then it was time to get Up!
My old man had a chiflidito
That irritated the world to
Wakefulness.

    Wheeeeeee! Wheeeeeee!

¡Arriba, cabrones chavalos,
Huevones!
    Y todavía la pinche
    Noche oscura
Y la jefita slapping tortillas.
      ¡Prieta! Help with the lonches!
      ¡Caliéntale agua a tu 'apá!
(¡Me la rayo ése! My jefita never slept!)
Y en el fil, pulling her cien
Libras de algodón se sonreía
Mi jefe y decía,
      That woman—she only complains
      in her sleep.[6]

Then we come to the third person contained within the concept of *la casa*—the child. The following poem by Alurista recalls the Chicano infant. Alurista also proclaims he will ensure that the child will smile in the sun.

chicano infante

envidio tu sonrisa
    rojos labios
    tiernos
envidio tu pelo
    sedosos mechones
    húmedos
envidio tu sudor
    beautiful child
brown eyed sun
    on the pyramid of joy
    contemplating
    Chicano infante
    niño de ilusión
envidio tu pureza
    tu candor
    tu gloria
tú eres feliz
    y lo serás
serás feliz
    y nadie
       ningún humano

nunca
        no lo permitiré
i won't allow it
i will protest
        i will yell
and you will hear
        and you will know
que no me dejo
and that you
you that are
        and your happiness spills
you will continue
        in your purity
        in your candor
        in your bliss
        in your happiness
objeto de envidia
tú eres
y lo serás
i will see to that
—you will smile (in the sun)[7]

These poems are representative of the Chicano poet's intent not only to remember an obligation but to recall the sources of strength, the original elements from which he came and from which he can once again regain that strength.

El barrio is another beautiful word that evokes a constant element in the lives of Chicanos. I have yet to know a chicano who dislikes or who is not moved by Raul Salinas' "a trip through the mind jail," wherein the *barrio* is an important protagonist in giving, conserving and cleansing the poet. Every Chicano poet I have read has written a poem directly or indirectly conceived with *el barrio* in mind. Perhaps to some literary critics this would be a *flaqueza*, but again the Chicano writer is involved in a ritual that takes him back to primal and basic elements of a specific people. Of the many poems dedicated to the *barrio*, I have chosen two: one from Alurista, "nuestro barrio," and one by Raul Salinas, "Journey II."

nuestro barrio

nuestro barrio
        en las tardes de paredes grabadas

los amores de pedro con virginia
en las tardes
                barriendo
dust about
        swept away in the wind of our breath
el suspiro de dios por nuestras calles
        gravel side streets of solitude
        the mobs from the tracks are coming
en la tarde
        mientras don josé barre su acera
        mientras dios respira vientos secos
                en el barrio sopla la vejez de chon
        y la juventud de juan madura
en la tarde de polvo
        el recuerdo de mi abuelo
        —de las flores en su tumba
        dust
                polvosas flores
blowing free to powdered cruces[8]

Journey II

They're tearing down the old school
        wherein i studied as a child
                Our Lady of Guadalupe ...
Parochial prison/Internment camp for
        underprivileged Mexican kids,
                soon to be pummeled by
merciless wrecking ball.
        What do i remember best?
        What childhood mem'ries
cling stubbornly to the brain
        like bubble-gum under a table?

        Saturday afternoon Confession:
(it was no sweat giving up the li'l tadpole sins,
        spittin' out the big bullfrogs was the hassle.)
                unlit & cramped confessional closet
with only shadowy profile of Padre José,
        ever ready to impose heavy

Our Father/Hail Mary sentence.
Catechism: Doctrina classes after school
    First Holy Communion Day!
        (i ingest
one of many sacraments to come
    & speak to the galaxies)
    white suit/padrino Chris/a ride in
        Posey's pre-war '38 Buick
The twins: Boffo & me fantazise,
    grown up—slaying dragons—planting corn
        if they would marry us.
Climbing, zooming heavenward, up rickety
    stairs into chamber of horrors/haunted
        house of learning . . . viewed by un-
suspecting boyzngirlz as transylvanian
    castle of doom.
        "No, 'Minga, those weren't black
ghosts flying around on lofty 5th floor
    balustrade, just Sisters' penguin-like
        habits; hanging out to dry."
The unforgettable recital: tribute to John Phillip
    Sousa, in abandoned subterranean lunchroom.
        All dress'd up like cadets. I played the
triangle. Big deal! The seamstress goofed on
    my uniform. Each time triangle went . . . ting!
        . . . oversized trousers slipped down
another inch. Trusty blue/gray lunchbox:
    opened many a coin slot
        on schoolyard bullies' heads.

Singing "God Bless America": would you believe?
    Competing for the lead with my friend Fernando . . . The
    one who, like Nash & cousin Albino, never
        returned that Saturday; from gathering palms
        for Palm Sunday . . . crushed beneath grinding
locomotive wheels.
    How unreal it all seems now.
    They MUST have gone to heaven;
how could any God deny them entrance?
    Such beautiful people . . . young plants
        who never lived to blossom.

With their deaths life lost all meaning.
    Fernando: my competitor in song—Albino: cohort
        in chasing girls—Nash: (good ol' thoughtful
           Nash)
never once forgot my birthday.
    How unfair ... unkindly
        they were stripped from my being.
"if only good people go to heaven when they die,
        i done blew my chance of ever seeing them again."

        Strutting birdbreast stuck way out, smoking
WINGS cigarettes. Great big eyes for Juanita what's-
    her-name. Treating demure Catholic young ladies
        to unpaid-for Kress's 5 & 10¢ birthstone rings
inducing them to smoke ... too soon busted!
    Reprimanded.
    Forced to kneel prostrate before giant crucifix and
        Sister Hermaneda. Tender knuckles kissed by
wooden ruler. Sorry, wrong rumba.
    Carlin's Place: our crowd o'rowdies jitterbugging
        me watching
"You got to ac-cen-tuate the positive, e-li-mi-nate the
    negative, don' mes with Mr. in-between."
    Sounds: Mercer, Woody & The Duke
"Couldn't make it without you, don't get around
    much anymore."

    A thousand merry harlequins dance happily/
nostalgically inside my head.
    The families whose sons n' daughters
        became priests & nuns.
I wonder what percentage of us
    turned nomadic children
        of the streets?
AGNES MARIE: because you were who you were
    i'd name a daughter after you, i still possess the
        comic valentine you sent me. The one of a
gawky/gangly gal in bathing suit & water-wings, which
read: "Lissen punk, you be mine or i'm sunk!"
    So many times i've seen you as i turned a corner/
    crossed a street, in so many different cities, but—

unlike Dante—the you i saw was never really you.

    The 1st hip priest encountered—Father Busch—
Father Green was also pretty much aware;
    in that long ago, before the era of NOW clergymen:
      BRIGANTI & GOERTZ.
"Polished Pebbles": worn-out operetta
    year-in-year-out performance by seniors
      at uptight Knights of Columbus Hall.
To this day i've yet to know
    who penned that lame libretto of corn!

    The sandpile in back of Joseph's Garage
the little pasture at the French Legation:
    first experiments with sex conducted there.
      Josie luring us to Confederate Cemetery for
advanced lessons. i chicken out and run. So,
    wherever you may be J., i apologize.
      i just wasn't ready.

Sister Armela:
    i've got news for you;
      Ivory Soap Don't Taste Worth A Damn!
And all i ever said was DAMN!!!
    The busted water fountain which i didn't bust.
      Ask God, He'll tell you i didn't do it.
Snitchin' Teresa said i did.

    E-X-P-U-L-S-I-O-N!

    Retaliation/paintbrush in hand/no longer
dull abandoned lunchroom. Red paint on sickly-green walls.
    Me an' my rappie—Joe Giddy—decorate the dingy
      cellar and defy the Gods.

"CATCH ME IF YOU CAN, YOU'LL NEVER TAKE
    ME
    ALIVE."—signed Mr. X ... "GOD IS DEAD AND
      BURIED
IN THIS DINER THAT NEVER FED ANYONE." "THE
EASTSIDE TERRORS STRIKE AGAIN."

> Yeah, i did it,
> you shoulda' never kicked me out, father.
> i loved the school in my own way.
> Even if it was mostly prayers, i still learned something.
> There's still a couple of guys
> i'm pretty tight with/communicate with: like
> Ol' St. Jude Thaddeus, who's had Miz' Hill.
> on her knees there 36 years;
> & St. Dismas, he's one of the fellows.
> He *knew* what was happening!
>
> There's more ... much more ... an infinite voyage
> on a route paved with invaluable gems
> to treasure forever.
> When i was out last time, i visited the old school
> once again. It had changed some. A section of
> the old spook house facade was gone, a modern
> cracker-box was in its place. i would have lingered
> to catch a few vibrations of that other world, but
> i was a sick poet that day. My only concern
> was the 4 caps of medicine someone had left under
> a rock for me. i thought of going back the next day.
>
> A prior commitment with the courts of law
> made this impossible.
> i won't be there for the razing,
> but i'll return when i'm an aged, wizened man.
> When freedom doves are on the wing again,
> i must go back and savor long the taste
> of spirits from another era (long before
> the fall of innocence), upon my famished heart.
>
> And if there is a parking lot
> erected on that sacred spot
>
> i'll blow it up with dynamite
>
> and think of everything
> it meant to me ... [9]

The third element, *la lucha*, is not only linked to but encompasses *la casa* and *el barrio*. *La lucha* is a struggle of cultures, dignified and undignified, a struggle of man and that which he creates, a struggle to tear away one's own masks and discover oneself. Most of all it is the struggle with exterior and interior inconsistencies that both repress and call forth powerful, centuries-old human frailties. This struggle, this will to continue, is also a constant element in Chicano literature. The difficulty is maintaining a human base through the struggle as one confronts other men and one's own "other."

The following are three poems by two Chicano poets, Alurista and Sergio Elizondo. The poems by Alurista, "must be the season of the witch" and "mis ojos hinchados," are freedom cries in the struggle between cultures and technology. The poem "My Tale" is from a Chicano epic poem, *Perros y Anti-Perros* by Elizondo, in which a Chicano in remembering unmasks himself and becomes the sum of his own circumstances.

My Tale

I move now
to Augusts of Great Wars
that tremble my breast
and dance my heart.
In a French stable
    a stone shack
    wine from dark bottles
I celebrate my freedom.
Shoulder patches their thing,
    rifles,
    bread

I sing my Chicano epic,
Chigueasumadre the world
and long live the
    so-called American democracy!
a hundred skirmishes I leaped in
    where the "cousins" couldn't,
against other wretched men
    who owed me nothing.
in faith,
new lustre upon my bronze,
I prattled in English.
I chowed down in gringo,
Lots of down, lots of up

plenty of money,
I rode cars:
The Miller band took me,
in trombones and saxophones
to the arms of the first [gringa]
and I said: "Aquí chingo."
They paraded all to hell
    in New York.
I and my body, alone.

Awaiting burial.
They denied me that in Three Rivers Texas.
The olive and arrow Eagle
buried me sacred.
But I and my ancient spirit
roam the land of my fathers.

    Brother, hand me the lira,
you with the twelve-string.
I have no hymn of glory . . .
let's see what we make of this.
I.
A soldier I went,
A man I returned.

    Dark through my parents'
        wings of passion,
    darker through the sun
        of my labors,
    white through the eyes
        of the Virgin,
    hot like the red chile.

She.
Rocks in the curves of her walking
Sings when she speaks.
In her brown skin
the sun burned the honey,
and
in her eyes,
the warmth of bees

that hover in the roses.

Friend: I have everything.
From now on,
the grapes that await me
    in the fields
friends of my harmony,
with tender hands
I caress as sisters.
Adam and Eve
two in one
in all these years
    they call history,
I am an Israeli
    of my vineyards.
I have a knife
for the sunglassed fatman
who guards my back
while silently
I work,
and peek ever slyly
at my girl.

Grapes of love
    I feel you leave me;
today I prefer
    my valiant self
and will no more complain.
Goodbye, goodbye, boss fatman,
I got things to do,
Chicana my soul,
gringos in my pockets,
a car at my side
like the eagle when I pounce
Now! Chingueasumadre, friend!
On the walls of my barrio
in big letters,
I write
so my eyes can delight:
I live, I enjoy, I fuck,
I love,

I take,
and on the corners
a 'Juana joint.
They cannot reach me,
I fly
and even if it is
the badges with new guns,
I leave them behind
and tell them
you-know-what,
while I paint myself CON SAFOS.[10]

must be the season of the witch

must be the season of the witch
 la bruja
 la llorona
she lost her children
 and she cries
en las barrancas of industry
 her children
devoured by computers
and the gears
must be the season of the witch
 i hear huesos crack
in pain
 y lloros
la bruja pangs
 sus hijos han olvidado
la magia de durango
 y la de moctezuma
 —el huiclamina
must be the season of the witch
la bruja llora
sus hijos sufren; sin ella[11]

mis ojos hinchados

mis ojos hinchados

flooded with lágrimas
de bronce
melting on the cheek bones
of my concern
  razgos indígenas
the scars of history on my face
  and the veins of my body
that aches
  vomita sangre
y lloro libertad
  i do not ask for freedom
i am freedom
  no one
not even yahweh
  and his thunder
can pronounce
  and on a stone
la ley del hombre esculpir
  no puede
mi libertad
and the round tables
  of ice cream
    hot dog
  meal ball lovers meet
to rap
  and rap
and i hunger
  y mi boca está seca
el agua cristalina
  y la verdad
  transparent
in a jarro
  is never poured
dust gathers on the shoulders
  of dignitaries
y de dignidad
  no saben nada
muertos en el polvo
  they bite the earth
and return
  to dust[12]

The ritual, the fiesta of the living I have presented here as a personal account of Chicano literature, may not be accepted by Chicano writers or critics; yet to me the act of writing is a personal ritual, a constant means of establishing contact with humanity and with one's origins. The ritual is simple yet complex. The bond is there, the cleasing is there, both for the Chicano writer and for his reader. These effects of the ritual are produced through simple forms such as *la casa* and *el barrio* and by the transgressive and ingressive concept of *la lucha*. Chicano literature presently dwells to a great degree on the past, whatever the genre, and is a remembering of our common human origins through the three specific elements discussed above. I do not think that literature is necessarily better when it speaks about man in general. Rather, I believe literature to be at its best when dealing with a specific individual. I do not mean that Chicano literature should have a "regional" or "costumbrista" basis but rather a profound *indagación* beyond these attitudes. It should, by drawing upon cultural origins, provide a perception of the world, of people, of oneself in awe of one's own life and its perplexities, its complexities and its beauty. At present, Chicano literature is specific for the most part, and more and more provides a profound, lasting focus upon a personal perception. It beckons one to the source.

> I am like a drunkard, I suffer, I cry
> I say and recall
> May I never perish, may I never die!
>
> Where there is no death, where one wins I go:
> May I never perish, may I never die![13]

Notes

[1] "In awe of the *other*" implies specific and general philosophical points of view. I make reference to becoming cognizant of the expansive and evolving thought, in our era, on this matter; the *other* in the bosom of reason itself, as the object of the sentimental and instinctive ego, as the moral activity of the ego, as found in the dialectics of the subjective spirit and the dialectics of nature, as an invention of the ego, as phenomenological reflection, et cetera. See Laín Entralgo's *Teoría y realidad del otro.*

[2] Tomás Rivera, . . . *y no se lo tragó la tierra.*

[3] Tomás Rivera, "Recuerdo, descubrimiento y voluntad" (From a paper presented at a Symposium on "Tomás Rivera and Chicano Literature," Indiana University, Bloomington, 14–15 April 1972). [Published in English and Spanish, and collected in the present edition. For the English translation of this passage see "Remembering, Discovery and Volition in the Literary Imaginative Process."]

[4] Alurista, "La casa de mi padre," *Floricanto en Aztlán*, (Los Angeles: Chicano Cultural Center, UCLA, 1971): 27.

[5]Ricardo Sánchez, "Recuerdo," *Canto y grito mi liberación*, (El Paso: Mictla, 1971): 63.

[6]José Montoya, "La jefita," *Aztlan, An Anthology of Mexican American Literature*, Stan Steiner and Luis Valdez, Eds. (New York: Vintage Books, 1972): 266–68.

[7]Alurista, "Chicano infante," *Floricanto*, 54.

[8]Ibid., "Nuestro barrio," 87.

[9]Raul Salinas, "Journey II," *Voices of Aztlan, Chicano Literature of Today*, D. Harth and L. Baldwin, Eds. (New York: Mentor, 1974): 192–96.

[10]Sergio Elizondo, "My Tale," *El espejo/The Mirror*, Herminio Ríos and Octavio Romano, Eds. (Berkeley, Ca.: Quinto Sol, 1972, 2nd ed.): 221–25.

[11]Alurista, "Must Be the Season of the Witch," *Floricanto*, 26.

[12]Alurista, "Mis ojos hinchados," *El grito*, 2.1 (1968): 3.

[13]"Brief Song from the Nahuatl," Rafael Jesús Gonzales, Trans. *El grito*, 5.1 (Fall 1971): 14.

Recuerdo, Descubrimiento y Voluntad en el Proceso Imaginativo Literario

En mi obra ... *y no se lo tragó la tierra* puse el énfasis en el recuerdo, en el descubrimiento y en la expresión de la voluntad. Fue mi empeño en que una voz colectiva expresara esta síntesis para que así diera fuerza a la idea de que siempre habíamos sido y éramos personas completas, y también reflejar que ahora que buscábamos la forma abstracta que representase a esta persona completa, se revelara no solo el empeño como humanamente total sino la propia persona Chicana como eso. Al repasar mis años de trabajador migratorio se me reveló la propia vida como esto —recuerdo, descubrimiento y voluntad.

Primeramente quisiera hacer algunas observaciones sobre el tipo de personas que se presentan en mi obra. Los personajes están ligados a la economía norteamericana como *migrant workers*. No creo que sea necesario presentarles las estadísticas del número de personas que en realidad se metieron o fueron metidas a los llamados trabajos migratorios. Las estructuras políticas y económicas que circundaban la vida de estas familias estará siempre en la historia como algo brutal, inaudito e inhumano. Quizás si se revelara todo, se observaría esta trágica página de la historia norteamericana como lo más funesto de un sistema frío, materialista y realmente inhumano. Hoy día existen aún los trabajadores migratorios pero en menos cantidad y ya con algunas protecciones por la ley. Pero, en fin, el trabajador migratorio siempre fue y seguirá siendo víctima de todos. Fueron y tal vez serán estas personas peores que esclavos. El esclavo es una inversión y se le protege. El trabajador migratorio nunca tuvo ninguna protección porque realmente no era ninguna inversión para el explotador y así trabajaba bajo las condiciones de la esclavitud, menos los beneficios más rudimentarios.

Sin embargo, ¿por qué es que no se nuló o no sufrió este hombre un anonadamiento completo? Creo que todo hombre le tiene amor a la tierra, así como al prójimo. La engendra. Le da y le saca vida. No obstante, el ser Chicano, al hincarse sobre la tierra y al engendrarla, le sacó y le dio vida. Sintió así una existencia simbiótica con la tierra y, si no comprendió las estructuras políticas, económicas o sociales que le circundaban y que trataban de reflejarlo, sí comprendió su propia relación con las realidades de la tierra, del sol, del viento y del agua. Sí comprendió también sus

From *Atisbos: Journal of Chicano Research* 1(1975): 66–77.

propias relaciones entre su gente y sintió algo más. Aunque las condiciones exteriores fueran inhumanas, el ser Chicano no se deshumanizó, al contrario, se hizo más humano. Mientras existió esta relación con la tierra el Chicano no se deshumanizó. Aunque se diera cuenta de que el ambiente exterior fuese inaguantable, siempre halló refugio en su propia gente y en la tierra quienes no le abandonaron. Hasta cierto punto rechazó también el sistema exterior, ya que se dio cuenta de que bajo ese sistema en que tenía que vivir, no había alguna indicación de que hubiera ganancias al actuar humanamente, ni al querer al prójimo sin interés. Este es el tipo de personaje que traté de representar en mi obra.

Las Raíces de la Literatura Chicana

Pasando ahora a la literatura chicana, ¿cuáles han sido las raíces de esta literatura? No podemos aseverar que esta literatura se empeñe en representar solo el ambiente rural. Este ambiente es solamente una raíz del barrio, etc. Creo que las raíces más auténticas de la literatura Chicana sean las del barrio y las del ambiente rural. Estas se han sentido y se han inventado mientras aquéllas que se vinculan a lo indígena o a lo mexicano a lo mejor solamente se han inventado, desde luego que no se niega aquí su autenticidad. Hay impulsos en todas las formas, en todas los géneros.

La literature chicana es un esfuerzo en darle forma, armonía, y unidad a la vida chicana porque se manifiesta ésta como vida que vale mientras esté sobre la tierra. Y así florecen el arte chicano, la literatura chicana, el drama —en fin se inventa y se futuriza el chicano como un ser humanamente total. Esto es de gran importancia para el suroeste, ya que es inconcebible la humanización de esta región sin la actuación propia de este segmento de la población de esta región. Pero, ¿por cuáles procesos se lleva a cabo la invención y la furturización?

El Recuerdo: Un Método de Narrar

En mi obra hice hincapié en los procesos del recuerdo, del descubrimiento y de la voluntad. Primeramente esto del recuerdo. Me refiero al método de narrar que usaba la gente. Es decir, recuerdo lo que ellos recordaban y la manera en que narraban. Siempre existía una manera de comprimir y exaltar una sensibilidad con mínimas palabras. También existía constantemente el inventarle nuevas ocurrencias. Esto, claro está, es lo que elabora la tradición oral. Aunque muchos de aquellos padres que andaban en los trabajos eran analfabetos, el sistema narrativo predominaba. Siempre había alguien que sabía los cuentos viejos —del gigante moro, del negrito güerín, etc. Luego, había siempre aquellas personas que interpretaban películas, que narraban sobre partes distintas del mundo, y siempre los cuentos de Aladín y su lámpara maravillosa. De esta manera, en los campos migratorios, se desarrolló una literatura oral. La gente busca refugio no solamente en la iglesia, o con sus hermanos, sino también al sentarse en ruedo y escuchar y narrar, y por medio de palabras escaparse a otros mundos, e inventarse también. Desde luego en los niños se desarrolló también una especie de mundo narrativo y en el tedio del trabajo de cada día se cristalizaron mundos.

Las narraciones orales se formulaban también sobre México, o sobre las costumbres, sobre la revolución de 1910. También, desde luego, se formulaban sobre lo fantasmagórico, los espantos, las ánimas, la llorona, el diablo, Juan sin miedo, las apariciones de mujeres con caras de caballo, los tesoros escondidos y las llamas que los anunciaban o las ánimas que los protegían. El pasado y el futuro se concretaban no como intrahistoria, que se conoce casi siempre por medio del estudio, sino como intrasensibilidad que se conoce por medio de la sensibilidad creada e imaginada. El recuerdo cada vez untado de imaginación fue capaz de proyectar esta intrasensibilidad.

Al recordar y al contar y al recontar, el elemento imaginativo y la sensibilidad se elaboraron, se prepararon y se inventaron. Así, fue esto no solamente intrasensibilidad sino intrainventividad. El recuerdo revela una vida, revela una imaginación, y así es aun una especie de incubación.

El Descubrimiento de Realidad

Usé en mi obra deliberadamente a personajes jóvenes o niños por la mayor parte. No cabe duda de que el major y más puro descubrimiento es el del niño que descubre su propia vida. Y, ¿qué es lo que aprecia más el niño sino la calidad, lo lógico, una narrativa real en la manera de que se ha narrado por tantos siglos? El niño por naturaleza se inclina al misticismo, pero a la vez requiere una consistencia verídica. Así, el niño en los trabajos migratorios se pone consciente de una intrasensibilidad y de la manera narrativa pero, claro, en su propia lengua o dialecto.

Hay que investigar más esto de la consistencia y esto del descubrimiento. No existe literatura sin raíces. No creo que se pueda escribir ficción buena acerca de algún hombre en general. Creo que en la literatura todo se unta de lo específico. Entre más esté el hombre en su ambiente, mejor se comprende por todos. Entre más nacional sea, más international se vuelve. Claro que hay que penetrar la capa de lo típicamente regional o nacional. Es decir, cuanto más se revela el hombre específico en su elemento dialéctico y natural, más se revela su universalidad humana. Por esta razón el mundo que se les revela a los niños es tan puro. Se conciernen los niños con las preguntas eternas. Cuando niños creo que todos nosotros preguntamos sobre lo que después encontramos en las obras de los hombres más sabios que han vivido sobre la tierra —la cuestión de la justicia, el propósito de la vida, el sufrir, el amor, etc.

El niño chicano así como cada hombre en su ambiente específico descubre ciertas realidades —a su familia, la lengua, lo propio. También, descubre las relaciones familiares, los principios de la iglesia. En fin se le presenta su mundo cultural, un mundo cultural que acoge, que reconstruye, en el que vive. Luego, llega a comprender las relaciones de los pueblos, de los barrios. Luego, cuando menos lo espera se le presenta la realidad de la ideología norteamericana. Y no es que no la haya percibido anteriormente, sino que percibía todo aquel mundo como un *film* —real pero no real, experiencia vicaria. De esta manera cae el niño en el descubrimiento de América.

El Niño Chicano: Un Colón Verdadero

El descubrimiento de América y de los "americanos" es algo desarraigador. El niño migratorio descubrió las estratas sociales. Descubre el sentir del no tener, del no deber ser, del no deber estar. El sistema educativo se le revela como una estructura en la cual él no debe estar, en la cual no debe ser pero en la cual se le obliga participar. Aquí hay peligro. Puede ocurrir una depersonalización. Ocurre y no ocurre. No ocurre cuando al estar al margen de las estructuras y al obligarse a la participación no necesariamente cae al limbo sino que llega a buscar y a encontrar refugio en el recuerdo. Y esto no es proceso perdido ya que puede ser período de incubación.

Permítanme elaborar esto del recuerdo y del descubrimiento de América con algunas observaciones personales. Pasé por una tradición oral. Antes del descubrimiento de América traía conmigo cuentos, narraciones, ideas sobre modales, en fin, una cultura ya bastante desarrollada para haber podido existir en paz con el prójimo respetándolo y a la vez amándolo. Sin embargo, desde el primer día en que me metí al mundo inglés, me encontré con ese mundo estructurado, prefabricado para mí, dentro de libros, dentro de palabras extrañas, dentro de otras sensibilidades. Recuerdo que ya en el primer año de universidad tenía que maravillarme en las novelas de Rölvaag en que se exaltaba la lucha entre los elementos naturales y los imigrantes suecos de Minnesota. A la vez reconocía que por lo que pasaban aquellos personajes de novela.

lo estábamos pasando nosotros en la vida real. Lo que tenía que vivir vicariamente era una realidad fuera de la estructura educacional. En mí la evolución fue, entonces, de la tradición oral a la tradición vicaria, luego al reconocimiento de que lo que debería ser vicario para el Chicano era en fin una realidad.

La Fuerza de Voluntad

Regresando al niño chicano, el niño del no tener, del no deber ser, del no deber estar. De este aparente anonadamiento brota una desesperación casi incontrolable, pero de aquí también se fortalece y se comprime la intrasensibilidad. Y de allí fuerza de voluntad. De la desesperación brota la esperanza a la fuerza de seguir viviendo. El proceso de descubrimiento, al pasar por las etapas de preparación, de incubación, y de iluminación antes de volverse verificación, se rompe. Es esta rotura la que hace que brote la fuerza volitiva, si es que no se depersonalice el niño. Al llegar a la ruptura es normal que haya un recogimiento a la etapa de preparación, de incubación y de iluminación. Es decir, en la ruptura no se pierde nada. En realidad se fortalece la preparación para el descubrimiento. Se examina la preparación oral, la incubación, y la iluminación. Se llega a comprender que todos estos procesos contribuyen a una persona completa y no solamente a una estructuración material fuera de la persona. Queda así el último paso, la verificación de esta persona completa en alguna estructura fuera de la propia.

En mi obra traté de preparar, de incubar, de iluminar y por fin de descubrir. De estos procesos pensé que saldría la voluntad. Creo que buscamos ahora mismo el último paso. Ya habiendo pasado por las etapas de preparación oral, de incubación y de iluminación, queremos ahora verificarnos en formas exteriores. Este impulso es un esfuerzo volitivo. Existe así un complemento entre recuerdo, descubrimiento y voluntad. El recuerdo y el descubrimiento del propio ser llevan a la fuerza volitiva, no obstante las estructuras que se le impongan. Hay que recordar que la literatura Chicana es solamente un esfuerzo entre tantos que señala el desarrollo intelectual de la raza y que subraya también los rasgos propios.

El Proceso Imaginativo

El recuerdo y el descubrimiento del Chicano migratorio pasaron por una etapa de incubación, de fermentación, de recogimiento en los procesos imaginativos. No obstante, al imponérsele las estructuras norteamericanas a estos procesos, en los cuales la lengua es de gran importancia, es evidente que las estructuras no pudieron romper la imaginación del Chicano y así no rompieron la intersensibilidad de la raza. No la rompieron porque al imponerse las estructuras norteamericanas con tanta fuerza y sin lógica, se intensificaron los procesos imaginativos, y así se exaltó y se reveló una voluntad.

En el último cuento de mi obra, *...y no se lo tragó la tierra*, "Debajo de la casa," el niño recuerda y descubre. Recuerda el año anterior. Pero también recuerda que existen otros años. También descubre que el existir es en fin una relación entre el recuerdo y el descubrimiento constante. Pero aún da otro paso más. Inventa. Se inventa. Al llegar a su casa se sube en un árbol. En el horizonte ve una palma. Se imagina que alguien está allí viéndole a él y por eso es que le saluda moviendo el brazo para atrás y para adelante. Esta acción respaldada en la inventividad y entre la intrasensibilidad es pura fuerza volitiva, es fuerza de voluntad que subraya una acción ya física.

Cualquiera que se meta a descubrir su propia vida por medio del recuerdo creo que encontrará la fuerza volitiva de inventarse continuamente como deseante de amar a todo hombre sobre la tierra. Unamuno, el gran filósofo español, nos dice que el hombre está deseante de Dios, que tiene un constante deseo de que exista un Dios. Thoreau, el gran pensador norteamericano, nos dice que todo hombre vive ideas de desesperación. ¿Por qué no subrayar también que lo más humano del hombre es poseer el deseo de amar al prójimo, al otro? Es por eso que puse énfasis en el recuerdo, en el descubrimiento y en la expresión de la voluntad. Estos procesos pueden llevar al deseo anterior. Quizás la literatura Chicana revele este empeño, sin embargo, al no ser así, sí revela al Chicano como persona completa. La intrasensibilidad, la propia invención, el recuerdo, el descubrimiento son procesos personales, de la persona. Todo esto es algo sagrado. Y es nuestro.

Remembering, Discovery and Volition
in the Literary Imaginative Process
🌿

In my work, ... *y no se lo tragó la tierra*, I emphasized remembering, discovery and the expression of the will. It was my intent that a collective voice should express that synthesis to reenforce the idea that we had always been and were complete persons and also to demonstrate that, as we search for the abstract form which represents this complete person, the effort should reveal itself as not only humanly total but also as distinctly Chicano. Recalling my years as a migrant worker, life itself was revealed to me in this way—remembering, discovery and volition.

First of all, I would like to make a few observations regarding the type of characters which appear in my work. They are tied to the American economy as "migrant workers." I do not think it necessary to present you with the statistics regarding the number of people who in reality got into or were forced into migratory work. The political and economic structures which surrounded the lives of these families will always appear in history as something brutal, outrageous and inhuman. Perhaps if everything were revealed, this tragic page in American history would be observed as the most pernicious in a cold, materialistic, and most inhuman system. Migrant workers still exist today but in fewer numbers and now have some protection by the law. But, in the long run, the migrant worker always was and always will be exploited. These people were and perhaps may be worse off than slaves. The slave is an investment and is protected. The migrant worker never had any protection because he was really not an investment for the exploiter and thus worked under the conditions of slavery without the most rudimentary benefits.

Nevertheless, why is it that this man did not suffer complete annihilation? I think that man has a love for the land as well as for his neighbor. He engenders it. He gives love and from it generates life. Notwithstanding, the Chicano, when he knelt upon the land and engendered love, generated and gave it life. He thus felt a symbiotic existence with the land and if he did not understand the political, economic, and social systems that surrounded him and that tried to structure him, he did understand his own relationship with the realities of the land, the sun, the wind, and the water. He also understood his own relationship among his people and felt something more. Although the exterior conditions were inhuman,

From *Atisbos: Journal of Chicano Research* 1 (1975): 66–77.

the Chicano did not become dehumanized; on the contrary, he became more human. As long as this relationship with the land existed, the Chicano was not dehumanized. Even though he realized that the external environment was unbearable, he always found refuge in that which never abandoned him—his own people and the land. To a certain point, he also rejected the external system since he realized that under the system in which he had to live, no indication was given to him that there would be any rewards for acting human or for loving his neighbor unselfishly. This is the type of character I tried to portray in my work.

The Roots of Chicano Literature

Going on to Chicano literature, What have been the roots of this literature? We cannot assert that it insists on representing only the rural environment. This ambient is only a root. There are other—the pre-Cortezian, the Mexican, the *barrio*, etc. I think that the most authentic roots of Chicano literature are those which deal with the *barrio* and rural surroundings. These have been felt and have been created, while the others, which are related to the Indian or to the Mexican, perhaps have only been invented, which does not negate their authenticity. There are impulses in all the forms, in all the genres. Chicano literature is an attempt to give form, harmony and unity to Chicano life because, as long as Chicano life exists, it manifests itself as meaningful. And thus Chicano art, literature and drama appear—in short, the Chicano creates himself and his future as a humanly total being. This is of great importance for the Southwest since the humanization of this region is inconceivable without the proper actuation of this segment of the population. But, by what methods are invention and futurization achieved?

Remembering: A Method of Narration

In my work I emphasized the processes of *remembering, discovery and volition.* I will discuss remembering first, I refer to the method of narrating which the people used. That is to say, I recall what they remembered and the manner in which they told it. There was always a way of compressing and exciting the sensibilities with a minimum of words. New events were also being constantly added. Needless to say, this is what the oral tradition is all about. Although many of the workers were illiterate, the narrative system predominated. There was always someone who knew the old traditional stories—*el gigante moro, el negrito güerin,* etc. Then there were always those who acted out movies, told about different parts of the world and about Aladdin and his magic lamp. An oral literature was, in this way, developed in migrant camps. People find refuge not only in the Church or with their brothers but also by sitting in a circle, listening, telling stories and, through words, escaping to other worlds as well as inventing them. It was natural that a type of narrative world developed in the children and worlds were crystallized because of the tedium of every-day work.

They created oral stories about Mexico, the customs or the Revolution of 1910. They also invented stories about the supernatural, ghosts, souls, *la llorona,* the devil, *Juan sin miedo,* apparitions such as women with horses' heads, hidden treasures, the flames that revealed where they were hidden and the spirits that protected these treasures. The past and the future were concretized, not as history which can be learned through study but as inner sensitivity which can be learned though creative and imaginative sensibilities. Remembering, each time abetted by imagination, was able to project this inner sensitivity.

By remembering, narrating and retelling, the imaginative element and the sensibilities were elaborated, prepared, and invented. Thus, this became not only inner sensitivity but inner inventiveness. Remembering reveals of life, an imagination and is thus still a type of incubation period.

The Discovery of Reality

I deliberately used in my work young characters or children for the most part. There is no doubt that the greatest and purist discovery is that in which a child becomes aware of himself as a person. And what does a child appreciate most if not quality, logic, a realistic story told in the tradition which has been handed down throughout the centuries. A child is naturally inclined toward mysticism, but at the same time, demands a consistent reality. Thus, the child in migrant work becomes aware of an inner sensitivity and of a way of narrating, in his own language or dialect.

It is necessary to delve further into the idea of consistency and that of discovery. Literature cannot exist without roots. I do not think it possible to write good fiction about some man in general. I think that everything is imbued with the specific. The more man is placed within his environment, the better he will be understood by all. The more national he is, the more international he will become. It is necessary to transcend that which is typically regional or national. That is to say, the more the specific man is shown in his natural and dialectic element, the more his human universality is revealed. for this reason, the world that is revealed to children is so pure. Children concern themselves with questions about the eternal. As children, I think all of us have asked ourselves about those things which we later find in the writings of the wisest men—the question of justice, the purpose of life, suffering, love, etc.

The Chicano child, as every man in his particular surroundings, discovers certain realities—family, language, things about himself. He also discovers family relationships, the teachings of the Church. In sum, he is presented with his culture, a culture he assimilates, reconstructs, and in which he lives. Later on, he learns about relationships between towns and *barrios*. Still later, when he least expects it, he is presented with the reality of American ideology. Not that he had not perceived it previously but he had seen that whole world as a film—real but not real, a vicarious experience. In this way, the child comes to discover America.

The Chicano Child: A True Columbus

The discovery of America and of Americans is somewhat shocking. The migrant child discovers social strata. He discovers the feeling of not having, of not existing, and of not belonging. The educational system is revealed to him as a structure in which he does not belong, in which he cannot exist but in which he is required to participate. There is a danger here. The child may become depersonalized. It occurs and it does not occur. Even though the child finds himself at the margin of these structures and is forced to participate in them, he does not necessarily go astray but instead looks for and finds refuge in remembering. And this is not a wasted process as it may be a period of incubation.

Allow me to elaborate on these ideas of remembering and discovering America with some personal observations. I was brought up in an oral tradition. Before my discovery of America, I carried with me stories, narrations, ideas about mores; in short, a well defined culture which enabled me to exist in peace with my neighbor, respecting him and, at the same time, loving him. Nevertheless, the first day I set foot in the Anglo world, I found myself with that structured world, prefabricated for me, within books, strange words, and other sensibilities. I recall that in the first year I was at the university, I was amazed by the novels of Rölvaag in which the struggle between nature and the Swedish immigrants of Minnesota was described. At the same time, I realized that what those characters were suffering in the novel, we were experiencing in real life. What I had to live vicariously was my reality outside of the educational structure. My evolution, then, went from the oral tradition to a vicarious tradition and then to the recognition that what should have been vicarious for the Chicano, was, in reality, life itself.

The Act of Volition

Let me return to the Chicano child, the child of not having, of not existing, and of not belonging. From this apparent nothingness, an almost uncontrollable desperation emerges while, at the same time, the inner sensitivity is fortified and compressed. And from that springs the act of volition. Hope and the will to keep on living arises from this desperation. The process of discovery, as it goes through the stages of preparation, incubation and illumination before becoming verification, is broken. If the child has not been depersonalized, it is this rupture which make the will emerge. When this rupture is reached, it is normal that the child recollect the stages of preparation, incubation and illumination before becoming verification, is broken. If the child has not been depersonalized, it is this rupture which make the will emerge. When this rupture is reached, it is normal that the child recollect the stages of preparation, incubation and illumination. That is to say, nothing is lost by the rupture; on the contrary, the preparation of discovery is fortified. The oral preparation, the incubation and the illumination are examined. The child comes to the understanding that all these processes contribute to the complete person and not only to the material structure outside of his own.

In my work, I dealt with preparation, incubation, illumination and, finally, discovery. From these processes, I thought that the will would emerge. I think that we are now searching for the final step. Having passed through the different stages, we want to verify ourselves by external forms. This desire is an act of the will. Thus, there exists a complement between remembering, discovery and volition. Remembering and discovery of oneself lead to volition, notwithstanding the structures which are imposed on it. We should recall that Chicano literature is only one effort among many which shows the intellectual development of *la raza* and emphasizes its characteristics.

The Imaginative Process

Remembering and discovery in the migrant Chicano passed through the stage of incubation, fermentation and recollection in the imaginative processes. Nevertheless, when the American structures were imposed upon these processes (in which language takes on great importance), it is evident that the structures were not able to disrupt the imagination of the Chicano and thus were not able to destroy the inner sensitivity of *la raza*. They did not destroy it because imposing the American structures so forcibly and illogically only resulted in an intensification of the imaginative processes and thus the will was nurtured and revealed.

In the last short story of my work ... *y no se lo tragó la tierra*, "Debajo de la casa," the child remembers and discovers. He remembers the previous year. But he also remembers that other years also exist. He discovers that existing is, in the long run, a relationship between remembering and constant discovery. But he goes further. He invents. He invents himself. When he gets home, he climbs a tree. He sees a palm on the horizon. He imagines that someone is there looking at him and that is why he greets him by waving his arm. This action, backed by inventiveness and within the inner sensitivity, is a purely volitional act, an act of the will that is emphasized by a physical action.

I think that anyone who seeks to discover his inner being by remembering will find the will to invent himself continually as desirous of loving all mankind. Unamuno, the great Spanish philosopher, tells us that man is desirous of God, that he has a constant desire for God to exist. Thoreau, the great American thinker, tells us that all men live lives of quiet desperation. Why not emphasize also that the most human thing possible for man is to possess the desire to love his neighbor, the other? It is because of that that I emphasized remembering, discovery and the expression of volition. These processes can lead to the aforementioned desire. Perhaps Chicano literature reveals this effort, however, if that is not so, it at least reveals the Chicano as a complete person. Inner sensitivity, self invention, remembering and discovery are personal processes. All this is something sacred. And it is ours.

Translated by Gustavo Valadez

Critical Approaches to Chicano
Literature and its Dynamic Intimacy

❦

Since the resurgence of Chicano Literature in the [19]60's, there has been an equal professional thrust to develop a critical attitude and affinity with the varied efforts by Chicano writers.[1] A nascent or renascent effort was judged almost immediately. At times it seemed that the critical effort came before the works themselves: anthologies were compiled before extensive works appeared. The critical approaches themselves differed and continue to evolve. The following is an analysis of this impetus.

Principally, there have been five types of approaches: 1) [the] structuring of the literature; 2) the Third World proletariat voice; 3) archetypal symbols and Chicano types; 4) cultural traditions and affinities; and 5) the Chicano writer and society, and *his* society in particular. In addition, the following will examine the idea of Chicano literature as fundamental knowledge and the dynamics of neutrality.

Structuring a Literature

The first attempts at criticism dealing with Chicano writings dealt primarily with the structuring of a literature: chronology, genres, perspectives, intentions, language. The writings of [Philip] Ortego, [Rolando] Hinojosa, [Luis] Leal, [Tomás] Ybarra [Frausto], Antonia Castañeda, and many of the efforts to anthologize a literature that is yet minimal[2] is and continues to be an effort to deal with control of symbols.

I believe all of us are aware that in complex societies we most commonly deal with power and symbol controls. Control gives power and provides more access to control of symbols and to other energy forms. In contemporary social science literature, the term structure appears principally as a noun or adjective. In literature, literary criticism dealing with the structuring of Chicano literature, there is a basic effort to consider structure as a verb. To say something is structured is to say that it has been taken out of someone's control. Structuring is a dynamic process present in all human activity. A physical act rests on the fact that there is cultural agreement as to content and meaning of words pronounced; there exists a legitimacy, an agreement and the recognition of an authority. The effort here, then, is to ascertain the aforementioned. Chicano

Previously unpublished

literature had to be structured. My own attempts of auto-criticism were desires to underline that we *had* a literature.

Chicano Literature as a Third World Voice

Chicano Literature is seen as an expression of a proletariat voice, perhaps a Third World voice coming from a group that, although fabricates [and] creates, grows and works in a consumer society; [and] is still desirous of, not identity, but [of] consumer goods in the most highly industrialized society in the world. The Chicano in this sense is seen as an analogy to the Third World colonized receptor. And it is hoped that the Chicano will recognize the power of the receptor.

The question or perspective becomes larger if one [applies] (critical) criteria to Chicano literature which can diffuse it and affect it pejoratively.[3] Let's make an analogy between science and technology, [and] academic and creative writing (the study of literature). Science is the search, as literature is, and technology is the academic institution, the application; and this involves the political and social world. The former is fundamental knowledge, the other is application of that knowledge. Knowledge is neutral; it is the process of understanding. What is done with knowledge is what is problematical. [Neither] the scientist nor the writer must be made into a type of priest. He/She is not. Science is part of modern culture. Society expects more and [more] from technology. It is impossible that the people understand it. Yet literature departs from the analogy at this precise point. Literature as fundamental knowledge of the human dynamics is understood by those who read. Thus there is that group of critics who search in Chicano literature such elements as change, revolutionary seeds, non-bourgeois affinities and existentialistic positions.

Symbols, Archetypes and Types

A third critical approach is one which has begun to be developed, the archetypal symbolism. [Arturo Madrid's] "In Search of the Authentic Pachuco"[4] is a brilliant approach to this type [of] critical awareness. Basically a literary approach, its impetus is to delineate all sides, attitudes and development of "characters" or "types" that appear not only in imaginative literature, but also in socio-anthropological studies. There exists, specifically in Madrid's intentions, a professional honest approach in defining said types. There is a very exact, persevering thrust to document "authentic" *stabs* at these character-types by Chicano writers.

I still recall "El Pete Fonseca," a story which I had initially included in ...*yo no se lo tragó la tierra*, being excluded from it. Both Herminio Ríos and Octavio Romano[5] were of the opinion that "Pete Fonseca," a pachuco-type, was presented in [a] derogatory manner and [was] negatively sensitive for Chicano literature at the time (December, 1970). I conceded, but "Pete Fonseca," and Don Laíto and Doña Bone ["La mano en la bolsa," *Tierra*], are my favorite characters-types which I have developed. I made and make no pretense at moral judgment and simply wanted to present them as amoral types. Judy Salinas'[6] effort in depicting "women" in Chicano literature, and Jan Gueder's[7] efforts are excellent studies of "Chicano women" developed by Chicana writers.

Culture, Tradition and Literature

In this approach, Chicano literature is seen also as an extension of a culture or cultures. It is argued that it follows traditional outlines of Hispanic attitudes, that its roots are more profound than these attitudes and are imbedded in pre-Columbian myth-archetypes, as Alurista proclaims. Its basic element may be, as stipulated by Frank Pino,[8] popular manifestoes. The social democratic spirit, non-political, at times "descuidado" [careless] is sensed as this.

In these critical approaches there is an intent to underline the idea of continuity, either of a Mexican culture or [of] a North American one. We can ask what are these cultures really? I have used the hundred-year-old Taine thesis of *race, moment, milieu*, at least to my satisfaction in attempting to delineate a continuity of the Mexican culture in Chicano literature. Charles Tatum[9] and Guillermo Rojas[10] have indicated in their studies the pervasive "Mexicanness" in several Chicano works. Not only is this pervasive because of language (Spanish in this case) but also because of styles, genres or ideologies. Most studies of this nature have attempted to prove a continuity of culture which involves Mexican, Mestizo or Hispanic elements. Not much has been indicated as to how North American culture is a continuity in Chicano literature.

The Chicano Writer and Society

Lastly, I should like to express a more recent preoccupation, and perhaps one that has been [present] all along. I refer to the perceptions revealed by [Arturo] Islas wherein Chicano literature is criticized indirectly by observing the societal pressures on the Chicano writer. No great work of fiction has been written by a group of people. Where is or what is in reality a collective spirit or consciousness? What is social consciousness? The dangers are clear. As writers and readers of Chicano literature, we must be able to differentiate between socio-political theory, philosophy and activity. There is no congruence here. Islas states that Chicano writers fall between two literary traditions, Anglo and Latin American:

> The Anglo writer may choose to become involved in political [and] social problems of the nation, but societies' notions about his role in relation to these problems do not demand a direct involvement. The Latin American resides within a context and literary tradition that doesn't allow that choice so readily. In Latin America it is assumed they will involve themselves as a matter of course with the social and political problems. When they don't, that stance is considered/perceived as a political statement and judged accordingly. Anglo American writers have not been influenced by the Latin American literary tradition; consequently, one cannot use the same criteria in judging.[11]

Does the Chicano writer, indeed, fall between two literary traditions of who *must* write Chicano literature?

Literary criticism on Chicano literature has thus addressed itself to 1) [the] structuring of the literature and gain [of] its control; 2) the pervasive social consciousness that a literature from a largely proletariat group provides; 3) the archetypes developing in the literature; 4) the extension of cultural content and the continuity [of] its roots, be they pre-Columbian or Hispanic; and 5) the Chicano writer falling into either an Anglo American or Latin American literary tradition, and consequently reflecting the literature that will be provided.

Dynamic Intimacy

All of these approaches have much significance to Chicano literature, and are indeed not surprising. I should like to reflect on one aspect that I find more and more pervasive: a dynamic intimacy. When I speak of intimacy here, I am relating the word to the notion of the human and spiritual person. This intimacy may have several characteristics, such as a) withdrawing into oneself; b) returning to oneself; c) consciousness of oneself; d) solipsistic withdrawal. None of these constitutes intimacy in my use of the term. I use the word rather as a manner of transcending oneself. "Ir hacia sí mismo" ["To go towards oneself"] does not signify that one is enough for oneself. Intimacy is not pure and simple solitude. To transcend oneself explicitly means to *tie* one's intimacy with another's.

Intimacy is paradoxical; it is a closing and it is an opening (ser en sí, ser fuera de sí [to be within oneself, to be outside oneself]). The basic dynamic intimacy elements in Chicano literature I find as the following: 1) the sense of remembering rather than an attitude of narrating; 2) the desire to present several levels of consciousness rather than one level of consciousness; 3) a presenting of a specific man/woman in a specific environment rather than attempting to represent a general or universal man; 4) more and more, attempting to present a human attitude rather than a racist, national one; 5) individual interpretations rather than a societal one; and 6) language of dialogs and the language of remembering.

Recently, Inés Tovar made me more aware of these intimate dynamics in Chicano literature.[12] At present she is writing on the whole question of aesthetics. Her questions are revealing of an attempt to get at these dynamics. Questions such as these:

1. What is man's relationship to the sacred or divine?

2. How is a writer's style integrated with his or her aesthetic?

3. What part does language play in the evolution of a Chicano aesthetic?

4. How does one determine who is a Chicano writer and who is not?

5. What does the education of a Chicano writer have to do with his aesthetic?

6. Who is a Chicano writer's audience?

7. What is the attitude of the Chicano writer to his audience?

8. What are unique Chicano literature features?

9. What is the dialectic working in your [Chicano] writing?

10. Is there a Chicano aesthetic?

Yet, I must ask: Is Chicano literature ready for all the ordeals?

The Ordeals of Civility and Chicano Literature

The ordeals of civility, as one Jewish writer puts it, are extreme. What one has to go through to appear authentic, learned, professional, critical. The ordeals of established norms are deadly, non-creative and dangerous. Especially for a new literature or for a literature that is experiencing some attention is this extremely dangerous. I almost wish that we did not have to discuss it and put it through these very ordeals.

Yet, what must/can one expect from a literature greatly developed from an academic perspective by those who have gone through these very ordeals. The study of science I equate with creative writing. Both are fundamental knowledge. The study of technology and the study of literature are applications through ordeals and are necessary. Somehow as we experience more literature written by Chicanos, we must be ever aware of the human dynamics, the dynamic intimacy of the writer and his science as fundamental knowledge. Fundamental knowledge is neutral. In literature, dynamic intimacy is found in this neutrality.

Notes

[1]I have reconstructed this article from a typescript, which is missing pp. 2–3, and an autograph version, and I have supplied the notes to this critical essay.

[2]Rivera is referring to the Chicano literature written since the 1960's. There is an extensive body of Mexican American and other U.S. Hispanic literatures written beginning with the chronicles of conquest, during the Spanish colonial period and after U.S. annexation of Mexican territories in 1848. This literature not only appears in published form—books, journals and newspapers—but as autobiographies, memoirs and other forms of testimonial literature that are continuously being recovered by scholars.

[3]The typescript and autograph have: "and pejoritize it."

[4]"In Search of the Authentic Pachuco: An Interpretive essay," *Aztlan* 4.1 (1974): 31–60.

[5]Editors of Quinto Sol Publications.

[6]At the time of the presentation of his essay as a paper, Dec. 1975, Rivera is perhaps referring to Judy Salinas' "The Chicana Image," *Proceedings of the Fifth National Convention of the Popular Culture Association*, St. Louis, MO, March 20–22, 1975; revised and amplified as "The Image of Woman in Chicano Literature," *Revista Chicano-Riqueña* 4.4 (1976): 139–48.

[7]Ernestina N. Eger's *A Bibliography of Criticism of Contemporary Chicano Literature* (Berkeley: University of California Studies Library Publications, 1982) lists only a Patricia A. Geuder, item 134: "Sociolinguistics and Chicano Literature," paper presented at the Rocky Mountain MLA, Laramie, WY. 12 Oct. 1973; and item 1120, "Address Systems in *The Plum Pickers*," *Aztlan* 6.3 (1975): 341–46.

[8]"Chicano Poetry: A Popular Manifesto," *Journal of Popular Culture* 6.4 (1973): 718–30.

[9]"Contemporary Chicano Prose Fiction: Its Ties to Mexican Literature," *Books Abroad* 49.3 (1975): 431–38.

[10]"La prosa chicana: Tres epígonos de la novela mexicana de la Revolución," *The Chicano Literary World 1974*, Felipe Ortego & David Conte, Eds. (Las Vegas, NM: New Mexico Highlands University, 1975): 59–70; rpt. in *Cuadernos Americanos* 34.3 (1975): 198–209.

[11]Probably from "Between Politics and Aesthetics: Problems in Chicano Fiction," unpublished essay; see Eger, item 457. Arturo Islas passed away before I could verify the source of the citation.

[12]Probably through correspondence with Rivera. Eger lists no publication or paper by Inés Hernández Tovar dealing with the question of Chicano esthetics.

On Chicano Literature

🌿

Cash bar, music, food (menudo), beer, raffling, a woodcut of Don
Pedrito Jaramillo, mixed drinks, a chance to buy samplings of Chicano
literature, all of this from 8 to 12 for the benefit of *Caracol* and Cecilio
García Camarillo. Who? What? When? Where? Three hundred or so
persons, dancing and thinking, a master of ceremonies, Max Martínez,
introducing the Chicano writers present—he said hello at least twenty
times, poet, poetess—finally someone listened. Merriment and Cecilio's
voice over the sound saying "Muy agradecido" ("Much obliged"). A fund
raiser for *Caracol*, over two and a half years in existence, monthly, for
thirty-six months, twenty-six pages for twenty-five cents, dying and resus-
citating with the moon cycles. Cecilio typing all night, somehow getting
the $115 together each month to pay the printing costs. Some money
comes from subscribers to pay for the bulk rate mail. Can you believe
it? *Caracol* out of San Antonio to where? Do Chicanos read? Isn't that
a racist statement? To where—universities, restaurants, homes, even to
Japan and Switzerland, Germany and Mexico, and, of course, Cuba and
to the Philippines and to places in South America, from Mario's and Los
Arcos in San Antonio to a little Mexican restaurant in Provo, Utah. The
motto of *Caracol* seems to be *Sí se puede* (It can be done). Cecilio says it
(writes it) on every issue of *Caracol*. In reflection, this motto, *Sí se puede*,
exemplifies the efforts of Chicano literature in the last decade. After all,
isn't all literature an expression of will, of a people, of a person, of an
attitude?—*Sí se puede*.

If I were writing a formal academic paper, I would write: During
the last ten years there has been a resurgence of publication of literature
written by Mexican-Americans (Chicanos) in the United States, mostly
written by writers in the southwest, although an effort has also been in
evidence from the midwest. The literature expresses itself in the common
literary genres, such as poetry, the short story, the essay, the novel, and
some drama. Especially the poetry, the short story and the novel have
shown great proliferation. Significantly, this literature has had an affinity with the Chicano movement which had its beginning in the late 60's.
The Chicano Movement is generally recognized as having an academic
bent, since it really has its beginning in academia—to wit, the Chicano
Movement in California. This movement, in the words of Nick Vaca, had
two irreconcilable positions. On the one hand, the Chicano Movement

From *Texas Books in Review* 1.1 (1977): 5–6.

proclaimed a Chicano cultural differentiation, a Chicano unique culture, which became/was a mystique; and on the other hand, the Chicano Movement demanded to partake from the System better education in the form of bilingual education, better economic participation in the System, equal distribution of monies, etc., for the Mexican-American people.

The Chicano writers of the last ten years are, for the most part, first-generation Americans and come from the working class. The majority are teachers. They write about the urban working class and the rural working class. The developed characters are Chicanos. They attempt to destroy stereotypes without creating others. They write about school and working experiences. They give Chicanos a heroic attitude and, most of all, extol the will and tradition of the Chicano through popular motifs. So much for the plot summaries.

Chronologically, it was the classic study on the Mexican-American corrido *With His Pistol in His Hand* by Américo Paredes, Professor of English and Anthropology at [the] U[niversity of] T[exas], Austin, that opened the way for Chicano literature. In 1957, there were few studies on any aspect of the Mexican-American creative or imaginative impulse. Certainly there were those studies by George I. Sánchez in pedagogy and the historical tradition as exemplified by Professor Carlos Castañeda, both of these professors at UT Austin, but there were few efforts since pre-depression times that revealed the spiritual history of the Chicano through imaginative means and manners. The book *With His Pistol in His Hand*, more than anything, presented a Mexican-American perspective. I still recall in the late 50's several of us, who were writing and attempting to write and publish, sought out the few examples of Chicano writers. We imitated North American writers, and as a consequence the efforts were continually stereotypes of even our own people.

In the early part of this last decade, 1966–76, Chicano literature has suddenly had a three part mission: *conservación, lucha e invención* (conservation of a culture, the struggle or fight for better economic, social, educational and political equity; and invention). The conservation of a culture aimed at the centric idea of possessing a distinct culture and thus a sense of identity. Ironically, the California writers hit hardest with the sense of identity. The Chicano writers from the west felt a deep sense of loss of culture. The Americanization process, because of a better school system than Texas, had dealt a major blow to the culture of the Mexican-Americans in California. In Texas this was not the case. Because of segregation policies through the 1950's, the Mexican-American in Texas suffered little isolation from his own culture. A Mexican institutionality seemed to prevail, especially in enclaves such as exist in San Antonio,

El Paso, Corpus Christi, the Valley, Austin and Houston. I still recall a moment when Rolando Hinojosa was asked about the loss of his identity because of Americanization. Hinojosa's reply was that he always knew he was a Mexican, "Texans never let you forget it." No loss of identity here. Aside from the identity question, there are other aspects which are part of the conservation attitude. One, of course, is the maintaining of a native language. Again the controversial social agent was the school. But through the 40's and the early 50's there were few Mexican-American educators that even espoused the idea of a Mexican-American or Chicano culture, much less its positive sides. The Spanish language was seen as pejorative to the social and economic mobility. Another aspect was the so-called value system that prevailed so much on the "personalismo" of the Mexican-American and the Chicano. This is the attitude exemplified for so many centuries by the Hispanic man—social democracy, a popular democracy vis-a-vis a political democracy. The important aspect of the value system of the Chicano was the interior person, the concept of *honra* (honesty) versus the concept of *honor* (honor). These attitudes which prevail in human relationships were for Chicano writers worthy of conserving. Also in this value system, the worth of the extended family and the attitude of personal relationships were to be more worthy than individual gain.

La lucha, the second mission—the stuggle—pertained to the economic, social, educational and political struggle against the System. The essay was the sword that would gut the belly of the shark, as Herminio Ríos has stated many times. The essay, in the words of Octavio Romano and Juan Gómez Quiñones, represents educational, social and historical writing, respectively. It is a dedicated fervor to right the educational history and the social history of a poorly documented people.

To document was to make things right. To document ourselves was to take the Mexican or the Mexican-American or the Chicano away from others and to return him to ourselves. This was not a solipsistic withdrawal, but rather a struggle to control through documentation. Legitimately, once a structure existed which we had created, the Mexican-American was ours and so was the Chicano, and thus a sense of intellectual liberation would come forth from documentation.

The third mission was to invent. To invent as one, is to love, so says Jorge Guillén. The third mission was to—to invent. Only through a self-invention, through the Chicano's own world view, could a true perspective be gained. What to invent? Through what genre? Does one destroy stereotypes by simply outnumbering others? The Manichean trap was omnipresent. Does one destroy stereotypes. Is it really possible?

By creating others? The important thing was the self-portrait, the self-invention. Language became a great preoccupation. Many works were written in English, many in Spanish, many through a bicultural-bilingual effort. A tradition began to surface during the last decade. What was this tradition? What is this tradition?

The frenetic effort of the late 60's revealed immediately two basic purposes of Chicano literature. *El Espejo/The Mirror,* edited by Octavio Romano [and Herminio Ríos] and published by Quinto Sol Publications in Berkeley, in 1967, indicated also an effort to anthologize a literature that was yet minimal. The purposes were there, however. On the one hand, there was an effort to demonstrate a proficiency; and on the other hand, there was an effort to educate Chicanos in their own literature. The effort to demonstrate a proficiency had a distinct didactic purpose. Through works of excellence, writers were to demonstrate the proficiency of the Chicano in creating works of merit. This proficiency would in turn destroy stereotypes. The literature was to be a literature to educate the total North American public, so that, stylistically, it had to be written in a style acceptable to that public. The essay, written in English, as a genre flourished. Octavio Romano, Herminio Ríos, Philip Ortego, led the way. Novelists such as Richard Vásquez, in his novel *Chicano*; José Antonio Villarreal, in his novel *Pocho*; and Raymond Barrios, in his novel *The Plum Plum Pickers,* created works in English. The effort to educate the Mexican-American was different. The Chicano was, of course, the basic theme, the basic substance. But the style and language were to be his very own. There was no accomodationist effort in this regard. There was no effort to acquiesce to the North American public. This type of intent flourished. Although there was no attempt to speak to the total North American public, perhaps this effort was the most original. This intent really led to experimentation with the Spanish, English languages, and with *caló* and *pachcano* [sic], etc. Writers such as Miguel Méndez, Jesús Maldonado, Alurista, Nephtalí de León, José Montoya, Ricardo Sánchez, came to the forefront. Clearly, their intent was to develop a strong literature, but with no intention to please any critical orientation. Writers such as Rolando Hinojosa, Cecilio García Camarillo, Rudy Anaya, Sergio Elizondo, Aristeo Brito, Raúl Salinas and, lately, Alejandro Morales developed without regard to concession to any critical bent, and write in either Spanish or English. In all cases, the Mexican-American is developed as a human being totally complete, with virtues, faults, inconsistencies, depravity, with heroic bent, and in amazement at these very same possessions.

In sensing the tradition of Chicano literature, one can easily ascertain thematic underpinnings, such as identity, alienation within a "foreign" system, the continual presence of a Mexican culture, acculturation and the agonies of assimilation as it occurs in schools and within other North American institutions. Also, as one can expect from writers whose age of reflection was spent within a working class environment, there exists a strong ethnic proletariat voice and, at times—especially in the early years of the decade—, a sense of Chicano nationalism. A prevailing theme is refuge as a reaction to prejudice, affronts, ignorance; or simply because of class powerlessness, the family—the home—, the barrio become human places and situations of refuge. There exists also a satiric and ironic view of those Mexican-Americans who move into the System without becoming conscious of/or willing to sacrifice for the working class. Within the syndrome of refuge and consciousness, there also prevails a saturation of suffering caused by oppression. Through all these there exists and there is a threat of escape, but of revelation—a documented revelation that brings influential freedom. Consciously and unconsciously, the tradition of Chicano literature reveals itself as precisely an effort at intellectual emancipation.

Throughout the southwest, then, for the last decade there has developed a Chicano literature. Chicano writers from Texas make a formidable list. In 1976, a sign of maturity and pride for the literature was signaled when the distinguished Chicano author, Rolando Hinojosa, was awarded the Premio Casa de las Americas, 1976, for his novel *Klail City y sus alrededores*. Hinojosa had previously received the 1973 Quinto Sol National Literary Award for his book *Estampas del Valle*. Other Chicano writers from Texas who have provided continuously an impetus for Chicano literature and letters are the following: Estela Portillo, drama and prose, El Paso; Ricardo Sánchez, poetry, El Paso; Raúl Salinas, poetry, Austin; Rolando Hinojosa, short story, novel, Kingsville [the Valley]; Tomás Rivera, recipient of the first Quinto Sol Prize, short story, Crystal City; Cecilio García Camarillo, Laredo and San Antonio, editor of *Caracol* and one of the outstanding poets of Chicano literature; Max Martínez, short story, novel, avant garde, Nixon and San Antonio; Evangelina Vigil, poetry, San Antonio; Gloria Guerrero, poetry, San Antonio; Reyes Cárdenas, poetry, Seguin; Carmen Tafolla, poetry, San Antonio; Nephtalí De León, poetry, drama, publisher of Trucha Publications, Lubbock; Dan Garza, short story, Dallas; Inés Tovar, poetry, Austin; René Cisneros, editor of *Tejidos,* Laredo and Austin; Jesús Maldonado, short story, poetry, the Valley; Luis Dávila, editor of *Revista Chicano-Riqueña* (Bloomington, Indiana), San Antonio; Frank Pino, poetry, short story, San Antonio; Alfred de La Torre, novel, San Antonio; Angela de Hoyos, poetry, San Antonio, and so many others. All of these writers have been published in *Caracol* during the last thirty months.

Caracol (Snail shell) symbolizes the capturing of endless echoes of a people. It symbolizes also an external outpouring of imaginative thinking. And certainly it symbolizes life and death. The benefit for *Caracol* on November 26, so human and real, wedded the ideas of imagination and reality. The survival of *Caracol* was to come from, among other things, the money from a raffle of a woodcut by César Agusto Martínez, Chicano artist from San Antonio. The woodcut was a representation of Don Pedrito Jaramillo, a renowned faith-healer and folk hero, curandero from the Texas Valley. No doubt Don Pedrito viewed the proceedings with a ritual knowledge. The ritual had full ingredients—music, dancing, food, a chance, a recognition of Chicano artists and writers, an immortal being Don Pedrito Jaramillo, and people. *Caracol* had come to life again. This is Chicano literature. Chicano literature will provide other firsts, because simply: *Sí se puede.*

The Great Plains as Refuge in Chicano Literature

The Great Plains have a special attraction to me as a person and as a fiction writer. I spent half of my first twenty years in one or another midwestern or Great Plains state. As a child and as a young man, I lived in Iowa, the Dakotas, Minnesota, Michigan, Wisconsin, and Ohio. My earliest recollections are of waking up on a farm in northern Minnesota close to the North Dakota border, where my parents and other relatives worked in the beet fields, surrounded by sounds that I hear even today. These sounds of the farm animals and the voices of working men continue to have a distinct and almost unique clarity and quality. I am beginning this essay in this very personal manner because I think that literature is a personal endeavor—whether you write it or read it.

The second largest migration of Mexican-Americans into what we called *el norte* occurred during the late 1920s and '30s. My parents and other relatives were among that group. Actually, we had ventured out of Texas in the years just before World War II; the largest migration came during the course of the war.

As a child I became aware of various differences between the people we worked for in Texas and the people we worked with in *el norte*. Perhaps just here in these words—worked *for* and worked *with*—is the main difference. Other differences that I noted were linguistic; in *el norte* I would hear languages other than English. I first realized what an immigrant was in the late 1940s in Duncan, Iowa. Previously, I had read some elementary historical accounts of how the great American experience had drawn together people from all over the world, but to me the first real immigrant was Peter Falada, a member of the Czech colony in Duncan. Upon our arrival he asked us one question: "When did your folks come over from the Old Country?" I was born in Texas and we were then spending half the year in the Midwest or the Dakotas, so, although we were strangers to Iowa, I had never considered myself an immigrant. But my father said, "I came from the Old Country in 1915." "We beat you by five years," was Falada's reply. For the first time I saw my father as an immigrant.

That summer I began to discover other immigrant groups who had

From *Vision and Refuge: Essays on the Literature of the Great Plains,* Virginia Faulkner with Frederick C. Luebke, Eds. Lincoln, NB: University of Nebraska Press, 1982: 126–140.

settled in this small town in north-central Iowa—Dutch, Swedes, Finns, and others. I also succeeded in getting Peter Falada and my father to talk of their experiences when they left "the Old Country" and came to the United States. They enjoyed profoundly telling tales of risks, hardships, survival, and of the challenges that earlier settlers faced with them. When we spoke in Spanish Peter Falada would become irritated and would remind us that we were in America. Then he would turn to his wife and children and speak in Czech, and they would all laugh. Our turn to be angry and our turn to tell them that they, too, were in America.

The annual experience of living away from a home base in Texas afforded me grounds for comparison when I developed my own ideas about environment and people. Economic necessity forced us to travel to places away from home and to come into contact with the inhabitants. Although the working conditions were hard, once we were back in Texas we could romanticize about the good land, *el norte*.

In freshman English I was introduced to what was later to be called ethnic literature. In the middle 1950s I had set out to search for, and perhaps find, something written by my own people. I was thirsty for descriptions that would reveal the hardships of a people who were searchers of work like us. Then, as part of a class assignment, I read *Giants in the Earth*. I am sure my professor was astonished by my interest and my desire to dwell on immigrant hardships and the naturalism of the novel, by my interpretations emphasizing the dignity of the common man, and—despite Rølvaag's specific ambience—the universality of the struggle. What my professor regarded as a vicarious experience on my part was a reliving and reconstruction of our own experience: as migrant workers in the forties and fifties, the Chicanos were giants in the earth. It was after reading Rølvaag that I decided I would one day tell the story of the Chicano migrant workers. The land, the people of the plains, and their drive to gain sustenance from the earth became a profound preoccupation.

Chicano literature has a deeply rooted tradition of intellectual emancipation. The myriad of underlying themes which focus on this tradition reveal the constant struggle to decolonize the mind of the Chicano. There is need to show a struggle, there is need to conserve a culture, and there is need to portray the Chicano as a whole human being, with all the frailties, virtues, and faults common to every man.

Among the many themes in Chicano literature that speak to the migrant experience is the concept of refuge. The refuge may be the family, a cultural home base, the Spanish language, the food, Mexican customs. At times, refuge is the idealistic notion of a more or less perfect culture that has ended, the cultural mystique of a past of pageantry, pomp, and learning. Then there is the refuge, mostly economic, that migrant people seek. For the seasonal migrant worker, the Great Plains was this kind of refuge. As Chicano literature interprets that aspect of Chicano life, several writers attempting to capture and document the experiences of the thirties, forties, and fifties depict the Great Plains variously as a utopia, a free state, as a place of exploitation, transient jobs and exhausting work, and as a desolate and impersonal region that drove one to turn inward. The people as well as the environment deserve to be written about, for life in the Great Plains is a solid part of the Chicano experience. The region was a place to go once you had made a decision that it was also your country, and once you sensed [this] you also had a future.

For the Chicano and for the Mexican of the latter half of the twentieth century, migration to the United States is a political, economic, and social act. Speaking of the exodus from Mexico to the deserts of the southwestern United States and a step farther on into the heartland. Ernesto Galarza, one of the foremost Chicano essayists, says: "It was not to flee the revolution as much as to flee their aftermath of defeat and frustration, that the landless came." In his analysis of the land system and social injustices that caused the migrations of millions, Galarza calls the exodus one of the great movements in history:

> Migration is the failure of roots. Displaced men are ecological victims. Between them and the sustaining earth a wedge has been driven. Eviction by droughts or dispossession by landlords, the impoverishment of the soil or conquest by arms, nature and man, separately or together, lay down the choice: move or die... The Mexicans who left their homeland in the six decades beginning in 1880 represented one of the major mass movements of people in the western hemisphere.[1]

The power, the material advancement, the sense of oneness with the human race which these migrants sought is a constant dream even to the present time. Although the great majority settled in California and Texas, a large segment went on into the Midwest. The three basic enclaves of Mexican Americans today are in Texas and California and Chicago.

The sense of drive and movement is caught realistically in the work of the renowned anthropologist Manuel Gamio, writing in the 1930s. In the real-life story of one of Mexican's travel and experiences, *The Personal Narration of Elías Garza*, he describes the transition from the Mexican to the Mexican-American experience:

> At that time I heard there were many good jobs here in the United

States and that good money could be made. Some other friends accompanied me and we went first to Mexico City and from there we came to Ciudad Juarez. We then went to El Paso and there we took a *reenganche* [contract] to Kansas. We worked on the tracks, taking up and laying down the rails, removing the old ties and putting in new, and doing all kinds of hard work. They only paid us $1.50 and exploited us without mercy in the Commissary camp, for they sold us everything high. Nevertheless, as at that time things were cheap, I managed to make a little money with which I went back to La Piedad to see my mother.[2]

Chicano literature covering the migrations of the late nineteenth and twentieth centuries treats three basic types of worker: the *vaquero* (cowboy), the *trasquilador* (sheep shearer), and the *traquero, trabajador del traque* (railroad hand). As Tomás Ybarra-Frausto states in his study "Cuando vino el alambre, vino el hambre" (When the [barbed] wire came, came the hunger):

> The life and experiences of these men who left an indelible imprint on the early Southwest [the Midwest and the Great Plains] are reflected in various forms of literary expression. They had their poets, their composers, and their makers of legends whose *corridos*, *coplas* [ballads], and stories distill the essence of their experience. The basis of their literary expression was a rich vocabulary dealing with the new phenomena they constantly came upon.[3]

During the 1800s approximately 70 percent of the section crews and 90 percent of the extra gangs (temporary replacements) on some railroad lines were composed of Mexican laborers, legally and illegally hired by agents of contractors.

"Los reenganchados a Kansas" (Contracted to Kansas) is a *corrido* about the thousands of men who traveled accompanied by their families and lived in boxcars while working on the track for the Sante Fe, the Rock Island, the Great Northern, or the Southern Pacific. Many of the present colonies and barrios, especially in the Great Plains, were originally settled by this group of migrants and immigrants who preceded the major migration of 1910. The *corrido*, in part, goes like this:

One day the third of September,
Oh, what an unusual day!
We left Laredo
Signed up for Kansas...

One of my companions
Shouted very excitedly:
"Now we are going under contract
To work for cash."

Run, run little machine
Along the Katy line,
Carry this party of laborers
To the state of Kansas City...[4]

[Un día tres de septiembre,
Ay, ¡qué día tan señalado!
Que salimos de Laredo
Para Kansas reenganchados...

Cuando salimos de Laredo
Me encomendé al Santo Fuerte,
Porque iba de contrabando
Por ese lado del puente.

Uno de mis compañeros
Gritaba muy afanado:
—Ya nos vamos reenganchados
A trabajar al contado.—

Corre, corre, maquinita,
Por esa línea del Quiri
Anda a llevar este enganche
Al estado de Kansas City...]

The final stanza of the *corrido* presents the Mexican view of U.S. labor unions as having a double standard. The *reenganchados* knew that since they we e not citizens of the United States they would receive no union benefits and were regarded simply as a means of increasing the numerical strength of the railroad unions, not as participating members.

From the turn of the century into the thirties, migration is an important theme in Chicano literature; indeed, it continues to be an important element in the 1970s.[5] In 1976 the Chicano writer Rolando Hinojosa Smith received the Premio Casa de las Américas for the best novel. That Hinojosa should be awarded this prestigious prize, never before given to a North American, stands as a distinct achievement for Chicano literature. His novel, *Klail City y sus alrededores* (*Klail City and its surroundings*), devotes some thirty pages to the joy and hope and agony and disillusionment of traveling, working and confrontation in the Great Plains and the Midwest.[6] One young man, P. Galindo, a native of the Texas [Rio Grande] Valley, has an idealized notion of what to expect, even though he has previously traveled to *el norte* and sought work there. He is confident that he will find work and that everything will turn out well. One chapter deals with the death of a young woman's parents in Cheyenne Wells, Colorado, and the lonely journey of the bereaved through western Kansas and eastern Colorado. In search of refuge, they have found death. Another character, the young man Gariva, has a truck which he names *El Rápido de Oklahoma (The Oklahoma Express)*. He paints the name on his truck and is himself called by that name. Oklahoma has a touch of the exotic to the people in the Texas [Rio Grande] Valley—that is, to the characters in the novel.

Throughout the novel (which actually is a collection of cameos lightly threaded together as a unifying device), Hinojosa attacks the Anglos bitterly and sarcastically. George Markham, Big Foot Parkinson, Van Meers, and Mrs. Elsinore, all Texans, are shown as grotesque, one-dimensional creatures. The author balances his characterizations of Texas Anglos, however, by portraying a midwesterner, Tom Purdy, as the epitome of goodness. He describes Tom thus:

> This man without any money, but with dedication and determination, without having anyone come and whisper in his ear, said: "Enough; no more"; and he began to repair the houses available for the Chicano migrants... He didn't talk to the federal or state government nor the press. Nor did he talk to those civic organizations that abound in almost every town in this country. No. He spoke with his wife and the two of them in silence and without hesitation began their chore for a group of people whom they didn't know and whose language they didn't speak... What was accomplished allowed La Raza to live with dignity.

One of the most important elements in Chicano oral history and oral literature is the *corrido*, the ballad. Just as Spanish literature has its roots in the romance, so Chicano literature takes its basic design from the concrete, simple narrative of this art form. Luis Valdez calls the *corridos* the songs of Exodus. He states: "'Wherever you go, you shall go singing,' the War God of the Aztecs, Huitzilopochtili, commanded the people. With the *corridos* of the Southwest, La Raza has been singing its history ever since."[7] The songs of Exodus are many. Most are laments at leaving behind a country, a family, a loved one. Then there are those *corridos*, such as the songs of the vaqueros, in which the poet expresses his own response to new experiences and new landscapes. For the purpose of this essay I will confine my discussion to *corridos* dealing with the hard life of the vaquero. "The Corrido of Kansas" focuses on the imminent presence of death and the dangers of the two-month cattle drive from Texas to Kansas. Its last stanzas describe the death of a young vaquero.

> The wife of Alberto Flores
> Comes up to ask the foreman,
> "Where has my son stayed,
> For I have not seen him arrive?"
>
> "Ma'am, if I were to tell you
> You would start to weep;
> Your son was killed by a bull
> On the gates of a corral.
>
> "Thirty pesos was his wages
> But it was all owed.
> And I have put in three hundred
> To have him buried.
>
> "All the drivers
> Went to accompany him.
> With hats in hand
> They saw him buried.
>
> "And now I say farewell
> With thoughts of my beloved.
> We come also to the end
> Of this cattle-driving song."[8]
>
> [La mujer de Alberto Flores
> le pregunta al caporal:
> "¿Dónde se ha quedado mi hijo,
> que no lo he visto llegar?"
>
> "Señora, si le dijera
> se pusiera usté a llorar;
> a su hijo lo mató un toro
> en las puertas de un corral.

"Treinta pesos alcanzó
pero todo limitado,
y trescientos puse yo
pa' haberlo sepultado.

"Todos los aventureros
lo fueron a acompañar,
con sus sombreros en las manos,
a verlo sepultar."

Ya con ésta me despido
con el amor de mi querida,
Aquí se acaban cantando
los versos de la corrida.]

The scene at the end of the *corrido* is Kansas. All the elements of humanity and dignity refer to the place where the tragedy occurred.[9] What makes the many variants of the *corridos de Kiansis* so appealing to the vaqueros themselves? Is it because Kansas represents a goal? Economic gain? As a land far away from the Texas Valley, is it an exotic place in the mind of the composer? Perhaps all of these.[10]

According to the renowned Mexican-American folklorist Américo Paredes, the cattle drives to Kansas were the inspiration for the oldest complete *corridos* from the lower Rio Grande border. They are among the oldest even in the Greater Mexican tradition. In his *Texas-Mexican Cancionero*, Paredes writes:

> Everyone has heard of the famous cattle drives to Kansas, the subject of many a Western. What is not so well known is that it was cattle owned by Mexicans and Texas-Mexicans (some legally obtained from them and some not) that formed the bulk of the herds driven north from the Nueces-Rio Grande area, the so-called cradle of the cattle industry in the United States. Not all cattle that went north were driven by Anglo cowboys. Many of the trail drivers were Mexicans, some taking their own herds, other working for Anglo outfits. The late 1860s and early 1870s was a period when a good many Mexicans still were *dueños* (owners) on the Texas side. In this respect they could meet the Anglo on something like equal terms. But the Texas-Mexican possessed something else that gave him a certain status—the tools and the techniques of the vaquero trade, in which the Anglo was merely a beginner. The Mexican with some justice could feel superior to the Anglo when it came to handling horses and

cattle, or facing occupational hazards such as flooded rivers. These attitudes were apparent in the *corridos* about the cattle drives to Kansas, pronounced "Kiansis" by border rancheros.[11]

No doubt intercultural conflict is reflected in the many variants of the *corridos de Kiansis*, but what is of greater significance is, first, that the conflict is expressed in professional rivalries rather than in violence between men of different cultures; second, that in Kansas the Mexican could meet the Anglo on equal terms; and third, that the Kansas-Mexican experience elevated the status of the Texas-Mexican because he had the tools and knew the techniques of the vaquero trade. Since the *Kiansis corridos* make no mention of armed conflict between Mexicans and Anglos, the oral tradition at least conveyed to the Texas-Mexican that a different kind of justice prevailed in the Great Plains. There were no armed forays against an unarmed people.

The migrant worker who came after the era of the cattle drive found a similar situation. Time after time Chicano literature tells how the small farmer from the Midwest and Great Plains is different from the Texas farmer. Certainly there is a historical reason for this difference. Armed conflict did not occur in the Great Plains as a result of regional or national politics; Great Plains settlers are themselves recent immigrants. But clearly it was working the land side by side with the person who owned it that pleased and gave dignity to the Mexican common laborer. It surprised the Mexicans that not only did the men who owned the land join them in the fields, but also the women. They were surprised to be invited to eat in the farmers' homes. In fact, the working of the land is a common denominator. The word filters back to Texas.[12] In the Midwest and the Great Plains a person's worth is determined by the amount of hard work he or she can do. Even children were able to understand this basic difference. In a short story of mine called "Los niños no se aguantaron" ("The Children Couldn't Wait"), a child longs to be up north rather than in Texas. The elemental need for water draws him to his death. He is shot "accidentally" by a Texas rancher for drinking water out of a cattle tank.[13]

The Great Plains is represented as a region where fair play is at least more common and where the natural environment, though harsh, is fought by all alike. A sense of isolation pervades Chicano literature set in the Great Plains. There are stories of the aimless wandering of a penniless family in search of work,[14] of illness striking a whole area, of truck accidents, of exploitation, of floods or droughts that prevent men from working, of hate. However, it is not hate directed at any one person but at an endless cycle of poverty, as in the poem "Odio" (Hatred), in which the poet sees the Chicanos as weeds.[15]

> Weeds rupture the marble
> And I laugh at the whiteness.
> Alone,
> daggers,
> knifing,
> soundless,
> unloved through death.
> Torn from the earth,
> left to dry,
> to die.
>
> Future in the seed.
>
> Stone upon stone
> of despair.
>
> Stone from which
> come the weeds
> who blade each other
> without love
>
> >   to be torn from the earth
> >   and thrown to the earth.
>
> The seed is here
> on the stone
> on my forehead.

Similar in setting is the poem, "The Child Cried," by Javier Aréchiga,[16] which exalts the hopelessness and feeling of futility of a common field laborer:

> The child cried
> No one noticed
> He tried to hold
> Pero nadie le ayudó
> [But no one would help him]
> He wanted water
> The others kept picking

He felt burned from the sun
Everybody was a picture
He died

If migrant workers remained in the Midwest or Great Plains, they usually moved from rural to urban areas. In the next two poems Aréchiga illustrates the fear, the indifference, and the loneliness not only of death but also of the unheeding urban steel mills.

Perdido (Lost)

I cried to what was
I saw nothing but concrete,
Rotten paper and wood not
Identifiable in the iron smoke

We screamed by ourselves
Panicking constantly,
Still there was nothing.

Many young swept with the big
Smack.
Forgotten by La Malinche ... [17]

La Bruja (The Witch)

She appeared so mysteriously
without warning and waiting
without compassion
without

Clanging, clanging and steel
the grinding, grinding of machinery
without warning and waiting
without love
without compassion
without

She uncovered herself
sickness attaching ...

Ringing, ringing of noise

The floating, floating of faith
the injuries

She disappeared
knowing that all had been accomplished.

The Chicano literary movement of the last decade swept from west to east, starting in California and ending in Texas. A midwestern Chicano enclave also made its presence felt. In Gary, Indiana, the *Revista Chicano-Riqueña*[17bis] began to flourish in the early seventies. I mention this to illustrate an inherent cultural attitude on the part of the Chicano. The educational institutions of the Midwest and, to some degree, of the Great Plains, although not seriously attacked by Chicano students, felt the reverberations of conflicts in the Southwest.[18] The Chicano student who was becoming increasingly aware of his own historical traditions and who was confronted by the demands of Chicanos in other parts of the country that he raise his level of consciousness also reacted. Thus we have writings by Chicano authors stressing the need for those who have had no definite commitment to become involved, even though the issues do not directly affect them. Failing to do so is a kind of refuge by default.[19]

The seeking of refuge after 1848 was a constant preoccupation for Tejanos (Texas Mexicans), especially throughout the nineteenth century. Nepomuceno Cortina's raid on Brownsville in 1859 and his subsequent defeat by the U.S. Army had set a pattern for other Texas-Mexicans who were forced into violent protest against exploitation and injustice. Inevitably, the weight of American authority was too much for a Texas-Mexican to fight. If he was not killed or capture, the man who "defended his right" had either to seek refuge across the Rio Grande in Mexican territory or go to *el norte.*

In the 1880s the land to the north again offered economic advantages, and this fact, coupled with the idea of competing on even terms as a cowhand or a railroad worker, presented an alternative that was more appealing than what was available in Texas.

Among the immigrants from Mexico during the revolution of 1910 to 1920 were peons fleeing a *hacendado* system, but in Texas they found an even more rigid and cruel ranching system. The peasants who made their way into the Great Plains and the Midwest in some cases found conditions of farm unlike any previously known to them. At times they worked and ate with—and in many cases shared the homes of—the landowners, and they would never be the same again. Upon returning from their refuge, they would talk of the great opportunity and the hard work that they found in the Great Plains and the Midwest, where, according to them, the dignity of the common man was an accepted fact.

But the refuge had its drawbacks. There was isolation from their own culture. There were subtle prejudices. The Chicanos did not own the land. They were few in number. There was a cultural loss. There was change. Still, Chicano literature is replete with examples demonstrating as historical fact that the Great Plains and the Midwest provided an escape (sometimes an illusion), a terrain, and a host society that tested an individual but offered him or her a better opportunity to compete on equal terms.

For two decades in my own life, the shout every spring of *Vámonos p'al norte* opened up visions of adventure, work, money, new people to meet, new situations, new land. It is impossible to imagine Chicano literature without the migrant worker. And it is impossible to imagine the migrant worker without the myriad notions of a refuge in the Great Plains. The idea of refuge is, above all, one more step toward the intellectual emancipation that is basic to the tradition of Chicano literature.

Notes

[1] Ernesto Galarza, "The Roots of Migration," *Aztlan: An Anthology of Mexican American Literature.* Luis Valdez and Stan Steiner, Eds. (New York: Vintage Books, 1972): 128.

[2] Manuel Gamio, "Narración personal de Elías Garza," *Literatura Chicana; texto y contexto,* Antonia Castañeda Shular, Tomás Ybarra-Frausto and Joseph Sommers, Eds. (Englewood Cliffs, New Jersey: Prentice-Hall, 1972): 19.

[3] Tomás Ybarra-Frausto, "Cuando vino el alambre, vino el hambre," *Literatura Chicana,* 208.

[4] "Los reenganchados a Kansas," *Literatura Chicana,* 222–23.

[5] Rolando Hinojosa-Smith, "E Pluribus Vitae," *Revista Chicano-Riqueña* 1. 2 (1973): 14, 15.

[6] Rolando Hinojosa-Smith, *Klail City y sus alrededores* (Havana: Casa de las Américas, 1976): 88–106.

[7] Luis Valdez, "Songs of Exile," *Aztlan,* 131.

[8] "El corrido de Kiansis," *Literatura Chicana,* 210–11.

[9] Francisco Ríos, "The Mexican in Fact, Fiction and Folklore," *Voices* (Berkeley, California: Quinto Sol Publications, 1971): 59–73.

[10] Antonia Castañeda Shular, "Lo mero principal," *Literatura Chicana,* 93–94.

[11] Américo Paredes, *A Texas-Mexican Cancionero* (Urbana: University of Illinois Press, 1976): 25–26.

[12] Tino Villanueva, "De sol a sol," *Revista Chicano-Riqueña* 2. 2 (1974): 17–18.

[13] Tomás Rivera, ... *y no se lo tragó la tierra / ... And the Earth Did Not Part* (Berkeley, California: Quinto Sol Publications, 1971).

[14] Tomás Rivera, "Las salamandras," *Festival de Floricanto* 1 (Los Angeles: Southern California Press, 1976): 23. *. . . y no se lo tragó la tierra / . . . And the Earth Did Not Devour Him* (Houston: Arte Publico Press, 3th ed.; 1991).

[15] Tomás Rivera, "Odio," *El grito* 3 (Fall 1969): 60.

[16] Javier Aréchiga, "Poetry," *Revista Chicano-Riqueña* 1. 2 (1973): 25–28.

[17] La Malinche is the name bestowed by the Aztecs on Doña Marina, a woman given to Cortez before the capture of what is today Mexico City in 1519–20. She symbolizes the surrender of one culture to another.

[17bis] *Revista Chicano-Riqueña*, now *The Americas Review*, published by Arte Publico Press.

[18] Raúl Salinas, "A Trip through the Mind Jail," *Aztlan*, 339–44.

[19] Frank Pino, "El teatro," *Revista Chicano-Riqueña* 1. 2 (1973): 11–13.

Chicano Literature: The Establishment of Community

I took the idea for this study from a lecture by Robert Hine, a professor of history at our University of California at Riverside. During the spring of 1980, at the 29th Annual Faculty Research Lecture titled "Community, Utopia and The Frontier," he established the essence of community in the American West. As I listened to his presentation his ideas became very relevant to Chicano literature in the last ten years in a variety of ways. So I titled this presentation "Chicano Literature, 1970–1979: The Establishment of Community."

In the last ten years Chicano literature has established community, myth and language. Or at a minimum, it has reflected the urge and desire to establish such elements of the Chicano ethnic group. The flourishment and the now documented last ten years of literary effort reveal these very attitudes, problems and the very exact efforts of the exteriorization and the imaginative and inventive efforts of the Chicano. The different genres extol also the most important literary enterprises, the struggle for intellectual emancipation. The Chicano community will never be the same again. It is a changing, dynamic community. We in the Chicano community realize this and we are also aware that the changes will be broader and faster in this decade. Chicano literature will reflect this as it has done so for the past decade.

The anxiety to have a community, the urge to feel, sense, and be part of a whole was the most constant preoccupation and need for Chicano students and faculty alike in academia in the past ten years. Surely this was also the case for the Chicano community outside the walls of academia (or was it not? I do think we have to ask the question) which was trying to form something out of a very diffused nation or a very diffused tribe. Chicano literature as it began to flourish in the 50's and 60's revealed a basic hunger for community (*hambre por una comunidad*). Here was a group of kindred people forming a nation of sorts, loosely connected politically and economically and educationally but with strong ties and affinities through its folklore and popular wisdom. Also there were ties through varying degrees of understanding of its historical precedence and a strong tie because of its language. Yet the political and social organiza-

From *A Decade of Chicano Literature*, Fernando de Necochea, Francisco Lomelí, Roberto G. Trujillo, Eds. Santa Barbara, CA: Editorial La Causa, 1982.

tions of the Chicanos were weak within and existed within sophisticated North American and Mexican societies that really had not cared about the development of the group itself. Clearly, the impetus to document and develop the Chicano community became the essential *raison d'etre* of the Chicano Movement itself and of the writers who tried to express that.

The different *planes* that were evolved called for the establishment and betterment of the Chicano community above all else. One of the most important goals was to establish a *lugar* or a place. Aztlán became the place in most writings. Myth or not, the urge to have, to establish, and to nurture a place of origin, of residence became the most important need to meet. This was not surprising. This deep need for community revealed basically a colonized mind and a deprived, powerless class. The Chicano had to begin decolonizing the mind. The start, the beginning steps, were to declare a place of residence—to establish a community and to document that community. As Martin Buber has stated, "Community is the aspiration of all human history." And Chicanos were human, and Chicanos had a history. And very definitely, in the late 60's and early 70's, I believe that the Chicano community began to aspire very deeply for its sense to community.

I want to digress briefly to elaborate the idea of community in the U.S. and especially in the West. I am quoting and paraphrasing Robert Hine's effort in delineating community, utopia, and the frontier for American society as a whole. I want to take these concepts and apply them to Chicano Literature—the effort itself, its content, and its form.

Professor Hines states the following:

> In 1930, Wheatland, Missouri was probably as typical a small town as one could find. The citizens were well knit. They were asked if their pioneer ancestors were any more well-knit than they. The answer was yes. They were downgrading the present (1940's). Hundreds of others were saying that society was prevailingly alienated, fragmented, atomized; and they would look back at a pioneer past and say the past was better. Also, in the scholarly area, distinguished people like Yi Fu Tuan, in his work *Landscapes of Fear*, describes a type of innocent, fearless past which became alienated from its natural environment and sinks into an anxious present. Samuel B. Warner, Jr. finds that most people living in the modern world, particularly in the large urban settings, feel as if they are existing in a clearing in a vast wilderness—that wilderness is the city. The only thing that they can know is the small clearing. And this has happened, says Warner, because the city has chosen deliberately to

ignore its goal of community in favor of other goals. And these other goals are competition and innovation. The citizens of Wheatland, Missouri and others in 1980 are examples of people who are thinking about what is known as modernization theory—a theory that says roughly that we are engaged in accelerated economic growth associated with a psychology of getting ahead, a psychology of production, and that this leads inexorably toward the destruction of community for American society as a whole. On the other hand, there are large numbers of scholars who are pointing over and over again at a very strong community in the modern world. Scott Greet, Robert Redfield, and even Oscar Lewis find particularly among kinship groups in modern cities strong elements of community.

Now, what is community? According to Robert Hine, community is the following:

> All definitions of community argue that first of all, community is a place [*un lugar*], a geographical location where they know people, know that the sun will come out behind a particular place, the formation of clouds; the place may be architectural features, a barrio, a nick on a building, color, age, material things, all of which express continuity [*una continuación de las cosas y así del espíritu*]. Secondly, community is a set of personal relationships. These are usually related to the size of the community but the primary thing is the personal relationships that must be primary in a community. Rebecca West says that "the community is conversation." [*La comunidad es conversación; la comunidad es platicar.*] Thirdly, the community is values. The value of the group over the individual. These values say that the whole is more than the sum of each of its parts. As a community works out [sic], as these elements come into play, there is a tension of individuals versus the group. There are the tensions of a family within a community. And within the family itself is the basic building block. The family is also different elements—class, hierarchy, and it is class and hierarchy which make for the strong building power in the community. The ideal community is one which can make all these factor work [*valores, conversación*].

If we take Professor Hine's definition and place it parallel to structures, plots, ethos, motivation, characterization, etc., of Chicano literature of the past 10 years, there is an almost exact correspondence. Works such as *Bless Me, Ultima, Estampas del Valle, ...y no se lo tragó la tierra, Revolt of the Cockroach People, The Road to Tamazunchale, El diablo en*

Texas, *Peregrinos de Aztlán*, *Caras viejas y vino nuevo*, are explicit in their urge for community and as such they are moods of community. Likewise in many works of poetry and short fiction, the basic preoccupation is *el lugar*, *la comunidad*. If in Spanish, and to a lesser extent in Mexican literature, there has been a tendency for the action of the literary work to overimpose itself to the thematic underpinnings, I believe that in Chicano literature of the last ten years that the idea of community has imposed itself on the action and theme of literary works. (*Las ganas de tener comunidad han sido muy fuertes.*) I also believe that specifically in the theatre this is the case. (*El pueblo se sobreimpone.*) Community was a major preoccupation for the literary festivals such as *Flor y Canto* and *Canto al Pueblo*. There was a constant preoccupation that the community partake as well as participate in the *certámenes*—fully involved in the presentations or in the audience.

The community is place, values, personal relationships, and conversation. What better description than this is there to define a work by such a distinguished Chicano writer as Rolando Hinojosa-Smith where we find *lugar*, *modales*, *relaciones personales*, *conversación* as constant motifs. I think that it was because of the strong urge to establish a community that Chicano literature imbued itself with the preoccupations and the notions of proficiency and didacticism, especially the latter. As part of that communal urge to establish residence here was the strong desire to teach the people (*el pueblo*) in a meaningful manner through literary works while at the [same] time to the total North American public.

In the last ten years in poetry, theatre and short fiction, and in the novels, I perceive an effort, at times overly obvious, to deal with the traditional beliefs, customs, sayings, constant allusions to the supernatural, legendary symbols. These are the elements of coherence of the Chicano community and the writer utilized these common denominators to give form to an amorphous group. The Chicano writer took on the responsibility to document and preserve what sometimes existed quite unreflectively among "la gente." The writer speaking from the community, through characterized members, thus extracted the wisdom, the advice, and counsel from the community. This has been considered by many critics as a flaw in Chicano writers. I do not think it is a flaw. I contend that the more definite and national the person in a literary setting, the more universal the motivation and the more revealing of original elements of human perceptions and motivations he or she possesses. In this manner both place and person exist as primary units that hold basic original elements of humankind, that is, the total crystallization of passions—love, hate, joy, *tristeza*, etc.

The following two short pieces are both by Rolando Hinojosa-Smith. These are written some eight years apart. They have a basic theme. They reflect not only an evolution but a difference in style and emphasis and sensitivity. The first is titled, "La Güera Fira" and is found in *Estampas del Valle* and the other is a poem titled, "Old Friends" from *Korean Love Songs*:

Fira the Blond

Without beating around the bush: Fira the Blond is a whore. She doesn't pretend to be a whore (like maids do) nor does she whore around (like society women); no. Fira's a whore and that's that. There's more. Fira has blue eyes, short hair which she doesn't dye and a figure that would stop the hiccups of don Pedro Zamudio, the parish priest.

Fira isn't from around here. She's from Jonesville-on-the-River. The daughter of a Mexican woman from Jonesville and an Anglo soldier from Fort Jones: she wasn't the first to leave nor the last, but, truthfully, she certainly has to be the most beautiful woman of the Valley. (The person who really knows a lot more about the people of Jonesville is don Américo Paredes.)

Fira is a serious woman who carries her whoredom like school girls carry their books: naturally. After she bathes, she smells of soap and water and when she goes to work, the curls by her temples are still wet.

She works in the tavern owned by Félix Champión, an illegitimate son of my Uncle Andrés. She neither dances nor struts from table to table nor flirts nor carries on. Don Quixote used to say that being a go-between was serious business; that may be, but the occupation of being a whore in a simple tavern of a one horse town is nothing to laugh about either.

The women of Klail know who she is and what she is and that's it. If they gossip, that's it. If they gossip, that's their business; but the majority don't gossip. Women usually tend to be understanding when they feel like it.

The only bad part of it all is that Fira won't last much longer in Klail: it's too small and, to tell the truth, money's scarce around here.

I believe that folkloric elements and popular expressions are clearly noted in the development of this unique character, and that the same is to be noted in several of the anecdotes and vignettes of this work.

About eight years later, Hinojosa wrote a poem, "Old Friends," that deals with the same theme, but from a much more personal vantage point and somewhat more stylistically refined, and written in English:

Old Friends

In Honshu, the bigger island,
The southern Japanese businessmen call their whorehouses
Emporiums. Off Baron Otsuki boulevard,
In Southeast Kobe, are five emporia, all in a row.

The nominal owner of Shirley's Temple of Pleasure Emporium
Is middle-aged Tomiko Sambe.
She prefers to be called Shirley.
And when she says it, it doesn't sound anything like that.
(Here, on an earlier medical R&R
Tomiko replaced my lost dress Army shoes.
For a week or two, with black navy shoes of proper fit.)
My good acquaintance here, Mosako Fukuda,
Has a brother named Hideo who's a medical student in Nagoya.
Mosako, native to the Kobe-Kyoto-Osaka Triangle,
Visits her parents in Nara every ten days or oftener, and always
When the cycle comes and lays her low.
There's no pretense here:
Her parents know where she works
And I, learning the ways of the world,
Do not add insult to their injury
By visiting their home. I know of them and of Hideo through
        her.
And, like the popular song now,
'She's never been to Tokyo,
Hokkaido is out of the question.
She's been once to Kyushu, but never to Shikoku.'

She loves to walk, and she loves the parks.
We go and stay until the familiar shimbun!—enough—
Enough, she says, and we walk back to Shirley's.

And now, midday of the sixth day of R&R, and
Despite what Berman claimed,

The shoulder's stiffened up again, thus
Making this just one more of Mosako's love duties.
As she starts on the shoulder,
She hums and sighs, and
When she tickles *me, she* laughs. I laugh, too,
And after this, the usual bath and mat and bath again.
We're a likely pair, we are; and I'm certainly no Pinkerton
To her Butterfly, but I *have* come to say goodbye. Later
    tonight,
We'll go shopping and then I'll leave with nine days left on
    my R&R.

Early next morning,
The World War II vets sweep the Temple of Pleasure Empo-
    rium
While we enjoy a quiet breakfast of pastry and tea.
Tomiko, who prefers to be called Shirley,
comes in and we shake hands, Western style. After her tea,
We take long, full bows just like the old friends that we are,
And Mosako will walk me to the K-K-O Railway less than
    three blocks away.
She holds my pass, my ticket, and the money;
She puts them in my pocket, in a flowered envelope, and then
I surprise her with yet another fan (which she needs like a
    hole),
But she takes it, and her eyes close when she smiles.
Then her eyes and mine open wide when the train surprises
    us, and
we watch
The rushing crowds.
Gently with her fan,
She pushes me away, and
again her eyes close
When she smiles. She turns
Walks away, carefully opening and studiously closing the fan
As the train rears back before
Moving on. I look for a familiar patch or face.
And finding none,
I remove my cap in time to catch the last
Faint smell of the tea and pastry
Prepared by my old friend.

As we recall these two pieces, in "La Güera Fira" we have examples of the type of cameos we find throughout *Estampas del Valle.* I believe Hinojosa, among other things, attempts to build a community by the development of so many of these characters. He creates a true community in *Estampas* above all else. The language itself is the language of conversation. (*Es una conversación con gusto.*) The elements of the community and the acceptance by the community of la Güera Fira as part of its existence is very exact. La Güera Fira makes up part of the whole of which the group is made. She fits. The language is oral—descriptive and realistic.

In "Old Friends" we have an example of an impressionistic endeavor. Here we have the language and the sense of reflection. Also well-understood is the attitude of acceptance and thematic intent to reveal acceptance of relationships and mature perspectives of men and women. It is also a very subjective poem although it appears to be very realistic. It is not the building or re-building of a community. Although these two pieces are different, there are elements, common denominators, that are part of both which have elements of folkloric intent. One is the concept of cohabitation (*vivir y dejar vivir*). That is, the acceptance in the community of all types of people without signaling out a pejorative or positive value as to the role of people in the community. There is no attempt to denigrate anyone because of the state or position in the community. There is the wisdom of acceptability and the wisdon of relationships between men and women, no matter what their position, social class, rank or endeavor. And more specifically there is the respect for individual condition and situation. The folkloric elements of Chicano literature that were so apparent in the early part of this decade still carry forth in several ways the wisdom of the Chicano community. I believe it is the folkloric and oral language that brings forth the wisdom of the people. Literature in this sense becomes the history of customs.

Perhaps the most important element of Chicano literature is that it was able to capture from the beginning of the decade this very wisdom of a very disparate and amorphous nation of kindred group. It was able to do that because there was hunger not only in the community but in the Chicano writer to create a community. Up to the present time, one of the most positive things that the chicano writer and Chicano literature have conveyed to our people is the development of such a community. We have a community today (at least in literature) because of the urge that existed and because the writers actually created from a spiritual history, a community captured in words and in square objects we call books.

Richard Rodriguez' Hunger of Memory as Humanistic Antithesis

≋

Although I was born in Texas, had lived in many states in the Midwest and had not lived in any Spanish-speaking country, my public voice as well as my private voice was Spanish through my first eleven years. It was in the fifth grade, that *eureka*! to my surprise, I started speaking English without translating. I suppose that at that time I had two public voices as well as two private ones.

Hunger of Memory: the Education of Richard Rodriguez (Boston: D. Godine, 1981) is an exceptionally well written book. It is a profound book, a personal expression which one learns to respect for its sensibility. To respect this type of sensibility is something I learned in the Spanish-taught "escuelita," which I attended before entering public school at age seven. What Richard Rodriguez has written has great value. However, I have difficulties with concepts in the book which I consider anti-humanistic. For several reasons I consider *Hunger of Memory* as a humanistic antithesis. This book has been controversial for the Hispanic in general and in particular to the Mexican-American or Chicano. This has been the case much more so, I think, because it seems to be so well accepted by the North American public as a key to understanding the Mexican-American and debates related to bilingual education and affirmative action. Thus, it is important to define and perceive the book from different vantage points. Hispanics, Chicanos, and Latinos are not a homogenous group. They are as heterogenous a kindred group as any that exists in our present society. They are at different levels of development, perception, understanding, and as complex and therefore as complete as other human beings. Richard Rodriguez' book is a personal expression, an autobiography, and it must be understood as that in its singularity. It should not be used as a single way or method of understanding the bilingual, bicultural phenomenon of the Hispanic group.

I do not know Richard Rodriguez. I have seen him on television. I have read *Hunger of Memory* three times. I intend to read it again for it has much to offer. The work becomes more with each reading.

Richard Rodriguez' essays have a style and tone which complement and establish his concepts. *Hunger of Memory* establishes its tone through patterns based on the ideas of silence and the centrality of language—

From *Melus*, 11. 4(1984): 5–13. Winter 1984.

silence versus non-silence, silence and active language, silence and culture, silence and intelligence. The aggregation of silence seems to indicate that if a person does not speak, he/she lacks intelligence. This is a view generally held by many teachers in the classroom: how can one judge silence? If a child's hand does not go up, if a question is asked, the teacher's perception is usually that there is a lack of intelligence. Richard Rodriguez insists on the presence of his signal-silence and the public voice. If a person does not speak he/she does not have a public voice. How can one have a personal voice only in silence as the only true aggregate? The author indicates that Spanish was and is his personal voice. But it is an inactive passive voice that became neutered, sterile, and finally silent—dead.

I find underlined throughout the text a negation of what is fundamentally the central element of the human being—the cultural root, the native tongue. As one reads each essay, one progressively recognizes that what is most surprising for Richard Rodriguez is that silence and his basic culture are negative elements, regressive ones. This pattern of negation is softened somewhat when he thinks of his parents and his love for his parents, but he ultimately comes to the thesis that this silence and the consequent inactive community is something regressive or negative. This dealing with silence reminds me of my efforts in struggling with this phenomenon of silence when I studied in Mexico and lived with Mexican families; especially in the rural communities, where I tried to write about what I considered the impenetrable face/masks and their silence. But I never thought for a moment that their masks did not conceal an imagination or thought processes, not that they were not developing and inventing constantly their own world view and perceptions. And that, although they were not speaking to me and hardly to each other, they were not actively thinking. Richard Rodriguez delves into silence, and writes from silence as he himself tells us, "I am here alone, writing, and what most moves me is the silence." Truly this is an active task for him. Yet, with regard to his own family, he sees this silence as a non-force. He finally concludes simplistically, unfortunately, that his personal voice is Spanish and that his active voice is English. Surely, this is a humanistic antithesis.

It is necessary at this point to call attention to his development as a writer. He grew up and was taught in the humanities. The humanities have a clear base—at a minimum the explaining or aiding in the elaboration of a philosophy of life. Surely by the time one is twelve years old or so one has a philosophy of life. By then one has formulated and asked all the great philosophical questions and has even provided some answers. Whether one asks and answers in English or Spanish or in any other tongue is not important. The humanities, and certainly the study of literature, recognize this. As an educated scholar in literature, certainly, and much more so as a Renaissance scholar, Richard Rodriguez should know this. But his thoughts do not recognize this fundamental philosophical base. Clearly as a youngster of twelve or thirteen years of age he could not have, but certainly as an academic he could have reflected on the realities of his life, on the sensibility, and on the importance of what he did not know then and what he must now know. The humanities are also, to put it simply, a search for life, a search for form, but most significantly a search for wisdom. In this regard Richard Rodriguez starts out well. His search for life and form in the literary form of autobiography has as a premise the basic core of family life. But then Richard Rodriguez struggles with the sense of disassociation from that basic culture. Clearly, he opts to disassociate, and, as a scholar, attempts to rationalize that only through disassociation from a native culture was he to gain and thus has gained the "other," that is, the "public" world. Without wisdom he almost forgets the original passions of human life. Is he well educated in literature? For literature above all gives and inculcates in the student and scholar the fundamental original elements of humanistic endeavor without regard to race or language, much less with regard to a public voice. The most important ideas that the study of the humanities relate are the fundamental elements and values of human beings, regardless of race and nationality. Ultimately, the study of the humanities teaches the idea that life is a relationship with the totality of people within the circumstance.

Then we come to the question of place and being. In Spanish there are two verbs meaning "to be," *Ser* and *Estar*. This is quite important to *Hunger of Memory*. Being born into a family is equal to being, *Ser*. Education and instruction teaches us to be, *Estar*. Both are fundamental verbs. *Ser* is an interior stage, and *Estar* is an exterior one. To leave the *Ser* only for the *Estar* is a grievous error. Richard Rodriguez implies, at times explicitly, that the authentic being is and can only be in the *Estar* (public voice) and only there is he/she complete. And further, he states that authenticity can only come by being an exterior being in English in the English-speaking world. In the Hispanic world, the interior world of *Ser* is ultimately more important than the world of *Estar*. *Honra*, honesty, emanates from and is important to the *Ser*. Richard Rodriguez opts for the *Estar* world as the more important and does not give due importance to the world of *Ser*. He has problems, in short, with the world from which he came. Surely this is an antithesis to a humanistic development.

As with memory, the centrality of language is a constant pattern in the book. For the Hispanic reader the struggle quickly becomes English versus Spanish. His parents do not know the grand development of the Spanish language and its importance beyond their immediate family. However, Richard Rodriguez should, as an educated person, recognize this grand development. Surely, he could have given credit to the development of a language that has existed over six hundred years, which has elaborated a world literature, which has mixed with the many languages of the American continents, which is perhaps the most analytical of the romance languages, and which will be of such importance in the twenty-first century. Instead Richard Rodriguez flees, as a young man, from this previous human achievement. This fleeing is understandable as a symbol of the pressures of the Americanization process. Yet, as a formally educated scholar, reflecting upon that flight, he does not dare to signal the importance that the language has. Instead he sees it as an activity that has no redeeming value. He gives no value to the Hispanic language, its culture, its arts. It is difficult to believe that as an educated humanist he doesn't recognize the most important element of Hispanic culture—the context of the development of the distinct religions in the Spanish peninsula—the Judaic, the Christian, and the Moorish. These distinct cultures reached their apogees and clearly influenced Spanish. As a humanist, surely he must know this. The Hispanic world has elaborated and developed much in the history of ideas. Richard Rodriguez seems to indicate that the personal Spanish voice lacks the intelligence and ability to communicate beyond the sensibilities of the personal interactions of personal family life. This is intolerable. Hispanic culture has a historical tradition of great intellectual development. He does not recognize the so-called "original sin" of the American continents. What is this *pecado original* that Hector Murena wrote about so eloquently? It is simply the act of transplanting the European cultures to the American continents. The conquest by the Europeans of what is today Hispanic America is one of the most fundamental struggles for justice. The *Laws of Burgos* (1511–1521), established in Spain before the conquest of Mexico, held above all that the Indian was a man of the world. This was a fundamental axiom. The evolved mestizo nations struggled through a racist colonial empire, but there was a mixture of races. This was less evident in the English-speaking world. I mention this because it appears to me that one of the greatest preoccupations of Richard Rodriguez is that he "looks" Indian. He speaks of his father as looking and being white. He speaks of his mother as looking Portuguese. It surprises me that as an educated humanist in 1982 he would still have that type of complex, colonized mind. He feels out of place in Bel Air in L.A. because he looks

Indian. He worries about what or how he will be perceived by the "Anglo." These are honest and sincere perceptions. I respect his feelings. He does, however, remind me of students I had in the 50s and 60s who were struggling with their brownness.

The Hispanic colonial period evolved a racism based mainly on color and, of course, class. The colonial mind was preoccupied with color. When a child born to a couple was darker than the parents, he/she was called a *salto atrás*, a jump backwards, but if the child was lighter, he/ she was considered a *salto adelante*, a jump forward; and if the child was the same color as the parents, a *tente en el aire*, suspended. At times Richard Rodriguez clearly illustrates a colonized mind. His reactions as a young child are understandable. As a writer, however, while interpreting these sensibilities well, he fails to analyze those pressures that force conformity and simply attributes negative values to the language and culture of his parents, who have, as he states "no-public-voice."

It is well to recall briefly the formation of the Mexican nation and its history as it went from a political to an intellectual emancipation from 1811 to 1917. It took the Mexican nation over 100 years and 50 civil wars to evolve an independent, clear, and creative character. It is a unique nation. By 1930 the Mexican character was distinct—its art, music, literature, and culture were unique. It had developed a unique identity and character; it had accepted the *mestizo*. Surely, Richard Rodriguez must recognize, now that he is educated, that his parents came from a culture that was distinctly Mexican, and non-imitative, that his parents represent a culture with a singular identity. He offers, however, no recognition of the cultural uniqueness of his parents. Mexican culture had gone through its colonial and imitative period, its struggle for intellectual emancipation, and had arrived as an authentic, unique nation. His parents, therefore, recognize much better than Richard Rodriquez who the "gringos" are. This is a constant motif in the book. His parents know who they are themselves. They are no puzzle unto themselves. Richard Rodriguez says that change is a constant and should be constant and he argues that in order to change or to have the dynamics of change it is necessary to leave behind his Mexicanness, represented by the silence of the personal voice, the non-public voice, and his distinct cultural attributes. By gaining the other public voice, he asserts, he will become more authentic. Truly, this is antithetical to a humanistic education.

Richard Rodriguez' views remind me of two excellent books. The first one was published in 1930 by Samuel Ramos, *El perfil del hombre en la historia de Mexico* (*The Profile of Man in the History of Mexico*), and the other was published in 1950 by Octavio Paz, *El laberinto de la soledad*

(*The Labyrinth of Solitude*). *El perfil* discusses the inferiority complex of the Mexican. *El laberinto* reflects on the silence and the bursting out from that silence of the Mexican psyche. They are books eloquent in their perceptions of silence and the negativistic attitudes about the Mexican psyche. Samuel Ramos writes about *el pelado*; Octavio Paz has a marvelous chapter on *el pachuco* and now with Richard Rodriguez there is a total book on *el pocho* or what he considers to be *el pocho*. *El pelado, el pachuco* and *el pocho* can be considered alienated persons at the margins of culture. They do not represent the totality of the Hispanic culture in general, nor, in particular, the Mexican or Mexican-American culture. These are books about extreme people. What the *pelado*, the *pachuco*, and what Richard Rodriguez symbolize is a type of graffiti. By saying this, I do not seek to demean Richard Rodriguez' endeavor at all, but simply to point out that the most important element of graffiti is that it is an expression. Done in silence. Powerful. Exact. It calls out attention to itself as if saying "I want you, the passerby, to understand me. I am at the (extreme) margin. I want to be; I hunger to be part of your memory." Graffiti beckons us. It calls to tell us that they *are* us—in an extreme way, that they exist between cultures, but outside a culture.

In spite of its humanistic antithesis, *Hunger of Memory* has an authentic dimension. Perhaps the most important element here is that Richard Rodriguez is a reflection of a North American education. Is he a reflection of the English professor or the place of preparation which doesn't really give him perceptions other than those of the English-speaking world? There is, ultimately, I believe, a lack of understanding of world culture; especially lacking is an understanding of the Hispanic world. It is a reflection of a North American education. He calls himself Caliban in "Mr. Secrets." Who is Caliban? He is a slave, a monster, a character in Shakespeare's last play. Caliban represents the puppet, the person who is controlled. Caliban in *The Tempest* was driven by material instincts only. "Mr. Secrets," the last chapter, is especially clear on this concept. Is Caliban a reflection of a North American education? Is it an indication of an education which refuses to acknowledge as important only that which is tied to the northern European cultures? Is it an attitude of non-inquiry in the teaching of humanities? Aren't racist impositions, Adamic and nativistic concepts and attitudes quite prevalent?

The great surprise of many of our students who study abroad is that of finding out that not everything is originated (truly) in the United States, and that in reality our cultural history is quite short and in many instances limited. Richard Rodriguez is saying that he now has a public voice, an authentic one. Before he did not. He now believes that he is more real, and this is absurd. The dimension that Richard Rodriguez gives the North American public in his book fits well within North American intellectual circles because he has ironically justified his context by "being" not one of "them," but rather by having become one of "us." The North American public accepts Richard Rodriguez quite well and much in the same manner that it accepted Oscar Lewis' studies of the poor in Puerto Rico and Mexico. In this manner, knowledge of the unknown is accepted, simplified, and categorized. One has to ask if Richard Rodriguez has a community now? Did he have a community in the past? Does he think that now because he has published and has been accepted as a good writer that he now has community? Richard Rodriguez exists between two cultures, but he believes it more important to participate in one world than the other. But it is possible to participate in many worlds profoundly and, without losing, but rather gaining perception and appreciation from all.

I want to place in opposition to Richard Rodriquez' work a body of Chicano literature which has precepts as profound and as well writen. This body of expression has not had the same acceptance. Some of it is written in Spanish, some in English, and some in a mixture of both languages. It is not recognized well, basically because the works have not been published nor merchandized by major American publishing companies. In these Chicano works there is little hunger of memory, and much hunger for community. If Richard Rodriguez has hunger of memory, Chicano literature hungers for community. Those who labored, in the 1960s and 1970s and into the 1980s to establish a literature, accepted the task to develop a literature in the United States and that it was to be in languages understandable primarily to the Mexican-American community. The endeavor was a basic challenge to North American literary dominance. In 1965, there were few works written by writers of Mexican extraction in the United States. There were no courses being taught in Chicano literature. Today there are courses taught in Chicano literature in a total of 135 universities at the undergraduate and graduate level. It is recognized as a body of literature either as part of Mexican literature, as part of American literature, or as an offshoot of Hispanic-American literature. It has several intellectual bases, but this literature does not interest Richard Rodriguez even as a curiosity—even though, paradoxically, he is now inextricably part of that contribution.

The Chicano writers I have in mind were hungry for community. The manner of establishing that community was through remembrance and rediscovery of commonalities of the culture plus the need to accept the community in all its heterogeneity—that is, with all its virtues, with all its flaws, with all its energy, with all its apathy. It was important to recognize and to develop the basic elements of our community. Martin Buber's idea that "Community is the aspiration of all human history" was clearly before us. The Mexican-American as part of human history" had to develop that community, to be part of it, or leave it. Rebecca West says that "Community is conversation," and the Mexican-American community has not been silent since then. What the Chicano writer did was establish a community where there was a definite place, where dialogues could develop, and where the values of the community could be elaborated. There was little concern regarding acceptance by the larger/majority population. There is a more visible Chicano/Mexican-American community today because Chicano writers aided in underlining the realities that made up the community. Clearly Richard Rodriguez regards that community as living in silence. Actually that is why he is very alone. What one senses in *Hunger of Memory* is that his parents no longer speak. Ironically his parents speak louder than he. The sensibility of his writing effort, I dare say, does not come only from his training in the English language, but from those early day experiences when he was taught, I am sure, the way to invent himself in the world by his parents.

I said earlier that Richard Rodriguez reminds me of students I had in college in the 1960s who were embarrassed to organize themselves, who did not want to bring their parents to college to participate in college activities because their parents wouldn't know how to dress, and students who hardly respected the few Chicano professors who were then around. Truly, these students had the same type of colonized mind dramatized by Richard Rodriguez—honest, authentic, and naive, particularly at this later date.

What *Hunger of Memory* therefore reveals is one more step in the intellectual emancipation of the Mexican-American. It represents a significant intellectual step because such views are so clearly articulated. His parents know who they are, who they were, and who the gringos were. They didn't stop talking to him because they didn't understand him, but because he no longer saw the significance of their life. Richard Rodriguez lost the memory of all the philosophical questions they had helped him face and answer long before he walked into the English-speaking world. A writer is lonely only if he has lost the sense of his community's aspirations and the integrative values. His parents are the thesis of his statement. Sometimes, he feels frustrated because they have not read García-Márquez, Rubén Darío, but then he never read these writers to them. He hungers for a memory that could be so close, yet he doesn't seem to realize that satisfying this appetite is within reach.

Hunger of Memory is thus a humanistic antithesis for several reasons.

First, because its breadth and dimension is so narrow, unaware as it is of the traditions that should inform it. Second, it is ultimately an aggregation of cultural negations. Richard Rodriguez prizes as authentic only that which he learns in the classrooms. Third, he underlines the silence of culture as negative. Finally, Richard Rodriguez believes that it is only through English that he thinks he can elaborate what is correct and not correct for the community as a whole.

In his last chapter, "Mr. Secrets," as the family is leaving, and everyone is standing outside, his mother asks him to take a sweater to his father because it is getting cold. The last words of the book are "I take it [the sweater] and place it on him. In that instant I feel the thinness of his arms. He turns. He asks if I am going home now, too. It is, I realize, the only thing he has said to me all evening."

Here Richard Rodriguez tells us that his father has been silent all evening. What he doesn't tell us is that he (Richard Rodriguez) has also been silent. He does not tell us about *his* own type of silence. If he has a hunger of memory it is mainly because he does not choose to communicate his more intimate memories. Can anything be that painful? Where is the real *honra*, the real *Ser*? The only positive cultural attributes which he signals throughout his book are those relative to the English-speaking world. Richard Rodriguez understands the needs for memory, but does not dare recover it totally. Why? The title is the thesis, but the content is the antithesis of the very title. This is a classic work, 1930 Mexican vintage, clearly seeking approbation of an inferiority complex. As Samuel Ramos stated in *El perfil del hombre*, it is not that the Mexican is inferior: it's that he thinks he is inferior. This was the legacy of Spanish colonization. Richard Rodriguez apparently decolonizes himself by seeking to free himself from a personal voice, but in so trying he will likely enter another colony of despair.

Appendices

La casa grande del pueblo

La llegada fue de noche. Se veía la casa blanca, sin
luz, pero se veía enorme. Duramos cinco días
para llegar a la casa grande. Salimos un martes
de Texas. "en martes no te embarques." Llegamos
al estado de Kansas y se nos acabaron las estampillas
para la gasolina. También no teníamos en que
comprar dos llantas. Y estuvimos un día entero en
las afueras de Kansas City. El abuelo fue el que
llamó a la compañía azucarera en Minnesota y
consiguió más estampillas y un poco de dinero para
comprar las llantas. Estuvimos allí sentados en
la orilla del camino. En realidad nos tocó suerte
porque aunque era en abril, a mediados, el
sol nos calentó lo suficiente para estar a gusto.
Pudimos destullirnos un poco, y nos echamos
unas andadas por el ferrocarril. No estuvo
mal. Ya cuando conseguimos todo entramos y
pasamos por Kansas City y dos días después,
estábamos ya en Iowa, en Hampton, en la casa
Grande.

No podíamos creer lo blanco y lo enorme de la casa.
"Fíjese nomás, compadre, estos hombres sí que son
buenos. Fíjese nomás la casa que nos han dado.
Pero, usted cree compadre, está seguro de que esta sea
la dirección. Sí, oiga, aquí merito vamos a
vivir, aunque le sea increíble. Aquí en el centro.

From the autograph manuscript of "La casa grande del pueblo."

Las estampas inéditas

❧

Como Rivera ha explicado, la estampa o anécdota "a veces se puede ligar bien al cuento que precede pero no necesariamente. Sirve de ligazón para la obra total" (Documento, Archivos Tomás Rivera). Las estampas llevan en sí, más bien, resonancias de uno o más relatos. "Mingo y Pancha", por ejemplo, repite una característica de "El Pete Fonseca": "Decía papá que era muy recargue" y reitera un pasaje de "Zoo Island" donde don Simón habla con tres jóvenes que lo entrevistan para levantar un censo de los chicanos en una granja y de esta manera ver si son suficientes para formar un pueblo:

—¿Por qué no habla usted mucho don Simón?
—Esto es para el censo ¿verdad que no?
—No.
—¿Para qué? ¿Apoco creen ustedes que hablan mucho? Bueno, no solamente ustedes sino toda la gente. Lo que hace la mayor parte de la gente es mover la boca y hacer ruido. Les gusta hablarse a sí mismos, es todo. Yo también lo hago. Yo lo hago en silencio, los demás lo hacen en voz alta.

Mingo y Pancha

Mingo y Pancha llegaron al rancho en julio. Se notó luego, luego que les gustaba hablar de más. También se la recargaban mucho. Lo que le gustaba más a ella era platicar de su luna de miel. Decía que por toda una semana habían comido en restaurante. Y nada de frijoles y tortillas, nada más habían comido papas revueltas con huevo y pan blanco. El también decía que una vez había rendido a Roy Rogers en Fort Worth.

* * *

Algunos episodios, y estampas también, de *Tierra* expresan o implican los percances del camino a que están sujetos los chicanos en su nomadismo laboral. Valgan, por ejemplo, el episodio "Cuando lleguemos" y la estampa "Diez y seis muertos". La acción de "Zoo Island" tiene lugar en Iowa, desde donde parece haberse emprendido el viaje que se narra a continuación. También en "La cosecha" los chicanos ya están para volver a Texas: "Los últimos de septiembre y los primeros de octubre. Ese era el mejor tiempo del año. Primero, porque señalaba que ya se terminaba el trabajo y la vuelta a Texas". La estampa siguiente expresa lo que bien pudiera haber sucedido a esta gente.

La volteada

Dos semanas antes de regresar a Tejas fue al pueblo y se compró un carro. Llevó a un chofer para que lo trajera para el rancho porque él no sabía manejar. Su hijo mayor tenía apenas los trece años y él tampoco sabía. Trató de aprender y de enseñar a su hijo pero no pudieron aprender en dos semanas. Cuando se llegó la partida para Tejas le dijo a su hijo que él tendría que llevarse el carro porque él ya estaba muy viejo y no podía ver muy bien. Se fueron como a veinte millas por hora y realmente la única dificultad que tenía su hijo era cuando se arrancaba de algún lugar. Era puro saltar hasta que no se iba parejito. En Des Moines casi le dio un ataque de nervios al niño. Pero después que pasaron a Kansas City cogió tanta confianza que empezó a leer los letreros al lado de la carretera. Fue cuando se volcaron.

* * *

En "El Pete Fonseca", el protagonista Pete ha decidido casarse con la Chata y piensa en las maneras de ganar dinero. Una manera es ir al basurero para buscar alambre de cobre para vender: "También decía que le caían bien los niños de la Chata. Se podían comprar una ranfla y luego los domingos se podían ir a pasear, al mono, a pescar, al dompe a juntar alambre de cobre para vender".

El alambre de cobre

Como había llovido tuvieron ocasión de ir al pueblo. Estaba muy mojado para entrar a la labor así que muy temprano andaban viendo los carros de segunda. Vieron pasar un carro con una trailer llena de alambre de cobre e immediatamente la siguieron. El alambre lo podían vender a cinco centavos la libra y a lo menos llevaban unas cien libras porque el bulto estaba muy grande. Adivinaron también que seguramente iban a tirar el alambre y en realidad el carro cogió el camino hacia el basurero. Ya para llegar se metió en un rancho. E-llos lo siguieron. El ranchero les dijo que allí vivía. Ellos le preguntaron que si tenía trabajo.

* * *

Crystal City, Texas, donde nació Tomás Rivera tiene fama de ser un centro importante en la cultivación de acelga, o sea, espinacas. Para la promoción de este producto, este pueblo agrícola hizo construir una estatua gigantesca de Popeye, figura de los *cartoons*, que obtiene una fuerza extraordinaria al comer espinacas, y el pueblo celebra la cosecha de espinacas con una fiesta que incluye un desfile. En cuanto a *Tierra*, esta estampa hubiera marcado el punto de partida al norte, el tránsito del regocijo a la miseria.

[Popeye]

El paseo cada año de Popeye les gustaba a todos. Siempre iban dos o tres trocas cargadas de chicanos con el cuchillo de cortar acelga en una mano y una mata bien escogida en la otra. También llevaban cajas de acelga en un rincón. A muchos les gustaba llevar a sus hijos en las trocas para que le dijeran *adiós* a toda la parentela.

La casa grande del pueblo

La llegada fue de noche. Se veía la casa blanca, sin luz, enorme.[1] Duramos cinco días para llegar a la casa grande. Salimos un martes de Texas. "En martes no te embarques". Llegamos al estado de Kansas y se nos acabaron las estampillas para la gasolina. También no teníamos con qué comprar dos llantas. Y estuvimos un día entero en las afueras de Kansas City. El abuelo fue el que llamó a la compañía azucarera en Minnesota y consiguió más estampillas y un poco de dinero para comprar las llantas. Estuvimos allí sentados en la orilla del camino. En realidad nos tocó suerte porque aunque era en abril, a mediados, el sol nos calentó lo suficiente para estar a gusto. Pudimos desentullirnos un poco, y nos echamos unas andadas por el ferrocarril. No estuvo mal. Ya cuando conseguimos todo entramos y pasamos por Kansas City, y dos días después estábamos ya en Iowa, en Hampton, en la casa grande.

No podíamos creer lo blanco y lo enorme de la casa.

—Fíjese nomás, compadre, estos hombres sí que son buenos. Fíjese nomás la casona que nos han dado.

—Pero, ¿usted cree, compadre? ¿Está seguro de que ésta sea la dirección?

—Sí, oiga, aquí merito vamos a vivir, aunque le sea increíble. Aquí en el centro. Eso es lo que nos dijeron, compadre. Usted mismo oyó lo que dijo el viejo, y ésta es la dirección ... Vieja, saca la cabeza para fuera para que veas la casa que nos vamos a aventar este año ... Usted fue conmigo, compadre, cuando fuimos a hablar con el viejo. Recuerde que sólo nos advirtió que solamente cogiéramos un cuarto para las tres familias. Pero se imagina cuántos cuartos tendrá, compadre, y lo grande que serán.

—No me puedo imaginar, serán grandísimos los cuartos. Bueno, pues ya veremos. Oiga, compadre, ¿y habrá alguien ya viviendo aquí?

—No, somos los primeros que vamos a ocupar la casa. Pero, qué grande está. Vamos a entrarle.

—Oiga, compadre, hasta parece que espantan. Mire nomás qué grande está.

—No tenga miedo, hombre.

La casa no espantaba al principio. Nos bajamos de la troca. Éramos tres familias. La familia de mi abuelo, la de mi tío, y la de nosotros. Nos bajamos[a] y entramos. Tenía un corredor, un portalón que casi le daba la vuelta entera a la casa. Nos metimos y prendimos las luces y examinamos la casa cuarto por cuarto. Tenía unas ventanas enormes. Subimos al segundo piso que también tenía unas ventanas enormes. Desde allí podíamos ver por toda la calle las hileras de luces. Se veía un puente y al lado un camposanto y lo que parecía una escuela. Nos entró más gusto que nada.[2] No podíamos creer el estar en una casa así. De ricos. Las luces de la calle, los carros que pasaban al lado de la casa y enfrente de la casa, y estábamos contentísimos.

Después de que pasamos un rato examinando, salimos de la casa y metimos nuestros liachos.[b] Examinamos la casa con cuidado otra vez y allí estuvimos. Ocupamos tres cuartos, uno para cada familia, abajo. La casa tenía once cuartos. En el piso de abajo tenía un baño, una cocina, una sala, y tres recámaras. En el piso segundo tenía un baño y cuatro recámaras. Decidimos ocupar tres cuartos esa noche porque no había otra gente allí. También decidimos que, cuando viniera la demás gente, escogeríamos el cuarto que tenía una puerta que daba al baño. El baño tenía dos puertas, la que daba al cuarto, que iba a ser el de nosotros, y la que daba a la cocina. El segundo piso sería para solteros según nos dijo el viejo.

Esa noche desperté varias veces y oí[3] el crujido de la madera en la casa y me empecé a imaginar los cuartos solos y vacíos, huecos, vacíos sin gente, y allí nos dormimos a gusto. Dormimos muy a gusto, primero, porque veníamos muy cansados de tanto viajar, y, segundo, porque no podíamos comprender el tener una casa tan elegante como en la que estábamos. Nos parecía algo formidable.

Cuando amaneció el siguiente día, el asombro para nosotros fue aún tan fuerte como cuando llegamos. Al despertar y luego al andar por toda la casa, y luego al salir y ver la casa de día y examinarla y ver la tremenda yarda que tenía alrededor, y los árboles tan grandes en el fondo del solar, y luego[4] ver que estábamos en una vecindad realmente elegante donde había otras casas tan elegantes como la nuestra nos era increíble.[5]

Teníamos una casa grande en el pueblo.[6] Lo único que me sorprendió a mí y lo que me dio miedo fue el sótano. Grandísimo. Me pareció como que[7] la casa lo estaba escondiendo y guardándolo para alguna ocasión.[8] Lo encontré oscuro y frío. Hasta[9] parecía estar lleno de algo.

* * *

Este relato parece ser la introducción a la segunda novela de Rivera, *La casa grande del pueblo*, que el autor, según correspondencia suya y una entrevista, había terminado en borrador alrededor de 1975–76: "hace tres años que terminé otra novela, *La casa grande del pueblo*, pero no la he repasado", (Javier Vásquez-Castro, "Tomás Rivera", *Acerca de literatura: Diálogo con tres autores chicanos* [San Antonio, M&A Editions, 1979]: 51–52): No se ha podido encontrar el manuscrito de la novela entre los documentos literarios del finado autor. De este relato hay un manuscrito autógrafo y otro mecanografiado; éste lleva la notación autógrafa: "Original 4-1-75". La acción del relato tiene lugar durante o poco después de la Segunda Guerra Mundial, puesto que hay referencias a cupones, "estampillas", para la compra de gasolina, producto racionado durante este período.

Variantes del ms. autógrafo:
[1]pero se veía enorme.
[2]Nos entró a todos una alegría increíble.
[3]oía
[4]No consta en el ms.: los árboles tan grandes en el fondo del solar, y luego
[5]aún increíble.
[6]El ms. agrega: y era una maravilla.
[7]lo que
[8]lo tenía guardado para algo.
[9]oscuro, frío, pero

* * *

[a]Ambas versiones tienen: abajamos; que cambiamos a: bajamos — para corresponder con el "bajamos" de arriba.
[b]*liachos*: petates.

Era muy llorón

Al terminarse el rosario, la novena, mejor dicho, salieron todos para fuera de la casa y se empezaron a dirigir a sus casas. Parecía que la noche les invitaba a platicar y así se formaron algunas conversaciones. Era muy llorón. Cuando se casó m'ijo, lloró toda la mañana. Y yo le decía, que qué tenía que para qué lloraba. Ya sé que se sienten los hijos, pero no era para tanto. Y ustedes recuerdan que él era muy enérgico, pues también era muy llorón. Es que era muy sentimental mi viejo. Dios lo tenga en paz. La primera vez que lo vi llorar fue después de que le había dado unas patadas al más grande. Me dijo que le entró el coraje y no pudo aguantarse, y pues ahí lo tienes, llorando solo en el cuartito de dormir. Es que era muy sentimental. Y luego cuando se murió su amigo Adolfo, también. Recuerdo que cuando estábamos en el camposanto se le rodaban las lágrimas por los cachetes. Y luego m'ijo, el más grande, le preguntó que para qué lloraba. No le dijo nada, nomás se le quedó viendo con coraje. Y luego cuando se acabó el entierro y que ya íbamos saliendo del camposanto, como que le quiso hacer burla m'ijo a su papá, y se erizó mi viejo y le dijo que nomás los hombres de deveras lloraban. Que los meros hombres eran los que sentían. Y yo le creí. Porque, aunque era muy llorón, mi viejo era muy hombre. Eso sí lo sé. A mí nunca me dio o me dijo nada para yo no creer en él. Es que era muy sentimental. Y por eso cuando me abrazaba hasta se le rozaban* los ojos de lágrimas, y yo sabía y sentía que me quería mucho. Y por eso le quise. Era como si cada mañana podría yo despertar segura de que habíamos dos en todo esto que le llamamos mundo, que pertenecíamos y hasta se me hacía que nosotros éramos el centro de todo; como que al despertar por la mañana y al abrir los ojos reconocíamos los dos que enfrente estaba todo, de la nariz para adelante. Y después de que vinieron los hijos, siempre nos preguntábamos lo mismo, que cómo estarían los niños. A que mi viejo, era muy llorón, pero eso nomás mis hijos y yo lo sabemos.

*Así en el ms.; quizás ha de ser: rebosaban.

Notes

Introduction

[1] "The Great Plains as Refuge in Chicano Literature."

[2] Tomás Rivera, ... *y no se lo tragó la tierra/* ... *And the Earth Did Not Part*, Herminio Ríos, Octavio I. Romano-V., trans. (Berkeley: Quinto Sol Publications, Inc., 1971; ... *y no se lo tragó la tierra/* ... *And the Earth Did Not Devour Him*, (3rd ed.), Evangelina Vigil-Piñón, trans., in this collection.

[3] See Rafael Grajeda, "Tomás Rivera's ... *y no se lo tragó la tierra:* Discovery and Appropriation of the Chicano Past," *Hispania* 62.1 (1979): 71–81; rpt. in *Contemporary Chicano Fiction*, Vernon E. Lattin, Ed. (Binghamton, NY: Bilingual Press/Editorial Bilingüe, 1986): 113–25; Joseph Sommers, "From the Critical Premise to the Product, Critical Modes and their Applications to a Chicano Literary Text," *New Scholar* 6 (1977): 67–75; rpt. in *Modern Chicano Writers*, Joseph Sommers and Tomás Ybarra-Frausto, Eds. (Englewood Cliffs, NJ: Prentice-Hall, 1979): 74–85; José D. Saldívar, "The Ideological and Utopian in Tomás Rivera's ... *y no se lo tragó la tierra* and Ron Arias' *The Road To Tamazunchale,*" *Crítica* 1.2 (1985): 100–14; Ramón Saldívar, "Beyond Good and Evil: Utopian Dialectics in Tomás Rivera and Oscar Zeta Acosta," *Chicano Narrative, The Dialectics of Difference* (Madison: The University of Wisconsin Press, 1990): 103–31; and Julián Olivares, "The Search for Being, Identity and Form in the Work of Tomás Rivera," *International Studies in Honor of Tomás Rivera*, Julián Olivares, Ed. (Houston: Arte Publico Press, 1986 [*Revista Chicano-Riqueña* 13.3-4, 1985]): 66–72.

[4] The information with regard to Rivera's parents is taken from his article, "We are all immigrants," *San Antonio Express-News* (September 7, 1975): 5-6H. Except for the biographical content, synthesized here, the remainder of this article is duplicated in his essay, "The Great Plains as Refuge in Chicano Literature."

[5] See Bruce Novoa, "Tomás Rivera," *Chicano Authors: Inquiry by Interview* (Austin: University of Texas Press, 1980): 140–41.

[6] Rivera's short fiction, including two previously unpublished stories, "La cosecha" and "Zoo Island," was collected in my bilingual edition, *The Harvest, Short Stories/La cosecha, cuentos* (Houston: Arte Publico Press, 1989); Rivera's poetry appeared in my edition of *The Searchers: Collected Poetry* (Houston: Arte Publico Press, 1990). The contents of these editions, as well as portions of their respective introductions, are included in the present edition.

[7] I shall refer to the third edition, 1991, in this collection.

[8] The sources are given in the section of Rivera's essays.

[9]A portion of this discussion was first published in my "The Search for Being, Identity and Form in the Work of Tomás Rivera."

[10]Rivera did not list the titles of the vignettes in the published version of *Tierra*, but did list their titles in a primitive index. They are, as appearing sequentially in *Tierra*: "El agua y los espíritus" ["The Water and the Spirits"], "Con los espíritus" ["With the Spirits"], "Cerca de Japón" ["Close to Japan"], "De jodido no paso" ["I can't get any worse"], "La peluquería" ["The barber shop"], "El ministro" ["The minister"], "El abuelo" ["The grandfather"], "El botón" ["The button"], "El día del casamiento" ["The Wedding Day"], "Diez y seis muertos" ["Sixteen dead"], "Las tarjetas de Barcelona" ["Postcards from Barcelona"], "Figueroa," "Bartolo"; see my "Los índices primitivos de ... *y no se lo tragó la tierra* y cuatro estampas inéditas," *Crítica, a Journal of Critical Essays* 2.2 (Fall 1990): 208–22.

[11]Rivera clarifies this in a note to "El año perdido": "El año puede significar lo estáticamente cronológico y simbolizar tambien todo el tiempo que ha existido el personaje" ["The year can signify the statically chronological and also all the time that a character has existed"], from a document titled "El cuento" ["The Short Story"], Tomás Rivera Archives, Tomás Rivera Library, University of California, Riverside.

[12]For a more extensive discussion of the evolution of *Tierra*, see my "Los índices primitivos..." and my "'La cosecha' y 'Zoo Island' de Tomás Rivera: Apuntes sobre la formación de ...*y no se lo tragó la tierra*," *Hispania* 74.1 (March 1991): 57–65.

[13]"...yo trato de describir en ...*y no se lo tragó tierra*, que abarca los años '40 y '50, la explotación del trabajador agrícola, la situación de la iglesia católica en su esfuerzo, directo en indirecto, por mantenernos sumisos...aquel sacerdote que es incapaz de reconocer que las personas tienen derecho a ciertas libertades, y el inculcarles a ellos un sentimiento de culpabilidad, no es admirable" ["...I endeavor to depict in ...*y no se lo tragó la tierra*, that deals with the '40's and '50's, the exploitation of the agricultural worker, the situation of the Catholic Church in its effort, direct and indirect, to maintain us submissive... The priest that is incapable of recognizing that people have the right to certain liberties, and who inculcates in people a feeling of culpability, is not an admirable person"], Javier Vásquez-Castro, "Tomás Rivera," *Acerca de literatura: Diálogo con tres autores chicanos* (San Antonio: M&A Editions, 1979): 50.

[14]It is possible to include within the internal obstacles the institutions of machismo and patriarchy prevalent in Chicano society; see Patricia de la Fuente, "Invisible Women in the Narrative of Tomás Rivera," and Sylvia S. Lizárraga, "The Patriarchal Ideology in 'La noche que se apa-

garon las luces' ['The Night the Lights Went Out']," both in *International Studies in Honor of Tomás Rivera*, 81–89 and 90–95, respectively; and Olivares, "Apuntes," 58.

[15]"The Ideological and the Utopian in Tomás Rivera's *…y no se lo tragó la tierra* and Ron Arias' *The Road to Tamazunchale*," 103.

[16]"Beyond Good and Evil, Utopian Dialectics in Tomás Rivera and Oscar Zeta Acosta," 84.

[17]See Juan Rodríguez, "La embestida contra la religiosidad en *…y no se lo tragó la tierra*," *Pacific Coast Council on Latin American Studies Proceedings: Changing Perspectives in Latin America* 3 (1974): 83–86.

[18]The original titles of these stories are, respectively: "El niño que tenía sed" and "y no se lo comió la tierra"; see the ff. note.

[19]For a discussion of this development see my "Los índices primitivos…," 212–14.

[20]On the story "Debajo de la casa," Rivera states: "Es en sí una recopilación de los acontecimientos de las voces que ocurrieron o se oyeron…antes, y así representan también el esfuerzo colectivo que no solamente junta sino inventa las vidas chicanas" ["It is a compilation of the events, of the voices, that occurred or were heard…before, and thereby also represent the collective effort that not only unites but invents the Chicano lives"], from a document titled *Y no se lo tragó la tierra*, Tomás Rivera Archives.

[21]"The Discourse of Silence in the Narrative of Tomás Rivera," *International Studies in Honor of Tomás Rivera*, 106.

[22]Rivera goes on to explain this statement: "El esclavo es una inversión [A slave is an investment] so you protect him to keep him working. A migrant worker? You owe him nothing. If he came to you, you gave him work and then you just told him to leave. No investment. If he got sick, you got rid of him; you didn't have to take care of him. It was bad, labor camps and all that" Bruce-Novoa, 148, 150–51.

[23]On fragmentation in the Chicano novel as a means to social and cultural reintegration, see also John C. Akers, "Fragmentation in the Chicano Novel: Literary Technique and Cultural Identity," *International Studies in Honor of Tomás Rivera*, 121–35.

[24]"Language and Dialog in *…y no se lo tragó tierra*," *International Studies in Honor of Tomás Rivera*, 53–54. On the formal repercussions in *Tierra* of orality, Rivera affirms: "Lo oral implica immediatamente la limitación del tiempo. El narrarse oralmente limita la extensión de la narración por razones físicas fáciles de comprender. También lo oral limita la complicación de la trama. El poder mantener una trama demasiado rebuscada se hace una imposibilidad no solamente para el narrador sino para el

oyente. Lo oral implica aún otro aspecto—el estilo, la manera de narrar. Se tiene que narrar sin perder palabras. Estas limitaciones se vuelven ventajas en un cuento bien escrito" ["Orality immediately implies temporal limitations. Orality limits the length of the story, for physical reasons easy to understand. Orality also limits plot complication. It becomes an impossibility to maintain plot complexity, not only for the narrator but also for the listener. Orality implies still another aspect—style, the manner of narrating. One has to narrate without losing words. These limitations can become advantages in a well written short story"], "El cuento," Tomás Rivera Archives.

[25]From a document titled "Commentary about: *And the Earth Did Not Part/ ...y no se lo tragó la tierra*," Tomás Rivera Archives. On the novelistic structure of *Tierra*, see the criticism listed in n. 2.

[26]See "Los índices primitivos..." and "Apuntes hacia la formación de...*tierra*."

[27]See Arturo Madrid-Barela, "In Search of the Authentic Pachuco: An Interpretive Essay," *Aztlan* 4.1 (1974): 31–60; Lauro Flores, "La Dualidad del Pachuco," *Revista Chicano-Riqueña* 6.4 (1978): 51–58; Rafael Grajeda, "The Pachuco in Chicano Poetry: The Process of Legend-Creation," *Revista Chicano-Riqueña* 8.4 (1980): 45–59.

[28]The English version has 1948. In a primitive typescript of *Tierra*, which contains "El Pete Fonseca," Rivera deleted 1948, and replaced it with 1958, which is how it appeared in the published Spanish version. See the note to this story.

[29]"El cuento," Tomás Rivera Archives. Rivera appears to have used this document in his literature courses. The discussion of the types of "conflicts" is not original and appears, in various forms, in books on literary criticism, especially those for students. In any event, these conflicts are central to Rivera's narrative.

[30]In the story, the salamanders—with their blackness and the milky fluid that oozes from their body—appear to symbolize the dualities of life and death. This duality is generated in the text. In Mexican mythology the salamander, *axolote*, symbolizes good and evil, life and death, earth and water. Cognizant of this mythological treatment, Alurista employs the salamander in "Trópico de ceviche," in *Nationchild Plumaroja* (included in Alurista, *Return: Poems Collected and New* [Ypsilanti, MI.: Bilingual Press/Editorial Bilingüe, 1982]: 72–75), and Octavio Paz employs it as the title of a book of poetry, *Salamandra*. Nowhere in Rivera's work do we note the *indigenismo* motifs that characterize much of the Chicano literature of the 1960's and 70's. In an interview Rivera explains why the indigenous theme does not enter into his work: "Meterme

a un mundo psicológico indígena me es completamente imposible. En general lo veo como una cosa académica...nunca he tenido ese deseo de relacionarme con el pasado prehispánico. En el '68, muchos escritores, especialmente los poetas, empezaron a usar aquellos símbolos mitológicos indígenas, elaborando una especie de misticismo que trataba de presentar el período pre-cortesiano como un momento ideal, pero que no lo fue, en mi opinión, porque no ha habido ninguna época ideal en ninguna cultura; entonces, es imposible para mí identificarme con ese sentimiento idealista pre-colombino. Es imposible. Por eso no elaboro temas indígenas," ["It is completely impossible for me to enter into the indigenous psychological world. In general, I see this as something academic... I have never desired to relate to the pre-Hispanic past. In '68 many writers, especially poets, began using indigenous mythological symbols, elaborating some sort of mysticism that attempted to present the pre-Cortesian period as an ideal time, but it never was, in my opinion, because there never has been an ideal epoch in any culture; therefore, it is impossible for me to identify myself with that idealistic pre-Columbian sentiment. It's impossible. That's why I don't employ indigenous themes"]. Javier Vásquez-Castro, "Tomás Rivera," *Acerca de literatura*, 46–47. See Thomas Vallejos, "The Beetfield as Battlefield: Ritual Process and Realization in Tomás Rivera's 'Las salamandras'," *The Americas Review* 17.2 (1989): 100–109.

[31]The reader will find a similarity between this dialogue and a passage from "Es que duele"/"It's that it Hurts," from the novel *Tierra*.

[32]A similar experience is expressed in the concluding narrative of *Tierra*, "Debajo de la casa"/"Beneath the House."

[33]"Zoo Island" is an instance of code-switching, which in literary discourse is often a rhetorical device with an ideological motivation and with an evaluative function; see Rosaura Sánchez, *Chicano Discourse: Sociohistoric Perspectives* (Rowley, MA.: Newbury House Publishers, Inc., 1983): 171–72.

[34]See also "The Searchers."

[35]Rolando Hinojosa told this editor that, in reality, the large house was a two-story Army surplus barrack.

[36]With the selection of the narratives that would make up the final draft of *...y no se lo tragó la tierra*, Herminio Ríos began the English translation, *...And the Earth Did Not Part*, "in collaboration with the author, with assistance by Octavio I. Romano-V." (xix). Those narratives that were excluded and subsequently published—"El Pete Fonseca," "Eva y Daniel"—were probably translated by Rivera himself. The former was written first in Spanish, but it was first published in English as "On the Road to Texas: Pete Fonseca." "Eva y Daniel" was published in a bilin-

gual format. The narratives from *Tierra* that remained unpublished were not translated until their inclusion in this collection. With regard to the remaining stories, first, it is uncertain if "En busca de Borges"/"Looking for Borges" was written first in Spanish or English. It appeared first in English in the inaugural issue of *Revista Chicano-Riqueña*, 1973, then in Spanish two years later. "Las salamandras" was written in Spanish and first published in 1974, with the English translation appearing alongside the Spanish version in 1975. The last story he wrote was "La cara en el espejo," appearing in 1975, and published in English as "Inside the Window" in 1977. Rivera's "On the Road to Texas: Pete Fonseca" and "Looking for Borges" remain essentially intact. With both stories, I have expanded their conclusions to coincide with their Spanish versions. Rivera's English translation of "El Pete Fonseca" cuts short the conclusion of the Spanish version, which was published later in *Revista Chicano-Riqueña*. I have translated this conclusion ("I remember that Pete appeared out of nowhere...") because it repeats the exposition, which together, frame the story and give emphasis to the mythic configuration of the pachuco. In "En Busca de Borges," Rivera added a phrase at the end, which makes his anti-Borgean stance more manifest. This has been translated as: "...with a look of hope on their face which at times seemed idiotic." With "Eva and Daniel" I translated and added a sentence that was missing from the English version ("There were some very heated discussions but, finally, Eva's parents consented to their marriage"). I have made minor revisions to "Inside the Window" and even less to "The Salamanders" for the purposes of clarification and readability. In the case of "The Harvest" and "Zoo Island," I have supplied the complete translations.

[37]It is assumed that these are precisely the reasons that the Nobel Committee never awarded Borges the Nobel Prize in Literature.

[38]In the correspondence that accompanied this story, submitted for the inaugural issue of *Revista Chicano-Riqueña*, Rivera tells Nicolás Kanellos, editor, that he was teaching a creative writing course at The University of Texas, San Antonio, and that he wrote "Looking for Borges" as an example and stimulus for his students. Although the story was first published in English, like "Pete Fonseca," it is possible that Rivera originally wrote it in Spanish. The editor of the review *Caracol*, in his note to the story "Salamandra," mentions that Rivera had told him that "all his prose is written in Spanish. The only things that come out in English are some of his poems," *Caracol* 1.6 (February, 1975): 16. Sommers affirms that, in addition to Juan Rulfo's obvious influence, there is a Borgean influence in *Tierra*: "What needs to be affirmed is that Rivera's knowledge of the

themes and techniques of writers such as Borges and Rulfo is deployed so as to meet the challenge of his literary project, involving the narration and interpretation of rural Chicano existence, as understood by the author in 1970. Thus the thematic cluster found in Borges which posits the inseparability of the subjective from the objective, the difficulty of finding truth in empirical data when the causal explanation is located in the mind of the investigator, and the vulnerability of logic and reason to the more profound categories of the subsconscious and the instinctive, marks the points of departure of Rivera's novel. The boy, like a character in Borges, is immersed in the mystery of self-consciousness, the origin of the thought process and the fallibility of memory. The answers, it seems to him, are locked up in his own being, in his own incapacity to separate dream from reason and to order the past. But the process of the novel, which is the narration of experienced Chicano reality and the struggle to recuperate fragmented time, is Rivera's finding of a way out of the perplexities and the labyrinthine dilemma posed by Borges," "From the Critical Premise to the Product..." (76). Borges' presence as a Visiting Professor at the University of Oklahoma during part of the period that Rivera was there studying for his doctorate helps explain, in part, his literary influence on him. Nonetheless, as Sommers points out, Rivera's emphasis on experienced reality and his faith in the power of memory and volition to find meaning in life distinguishes him from Borges' pessimism (see Rivera's "Remembering, Discovery and Volition in the Literary Imaginative Process"). For Rivera, there are indeed truths, but they can only be found in the realities of the human condition and through socially committed literature. The concluding phrase of the Spanish version of the story, in all probability added after its publication in English, patently demonstrates that Rivera had later definitively distanced himself from Borges' ethics.

[39]In researching Rivera's unpublished poetry, I have sometimes felt as if I were searching through his wastebasket (an act of discovery in his refuse?), possibly publishing some poems that Rivera may have wanted to discard. Those poems, some incomplete and some drafts, that I do not include in this collection and which I wish to document are:
"Blankness and Darkness"
"Shoes Thump"
"For Rhonda Burnam"
"In the Park"
"To err is human, to forgive divine"
"Lack of Symbols"
"The Fibre Content"
Untitled, first line: "That building is called a skyscraper. It is very

tall."

Untitled, first line: "She goes to communion every Sunday and confesses every Saturday."

Untitled, first line: "You will now forget the past."

[40]For a fuller discussion of "The Searchers," see my "The Search for Being, Identity and Form in the Work of Tomás Rivera."

[41]For the translation of the Spanish text in "The Searchers," see the "Notes to the Poetry."

[42]Two essays, "Into the Labyrinth: The Chicano in Literature" and "Literatura Chicana: Vida en busca de forma," are essentially the same. The latter is a shortened version of the former, and lacks the important concept of the labyrinth. Except for a brief portion of "Literatura Chicana," which I have taken from the published translation, "Chicano Literature: Life in Search of Form," and have incorporated in "Into the Labyrinth," I have excluded this essay from the current edition.

[43]I have not found the drafts of other papers which appear in Rivera's *curriculum vitae*: "Perspectives: Chicano Literature," MLA December, 1973; "Biculturalismo y estructura creativa como emancipación intelectual," MLA Minority Commission, Dallas, October, 1976. His CV also indicates two articles which I have not been able to locate: "Perspectives on Chicano Literature," which Rivera lists as having appeared in *Sociological Abstracts* (Southwestern Sociological Association and Southern Sociological Society), "Spring Issue, 1972, 10pp." (as noted in CV); and "The Writings of Hinojosa-Smith: Integrity," noted in the CV as "(to be published) *El cuaderno* (T[exas] A[ssociation of] CH[icanos in] E[ducation]), Vol. 2, University of Nebraska-Lincoln" (sic).

[44]Which explains why the book was readily accepted for publication by a mainstream press.

[45]For the literary expression of this concept, see Rivera's "Zoo Island."

[46]Document, Tomás Rivera Archives

[47]*"With His Pistol in His Hand," A Border Ballad and Its Hero* (Austin: University of Texas Press, 1958).

[48]The cultural analysis of a great part of Chicano literature is, as Sommers affirms, "incomplete if the concept of class is not taken into account: the all-important factor of class [is] a factor which shapes and influences the process by which cultural expression is generated. For example, the experience of the migratory cycle is fundamental to the cultural content of ... *y no se lo tragó la tierra*. However, to understand this cultural content in its genesis and its full import as a series of responses to the problems of adversity, it is necessary to account for the particular nature of seasonal forms of agricultural production; the migratory labor

system is not merely tolerated, but imposed on a large segment of Mexican-descended population. Were this system of exploitation to disappear, new forms of cultural expression would soon manifest themselves, as indeed has been the case when the rural Chicano population has gravitated to urban areas in search of improved social conditions" (68). For a detailed discussion of the relation between class and culture, see Juan Gómez-Quiñones, "On Culture," *Revista Chicano-Riqueña* 5.1 (1977): 29–47.

[49]In his *curriculum vitae* (March 27, 1984), Rivera states: "Up to the time I started my teaching career [1957], I was part of the migrant labor stream that went from Texas to various parts of the Midwest. I lived and worked in Iowa, Minnesota, Wisconsin, Michigan, and North Dakota," Tomás Rivera Archives.

La cosecha / The Harvest

Las salamandras

Mester 5.1 (University of California, Los Angeles, 1974): 25–26; reimpreso en: *Caracol* 1.6 (febrero de 1975): 14–16, publicación bilingüe con los títulos de "Salamandra"/"Salamander"; *Kaleidoscopia* 3 (Universidad de las Américas, verano de 1975); *El Cuento: Revista de la Imaginación* 70 (México, julio-diciembre de 1975): 379–81; *Festival de Flor y Canto I: An Anthology of Chicano Literature*, Alurista, et al., Eds. (Los Angeles: University of Southern California): 22–23.

[1]En *Mester* y en los reimpresos no hay ruptura del párrafo; división del editor.

[2]*Mester* y reimpresos: "echaron"

[3]"húngaros"—gitanos.

[4]*Mester*: "El dinero ya casi se nos había acabado y nos fuimos al oscurecer..."

[5]Aparte del editor; véase n. 1.

[6]*Flor y Canto*: "Sentados todos en el carro a la orilla del camino. Hablamos un poco."

[7]*Flor y Canto*: "Estábamos cansados. Estábamos solos. Solos. Solos Estábamos.

[8]Véase n. 1.

[9]En *Mester* y reimpresos: "...a mi gente, pero esa madrugada..."; puntuación del editor.

[10]"...a mi gente dormida y esa madrugada ..."; puntuación del editor.

[11]*Mester, El Cuento*: "abajara" (voz popular, prótesis de la *a*). Todos coinciden en el uso de "bajara" al fin del mismo párrafo.

[12]Este renglón y el anterior ("Nos enseñó los acres...") se omiten en *Caracol*.

[13]*Flor y Canto*: "...al pie del fil..."; aparte del editor, véase n. 1.

[14]Se omite este renglón en *Flor y Canto*.

[15]"...en las colchas, al ver fuera de la carpa..."; puntuación del editor.

El Pete Fonseca

Primera publicación en inglés: "On the Road to Texas: Pete Fonseca," *Aztlan: An Anthology of Mexican American Literature*, Luis Valdez and Stan Steiner, Eds. (New York: Alfred A. Knopf, 1972): 146–54; reimpreso en: *Voices of Aztlan: Chicano Literature of Today*, Dorothy E. Harth and Lewis M. Baldwin, Eds. (New York: New American Library, 1974): 52–58; reimpreso en español como "El Pete Fonseca" en: *Revista Chicano-Riqueña* 2.1 (1974): 15–22, y en *A Decade of Hispanic Literature: An Anniversary Anthology, Revista Chicano-Riqueña* 10.1-2 (1982): 251–57.

[1]*RCR*: "renegando."

[2]*Caló*: "chale" —quieto, "nel" —no, "simón" —sí.

[3]"recargue" —engreído.

[4]"Spam" —marca de jamón enlatado.

[5]"trailer" —remolque, caravana.

[6]Suplo "de la trailer" para completar el sentido.

[7]Austin (Texas).

[8]*Caló*: "ranfla" —carro; "mono" —cine; "dompe" —basurero.

[9]*RCR*: "Les dieron el paso ya"; mss. "El Pete Fonseca" y "Mario Fonseca" (véase la nota 14): "Les dieron el pase ya"; (cf. "el pase", en "Eva y Daniel").

[10]Mason City (Iowa).

[11]*RCR*: "la chata"; *Aztlan*: "the cops". Es evidente la errata: "la ch*o*ta" [la policía] > "la ch*a*ta". Los mss. "El Pete Fonseca" y "Mario Fonseca" (véase la nota 14) tienen: "andaba diciendo que *los empleados* le habían quitado todo el dinero y el carro" (énfasis mío). El ms. autógrafo, "El Pete Fonseca", tiene "los empleados" con tachadura y enmienda de "la chota". El manuscrito mecanografiado que Rivera entregó para este número de *RCR* no se encuentra en los archivos de la editorial. Para esta edición pongo "la Chata", con mayúscula.

[12]Albert Lea (Minnesota).

[13]"ronchita"—dinerito, ganancia.

[14]*Aztlan:* "[19]48". En los Archivos de Tomás Rivera existen seis manuscritos autógrafos y mecanógrafos de este cuento. Dos mss. son fotocopias de un mismo original mecanografiado, el cual no se encuentra entre los documentos de los archivos. Las fotocopias reproducen las tachaduras y enmiendas al original. Por lo que atañe a las fechas de "[19]'58/[19]'48", las dos fotocopias reproducen idénticamente la fecha de "'48", su tachadura y el sobrescrito de "'58". Parece que estas fotocopias, a su vez, fueron enmendadas y luego fotocopiadas de nuevo, ya que las dos también presentan distintas tachaduras y enmiendas. Uno de estos mss. lleva el título de "El Pete Fonseca", título escrito a mano, y el otro lleva el de "Mario Fonseca", escrito a máquina. En ambos casos, parece que el título fue agregado a la versión fotocopiada. En cuanto al ms. "Mario Fonseca", todo caso del nombre de "Pete" ha sido tachado y enmendado a mano con "Mario". Hay tres mss. autógrafos, dos en español y uno en inglés, todos con el título de "El Pete Fonseca". De los mss. en español, uno tiene la fecha de "'58", y el otro el de "'48", con tachadura y enmienda de "'58". Aquel ms. parece ser anterior a éste, ya que el segundo es una versión ampliada y enmendada de la primera. El autógrafo en inglés tiene la fecha de "'48". El último ms., mecanografiado, tiene el título de "El Pete Fonseca", pero en el texto aparece el nombre de "Mario" con tachadura y enmienda de "Pete". Este ms. tiene una conclusion más breve que los otros y no indica fecha alguna. Desde el punto de vista biográfico, el año de [19]48 sería el apropiado por corresponder así a la adolescencia de Rivera, nacido en 1935. En una entrevista [*Salvador Rodríguez del Pino with Tomás Rivera*. Video recording. Santa Barbara: University of California, Television Services, 1977], Rivera declara que el protagonista de ... *y no se lo tragó la tierra* tiene trece años. Recordemos que "El Pete Fonseca" formaba parte de la versión original de *tierra*. Para 1958 Rivera ha dejado el trabajo migratorio; véase la nota 17 a la introducción. La conclusión de la primera publicación en inglés (*Aztlan*), es más breve, faltando toda la parte que corresponde y que comienza con "El Pete, recuerdo que llegó como la cosa mala..."

Eva y Daniel

Publicación bilingüe, "Eva y Daniel"/"Eve and Daniel", en *El Grito* 5.3 (1972): 18–25; reimpreso sólo en español en: *Mosaico de la vida*, Francisco Jiménez, Ed. (New York: Harcourt Brace Jovanovich, Inc., 1981): 66–70; *Nuevos Horizontes*, José B. Fernández and Nasario García, Eds. (Lexington, MA.: D.C. Heath and Company, 1982): 22–26; reimpreso en inglés: *English in Texas* 10.2 (1978): 38–39.

[1]Análisis de la sangre.
[2]*El Grito* y en reimpresos: "Pero es que no porque pasa uno el examen se lo llevan".
[3]"*no* descansó hasta que *no* los había tronado todos él mismo": giro popular de expresión afirmativa.

La cosecha

[1]Falta en "La cosecha" (1989): "de que si les fue bien o mal",
[2]*quedrá* (querrá): variante dialectal.

Zoo Island

[1]Falta en "Zoo Island" (1959): "tremendas".
[2]*son-of-a-bitches*[sons-of-a-bitch]—hijos de puta.
[3]"parquenrich": parque zoológico de San Antonio: Brackenridge Park Zoo.
[4]*Caló*: "maderistas"—jactanciosos.
[5]"güerquitos" (huerquitos)—niños.
[6]"la Jenca", el hermano de Tomás Rivera: Henry > Hank > Jenca; "la Chira", amigo de Tomás Rivera y de Henry: Jitter[bug] > Chira. La Chira pereció en Corea. El editor le agradece a Rolando Hinojosa esta información.
[7]El término "rancho" tiene tres significados en el español de los Estados Unidos: (1) rancho de ganado; (2) finca agrícola: "farm"; (3) un pequeño poblado: "settlement". En todos los cuentos, y también en los episodios de …*y no se lo tragó la tierra*, se emplea "rancho" en el sentido de "finca"; claro está, que en este cuento también se emplea como "poblado".
[8]*Colmarle el plato a uno*—fastidiar, molestar demasiado.
[9]"Zoo Island", alusión a una antigua cantera rodeada de un foso, la cual habitan una cantidad de monos. Esta parte del Brackenridge Park Zoo es el famoso "Monkey Island".
[10]El ms. tiene 89 1/2 (pero: 86 + Don Simón + el niño recién nacido + el niño por nacer (que cuenta por 1/2) da un total de 88 1/2).

La cara en el espejo

Flor y Canto II: An Anthology of Chicano Literature, Arnold C. Vento, Alurista, José Flores Peregrino, Eds. (Albuquerque: Pajarito Publications, 1979; publicación tardía de "Festival Flor y Canto II", Austin, Texas, marzo de 1975); reimpreso en inglés, "Inside the Window", en *Caracol* 3.2 (agosto de 1977): 17–18.

[1]*Flor y Canto*: "el abuelo". La publicación en inglés tiene "my grandfather" que he utilizado aquí como "mi güelito", siguiendo la pauta establecida dos renglones arriba.

[2]"Arriba el norte", letra y música de Felipe Bermejo, *Cancionero mexicano: Canciones mexicanas y canciones que han tenido gran popularidad en México*, I (México, D.F.: Libro-Mex Editores, S. de R. L., 1980): 115.

[3]*Flor y Canto*: "del bravero". Aquí se confunden los versos de "El Bravero", de Victor Cordero Beltrán:

Ábranla que ahí va el machete
y de escudo mi sombrero;
yo no temo a la muerte,
tengo fama de bravero

Y soy de León, Guanajuato;
no vengo a pedir favores,
y ando tomando hace rato
junto con mis valedores.

Los mejores corridos mexicanos (México, D.F.: El Libro Español, 1972): 147.

[4]*Flor y Canto*: "...tan lejos que se me hace, de donde yo venía".

[5]*Flor y Canto*: "...en toda la torre, luego, después..."

[6]*Flor y Canto*: "la cara era Chuy".

En busca de Borges

Publicado primero en inglés, "Looking for Borges", en *Revista Chicano-Riqueña* 1.1 (1973): 2–3; reimpreso en español, "En busca de Borges", en *Caracol* 1.10 (junio de 1975): 14–15; *Kaleidoscopia* 3 (México: Universidad de las Américas, verano de 1975).

[1]La versión española agrega a la conclusión: "con una cara de esperanza que a veces me parecía imbécil".

The Searchers: Collected Poetry
Bibliography

Abbreviations:

AL *Alaluz, Revista de poesía y narración* 12.1 (1980): 80.

AML *We are Chicanos: An Anthology of Mexican-American Literature.* Philip D. Ortego, Ed. New York: Washington Square Press, 1973: 184–87.

AOP *Always and Other Poems.* Sisterdale, TX: Sisterdale Press, 1973.

CS *Cafe Solo* 8 (1974): 31–32.

EE *El espejo/The Mirror.* Octavio Romano-V. and Herminio Ríos C., Eds. Berkeley, CA: Quinto Sol, 1972, 2nd edition: 237–44. Reprint of *EG.*

EG *El Grito* 3.1 (1969): 56–63.

ET *English in Texas.* (Texas Joint Council of Teachers of English) 10.2 (1978): 33, 35.

EL *Ethnic Literatures since 1776: The Many Voices of America. Proceedings of the Comparative Literature Symposium 9,* Vol. I. Wolodymyr T. Zyla & Wendell M. Aycock, Eds. Lubbock: Texas Tech Press, 1976: 27–31.

FLQ *Original Works, A Foreign Language Quarterly* (Norman, OK: 1967): 10.

NB *The New Breed: An Anthology of Texas Poets.* David Oliphant, Ed. Malta, IL: Prickly Pear Press: 1973: 138–43.

QE *El Quetzal Emplumece.* Carmela Montalvo, Leonardo Anguiano & Cecilio García-Camarillo, Eds. San Antonio, TX: Mexican American Culture Center, 1976: 246–53.

RCR *Revista Chicano-Riqueña* 1.1 (1973): 17–18.

SD *Songs and Dreams.* Joseph A. Flores, Ed. West Haven, CT: Pendulum Press, 1972: 80.

A Blas de Otero: *AL*
Alone: *CS*
A Most Tired Word: *AOP/QE*
Another Me: *AOP*
Always: *AOP/CS*
Autumn and Winter: *AOP*
Child, The: *ET/RCR*
De niño   De joven   De viejo: *EE/EG/QE*

Ennui: *AOP*
Eyes of a Child, The: *AML*
Hide the Old People or American Idearium: *EE/EG/QE*
Me lo enterraron: *EE/EG/FLQ/QE*
M'ijo no mira nada: *EE/EG/QE*
Overalls, The: *AOP/CS/NB*
Odio: *EE/EG/QE*
Past Possessions: *AOP/AML*
Perfection of Perfections: *AOP*
Poetics: *NB*
Rooster Crows en Iowa y en Texas, The: *EE/EG/ET/NB/QE*
Run, Puff, Run, Run: *AOP/QE*
Searchers, The: *EL*
Seeds in the Hour of Seeds: *AOP*
Siempre el domingo: *EE/EG/NB/QE*
Soundless Words: *AOP/AML/CS/QE*
This Solitude: *AOP/QE*
When Love To Be: *AML/ET/RCR*
Young Voices: *AOP/ET/RCR/SD*

De niño   De joven   De viejo

EE, EG: l. 36: "Los pasos cauteles" appears to include an erratum. The line should read: "Los pasos cautos" or "Los pasos cautelosos." Ll. 42–43: "Las miradas abajo / pensadas sentencias," "abajo" does not appear to be a preposition introducing "pensadas sentencias," in which case it would be "bajo" or "debajo de" as is the case with the preposition "detrás [de]" (l. 44). It is clearly an adverb, with "pensadas sentencias" in apposition to "las miradas abajo." Following the pattern established in the rest of the poem (e.g. ll. 40–41: "La ventana cerrada. / La mañana caliente…" and ll. 62–63. "Los sueños pasados, / los viejos amigos,") and to avoid confusion, I insert a comma: "las miradas abajo, / pensadas sentencias."

M'ijo no mira nada

In the typescript of II. A (see Chronology), this poem has a variant of the same poem published in El Grito. Line 6 of the published version has the child responding in Spanish: "¿Por qué pelea?," whereas his other responses to his father are in English. The variant gives for the same line: "Why does he fight?" While we cannot know the reasons why Rivera chose the published version, thematically and structurally it would seem that the variant given would have been the more appropriate. On one level, the poem deals with the linguistic and cultural alienation that can occur between Spanish-speaking parents and their children who choose not to retain or speak Spanish and seek assimilation into the English-speaking majority society. The unpublished version would have emphasized this cultural and linguistic drifting.

Seeds in the Hour of Seeds

Cf.: "Bartolo passed through town every December when he knew that most of the people had returned from work up north. He always came by selling his poems. By the end of the first day, they were almost sold out because the names of the people of the town appeared in the poems. And when he read them aloud it was something emotional and serious. I recall that one time he told the people to read the poems out loud because the spoken word was the seed of love in the darkness."

Young Voices

There are two primitive versions of this poem; one is "Love Seeds" (II.C.3) and the other, earlier, has a Spanish title, "la voz," although the text is in English. The most significant variant in the latter is the line between the third and fourth stanzas, which Rivera eliminated in his second draft:

REMEMBER, CHICANO,

the voice
is the love seed
in the dark

The Overalls

CS, NB, l. 9: "and the sound of clods"; CS, ll. 17-18: "the crushing / vapor»

Alone

A primitive version of this poem has three lines which Rivera eliminated from the conclusion of his final draft: "yet, they only remind me / that I am alone / forever"

A Blas de Otero

AL: ll. 1-2 present some confusion to the reader. As published in AL, the first word of the initial line begins in lower case, "la cicatriz del pecado original / Anonada la justicia y" (sic). The first word of the second line, corrected in this edition as "Anonadada," begins in upper case, as does the first word of the second and third stanzas, which seems to indicate that the word beginning in upper case introduces a stanza. The first line, "la cicatriz del pecado original," repeated in l. 21, may have been intended to function as an epigraph; at least it expresses a concept—reflecting the religious crisis of Otero's first books—which the rest of the poem glosses, comments or elucidates. In this regard, then, for this edition I have commenced the first line in upper case and have closed it with a colon, "La cicatriz del pecado original:"

The Searchers

I:12-15, 21-24 are popular children's rhymes found in Mexican/Chicano culture: "naranja dulce ... que yo te pido": "sweet orange / a lemon cut / your embrace / is all I crave"; "A la víbora ... por aquí pueden pasar": "Oh, the serpent, serpent / of the sea / of the sea / through here you [children] may pass."

I:38, "Hay, ese vato, chíngate": "Hey, guy, go to hell."

I: 39, "terrón": clod of dirt.

II: 10-12, "Tierra eres ... volverás": "Dust you are / dust you will be / and to dust you will return."

II:13-24, "Una noche caminando ... alumbran allí": "One night walking / a dark shade I saw / I withdrew from her / and she drew close to me. / What are you doing, sir? / What are you about here? / I am searching for my wife / who has been lost to me. / Your wife is no longer here, / your wife is now dead; / four candles white / are burning over there."

IV:32, "No estamos solos": "We are not alone."

VI:40, 42, "Pan dulce": sweet bread, pastry.

Searching at Leal Middle School

ll. 54-70, "Away in the dump yards ... and magazines": "There is one book which especially impressed me: In *Darkest Africa* by Henry M. Stanley. I found it myself in the dump, you see; a two-volume collection of Stanley's expedition into Africa in search of Dr. Livingstone. Of course, I didn't know anything about history at the time, or the exploration of Africa, but with the books came maps of the terrain through which Stanley had to travel. The text was a diary, a day-by-day account of what to Stanley was the discovery of Africa, with all the details, like how much food they ate, how far they had traveled, all those things. It fascinated me. It was better than going to a Tarzan movie. It carried over into my own life, because I started making maps of the terrain we traveled, and my brothers and I would explore and draw maps. It became a living thing. I haven't read them for a long time, but that title stuck in my memory because of the exploratory aspect ... I still have those books at home ...

That was back in 1944; I was about nine," Bruce-Novoa, *Inquiry* 143; see "Notes to the Introduction," note 5.

Rivera sent a copy of this poem to a student at Leal Middle School, stating in a cover letter: "I really enjoyed participating with you and the other students at Leal Middle School yesterday. Many of you are interested in poetry writing, reading and reciting. Keep up the interest. The study of literature and the reading of literature, as you now know, is one of my greatest interests. It is so because it reveals original elements that we all have as people. After I talked to the three groups of students at Leal Middle School, I came back to my office and wrote the following poem which I titled *Leal Middle School.* I have attached it here"(December 18, 1975).

Finally Life Began

Rivera does not translate one line from the Spanish version, the first of the final stanza, which would be: "Now that I've found my life, I'll search for others."

Through the Window

There are two primitive versions; the one that appears to be the earliest, an autograph, is titled "Life drops,"while the second draft, typed, is titled by hand, "Window," above the struck typed title of "Reincarnation." This version has a concluding line, eliminated in the final version, of a single word: "Death."

Chronology

I. 1967: "Me lo enterraron"

II. 1967–69:

A. *El Grito*

"De niño   De joven   De viejo"

"Hide the Old People, or American Idearium"

"M'ijo no mira nada"

"Odio"
"The Rooster Crows en Iowa y en Texas"

"Siempre el Domingo"

B. From the same typescript containing the above are the following unpublished poems:

"El despertar"

"En la hora de las semillas"
"Las voces del olvido"
"Nacimiento"
"Soy una palabra"

C. Four-page typescript, unpublished:

1. "Do Not Forget Me"
2. "You Have Seen Me"
3. "Love Seeds"
4. "Window"
Each page of this typescript of group C bears the autograph:

1 of 4
Tomás Rivera
541 Sooner
Norman, Okla.
Rivera lived at this address between 1967–69. Numbers 2–4 are primitive drafts of "Always," "Young Voices" and "Through the Window," respectively.

D. "We Didn't Bury Him," translation of "Me lo enterraron."

E. Among Rivera's literary documents, in the
Tomás Rivera Archives, there are three autograph indices of his poetry. The one that appears
to be the oldest lists most of the above poems and
includes titles or primitive titles of poems subsequently published in *AML, AOP, CS* and *RCR*:

"Alone," *CS*
"Past Possessions," *AOP*
"Reach Beyond the Eyes of A Child" ("The
Child"), *RCR*

"Run, Puff, Run, Run," *AOP*
"Seeds in the Hour of Seeds," *AOP*
"Solitude" ("This Solitude"), *AOP*

"Soundless Words," *AOP*
"The Word Is Tired ("A Most Tired Word"),
AOP
"Things" ("Ennui"), *AOP*
"Young Voices," *RCR*

F. The same index contains the following poems
which remained unpublished:

"Desátate"
"Estoy como estás"
"Fake or Fink"
"Finally Life Began"
"My Life"
"Palabras" (under the primitive title of "En esta
hoja blanca")
"[I Go to Church at] Veteran's Place"
"La vida por fin empezó" is not listed, but exam-
ination indicates that it was written before its
translation, "Finally Life Began."

III. March 1968: "Palabras"; dated autograph.

IV. 1969–1972:

A. *Revista Chicano-Riqueña* (Spring, 1973):

"The Child"
"When Love To Be"
"Young Voices"

B. Group A was selected from a group of poems that Rivera submitted to *RCR*, and some of which remained unpublished:

"A Flower"
"Another Day"
"Not Unlike the Wind"
"Through the Window"

C. Groups A and B were selected from a typescript that includes the unpublished poems:

"Awakening" (trans. of "Nacimiento," II. 1967–69, B.)

"To Walk Beyond the Door" and poems published in *AOP* (1973): "Always," "Another Me," "Perfection of Perfections."

D. *Always and Other Poems* (1973)
"A Most Tired Word," (II. 1967–69, E.)
"Always"
"Another Me"
"Autumn and Winter"
"Ennui," (II. 1967–69, E.)
"The Overalls"
"Past Possessions" (II. 1967–69, E.)
"Perfection of Perfections"
"Run, Puff, Run, Run" (II. 1967–69, E.)
"Seeds in the Hour of Seeds" (II. 1967–69, E.)
"Soundless Words" (II. 1967–69, E.)
"This Solitude" (II. 1967–69, E.)
"Young Voices"

E. "The Eyes of a Child" (*AML*, II. 1967–69, E.)

V. By 1976: "The Searchers," *Ethnic Literatures Since 1776.*

VI. Dec. 11, 1975: "Searching at Leal Middle School," dated typescript.

VII. 1979–80: "A Blas de Otero," *AL* (Blas de Otero: † 1979).

VIII. With the exception of specifically dated poems, all other poetry in Part II was probably written between 1967–72.